# ABOUT THE AUTHOR

For five decades, award-winning writer **Brad Steiger** has been devoted to exploring and examining unusual, hidden, secret, and otherwise strange occurrences. A former high school teacher and college instructor, Brad published his first articles on the unexplained in 1956. Since then he has written more than two thousand articles with paranormal themes. He is author or coauthor of more than 170 books, including *Real Vampires, Night Stalkers, and Creatures from the Darkside; Real Ghosts, Restless Spirits, and Haunted Places; The Werewolf Book; Conspiracies and Secret Societies,* and with his wife, Sherry, *Real Miracles, Divine Intervention, and Feats of Incredible Survival.* Brad's *Otherworldly Affaires* was voted the Number One Paranormal Book of 2008 by Haunted America Tours.

# OTHER VISIBLE INK PRESS BOOKS BY BRAD STEIGER

*Conspiracies and Secret Societies: The Complete Dossier*
With Sherry Hansen Steiger
ISBN: 978-1-57859-174-9

*Real Ghosts, Restless Spirits, and Haunted Places*
ISBN: 978-1-57859-146-6

*Real Miracles, Divine Intervention, and Feats of Incredible Survival*
With Sherry Hansen Steiger
ISBN: 978-1-57859-214-2

*Real Vampires, Night Stalkers, and Creatures from the Darkside*
ISBN: 978-1-57859-255-5

*The Werewolf Book: The Encyclopedia of Shape-Shifting Beings*
ISBN: 978-1-57859-078-0

# ALSO FROM VISIBLE INK PRESS

*Angels A to Z, 2nd edition*
by Evelyn Dorothy Oliver and James R Lewis
ISBN: 978-1-57859-212-8

*Armageddon Now: The End of the World A to Z*
by Jim Willis and Barbara Willis
ISBN: 978-1-57859-168-8

*The Astrology Book: The Encyclopedia of Heavenly Influences, 2nd edition*
by James R Lewis
ISBN: 978-1-57859-144-2

*The Dream Encyclopedia, 2nd edition*
by James R Lewis and Evelyn Dorothy Oliver
ISBN: 978-1-57859-216-6

*The Encyclopedia of Religious Phenomena*
by J. Gordon Melton
ISBN: 978-1-57859-209-8

*The Fortune-Telling Book: The Encyclopedia of Divination and Soothsaying*
by Raymond Buckland
ISBN: 978-1-57859-147-3

*The Handy Religion Answer Book*
by John Renard
ISBN: 978-1-57859-125-1

*Hidden Realms, Lost Civilizations, and Beings from Other Worlds*
by Jerome Clark
ISBN: 978-1-57859-175-6

*The Religion Book: Places, Prophets, Saints, and Seers*
by Jim Willis
ISBN: 978-1-57859-151-0

*The Spirit Book: The Encyclopedia of Clairvoyance, Channeling, and Spirit Communication*
by Raymond Buckland
ISBN: 978-1-57859-172-5

*Unexplained! Strange Sightings, Incredible Occurrences, and Puzzling Physical Phenomenam, 2nd edition*
by Jerome Clark
ISBN: 978-1-57859-070-4

*The Vampire Book: The Encyclopedia of the Undead, 2nd edition*
by J. Gordon Melton
ISBN: 978-1-57859-071-1

*The Witch Book: The Encyclopedia of Witchcraft, Wicca, and Neo-paganism*
by Raymond Buckland
ISBN: 978-1-57859-114-5

**Please visit us at visibleink.com.**

# REAL ZOMBIES, THE LIVING DEAD, AND CREATURES OF THE APOCALYPSE

# REAL ZOMBIES,
## THE LIVING DEAD,
## AND CREATURES
## OF THE APOCALYPSE

### BRAD STEIGER

VISIBLE
INK
PRESS

Detroit

# REAL ZOMBIES, THE LIVING DEAD, AND CREATURES OF THE APOCALYPSE

Visible Ink Press®
43311 Joy Rd., #414
Canton, MI 48187-2075

Visible Ink Press is a registered trademark of Visible Ink Press LLC.

Most Visible Ink Press books are available at special quantity discounts when purchased in bulk by corporations, organizations, or groups. Customized printings, special imprints, messages, and excerpts can be produced to meet your needs. For more information, contact Special Markets Director, Visible Ink Press, www.visibleink.com, or 734-667-3211.

Managing Editor: Kevin S. Hile
Art Director: Mary Claire Krzewinski
Typesetting: Marco Di Vita

Front cover art by Ricardo Pustanio; back cover photograph Shannon McCabe

ISBN 978-1-57859-296-8

**Library of Congress Cataloging-in-Publication Data**

Steiger, Brad.
    Real zombies, the living dead, and creatures of the Apocalypse / by Brad Steiger.
        p. cm.
    Includes bibliographical references and index.
    ISBN 978-1-57859-296-8
    1. Zombies. I. Title.
    BF1556.S735 2010
    398'.45—dc22

                                        2010007048

Printed in the United States of America

10 9 8 7 6 5 4 3 2 1

# CONTENTS

# CONTRIBUTORS

Thanks to the following gifted artists for contributing original illustrations to this publication.

### Ricardo Pustanio

Ricardo Pustanio is an enduring icon in the world of New Orleans Mardi Gras float design and local artistry. Today his phenomenal creative talents are witnessed by thousands upon thousands of locals and tourists who throng the streets of New Orleans each year to catch a glimpse of one of the oldest and most prestigious parades of the season, the Krewe of Mid-City. And according to Ricardo, "The best is still to come!"

Born in New Orleans, Ricardo is the third son of local golfing legend Eddie "Blackie" Pustanio, a well-known icon of the sport. When Ricardo was baptized, the famous "Diamond Jim" Moran was hailed as his godfather and all the major golfing pros who visited the elder Pustanio at his City Park Golf Course digs bounced little Ricardo on a famous knee at one time or another.

Like nearly every child brought up in the city of New Orleans, Ricardo was brought out by his parents to enjoy the pageantry and revelry of the great old-line Mardi Gras parades. These halcyon Mardi Gras days of his youth were Ricardo's first taste of the passion that would become the artistic pinnacle of his later career. During the 1960s Ricardo's entries won First Place and rode with the King of Mid-City three years in a row: a true precursor of things to come.

The winner of many art competitions throughout his life, his earliest prize-winning work was created while Ricardo was still in Kindergarten. From an early age, Ricardo's work was distinguished with prizes and praise. the piece hung in the children's area of the New Orleans Museum of Art for many years; other early works could be found on display in the New Orleans Cabildo. Most are now in private art collections in New Orleans and across the United States.

In the early 1970s Ricardo began a long association with local New Orleans radio station WRNO-FM, where he distinguished himself as Art Director for many years.

**Ricardo Pustanio works on one of his popular Mardi Gras floats.**

Ricardo's special style was also very visible in his work on numerous backdrops and displays for the 1984 New Orleans World's Fair; several of his original pieces from that fair have garnered high prices at auctions throughout the United States and Europe.

Ricardo served Le Petit Theatre du Vieux Carre as Technical Director for its 1992–1993 season, during which he contributed his considerable artistic talents to the creation of scenery and backdrops for the season's major productions, including *West Side Story* and *The Baby Dance.* For the latter he created a giant 60 foot by 30 foot papier maché pyramid, one of the highlights of the season. Ricardo's set designs for the productions of *King Midas and the Golden Touch* and *The Snow Queen* each won him numerous awards.

In 1992 Ricardo began his long association with William Crumb and the Children's Educational Theatre. His work on scenery and backdrops has toured with the company in 13 major productions across the United States, and he continues to contribute his talents to the organization to this day. Ricardo has also donated his time and talent to a number of nonprofit organizations, including the Save Our Lake Foundation and the March of Dimes.

Ricardo displayed his talent with scenic design in some of the best-known, locally produced films, including *Angel Heart,* starring Mickey Rourke; *The Big Easy,* starring Dennis Quaid and Ellen Barkin; Anne Rice's *Interview with the Vampire,* starring Tom Cruise and Brad Pitt; and most recently in the much anticipated *A Love Song for Billy Long,* which stars John Travolta and was filmed on location in historic New Orleans.

Ricardo has conceptualized and designed numerous book covers and illustrations for major works of science fiction and fantasy; he was voted Best New Artist of the Year at World Cons held in New Orleans and Amsterdam, Holland. Ricardo has also illustrated children's books, created portraits and artwork for private clients across the United States and in Europe, and has to his credit three original action comic books, the illustration and design of the long-running International Middle Eastern Dancer magazine, and several decks of personalized Tarot cards.

Ricardo has said, in reflecting on his artist achievements: "I have paid my dues many times over the years and I am always in a constant state of expectation: I can't wait for the next challenge, the next thing to approach me. I am probably most proud of my work with the Krewe of Mid-City in recent years, because they have allowed me an unlimited palette to create with: the only limit is my imagination, and as you see, that has never had any limits!"

Ricardo Pustanio's hands have been busy creating artworks that have brought joy and pleasure to literally thousands of people over the years. It is no wonder that Ricardo has been named one of The Hardest Working Mardi Gras Artists in the City of New Orleans and in the history of Mardi Gras design.

### Bill Oliver

Artist Bill Oliver is also a musician, composer, and award-winning song writer. His music is sometimes reflective and moody, and his compositions, like his art, often act as "sound photographs" that capture a moment of life and freeze it in time for further contemplation—even if that moment of contemplation involves a vampire, zombie, UFO visitor, or a werewolf.

**Bill Oliver**

Oliver resides in Vancouver, British Columbia, where he has nourished a life-long interest in the paranormal, UFOs, the metaphysical, and all things esoteric, stemming from many personal experiences. His enthusiasm for pursuing the unknown brought him into personal contact and interview opportunities with experiencers in all aspects of the paranormal. These encounters have had significant influences on much of Bill's work.

Brad Steiger first became familiar with Oliver's exciting artwork when the Canadian won the Christmas Art contest on the Jeff Rense Program in 2005. In the Art contest for Halloween 2006, Bill won honorable mention.

As the two men became better acquainted, Steiger was honored to learn that he had been one of Oliver's boyhood heroes with his work on the paranormal, the esoteric, and things that go bump in the night.

"To be reading one of Brad's classic books one day and being asked to do some art for one of his new books another is truly paranormal," Oliver said.

Visit Bill Oliver's website at http://www.boyso blue.com/.

### Chris Holly

Chris Holly lives on Long Island, New York, where she presently writes and publishes the site Endless Journey with Chris Holly's Paranormal World and the Knightzone.

**Chris Holly**

**Laura Lee Mistycah**

**Alyne Pustanio**

**Angela Thomas**

Although Chris has spent a life building different entrepreneurial ventures, her one true passion has always been writing. She feels it is her destiny to relate true events of the paranormal to the world.

Chris is grateful to all her readers and reads the emails sent to her concerning the world of the paranormal. "I always read every email sent to me and try hard to respond to each and every one who takes the time to write to me." You can reach Chris at chrishollyufo@yahoo.com, http://endlessjrny.blog spot.com/, and http://www.fttoufo.com/chrishollysparanormalworld.htm.

### Laura Lee Mistycah (Witchy Woman)

Laura Lee is the author of three books and is working on two more. She has been on the cutting edge of Healing Arts for over 25 years and has developed many techniques that have facilitated instant healing and pain relief. As a professional consultant, psychic, and Ghost Buster, Laura Lee has clients all over the world. She is also the steward of "The Knights of Mistyc House," and teaches Knights Training courses for First Wave Indigos. You can visit her site at http://www.mistychouse.com/.

### Alyne Pustanio

Folklorist and occultist Alyne Pustanio is a New Orleans native whose roots go deep into the local culture; and it is from that proverbial "gumbo" that she draws her inspiration for most of her tales of terror and fascination.

A descendant of Portuguese and Sicilian immigrant families who trace their ancestry to European Gypsies, Alyne was exposed to the mysteries of the occult at an early age. Two great-grandmothers were gifted and sought out mediums, and another relative is a verified psychic; however, Alyne credits her mother—an avid spiritualist—with inspiring her lifelong interest in the supernatural and unexplained.

These interests, combined with her avocations in folklore and history, result in a validity and passion that is immediately obvious in all her writings. Visit http://www.hauntedamericatours.com.

### Angela Thomas

Angela Thomas, also known as Oct13baby, is known world-wide for her accurate psychic readings, and her advice is widely sought by those who need honest and ethical insight into their physical, emotional, and spiritual problems. In addition to being a world-renowned psychic reader, Angela Thomas is also co-host of P.O.R.T.A.L. Paranormal Talk Radio, a weekly paranormal radio show devoted to bringing its audience the most fascinating information in the paranormal world. Email her at oct13baby@aol.com.

### Lisa Lee Harp Waugh

Lisa Lee Harp Waugh is a professional Necromancer and founder of the Sorcerers Guild of greater Houston, Texas. She has been practicing and conducting rituals for over twenty years. In addition, she is an accomplished writer and her work appears regularly in *Haunted America Tours* (http://www.haunted americatours.com).

When Lisa Lee lived in Galveston about 16 years ago, she became involved with the Hoodoos-Voodoos of the area and new techniques were revealed to her regarding communication with the dead. Later, she was baptized and trained in the secret dark religion by Bianca, the Voodoo Queen of New Orleans. Lisa Lee lived in New Orleans for three years until she learned as much as possible about spells, hexes, and how to Hoodoo-Voodoo people. You can email her at lisawonthebay@aol.com.

**Lisa Lee Harp Waugh**
(*art by Ricardo Pustanio*)

### Paul Dale Roberts

Paul Dale Roberts is the General Manager/Ghostwriter of Haunted and Paranormal Investigations International. He is a prolific writer who has investigated ghosts, werewolves, witches, vampires, and demons. Paul Dale Roberts is also the "ghostwriter" for Shannon McCabe's Haunted and Paranormal Investigations International (http://www.HPIparanormal.net); Paul's Lair/HPI is now found at http://www.shannonmccabe.com; you can email him at Pauld 5606@comcast.net.

**Paul Dale Roberts**

### Shannon McCabe

Shannon McCabe, "Ms. McCabe" is president of Haunted and Paranormal Investgations Internation (HPI), which seeks hard evidence to support alleged hauntings. Her complete biography can be found at http://www.ShannonMcCabe.com.

### Pastor Robin Swope

Pastor Robin Swope, who is known as the Paranormal Pastor, has been a Christian minister for more than 15 years in both Mainline and Evangelical denominations. He has served as a missionary to Burkina Faso, West Africa, and ministered to the homeless in New York City's Hell's Kitchen. He is the founder and chief officiant of Open Gate Ministerial Services and a member of St. Paul's United Church of Christ in Erie, Pennsylvania. Visit his blog at http://theparanormalpastor.blogspot.com.

**Shannon McCabe**

### Jackie Williams

Jackie Williams (http://www.spiralfirestudio.com) is a psychic and natural spirit medium, able to see and communicate with spirits and often drawing those she has come into contact with. She is a member of House Kheperu in the Priest caste and teaches classes on energy work, spirit communication, art and energy, and performs energy body readings/manipulation and cleansings. An award-winning artist with over ten years of professional experience in illustration and manuscript illumination, her latest project is the *Watcher Angel Tarot* with psychic Michelle Belanger,

**Pastor Robin Swope**

Jackie Williams

author of *Walking the Twilight Path* and *The Psychic Energy Codex* at http://www.michellebelanger.com.

## Lance Oliver

A native Texan, young Lance Oliver experienced several kinds of paranormal phenomena, including three vivid OBEs to a higher dimension of existence, as well as a visitation by some dark specter, seen through the slats of his bed. Overall, these experiences seemed to lean more toward a positive nature than a negative one.

Through his years attending high school, Oliver's fascination with the unexplained grew, prompting him to join the Mutual UFO Network (MUFON). Later, Oliver had the privilege of being personally trained by the organization's founder, Walt Andrus. After becoming an official UFO Field Investigator, he later was chosen to be the State Section Director of Tarrant County for MUFON.

After moving to Denton, Texas, he founded the Denton Area Paranormal Society (DAPS) in the fall of 2004. With the help of his wife, Mary, and several others, Oliver has positioned the organization to research and investigate numerous urban legends and reports of things that go bump in the night. He can be reached at orb-hunterx@yahoo.com.

## Julia Cole

Julia Cole has become known as *The Empress of the Known & Unknown Universes*[TM], and devoted herself to bringing enlightenment and inspiration around the globe by providing spiritual guidance to those seeking a deeper understanding. In her personal empowerment consultations, Julia provides in-depth advice and teaches clients to tap into their own inner-strength and achieve a more fulfilling and joyful life.

As a psychic medium, Julia brings healing and comfort by serving as a liaison between those here in the physical realm and those who have crossed over into the spiritual planes of existence.

Julia's weekly radio talk show Namaste Beloved[TM]; is heard on Blog Talk Radio every Friday evening starting at 9:00 PM Eastern. Julia Cole's email is namaste.beloved@gmail.com.

## Tuesday Miles

Tuesday Miles is an experienced psychic medium who is known to have had exceptional experiences with spirit entities. Tuesday's psychic abilities are multidimensional, which means that she can see spirit manifestations on all levels of the veil. Tuesday lives in a very active haunted house; she knows what it feels like having some unseen force enter into your life. One thing Tuesday teaches each of her clients is how to empower themselves. Tuesday believes that if you stand as a victim, the ghost will treat you as a victim, just as any human bully would do. Tuesday has made a promise that she has yet to break—if someone needs help with a paranormal situation, she will not turn her back on the client. She will do everything that she can to get that person some help. Tuesday Miles' personal website is http://www.Tuesdaymiles.com.

## Wm. Michael Mott

Wm. Michael (Mike) Mott is a freelance artist who writes both fiction and non-fiction. His artwork and writing have appeared or been featured in many publications. He has created artworks and graphic designs for mass-market book covers, posters, brochures, packaging, CD-ROM covers and art collections, and digital/web-based media, and has won several design awards, from regional Advertising Federation awards for printed material to awards for website graphics and design. His artwork has been featured in the exhibition "In Dreams Awake: Art of Fantasy" at the Olympia and York Gallery, New York City, 1988; at the 1987 World Fantasy Con, Con*stellation, the DragonCon 2001 art show, several one-man exhibits, and digital galleries in various venues. He also researches and writes on Fortean, folklore, comparative religion, and paranormal topics.

Mike is the author of the satirical fantasy novel *Pulsifer: A Fable* and its sequel, *Land of Ice, A Velvet Knife,* both soon to be re-released in one omnibus edition from TGS Publishing, as well as the nonfiction books *Caverns, Cauldrons, and Concealed Creatures* and *This Tragic Earth: The Art and World of Richard Sharpe Shaver.* His pulp fiction anthology of fiction, verse, and artwork, *PULP WINDS,* featuring an introduction by Brad Steiger, has been recently published by TGS (http://www.hiddenmysteries. com). Mike can be reached at admin@mottimorphic.com and at mottimorph@earth link.net. His website is http://www.mottimorphic.com.

## Ryan Mott

Fifteen-year-old Ryan Mott is the son of Mike Mott and is a budding artist and writer. He has a very fluid and natural drawing ability and a way with the written word as well. He shares his father's interests in history, myth, legend, and Fortean topics. He likes zombies, samurai, knights, dogs, and rock and roll. This marks the first publication of his artwork in a professional capacity.

# THE ZOMBIES ARE COMING

In 1965 when I wrote *Monsters, Maidens, and Mayhem: A Pictorial History of Hollywood Film Monsters* (Merit Books, Chicago), I included chapters on man-made monsters, vampires, werewolves, mummies, and Things from Outer Space, but I made no mention of zombies.

The book became successful enough for the publisher to request a sequel that same year. In *Master Movie Monsters* I elaborated on such topics as "Fantasy's Finest Hour," "Vintage Vampires," and "Mad Scientists and What They Hath Wrought." Once again, I included no discussion of zombie movies.

Why did I neglect to include the zombie, the dreaded creature of the undead, in two books about Hollywood monsters? Because American filmmaker George A. Romero had not yet scraped together a $114,000 budget, gathered some unknown actors and friends, and filmed an independent black-and-white horror film that was released in 1968 as *Night of the Living Dead*.

Before *Night of the Living Dead* birthed the way that motion picture audiences and popular culture would perhaps forevermore view the zombie, there had really only been two films of any note about zombies: *White Zombie* (1932) with Bela Lugosi, and *I Walked with a Zombie* (1943), the second horror film produced by Val Lewton, who was highly respected for his classic *The Cat People* (1942).

While *White Zombie* and *I Walked with a Zombie* have never exerted much influence on the mass audience, they were both set in the Caribbean, and they each made an effort to depict with some accuracy the legend of real zombies. Some critics have said that Lugosi's portrayal of the Voodoo master in *White Zombie* was one of his very best. The scene depicting the mindless zombies working in their master's sugar mill caught exactly the cruel exploitation of the undead slaves.

Jack Pierce, Universal Studios' top makeup artist (famous for the work he did making Boris Karloff's monster in *Frankenstein*), created unusually striking makeup for

Lugosi. Pierce also designed the head-to-toe costume and the make-up for actor Frederick Peters, who played the zombie, regarded by many as one of The Horror Hall of Fame's most frightening looking characters. Remarkably, *White Zombie*, in addition to the utilization of advanced camera, lighting, and sound techniques, boasted a full musical score—an impressive creative aspect that was lacking in Universal's greatest success in the genre, *Dracula and Frankenstein*.

Although zombies never gained the audience appeal and loyalty of the great monsters lineup of Universal Studios' Wolfman, Dracula, and the Mummy, *White Zombie* and *I Walked with a Zombie* actually depicted elements truer to the mythos of the real zombie than did *Night of the Living Dead*.

## Night of the Flesh Eaters

One of the titles that George Romero considered for his film was *Night of the Flesh Eaters*, which in my opinion would have been more appropriate and surely would have made the film no less frightening. The film is not really about zombies at all. The things staggering toward their victims from the darkness are not members of the undead who have been raised from their graves to serve as mindless slaves for a cruel taskmaster. Mysteriously, on this one fateful and grisly *Night of the Living Dead*, corpses crawl out of their graves to attack baffled and horrified victims.

When the film's principal characters take refuge in a farmhouse, they learn from an emergency broadcast on television that the murderers, who appear to be in some kind of trance, are actually the recently deceased who have been somehow returned to life and who are seizing the living and eating their flesh. None of the experts polled claim to be able to explain the hideous reanimation, but a science consultant persistently insists the cause of the dead rising from their graves is somehow the result of radiation from a Venus probe that exploded in the Earth's atmosphere.

As the night of horror progresses, the mindless, shuffling undead continue to advance in a seemingly unending army of monsters lusting for the blood of the living in the farmhouse. The film sustains a sense of genuine fear and helplessness that grips the audience and relentlessly never releases its grip. The fact that the film actually scares the viewer has made the *Night of the Living Dead* a film that horror buffs see over and over again.

Romero has never denied that he was greatly inspired by author Richard Matheson's novel *I Am Legend* (1954), in which a plague decimates Los Angeles. Victims of the terrible blight return to life as vampires, seeking to feast on the survivors, thereby killing and infecting them. One lone man struggles against impossible odds to stay alive and to preserve the human race. Matheson's novel was translated into film in 1964 as *The Last Man on Earth*, starring Vincent Price. (Subsequent adaptations of

It has become a popular group activity to dress up like zombies and gather to embark on zombie walks or dances. Here, Maria Eivers has applied the appropriate "undead"-type makeup in preparation for the San Jose Zombie Walk (*photo by Shannon McCabe*).

Matheson's novel have been *The Omega Man* [1971] with Charlton Heston, and *I Am Legend* [2007] starring Will Smith.)

Because Matheson's novel describes a plague that infected and killed people who later return as vampires to hunt the uninfected, Romero decided that his film should not utilize that same kind of monster. At the same time, he wanted to fashion his motion picture around an equally horrifying premise. After some deliberation, he decided that it would be truly nightmarish if dead people should no longer wish to be dead and suddenly rise from their graves to begin to kill the living.

Romero's film delivered enough terrifying action to stun its initial audience with the shock of raw realism that left many too frightened to leave the theater, but too numb with terror to stay. *Night of the Living Dead*, with its image of the grotesque mindless, lurching undead, became a classic horror film.

Although Romero decided against having the undead transform into vampires after their death, the stumbling, staggering corpses in his film do bite people and eat their flesh; and, vampire-like, their bloody victims become undead cannibals as a result becoming involuntary meals. The film was strongly criticized for its graphic and explicit content. Nonetheless, the archetype of the modern zombie horror film was born.

Groups of thousands of "zombies" have gathered to join zombie marches and parades. On Halloween 2008, 1,227 zombies joined to set a world record for the largest number of zombies dancing to Michael Jackson's "Thriller" (*photo by Shannon McCabe*).

Romero has gone on to make five zombie motion pictures, remaking *Night of the Living Dead* twice, most recently as *Night of the Living Dead 3D* (2006), directed by Tom Savini. It may be impossible to derive a completely accurate box office take for the initial *Night of the Living Dead*, but reasonable estimates indicate that it has grossed more than $30 million internationally. Romero has not forgotten his debt to the undead. He came full circle to the beginning of his success with the film *Diary of the Dead* (2008).

## Are Zombies Dancing Us to the Apocalypse?

*While George Romero brought the zombie into contemporary consciousness with* The Night of the Living Dead, *it seems unlikely that anyone could have predicted the enormous popularity of the creature in today's culture. Large numbers of our current population have gone "Zombie Nuts," which hopefully will not lead to anything more than role-playing and gathering in large groups to dress, dance, and act like the zombies do.*

*In today's zombie films, the mangled undead are much more agile than Romero's lurching creatures, who shuffle, drag their feet, and extend their flopping arms for balance. Today's zombies can run, fast.*

*Not only are the zombies becoming more agile on screen, you may encounter large numbers of pseudo-zombies dancing at the local mall. Even on days other than Halloween, large groups of the undead may appear everywhere from town squares to prison exercise yards to perform the famous "zombie dance" from Michael Jackson's music video "Thriller."*

On Halloween 2008, 1,227 of the undead filled the Old Market Square in Nottinghamshire, England, to set a new world record for dancing zombies. The previous record for zombie choreography had been set in Monroeville, Pennsylvania on October 28, 2007, with 1,028 participants. BBC News quoted Margaret Robinson, one of the organizers of the Nottingham zombie event, as saying that on that night the dancers were all zombies, all undead. She was covered in blood and very happy to be so.

On December 3, 2009, officials at the University of Colorado at Boulder warned that students who were caught walking around campus dorm buildings with Nerf guns could be arrested. More than 600 students had signed up to play the popular game "Humans vs Zombies" in which humans shoot the zombies with the sponge Nerf balls. When the Nerf guns were banned, the "human" participants in the battle resorted to using rolled up stockings.

The enormous popularity of the zombie in contemporary times has no doubt confused many individuals who try to balance their religious beliefs with a growing fascination for tales of a monster from the world of Voodoo and the undead. How should they respond to the ever-growing Cult of the Zombie? Is it possible that millions of people could become "zombified" after a great apocalyptic event? In the great majority of current motion pictures, books, games, and other media expressions, the zombies are themselves initially the victims of a great biological warfare, a mysterious virus, or some kind of mass pandemic that first kills them, then resurrects them with the uncontrollable desire to chomp on the uninfected and to create one big gory family.

Many of us who were reared in one of the Abrahamic monotheistic religions— Judaism, Christianity, and Islam—were told from our very early childhood that one day the graves would open and free the dead to face a day of judgment. Many of us who learned of this coming event in quite graphic detail were quite likely left with nightmares that convinced us not to walk through any cemetery at any time—night or day—for we were advised that this sudden raising of the dead could happen without any warning. No one—not even the wisest adult—knew the exact time when this awesome event might occur. As children, some of us envisioned terrible images of decaying corpses and skeletons pushing aside rotting coffins and reaching up through graveyard dirt to begin to run around in a kind of Halloween gone mad.

Because of our early religious conditioning, some of us, at some level of consciousness, have long expected a sudden onslaught of the undead rising from their graves.

And now, in a vast number of contemporary films, it seems as though the zombie is bringing on the Apocalypse, heralding Armageddon, the last great battle between the forces of Good and Evil—and if these zombie films are accurate, there won't be many unsullied humans left to fight the undead who will pursue them for their blood and their souls. To make matters worse, in these many dramatic presentations of a Zombie Apocalypse, there appears no sign of help from the promised legions of angels who are to arrive like the heavenly cavalry and save humanity from total destruction.

## Let Us Now Meet the Real Zombies

**R**eal *Zombies, the Living Dead, and Creatures of the Apocalypse* posits that a *real* zombie is not the victim of biological warfare, a blast of radiation from a space vehicle, or an unknown virus that escaped a secret laboratory. A real zombie is a reanimated corpse which has most often been brought back to life to serve as slave labor. Originating in West Africa as the worship of the python deity, Voodoo was brought to Haiti and the southern United States, particularly the New Orleans area. Voodoo holds that a supernatural power or essence may enter into and reanimate a dead body.

As my friend Lisa Lee Harp Waugh, a noted necromancer and writer, put it: "A Zombie is a soulless human corpse, still dead, but taken from the grave and endowed by sorcery with a mechanical semblance of life. It is a dead body, which is made to walk and act and move as if it were alive."

Voodoo lore actually has two types of zombie—the undead and those who died by violence. Those who adhere to the Afro-Caribbean spiritual belief of Vodun, popularized as Voodoo, are very cautious in their approach to a cemetery, for it is there that one is most likely to encounter the unfortunates wraiths who died violently and without adequate time for a proper ritual.

There is a third spirit that may be classified as a zombie—that of a woman who died a virgin. A terrible fate awaits her at the hands of the lustful Baron Samedi, Master of the Netherworld.

For those who embrace the teachings of Voodoo, the zombie, the living dead, are to be feared as very real instruments of a priestess or priest who has yielded to the seduction of evil and allowed themselves to be possessed by negative forces and become practitioners of dark side sorcery.

Waugh said that some Southern zombie-making rituals consist of digging up a fresh corpse from its tomb or deep grave: "The body is then fed strange potions and whispered to in strange chants," she explained. "Many individuals who have witnessed the evil, dark deed say that it is disturbing to view. You stand frozen in the shadows as a voyeur to some devil dark secret spell. You see a recently dead man being made into a zombie before your eyes."

Allowing that disturbing scene to linger a moment in one's mind, Waugh came up with an image much worse: "Picture the image of a beautiful Voodoo Queen riding a rotting corpse like a wild banshee, having dark magical sex in a graveyard. Certainly this would be a sight that you will never forget. Imagine the strange image as candles flair, and mosquitoes bite hard into your skin. Then the spell comes to a conclusion as the zombie corpse comes to life. At that moment the Voodoo Queen takes him into what seems to be a deep kiss—and bites off his tongue to make him her eternal slave."

Most contemporary experts on New Orleans Voodoo and zombies agree that the legendary Dr. John, believed to be a zombified Voodoo master, created the perfect zombie juices and powders to make a living, breathing zombie that will not die or age and be truly immortal.

Waugh commented that the most dangerous zombies are those that stay infants.

"Voodoo midwives often play this cruel trick on unsuspecting mothers who are about to give birth," she said. "The Voodoo Queens sit between the legs of the soon-to-be mother, as any midwife would, but they are chanting a secret spell."

"When the child is emerging from the womb, they will snatch them up at the second of birth. The cunning Midwife Queen will then break the child's neck and bite off the tip of its tongue as its soul hangs between the point of living and dead, thus making the *enfant diabolic* as they were called."

According to Voodoo lore, zombie children taken straight from the womb never age as mere mortals do. They may take over 30 years to grow into a beautiful girl or a handsome boy in its teens. Many Voodoo cultists insist that Marie Laveau, the queen of New Orleans Voodoo, never grew old because she was of zombie birth. Dr. John himself had performed her zombification at birth.

Zombie gumbo is a concoction that some people say Black Cat Mama Couteaux, a Voodoo Queen from Marshall, Texas, made to feed her zombie army each month. It usually consisted of dead animals found on side of the road, onion peelings, and scraps her dogs would not eat.

Marie Laveau fed her zombies a fine gumbo made with fish heads and scales and bones—and anything except banana peels which tend to constipate a zombie.

Some historians of Voodoo suggest that the origin of the word "zombie" may have come from *jumbie*, the West Indian term for a ghost. Others scholars favor the Kongo word *nzambi*, "the spirit that has resided in the body and is now freed" as filtering down through the ages as "zombie." Although

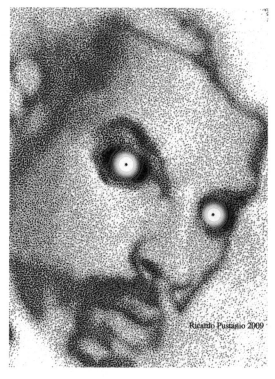

There are some who say that some Voodoo-Hoodoo Priests can "zombify" someone with a hypnotic stare and words chanted from Dr. John's "Black Book" (*art by Ricardo Pustanio*).

the practice of Voodoo and the creation of zombies was familiar to the residents of Louisiana before 1871, a number of etymologists believe that year is about the time that the word "zombi" entered the English language. The word that was originally used by the Haitian Creole people, these scholars maintain, was *zonbi*, a Bantu term for a corpse returned to life without speech or free will. There are others who argue quite convincingly that *Zombi* is another name for Damballah Wedo, the snake god so important to Voodoo. In other words, a zombie would be a servant of Damballah Wedo. A common ritual that creates a zombie requires a sorcerer to unearth a chosen corpse and waft under its nose a bottle containing the deceased's soul. Then, as if he were fanning a tiny spark of fire in dry tinder, the sorcerer nurtures the spark of life in the corpse until he has fashioned a zombie.

In Haiti the deceased are often buried face downward by considerate relatives so the corpse cannot hear the summons of the sorcerer. Some even take the precaution of providing their dearly departed with a weapon, such as a machete, with which to ward off the evil sorcerer.

There are many terrible tales of the zombie. There are accounts from those who have discovered friends or relatives, supposedly long-dead, laboring in the fields of

Marie Laveau, the greatest of all the Voodoo Queens of New Orleans, learned the power secrets of zombification from her mentor, Dr. John (*art by Ricardo Pustanio*).

some sorcerer. One story that went the rounds a few years back had the zombified corpse of a former government administrator—officially dead for 15 years—as having been recognized toiling for a sorcerer in the fields near a remote village in the hills.

The connotations of evil, fear, and the supernatural that are associated with Vodun (also "Voudou" and, popularly, "Voodoo") originated primarily from white plantation owners' fear of slave revolts. The white masters and their overseers were often outnumbered 16 to one by the slaves they worked unmercifully in the broiling Haitian sun, and the sounds of Voudou drums pounding in the night made them very nervous.

Vodun or Voudou means "spirit" in the language of the West African Yoruba people. Vodun as a religion observes elements from an African tribal cosmology that may go back 10,000 years—and then it disguises these ancient beliefs with the teachings, saints, and rituals of Roman Catholicism. Early slaves—who were abducted from their homes and families on Africa's West Coast—brought their gods and religious practices with them to Haiti and other West Indian islands. Plantation owners were compelled by order of the French colonial authorities to baptize their slaves in the Catholic religion. The slaves suffered no conflict of theology. They accepted the white man's "water" and quickly adopted Catholic saints into the older African family of nature gods and goddesses.

When Voudun came to the city of New Orleans in the United States, it became suffused with a whole new energy—and a most remarkable new hierarchy of priests and priestesses, including the eternally mysterious Marie Laveau. And, of course, with Voodoo came the chilling accounts of zombies.

Some Voodoo traditions maintain that the only way that people can protect themselves from a zombie is to feed it some salt.

Lisa Lee Harp Waugh said that the story of not feeding salt to a zombie is actually overrated. "Yes, it can destroy a zombie," she said, "but if given to them in moderation, it tends to keep a zombie frozen for a few years until its services are once again needed. A full dose of pure white salt—and that's about a full teaspoon today— would put an end to animated corpse in a minute or less. They usually fall to the ground with violent convulsions and all the fluid drains from their bodies."

## The Awakening of a Zombie

Recently, one of my colleagues, Paul Dale Roberts, told me of his interview with a man who claimed to have been turned into zombie: "Pete claims that when he was vacationing in Haiti, he had a fling with a Haitian girl, whose father is a Voodoo shaman of the island. When the Haitian girl saw him with another, he was a marked man.

"One night in a disco, he was stabbed in the arm with a hypodermic needle. He passed out and awakened in a coffin. He was buried alive. He was paralyzed, but aware of his surroundings. Later, he was dug up from his grave and used as a slave, picking sugar cane for six months. He somehow managed to get out of his comatose state of mind and escaped the island back to California. He claims to this very day that he has skin lesions on his arms, legs, and torso, because of his zombie transformation in Haiti."

When William Michael Mott, author of *Pulp Winds,* learned that I was doing a book on real zombies, he wrote a poem, "The Awakening of a Zombie," which aptly describes the classic and traditional fate of one chosen to be a zombie victim of a Voodoo sorcerer:

> Awake in the dark, closed in tight,
> Where am I? In what hole unfound?
> The memories of a funeral rite
> Still haunt my ears with mournful sound.
> And now I hear the digger come
> Shovel pounding like a drum
> Casket breaking, pale moonlight
> And falling clods blot out my sight.
> I must be dead! Can't move a finger
> As I'm pulled from the recent grave
> And I think I'd rather linger,
> Than become a zombie slave.
> The potion forced between my lips
> Brings tingling life back to my flesh
> And I'm led away from tombs and crypts,
> My gaping grave still moist and fresh.
> No urge for brains or bloody fodder,
> Just meager gruel, not born of slaughter
> And I barely recall Romero's films—
> As I fight just to move my limbs.
> This death-life is a sullen dream
> In which I mind each barked command
> And passing days of labor seem

An hourglass and grains of sand.
Poison of toad, and blowfish too
Went into that Voodoo brew
That I know is mixed into my gruel—
And I must eat, for reasons cruel.
I simply cannot disobey
And slowly, memories fade away
Of another time, or place, or land
When I wasn't dead—I'd been a *man*.
At night when torches gutter low
Into a shackled cell I go
And then I struggle to awaken
From an existence most forsaken.
The gruel's consumed by scuttling things
Before I bring myself to eat
So I eat the thieves that fill my bowl—
I've found a source of food, of meat.
A few more nights, the rats and roaches
Will fill my belly and free my mind
And someday soon, when dawn approaches
I'll burst these chains, to vengeance find!
A zombie terror from the grave
Will take the lives of those who preyed,
Turned a man into a slave,
Who watched his own humanity fade.
The price will then be paid in full
For when the foreman comes around
I'll take my chains and break his skull—
Then find the one who brought me down.
But I won't kill him, not then, oh no,
I'll take his tongue, then bind him tight
And deep into that hole, he'll go,
Beneath the dirt, and endless night.

### The Zombification Throne in New Orleans

Legend has it that each of the 23 cemeteries of old New Orleans has a Devil's Chair placed among its gravestones and crypts. There is, however, only one cemetery that has a Devil's Throne where the Voodoo folk, the witches, and all those seeking to make a pact with the Master of Darkness go to meet with him eye to eye. That awesome throne is located in St. Louis Cemetery Number 1.

Old Voodoo tales relate that Marie Laveau, the Queen of New Orleans Voodoo, learned the powerful secret of the chair from her immortal, zombified Voodoo master and mentor, Dr. John. Laveau's many followers tell how Dr. John would sit in the throne on nights when the moon was covered by clouds and converse with the Devil about the secrets of zombification, the power to turn someone into a zombie. According to some accounts, the Devil taught Dr. John over 100 rituals or hexes that would almost immediately transform a living or dead man into a real zombie.

The Devil's Throne in St. Louis Cemetery Number 1 is often called the Zombie Making Chair, because, according to Voodoo lore, it was while Dr. John was sitting on the Devil's Throne that his satanic majesty turned him into the first living, immortal zombie to walk the earth. Only the Devil himself would be able to bestow such powers upon a mortal.

Voodoo practitioners believe that if you sit on the Zombie Making Chair on a dark, moonless night and ask the Devil to transform you into a living zombie, you will live a healthy, immortal life and will not age, die, or be able to be hurt or maimed.

The catch to the bargain is that when Judgment Day comes and Satan is thrown into the dark, bottomless pit, it is you upon whom he will sit for 1,000 years.

# ZOMBIES VERSUS VAMPIRES

When a horror-buff friend learned I was doing a book about zombies, he remarked, "Well, you know, zombies are pretty much like vampires. They both need to feed on human blood."

I agreed that zombies "are pretty much like vampires" in the films *after* George Romero's *Night of the Living Dead* (1968) and the dozens of zombie movies that were spawned by that single low-budget, black-and-white, independent production.

"But," I stressed, "this is a book about *real zombies*, the undead that lie in their graves until they are summoned to serve their masters as mindless slaves. There are some stories of zombies that attack people on the orders of their masters; there are many accounts of dark side Voodoo sorcerers having been responsible for peoples' deaths; but I know of no accounts where shuffling zombies hunted humans to eat them. And no one becomes a zombie after having been bitten by a zombie—though a tetanus shot would certainly be in order."

It is quite easy to see how in centuries past the undead—whether zombie, vampire, ghoul, wraith, or restless spirit—may have been confused with one another.

No one can possibly derive an exact date when early humans first began to bury their dead. Controversy continues whether or not certain skeletal remains found in the caves of the Pleistocene epoch Neanderthals indicate that some kind of burial ceremony was conducted for the dead around 200,000 years ago.

Neither can anyone pinpoint for certain when the concept of an afterlife first occurred to primitive humans. It might be conjectured that when early humans had realistic dreams of friends or relatives who were dead, they might have awakened, convinced that the departed somehow still existed in some other world. Such an idea, whenever it first occurred, was undoubtedly taken either as reassuring and comforting or as frightening and threatening. The belief that there was something within each

The Draugre are the undead of the Scandinavian sagas. They incorporate aspects of the zombie in that they are animated corpses, and they are occasionally vampiric in their quest for blood. They also possess magical powers (*art by Bill Oliver*).

individual that survived physical death was either an exciting promise or a terrifying menace that eventually spread to humans everywhere throughout the planet.

Paleolithic humans (c. 250,000 B.C.E.) placed stones and other markings on graves, but we cannot determine for certain whether they did so to distinguish one grave from another for the purpose of mourning or to prevent evil spirits from rising from the burial place.

The fear of evil spirits also gave rise to the universal dread of cemeteries and the belief that burial grounds are haunted. Restless spirits, vengeful ghosts, ghouls, and vampires could lurk behind every grave stone or tomb.

The traditional vampire of legend was a corpse, wrapped in a rotting burial shroud, that has somehow been cursed by man or devil who has clawed free of its grave to satisfy its bloodlust for the living—quite often, family members or local townsfolk. The vampire in folklore appears as a grotesque, nightmarish creature of the undead with twisted fangs and grasping talons.

With each succeeding generation, the dark powers of the vampire grew. He could transform himself into the form of a bat, a rat, an owl, a fox, and a wolf. He was able to see in the dark and to travel on moonbeams and mist.

Mere mortals seemed helpless against the strength of the vampire—which could equal the strength of 10 men. What could the people do if they suspected that a vampire was rising from the grave or crypt at night to seek human blood?

Some homes liberally displayed wolfbane and sprigs of wild garlic at every door and window. Nearly everyone wore the crucifix about one's neck and placed others prominently on several walls—especially near windows.

And then there were the times when a few brave individuals hunted down the grave or coffin of the nocturnal predator and placed thereon a branch of the wild rose to keep him locked within. If that didn't work, then the only course of action remaining was to pry open the vampire's coffin during the daylight hours while he lay slumbering and pound a wooden stake through his heart, behead him, and burn the body—or, much safer, destroy the coffin while he was away and allow the rays of the early morning sun to scorch him into ashes.

## The Vampire that Terrorized an Entire Town

Real vampires are still being reported by honest and sober men and women in the twenty-first century. Recently I received a very strange and eerie account from a friend who is a professional journalist whose work appears in major newspapers in the United States. According to her, a friend from eastern Pennsylvania had told her something that she considered really earth-shattering.

Her friend said that he knew of a town in one of the New England states whose residents experienced the attacks of a vampire that was still active until late in the twentieth century. This "thing" had the entire town on edge, but it was the "in" secret of the community. If someone new moved to town (such as a teacher, medical professional, etc.), they were warned about what the townspeople would describe as possible attacks from escapees from a nearby asylum and not to be out late at night.

If someone were bitten, an elaborate chain of command would get the afflicted victims out of the area and to a protected place where they wouldn't wind up as the undead.

The person who told my friend this account was an art teacher, the son of a minister. "He is a thoroughly honest person, very kind and sympathetic," she said. "This is one of my few encounters with someone who had experienced the dark side."

She readily conceded that the experiences of the townspeople seemed like stories right out of a vampire movie or a novel. Horror writer Stephen King's *Salem's Lot* comes quickly to mind as far as plot," she said. "However in this case, it was only one

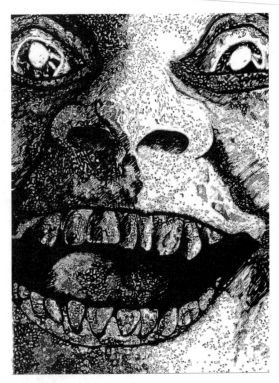

Real vampires differ from zombies in that they are the ones who enslave their victims, whereas the zombie is a victim who has been enslaved by a Voodoo Priest or Priestess (*art by Ricardo Pustanio*).

vampire or creature of the night. They had no idea of how to get rid of it. The creature seemed to strike spontaneously after long intervals of quiet—as if it had been out of town or something—and the entire population of the town was, at least on one level, aware of the situation.

"New people coming to the town usually never stayed long. If a teacher signed a contract, he or she was gone by the end of the year. New doctors, dentists, pharmacists, and lawyers would never buy homes or raise families there. They would commute and be there only on certain days, then usually leave before dark."

My friend told me that the only way that they finally got rid of this creature was to find its grave and pour several tons of cement on it!

"As far as I can recall," she said, concluding her account, "this seemed to work (but with vampires, for how long?)"

## From Grotesque Night Stalker to Sex Symbol

In 1897, Bram Stoker wrote a novel that would forever change the way people regarded vampires. In 1920, F.W. Murnau tried to obtain the rights to film Stoker's, *Dracula*. When his offer was refused, Murnau made the decision to film his own version (*Nosferatu*) with actor Max Schreck portraying Dracula as a loathsome bloodsucker, skittering about in the shadows with dark-ringed, hollowed eyes, pointed devil ears, and hideous fangs. With his long, blood-stained talons, his egg-shaped head and pasty white complexion, Schreck's Nosferatu seems to embody the creature of the undead as revealed by the collective nightmares of humankind throughout the centuries. One can only wonder if it is just an interesting coincidence that Schreck in German means "terror" or "horror"? E. Elias Merhige's *Shadow of the Vampire*, released on December 29, 2000, presented the unsettling premise that the monstrous Nosferatu (Willem Dafoe) who assumed the title role in the classic film by F.W. Murnau (John Malkovich) was, in reality, actually portrayed by a real vampire, rather than an actor.

Although *Nosferatu* remains a silent film classic and holds true to the traditional appearance of the vampire, Bela Lugosi's portrayal of Dracula as a sophisticated aristocrat owns the role in the minds of most *Dracula* aficionados. With a few close rivals—Christopher Lee, Frank Langella, Gary Oldman—Lugosi's is the first image that comes to mind when one discusses the infamous count. Lugosi first put on Dracula's evening clothes and cape on Broadway in 1927 for the popular stage play based on the novel. In 1931, he won the role for Tod Browning's motion picture version of *Dracula* and forever altered the image of the vampire in the popular consciousness from that of a hideous demon into that of an attractive stranger who possesses a bite that, while fatal, also promises eternal life.

In the twenty-first century, the vampire has become a sex symbol. Audiences were repelled by the image of the monster in *Nosferatu*. Some women were said to faint or scream during showings of *Dracula*.

Today the screams of teenaged girls during vampire movies is not due to shock or fear but are prompted by the same frenzied hysteria as that earned by rock stars. The male vampires are buff and handsome; the female vampires are gorgeous and seductive. Who wouldn't want to be bitten by these gods and goddesses and stay young and beautiful forever?

The zombie of today's films, games, and books is gaining on the vampire as the most popular of the grotesque creatures who chase down human prey and eat their flesh. However, the zombie may be resurrected, but not as a sexy beast, buff, handsome or beautiful. And the victim of a zombie, once bitten, shuffles about with a gaping wound oozing blood that surely does not improve his or her physical attractiveness or prompt sexual urges.

## The Awful Appetites of the Ghoul

The ghoul is often linked with the vampire and the werewolf in traditional folklore, but there are a number of obvious reasons why the entity has never attained the popularity achieved by the Frankenstein monsters, Draculas, and Wolfmen of the horror films. First and foremost is the nauseating fact that the ghoul is a disgusting creature that subsists on corpses, invading the graves of the newly buried and feasting on the flesh of the deceased. The very concept is revolting and offensive to modern sensibilities.

There are a number of different entities that are included in the category of ghoul. There is the ghoul that, like the vampire, is a member of the family of the undead, continually on the nocturnal prowl for new victims. Unlike the vampire, however, this ghoul feasts upon the flesh of the deceased, tearing their corpses from cemeteries and morgues. The ghoul more common to the waking world is that of the mentally unbalanced individual who engages in the disgusting aberration of necrophagia, eating or otherwise desecrating the flesh of deceased humans. Yet a third type of ghoul would be those denizens of Arabic folklore, the "ghul" (male) and "ghulah" (female), demonic "jinns" that haunt burial grounds and sustain themselves on human flesh stolen from graves.

Sgt. Bertrand, the infamous so-called werewolf of Paris, was really a ghoul, for rather than ripping and slashing the living, he suffered from the necrophilic perversion of mutilating the dead.

Ghouls are often linked to vampires and werewolves in popular culture. However, ghouls feed on the dead, not the living, invading the graves of the newly buried and feasting on the flesh of the deceased (*art by Bill Oliver*).

It is not difficult to envision how the legends of the ghoul and vampire began in ancient times when graves were shallow and very often subject to the disturbances of wild animals seeking carrion. Later, as funeral customs became more elaborate and men and women were buried with their jewelry and other personal treasures, the lure of easy wealth superseded any superstitious or ecclesiastical admonitions that might have otherwise kept grave robbers away from cemeteries and from desecrating a corpse's final rest.

Then, in the late 1820s, surgeons and doctors began to discover the value of dissection. The infant science of surgery was progressing rapidly, but advancement required cadavers—and the more cadavers that were supplied, the more the doctors realized how little they actually knew about the anatomy and interior workings of the human body, and thus the more cadavers they needed. As a result, societies of grave robbers were formed called the "resurrectionists." These men made certain that the corpses finding their way to the dissecting tables were as fresh as possible. And, of course, digging was easier in unsettled dirt. The great irony was that advancement in medical science help to perpetuate the legend of the ghoul.

## *Hare and Burke, Grave-Robbing for Profit— Dr. Knox, Buying Corpses for Science*

Early on, the most infamous of the grave-robbers were William Hare and William Burke, who supplied Dr. John Knox of Edinburgh, Scotland.

Hare ran an inn, and his friend, Burke, a small, portly cobbler, did his business in a shop near Hare's inn. Between them, the two men unearthed coffins from cemeteries and carried their contents from the grave to Dr. Knox's laboratory.

Burke and Hare had hit upon a goldmine. At 10 pounds per corpse (approximately 17 dollars in present U.S. currency) the two men could get rich in very little time, because Knox went through cadavers at an incredible rate. Ten pounds was more than an average 1820s working man could earn in six months. To keep pace with their greed, Burke and Hare had added their own special wrinkle to the wholesale corpse business: The goods they pedaled were always fresh because they would not wait for a "corpse" to die.

Returning to Hare's inn on a cold December night, the two men warmed themselves with a few tankards of grog. Burke joined his common-law wife, Helen, and Hare went to his kept mistress, Mag Laird. Together the foursome celebrated their newfound financial independence. Even though they had been in the cadaver business less than a month, their clothes had already become those of the rich.

All through the spring and into the summer of 1828, business boomed. Even though Knox had to reduce the going rate to eight pounds (approximately 13 U.S. dollars) during the hot months because of his need for ice, Burke and Hare figured that was fair enough.

With his newfound riches, Burke changed his taste in women. Helen was a bit frowsy, and, besides, he had his eye on Mary Paterson, a beautiful prostitute who had always been out of his financial class. Burke approached her as a prosperous businessman, then bought her a jug of gin. From there it was only a little jingle of coin to the home of his brother, Constantine, who collected garbage for the Edinburgh police.

Unannounced at his brother's house, Burke informed the bewildered man that he had some business to discuss with the ample-bosomed, blond-haired beauty. The door to the bedroom had not been closed long before the door of the house opened again and in barged Helen Burke, her eyes blurred with drink and her voice screeching hatred for her husband. Someone had told her of his leaving the grog shop with the beautiful streetwalker.

Helen ran to the bedroom and jerked open the door to find a frustrated Burke and a Mary Paterson who had fainted dead away from too much drink.

To further complicate matters, Hare had followed Helen Burke to brother Constantine's house, and, to avoid trouble, had quickly doled out a few shillings to get the man and his wife out of the way. Constantine protested, wondering what would become of Mary Paterson, but Hare assured him that all would be handled very smoothly. After promising Helen that he would see that her husband committed no unfaithful act, Hare also convinced her to leave.

The next day the medical students attending Dr. Knox's lecture and dissection laboratory were a little stunned by the dead beauty that lay under the doctor's knife. More than one of them had seen her before on the streets.

The medical students were not the only people who had missed the beautiful streetwalker. She had a steady friend, an Irishman named McLaughlin, who looked on himself as her protector. Though the big, burly man could not prove anything, he was sure that Mary had met with foul play, and he traced her vanishing trail right to a cobbler named Burke.

Even while McLaughlin went storming away uttering curses and promising extreme retribution if anything had happened to his Mary, Burke was suffering from further domestic problems. While trying to fulfill a special order from Dr. Knox for a 10-year-old boy and an old lady, he and Hare had unwittingly taken an idiot as a victim. The fact would have been inconsequential to Dr. Knox, but to Helen Burke, her mind clouded with drink and superstition, it was an evil omen—a curse in fact—and the two grim businessmen had all they could do to keep her from spilling the entire story while moaning in her grog. Even a vacation at the seaside did her no good, and Burke, Hare, and Mag Laird decided to leave Edinburgh and hide out in Glasgow. In their absence, Helen Burke managed to regain her callousness, and by the time the trio tiptoed back into Edinburgh a few months later, she had not opened her mouth.

> *The next day the medical students attending Dr. Knox's lecture and dissection laboratory were a little stunned by the dead beauty that lay under the doctor's knife.*

But the game could not be played much longer. When a neighbor ran across the corpse of an old lady, which was all tucked neatly away in Burke and Hare's chest ready for transport, the entire matter nearly exploded in their faces. Only Hare's quick action in moving the evidence saved the day.

The thorough Edinburgh police had been moving in on the dealers in corpses ever since the first missing-person report had come from that sector of the city. McLaughlin had come to the police reporting the disappearance of Mary Paterson, and subsequent questioning of medical students, who had seen her beautiful, cold body on Knox's dissection table, had made the officials suspicious of Burke and Hare.

The police made arrests at Hare's inn and simultaneously raided Dr. Knox's laboratory where they found the body of the old lady, which had recently been delivered. Although neither of the Burkes ever opened their mouths both Mag Laird and William Hare confessed, telling how the victims were lured to the inn, then suffocated. Even though Dr. Knox claimed that he had known nothing of the murders and was never brought to trial, the grisly publicity ruined his reputation and he faded into obscurity.

Of the four ghoulish grave robbers only William Burke paid with his life. Helen Burke, who had only circumstantial evidence against her, was released. Probably because they had so readily confessed to their roles in the crimes, both the Hares were set free. Mag died seven years later in France, but William lived to the age of 80 and died a beggar in London.

Burke himself remains with us to this day—a skeleton in the Edinburgh anatomy museum. The placard placed beside this stocky structure is decorated with a small skull and minces no words. It reads: *William Burke, The Murderer.*

## The Horrid Thing that Waited in Darkness

*Chris Holly, who is today a respected paranormal investigator, learned a dreadful truth when she was a teenager—that there are things beyond the ken of mortal men that prowl the darkness for their victims. In fact, it appears that the "thing"—vampire, ghoul, zombie, or reptilian monster—that pursued her, could well have ended her career as a researcher before it had a chance to begin.*

The following account is presented in Chris' own words:

I was 16 years old and had my junior driver's license, which meant I could drive until dark. It was summer and dusk came late—around nine o'clock. When we planned our days well and were lucky enough, we would arrange with the 18-year-olds who had full licenses to follow us home to drop off our cars before nightfall. They would then take us out in their cars for the rest of the night.

On a typical evening we would all hang out at the McDonald's in town. As dusk approached we would try to find the 18 year-olds willing to follow us home before the night took hold and the police sorted us out. Anyone caught driving with a junior license after nightfall would lose his or her driving rights altogether. Consequently, the hours between seven o'clock and nine o'clock became critically important each evening. If we did not have our "after nine" pals lined up by then, we were home for the night by nightfall.

**Paranormal investigator Chris Holly became a believer when she was a teenager and met a real ghoulish being.**

It was a Saturday night. My parents were off visiting my grandparents. I was allowed to drive my mother's convertible around with my pals until nightfall. I was to return the car to our house by 8:45—or else.

I was out with my two friends, Sally and Sara. We were hanging out with our other pals at McDonald's. My friend Sally's older brother agreed to pick us up at my house at 10 o'clock that night—after I had taken my mom's car home. He agreed to take us for pizza in town. It was a big deal to us at the time as my friend's brother was a 20 year-old. Being seen at the pizza place with him was a feather in our 16-year-old caps.

Time came for us to take the car home and so we headed to my house to meet Sally's brother. I drove the car home and parked it in the driveway in front of the house.

We all rushed to my front door as a few hours of cola drinking at McDonald's left us all in urgent need of the bathroom. The three of us ran to the bathroom across the hall from my bedroom and laughed as we yelled at each other to hurry up and swore off all additional cola drinking during future McDonald's visits. I was last in line and rushed into the bathroom as my two friends stood brushing their hair in the mirror.

My friend Sally stood straight up, turned completely white, and said to Sara and me, "I have a horrid feeling—we are not alone in the house. I think I heard something."

We all froze and listened. I thought I heard a sort of bump, too. I stood up and said, "Let's get out of here!"

The three of us blasted through the bathroom doorway, down the hallway, and out the front door. I slammed the door and locked it. Luckily, I had placed my keys into my pocket, but I left my pocketbook inside the house. We ran to the car and I backed it into the street. We quickly closed the convertible top and locked all the car doors. We were all in the front seat. We sat there terrified. I could feel my heart pounding with a fear I knew was real and warranted.

After a few minutes we thought maybe we were just suffering from "boogie-man" syndrome. I thought I should at least go back inside and get my pocketbook. Then I could call my parents and have my license and money with me as well. I was getting out of the car to go back to the house when something caught my eye.

As I lifted myself from the driver's seat and stepped outside the car, I thought I saw the front porch light flicker. My friend Sara stood beside me in the street as we looked up at the house. We watched as the light over the front door turned on and off—again and again.

I felt a fear I had never before known. Somebody was definitely inside the house and playing with us as well.

We jumped back into the car and locked the doors again. I started the car so we could go call the police and my parents. As I turned the ignition key with my trembling hand, I continued to watch this person inside our house proceeding to light up the living room.

As we pulled away, my friend Sally said, "Oh God, he is in your room! He turned on your light!"

I felt sick and angry all at once, knowing as I drove for help that someone was in my home, intentionally toying with us.

We reached the end of my street just as my friend's brother turned the corner on his way to pick us up. I blew the horn and told him to pull over. We all started screaming at once. He had brought two of his football pals with him and so we all decided to return to the house for one more look.

We both parked in the street and everyone watched as lights inside the house kept switching on and off every few seconds—first the kitchen, then the den, and then over to the living room. The front porch light was apparently turned on and off every time this intruder passed the switch inside.

The boys watched this taking place and clearly felt the same fear we did. My friend's brother decided we needed to call the police. He sent one of his friends in his car to call 911. We stayed locked in my mother's car—the three of us girls, Sally's brother, and Sally's brother's friend.

I decided to keep the motor running. At this point I was scared out of my mind. We watched as the light show continued. We sat silently waiting. The air was still. The only sounds we heard were the light chirping of summer crickets and the light hum of the car motor. Nobody said a word. We all knew we were being watched by and played with by some type of madman.

Sally finally broke the silence. She said, "Thank God you did not go back into that house."

I just sat frozen, ready to drive away if I needed to.

We sat there for what seemed an awfully long time, but in truth was only a few minutes. I was very fearful this person in my house would leave before the police arrived. We sat anxiously as the seconds ticked away and occupied ourselves by watching lights turning on—and now staying on—throughout the house.

Soon the house looked like a barn fire on a dark beach as every light appeared to be on—including outside floodlights and driveway spotlights. We again sat silently, watching.

Suddenly from deep inside the house came this animal-like, wild growling scream. I will never forget this nonhuman screaming until the day I die.

As this thing screamed it must have been pounding on the backside of the front door or a front wall. The house echoed this wild animal-like screaming and muffled banging with such force that I began to shake and cry. My friend's brother touched my shoulder from the back seat with his hand and said, "We need to leave. This is way too much for us to handle."

I was shaking so much I could barely place the car into gear. We started down the road but had rolled only a few yards when our friend returned with a police car following right behind him.

Coincidentally, my parents were turning the corner right behind the police car. I stopped my car and waited until the policeman was standing just outside my car door. I rolled down the window and then we all started to tell him what was happening.

The policeman looked up at the house to see the last of the light changes occurring. As he stood looking at the house, the creature inside let out one last howling scream.

The policeman reached for his side arm and whispered "Mother of God."

My parents ran to the side of our car, and the policeman asked my father for the keys to the house. He then withdrew his gun, called for backup, and started up the driveway toward the front door.

Before the policeman unlocked the front door, another policeman arrived. He ran to the front door to aid the first policeman, and they entered the house together.

We all stood outside watching as the policemen made their way through our house—this now eerie-looking building we girls had been giggling in just moments before. It again seemed as if a very long time passed—maybe 10 to 15 minutes—then one of the policemen called my father to the house.

Again, they seemed to be searching the house—this time all three of them. My dad eventually returned to the rest of us, still standing by the cars, and told my friend's brother to take all the kids directly home and to lock his car doors and not stop for anyone or anything.

As my friends drove away, my dad told my mother and me to get back into the car. He got into the car with us and quickly locked all the doors. He then told my mother and me that the policemen discovered the back door had been ripped open. He said the person who broke in had taken some of our clothing and makeup and thrown it around the house. My dad then looked at my mother in a way that told me there was something more he was not saying.

By this time there were many police cars around the neighborhood. I saw two policemen with a dog searching the neighbor's yard closest to our house. My friend Kim lived there with her family. We sat in the locked car for a long time. Both of my parents were upset and I was scared to death.

Finally a policeman appeared at our front door and motioned for my father to come back inside the house. My dad left us locked inside the car and did as the policeman directed. My dad talked with the policemen for a few minutes and then motioned for my mother and me to come inside the house as well.

When my mother and I walked into the house, one policeman and my dad took my mother by the arm to show her something down the hallway while another policeman tried to distract me in the living room. I wanted to stay with my parents, and so I started to walk toward the bedroom area where they had gone when my mom let out a horrible scream and burst into tears. I took off in a full run to where my parents were standing.

They were in my bedroom. I walked into the bedroom myself and saw my parents looking behind my open closet door. The policeman was

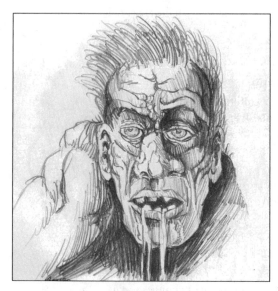

**Whatever thing had been in Chris Holly's house, it was clearly not human (*art by Wm. Michael Mott*).**

looking behind the door as well. I leaned forward and pushed the closet door closed in order to see what they were looking at in the space behind it.

On my bedroom floor, no longer hidden by the closet door, sat a little wooden chair my dad normally kept in his office behind the garage. Draped over the chair, as if someone had been sitting there holding it in his hand, was a long piece of brand new rope. It looked as if someone had just let it slip from his hands as he stood up to leave.

On the floor beside the chair were a long, sharp carving knife from the kitchen and some matches. My makeup had been used to paint strange marks and symbols on my bedroom wall. My nightgown was torn and thrown into the wastebasket next to my desk. On my bed was an outline where something had lain on it and left an imprint. Across my headboard on the wall were long claw marks where something had torn into the wall. I also noticed a putrid order lingering in the house.

*I could not understand what he was telling me. He repeated that someone or something with incredible strength grabbed the window frame and ripped the entire thing out of the wall of the house.*

I took it all in, despite my paralyzing terror, and then I looked one more time at the little chair and rope no longer hidden by the closet door.

I ran to the bathroom and vomited. My mom, crying, came in after me. I knew I had missed losing my life that night by the mere luck of my friends needing to use the bathroom. If I had entered the house alone, my life surely would have been taken. The question was, but by what?

The police stayed with us for hours. They did not pretend the incident was just a robbery or some silly kid staging a prank. I knew clearly, as they did, that I had barely escaped a cruel and untimely death. Police searched the area for hours that night. They scanned the house for fingerprints and took great care in recording the details of all we had seen and heard.

The police talked to my dad before leaving and told him they knew of another incident in the area with similar details. A woman had been lured into her basement by the unexpected sound of her washer and dryer running. She also heard the horrid screams of this vile intruder and ran for help. It was not the first time they had to deal with this, and we could tell the police were both concerned and frightened.

I slept on the floor in my parents' bedroom that night. In fact, I slept on their bedroom floor until my dad fitted all the windows and doors of the house with either heavy-duty locks or steel bars. I refused to go outside by myself or drive anywhere in the car alone. I was terrified.

My mother and I were sitting at the kitchen table when I could tell by one look at my dad's face that the *thing* had come back, that something once again was terribly wrong.

My father sat down and told us that my friend Kim had been sitting in the family room watching TV. She was home with her mother and little brother, sitting on the couch beneath the family room window, when something from outside the house grabbed the window—frame and all—and ripped it right out of the side of the house.

I could not understand what he was telling me. He repeated that someone or something with incredible strength grabbed the window frame and ripped the entire thing out of the wall of the house.

Kim had jumped up screaming as a long greenish-gray snake-like arm reached for her from outside the window shell. Kim claimed she felt what seemed like a claw skim across her neck.

Her mother heard all the noise from another room. She grabbed her husband's loaded rifle and ran into the family room where she saw the window ripped out of the wall and this hideous, reptilian arm reaching for Kim.

By this time Kim was on the other side of the room screaming. Her mother took aim and fired at the space where the window had been. She could not tell whether she hit it. Whatever it was ran away howling that same angry non-human scream when she fired the gun.

Once again the police searched the area. Dogs were used. Police cars covered the streets. Once again this creature escaped.

I remained terrified the rest of that summer. I refused to leave the house without another family member accompanying me. I refused to drive alone in my car. I never stayed home alone and progressed only as far as sleeping in my bedroom with the door open—provided my brother (who was home from college on summer break) or my parents kept a bedroom door open as well.

I went away to school the following year. I would never again spend time alone in that house. If my family went away, I would go out too and stay out until they returned. I never again felt safe in that house.

As far as I know, whatever entered our house that summer night was never caught or identified. I do know he or "it" intended to tie me up and hurt me. I do know he or "it" had little fear and enjoyed terrifying us that night. I also know he or "it" was beast-like and far from human given its loud haunting screams, incredible physical strength, reptile-like skin and putrid smell. I do know the monster that ripped the window and frame out of Kim's wall was the same monster that intended and tried to kill me.

I am thankful I ran out of the house that night, that I did not go home alone, and that my friends were there with me to help me think things through. Sometimes our fate is just a slight degree from being something we can or cannot survive.

That night fate gave me a helping hand. Many a day since I have pondered how lucky I was to survive that horrifying period. It haunts me still as I continue to wonder what type of creature I could have faced alone that night. We all often wonder from where did it come? And where did it go? I often think about this experience as one of the greatest mysteries of my life.

# MUMMIES AND ZOMBIES

Perhaps of all the classic monsters that have terrified theater audiences and groups gathered around campfires, the two most likely to be confused with one another are the mummy and the zombie. One thinks of curses and spells associated with both of these beings. Of course the principal difference is that the mummies pronounce curses upon those who disturb their elegant tombs, while zombies lie for a time in crude graves because a curse has been placed upon them.

When Boris Karloff emerged as Im-ho-Tep in *The Mummy* (1932), his 3,700-year-old reanimated body set out to punish those who had disturbed his tomb, as well as to reclaim his reincarnated lover. In *The Mummy's Hand* (1940) Universal Studios initiated the first of a series of films featuring the mummified High Priest Kharis, who is revived by a mixture of tana leaves. Kharis, first played by Tom Tyler, slowly shuffles toward his victims, but always manages to catch them, even though he is dragging one leg, and one arm remains bound to his mummy wrappings. In each of the four entries in the Kharis series, the lovely actresses who played his reincarnated lover from ancient Egypt were never able to escape his clutches, despite their appearing sound of body enough to easily outrun the shambling mummy. In 1942, Lon Chaney, Jr. took over the role of Kharis in *The Mummy's Tomb*. Chaney wrapped himself in gauze again in *The Mummy's Ghost* (1944) and *The Mummy's Curse* (1945)—always assuming the same shuffling gait that actors impersonating the undead have used in nearly every mummy and zombie movie made until quite recently. In *28 Days Later*, (2002) the zombies definitely run as they chase the survivors of a plague that has afflicted London.

As early religions began to teach that there was a spirit within each person who died that might someday wish to return to its earthly abode, it became increasingly important that efforts be made to preserve the body. Burial ceremonies, which had at first been intended solely as a means of disposing of the dead, came to be a method of preserving the physical body as a home for the spirit when it returned for a time of rebirth or judgment.

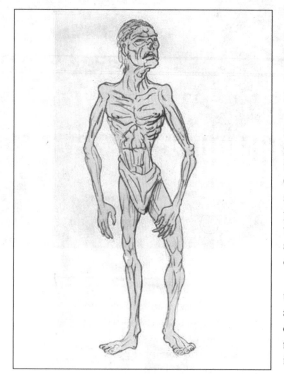

A real zombie is a reanimated corpse who has most often been brought back to life to serve as slave labor (*art by Wm. Michael Mott*).

The ancient Egyptians as a culture were pre-occupied with the specter of death. There was never an ancient people who insisted upon believing that death was not the final act of a human being, that "it is not death to die," with more emphasis than the Egyptians

Today, in many countries such as the United States, Canada, Great Britain, and the European nations, bodies are embalmed and every effort is made to preserve the body as long as possible. Coffins are sold to the bereaved families as dependable containers that will be able to preserve and protect the body of their beloved for centuries. The wealthier bereaved can afford crypts and vaults that are placed above ground and constructed of concrete or granite to contain family coffins.

Embalming the body of the deceased was practiced in ancient Egypt where the warm, dry climate assured its success. The Egyptians anointed, embalmed, and buried their dead, and made mummies of the men and women of power, rank, and importance.

To mummify, the Egyptians extracted the brain and the intestines, cleaned out the body through an incision in the side, and filled the body cavities with spices. The body was then sewn up and set aside to lie in salt for a period of 70 days. Then it was placed in gummed mummy cloth and fastened into its ornamental case. The poorer classes were not mummified but merely salted.

If the body of a vengeful mummy moves bereft of brain and other vital parts, there has to be a powerful spirit residing in or near the deceased that drives it. That spirit is known as the *Ka.*

In the cosmology of the early Egyptians, humans were considered the children of the gods, which meant that they had inherited many other elements from their divine progenitors than physical bodies. The *ba* or soul was portrayed on the walls of tombs as a human-headed bird leaving the body at death. During a person's lifetime, the *ba* was an intangible essence, associated with the breath. In addition to the *ba*, each person possessed a *ka*, a kind of ghostly double that was given to each individual at the moment of birth. When the person died, the *ka* began a separate existence, still resembling the body that it formerly occupied, and still requiring food for sustenance. Each person also had a *ren* or name, which could acquire a separate existence and was the underlying substance of all one's integral aspects. In addition to the facets listed above there was the *khu* or intelligence, the *ab* or will, the *sakkem* or life force, the *khaybet* or shadow, the *ikh* or glorified spirit, and the *sahu* or mummy. But the most important of all these was the *ka*, which became the center of the cult of the dead. It was to the *ka* that all offerings of food and material possessions were made.

When death came to the Egyptians, the physical body did not decay, for the greatest care was taken to preserve the body as a center of individual spirit manifestation. The body was carefully embalmed and mummified and placed in a coffin, on its side, as if it were only asleep. In the tomb with the mummy were brought all the utensils that a living person might need on a long journey, together with toilet articles, vessels for water and food, and weapons and hunting equipment to protect against robbers and to provide food once the initial supply was depleted.

About 1580 B.C.E., the *Pyramid Texts*, the oldest extant funerary literature in the world, dating back to as early as the Fourth Millennium B.C.E., and certain revised editions of those texts called the Coffin Texts, were brought together, re-edited, added to, and painted on sarcophagi and written on papyrus. This massive literary effort, the work of many authors and compilers, is known to us as the *Book of the Dead*, but to its creators as "The Chapters of Coming Forth by Day." Although there are many known copies of this ancient work, no one copy contains all the chapters, which are thought to number around 200.

By the time the text of the *Book of the Dead* was being copied on rolls of papyrus and placed in the tombs of the dead, a great social and religious revolution had taken place. Whereas the *Pyramid Texts* were meant only to be inscribed on the sarcophagi of the royals, it was now decreed that anyone—commoner or noble-born— who could afford the rituals would be entitled to follow the god Osiris into the afterlife.

The most important ceremony associated with the preparation of the dead was the opening of the eyes, mouth, ears, and nose of the deceased. This rite guaranteed life to the body and made it possible for the *ba* to re-enter its former dwelling.

The *Book of the Dead* also contained certain holy incantations that were designed to free the *ka* from the tomb and allow it to be incarnated again. The spirit might experience an existence as a hawk, a heron, or even a plant form, such as a lotus or a lily, moving along through various expressions of the life force until, after about 3,000 years, it could once again achieve rebirth as a human.

When an ancient Egyptian died, he or she expected to appear before Osiris, who would be waiting to pass judgment on him or her. The deceased would be led in by the jackal-headed god Anubis, followed by the goddess Isis, the divine enchantress, representing life, and the goddess of the underworld Nephthys, representing death. There were 42 divine judges to assess the life of the one who stood before them, and the deceased would be allowed to deny 42 misdeeds. Once the deceased had presented his or her case, Osiris indicated a large pair of balances before them with the heart of the deceased and the feather of truth, one in each of the pans. The god Thoth read and recorded the decision. Standing in the shadows was a monstrous creature prepared to devour the deceased, should the feather of truth outweigh his or her heart. In those instances when the heart outweighed the feather—and few devout Egyptians could really believe that their beloved Osiris would condemn them—the deceased was permitted to proceed to the Fields of Aalu, the real world, where the gods lived. Because humans were the offspring of the gods, the ancient Egyptians had no doubt about their immortality.

## *The Curse of King Tut*

With a legacy of hundreds of years of discovering mummies in their tombs and risking the curse placed upon the burial site, an extensive lore regarding grave robbers having activated spells that brought about their deaths had been built up throughout many generations. Several alleged supernatural occurrences associated with the discovery of the tomb of the pharaoh Tut-Ankh-Amon in 1922 launched the story of an ancient curse that could and would kill those who disturbed a royal mummy's resting place. The English archeological expedition led by Howard Carter came on the famous tomb by accident on November 4, 1922. What they had discovered was the ancient pyramid of a not-so-famous king of ancient Egypt named Tut-Ankh-Amon, who died at the age of about 18 from a blow to the head more than 3,300 years ago.

Although Tutankhamon had done nothing to distinguish himself in his brief life, the religious practices of Ancient Egypt made the pharaoh at once king and god. Believing in immortality of the body and the soul, these ancient kings had to prepare for death almost from birth to assure the existence of the *ka* (soul) throughout eternity. Though the embalming art was lost with the death of the ancient Egyptian culture, the tombs themselves show the craftsmanship of the Egyptian artisans. The *ka* of the dead king was provided with much gold and silver and many fine gems, so it could spend eternity in luxury. Thus the rich tombs of the ancient pharaohs became the targets of grave robbers, who relieved the dead kings of their riches.

Great precautions were taken to ensure that the tombs would not be pilfered. Slaves, who bent their backs building the royal sepulchers, were put to death. Priests, who held the funeral services, were sworn to secrecy; and the artisans, who had worked so diligently decorating the tombs, had their eyes put out as reward. The final protection placed on many tombs was a curse.

Some have argued that the tomb of King Tut did not have a curse placed on it at all, but Professor J.C. Mardrus, a French Egyptologist, not only declared that there was a curse, but maintained that he translated it from a tablet found at the entrance of the tomb. The "Stela of Malediction" read: "Let the hand raised against my form be withered! Let

**Several alleged supernatural occurrences were associated with the discovery of the tomb of Pharaoh Tut-Ankh-Amon in 1922 (*art by Ricardo Pustanio*).**

them be destroyed who attack my name, my foundations, my effigies, the images like unto me."

If there were an ancient curse condemning all those who defiled King Tut's tomb, what is the evidence of its effectiveness?

Howard Carter's canary was said to have been eaten by a cobra a few days after the opening of the tomb, a sign which the native Egyptian workers interpreted as the ancient power symbol of the pharaohs avenging itself on the golden bird of the Englishman.

Lord Carnarvon, the sponsor of the expedition, was bitten on the face by an insect shortly after the opening of the tomb and was dead within three weeks of pneumonia, which had complicated an infection.

An Egyptian present at the opening of the tomb, Sheik Abdul Haman, was dead within a few days after he had left the excavation site. Jay Gould, a tourist and friend of Lord Carnarvon, who had visited the tomb, died shortly after the Egyptian.

Woolf Joel, who kept a yacht on the river Nile and had become a friend of some of the men of the British expedition, died six months after visiting the tomb.

Sir Archibald Douglas Reid did not visit the tomb, but he died in February 1924 as he was about to X-ray the mummy.

Six years after the tomb was opened, Lady Carnarvon died of an insect bite in the same manner as her husband.

When the rumor of the curse began to spread, it was immediately communicated around the world. People in England, who had kept Egyptian artifacts in their families for centuries, readily turned them over to the British Museum. The ship on which the body of Lord Carnarvon was to be transported back to England with his wife had an almost complete cancellation of its passenger list.

The tally of King Tut's curse did not end with the deaths of the several people mentioned above. The grim record continued.

Professor Cisanova, of the College of France, and Georges Benedite of the Louvre in Paris, both died in Egypt and were associated with the excavations.

Albert M. Lythgoe, present at the opening of the tomb, died of a stroke on January 25, 1934, at the age of 66.

Sir William Garstin, also present at the opening, died in 1926.

An American, A. Lucas from the Museum of Natural History, died in 1929 at the age of 77. He was to have begun his retirement after assisting Carter in the field.

A tourist, Arthur E.P. Weigal, died of an unknown fever in 1934 at age 53.

The Hon. Mervyn Herbert, half-brother of Lord Carnarvon, who was present at the opening, died at age 48.

Richard Bethel, who assisted in opening the tomb, was 48 when he died in 1931. He had been in perfect health but died in his sleep during the month of November.

It is impossible to follow all of the tourists and journalists who visited the tomb, so an accurate tally of all those who violated of King Tut's privacy and paid for the intrusion with their lives cannot be considered final. Most accounts, however, place the score for the curse at 22 deaths.

Did those who died after enterting King Tut' tomb suffer from an ancient curse? (**Art by Wm. Michael Mott**)

Are these deaths the result of a series of strange coincidences? It must be observed that a number of those who died were somewhat advanced in age and would have passed on whether they had visited a pharaoh's tomb or a rose garden. The death of infection caused by insect bites is not terribly common, but it has been known to happen and may be completely unpleasant but natural, rather than supernatural. A number of contemporary researchers have also suggested that long dormant bacteria from the tomb could have taken up new residence in the lungs and other organs of those who opened or visited the ancient burial site.

There is little reason to doubt that the ancient pharaohs placed curses on their tombs to frighten away grave robbers from the fabulously wealthy treasures buried with them. And there are those who believe that the curses of the pharaohs somehow retain the power to project the icy fingers of death on those who dared to enter their sanctuary. Some scholars of the occult believe that the ancient Egyptian priests knew how to concentrate in and around a mummy certain magical energies of which we moderns possess little knowledge.

Were the deaths of those who entered King Tut's tomb the result of a curse or of a number of natural causes that, when they are presented collectively, only appear to have been the result of supernatural powers?

In 1932, 10 years after Tut-Ankh-Amon's tomb had been opened, Jack Pierce, Universal Studios' master movie monster maker, designed make-up for Boris Karloff, who played the reanimated mummy Im-Ho-Tep in *The Mummy*. The film became an instant classic horror film. One can only wonder, however, if the mummies would ever have invaded Hollywood without the legend of the Curse of King Tut.

### *The Manitou Grand Cavern Mummy*

I have written in previous books, such as *Worlds before Our Own*, of the mummified remains of men and women from a lost and unknown culture scattered throughout the United States. Some of these mysterious mummies are over seven feet tall and are estimated to be many thousands of years old.

And then there are those accounts of somewhat off-kilter doctors and scientists who have devised their own experiments in embalming and mummification.

Somewhere, right now, at a small country fair, a barker is chanting his old come-on and gullible small town folks are plunking down their hard-earned dollars to take a look at "The Marvelous Petrified Indian of Manitou Caverns."

The mummified remains they are viewing may be petrified, if you're willing to stretch a point a little, but by no stretch of the imagination is the shriveled package of skin and bones the remains of a Native American tribal member.

The Petrified Indian is Tom O'Neel, a rugged young Irish railroad worker who met an untimely death in a barroom brawl more than 100 years ago—and then his corpse became the victim of a bizarre experiment in frontier embalming and a pawn in a hoax that has carried his homeless remains across America ever since. A dime store wig gave Tom the needed long tribal warrior hair and an old tomahawk still rests in his mummified hands, but Tom O'Neel is no more Native American than General Custer.

The curious saga of Tom O'Neel began when his life ended during a wild shootout between railroad construction workers who poured into the suddenly booming town of Colorado City to lay track for the Colorado Midland Railroad in 1885.

The town coroner who pronounced Tom O'Neel dead was an amazing pioneer physician by the name of Dr. Isaac A. Davis, who had some theories about embalming and the preservation of bodies that had brought him a good deal of scientific note in medical circles of the day.

When attempts to locate relatives of the young railroad worker proved futile, Davis decided to use the body for some of his advanced embalming techniques and removed the corpse to a small stone shed in the city cemetery where he had housed chemicals and other instruments used for the normal preparation of the dead.

Dr. Davis believed that soaking a body in certain chemicals he had concocted, then drying the corpse in the mountain sunlight, could produce a cured body that would defy decay, much as the methods employed by Egyptian priests had preserved the remains of the ancient pharaohs.

For more than two years the frontier scientist alternately soaked and baked poor Tom O'Neel and injected chemical compounds into his lifeless veins.

Soon, the body began to take on the dark brown, leathery appearance of old cowhide and the once brawny figure of Tom O'Neel shrunk to a withered sack of skin and bones that weighed no more than 60 pounds.

It isn't quite certain what ultimate use Dr. Davis hoped to make of what he learned by experimenting on the remains of the young construction man, but death came to claim the doctor himself, and relatives hastened to be rid of the macabre mummy.

The family made a mistake, however, in selecting two local ne'er-do-wells to take the mummy to the cemetery for a decent burial. Quickly assessing the money-making potential represented by the mummy, the pair found themselves a black wig, some old Indian buckskins, several strands of beads, and managed to dress O'Neel's shrunken body. They found an old tomahawk to shove into the jar, and they headed off into the sunset to make their fortune as traveling showmen by exhibiting the remains of the "marvelous petrified Indian."

In the curious case of Tom O'Neel, a pioneering physician named Isaac A. Davis experimented with embalming fluids in an attempt to preserve the body of the man who died in an 1885 shoot out (*art by Ryan Mott*).

The project almost went awry at once when the two took some of the early proceeds of their ill-gotten gains and got roaring drunk, leaving Tom lying about in a Wyoming railroad depot unclaimed for several days.

When suspicious railroad officials opened the casket-like packing crate and discovered the mummy, sheriff's officers clapped the two budding showmen in irons for grave robbery.

Wires sent back to Colorado, however, turned up no incidents of grave robbing and the officials in Wyoming were happy to be rid of the grisly remains. No charges were filed.

The close brush with the law proved enough to discourage Tom's owners, however, and when an opportunity to sell the new circus attraction arose, the two partners leaped at it. Tom O'Neel began a new traveling career, this time with a tent show that also featured a two-headed calf and a five-footed goat.

There is no record of how many times the sun-dried remains of Tom O'Neel changed hands in the years that followed, but old newspapers of the era containing advertisements of the "Wondrous Petrified Indian of Manitou Cavern" are a witness to the long journey across the country in which Tom suffered the continuing indignity of exhibition at countless country crossroads.

One story has it that an old resident of Colorado City, back east for a visit, encountered the show with which Tom was then traveling and attempted to buy the corpse and provide it with proper burial. The compassionate man was turned down by the low-budget Barnum in charge, who claimed he was making a fortune with the petrified Indian.

Just where poor Tom O'Neel is right now isn't known, but chances are the long-dead Irish workman is still being displayed and represented as a relic from the mysterious path. His spirit must surely be horribly restless, and his Irish temper at full boil. We can only pity those sideshow tent gawkers if anyone accidentally breaks the jar and frees the Manitou Grand Canyon Mummy.

## Marking Burial Sites and Creating Cemeteries

The marking of graves goes back into remote antiquity. The ancient Hebrews buried their dead and used stone pillars to mark the graves. The Greeks often placed gravestones and various kinds of ornate sculpture on their burial sites.

The Assyrians (c. 750–612 B.C.E.) dug huge excavations which sometimes reached a depth of 60 feet into which they cast the bodies of their dead, one upon the other. Even when they began to place their dead in coffins, the Assyrians continued to pile one above the other in great excavations.

The Iberians, the original people who inhabited the peninsula where modern day Portugal and Spain exist, buried their leaders with great pomp and ceremony in chambers made of huge stones, covered over with earth. The bodies were placed in these megalithic chambers in a sitting posture. The Aryans, an Indo-European people, burned their dead and placed the ashes in urns shaped like rounded huts with thatched roofs.

Decorating graves with flowers and wreaths is an old custom which appears to date back to the earliest human burial observances. Wreaths made of thin gold have been found in Athenian graves during archaeological excavations. The Egyptians adorned their mummies with flowers, and paintings on the walls of tombs depict the mourners carrying flowers in their hands.

Not everyone who died in ancient Egypt was buried in a tomb. Although the Egyptians believed firmly in an afterlife, they were also of the opinion that only the powerful and important in the earthly life would have any notable status in the world to come. According to rank and wealth, those who were great in Egypt, and therefore likely to be important in the next life, were laid to rest in magnificent tombs with treasure, servants, food, and weapons to accompany them; the ordinary people were buried in rude stone compartments.

The rulers of the ancient city of Thebes—once the capital of upper Egypt (1580–1085 B.C.E.)—and their subjects never constructed massive pyramids to house their coffins, but cut their tombs from rock. As soon as a pharaoh would ascend the throne, his loyal subjects began the preparation of their tombs. Excavation went on uninterruptedly, year by year, until death ended the king's reign and simultaneously the work on his tomb—which also became a kind of an index revealing the length of his reign. These tombs, cut from the rock in the mountains in Upper Egypt, are still to be seen.

In sixteenth century Europe, it was customary to make wreaths of flowers from ribbon and paper and give them to the church in memory of the deceased. These artificial wreaths of long ago evolved into the contemporary mourning wreath of living flowers, usually brought by friends or relatives of the deceased and placed upon the grave.

## The Mummy with the Gray-Green Fungus

*Graveyards are reminders that we are mortals and that we will one day join those who rest below the well-manicured lawns. The crypts and mausoleums found in many cemeteries are another matter. For some reason, they seem to stir ancestral memories of ancient tombs and the restless undead that lie within their darkened confines.*

*Pastor Robin Swope, known as the Paranormal Pastor, was not always sequestered behind the pulpit and the comfort of his library. There was a time when he worked as a gravedigger, and he has shared two of these eerie experiences from those days and nights. In the following account, he tells of a most unusual occupant of a mausoleum near Pittsburgh:*

In the late 1970s a cemetery near Pittsburgh had built a new Mausoleum. It had been promised for years, and the salesmen eager to make a lucrative commission, had pre-sold crypts long before they were available. So many makeshift cement above-ground crypts were quickly built for those who had purchased mausoleum spaces and had passed on before they were built.

When the mausoleum was finished it was the job of the gravediggers to disinter the bodies and place them in their new crypts. It was a disgusting and dirty job, for many of the caskets leaked the liquefied remains of the deceased. To make matters worse for the gravediggers every body had to be physically identified by a mortician who had originally embalmed the victim—and not just by their clothing or jewelry—to make sure the corpse in the casket was the person named on the makeshift crypt.

The supervisor remembered each decaying face, for they were burned in his memory, but one stood out. Most of the bodies had long since dried up and become desiccated. If any flesh was left [it] was almost tanned leather hanging off the boney skeleton. Some looked as if they were made out of [gelatin] as the corpse had decomposed into a liquid goo. But one was odd.

When they opened the coffin of the old man it was like he had just been laid to rest. Except for one disturbing and obvious fact. He was covered with a furry grey-green fungus. All his flesh had been eaten by the fungus but it held the shape of his face so well it shocked the superintendent and the undertaker. Except for the odd color and the fleece-like look of his skin he looked like he might just open his eyes or mouth at any moment.

They quickly got over the initial shock and noted that, yes, he was who he was suppose to be, and they put the coffin in the second level in the back of the newly constructed mausoleum.

Monday morning when the maintenance crew came to open up the office they noticed the mausoleum door was open. As they neared the open door they immediately knew something was wrong. Something was smeared on the glass door of the mausoleum, and as they looked inside, one of the crypts was open.

And it was empty.

Fearing the disgusting work of grave-robbers they went to call the police, but as they rounded the corner to head back to the office they passed the old makeshift cement crypts.

One was open and it held a casket.

It was the casket of the mold man, right back in the place he had been interned for the last five years. To be sure everything was all right and they did not have a grave robber playing a joke they opened up the coffin.

The body was still there and the jewelry he wore was still intact. They called the police, but there was nothing the officers could do other than file a vandalism report. The body was placed back in the mausoleum.

After they sealed up the crypt again, the staff noticed that the smear on the door was the same color as the mold that covered the man. Also disturbing, there seemed to be small pieces of the stuff on the carpet that covered the floor from the crypt to the doorway. The body did not look molested at all, and the casket had shown no visible signs of forced opening, but it was still very disturbing.

Two weeks later, it happened again. Everything was the same, the crypt was opened and the casket was found resting in its old spot. Even the smear and pieces of mold scattered here and there were the same.

But one thing was different this time. It had recently rained and the ground was soft. A single trail of footprints ran from the mausoleum to the makeshift crypt.

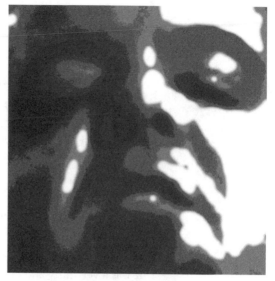

One body in the mausoleum was peculiar. Though the flesh had decayed, the corpse was covered in a green fungus that mimicked the features of the once-living man (*art by Ricardo Pustanio*).

And they were almost erased by the tracks left by the dragged coffin.

There were only a single set of tracks.

And it was then that they noticed the handles of the coffin were also smeared with the gray-green mold.

It was if the mold man had somehow [come] out of the coffin and dragged it back to his original resting place.

But that was physically impossible. Wasn't it?

Nevertheless a close look at the corpse and the fallen mold made everyone present shiver. They were the same material.

Once again the body was laid to rest in the mausoleum, and the funeral director brought in a Catholic Clergyman to give Last Rites and a blessing on the tomb.

Mold man stayed put this time.

The maintenance crew always gave his crypt special attention.

They always feared that one morning they would find it open again, and see the evidence of mold man once again walking the earth.

When you work at a cemetery for any length of time and meet others who have lived the life of a gravedigger for years, you hear some strange and unexplained stories.

And you hope that you are not the next one to come in the next morning with fear in their eyes and tell the others, "You are not going to believe this, but...."

## The Thing that Moves at Night

*As explained in the notes before the previous account, before Robin Swope became a pastor, he worked as a gravedigger. Although one does what one has to do to keep food on the table, Swope did not particularly relish his days on the job. It was enough to enable one to believe easily in zombies and restless spirits.*

*Here is another story from the Paranormal Pastor, Robin Swope:*

I was a gravedigger. A lot of people get much pride by having a jacket or shirt that display those words upon it with casual recklessness, but I was never too proud of the occupation.

It was a very dirty and disturbing occupation. With every worm that I smashed into the ground with our dirt tamping machine I could not but think of the human flesh we sent to the grave below. The worms were pink mutilated flesh smashed into ground by no will of their own, such as we will all be. When you are in such a disturbing occupation you have no one to turn to but your coworkers to relay you stories of the strange and unusual.

Perhaps you do so to find sanctuary, to help you cope, to help you think you are not going insane. Needless to say I was told quite a few stories.

For some reason the most startling stories center in the location of Mausoleums.

The graveyard where I was employed for six years was in Erie County Pennsylvania. It has a large Mausoleum in its 80 acre confines. It is distinctive because it is the only Protestant Mausoleum in all of Erie County. Many well to do Protestant families are buried there in the simple T-shaped building.

In the late 90s one of the gravediggers was placing a body into one of the crypts. To do this you need a casket elevator— a simple device that raises the casket to the crypt level so the coffin can be slid into its niche. Since many crypts are at high levels, the device is an essential tool for any Mausoleum.

In this instance, the superintendent and his helper were on the fourth level, about 30 feet off the ground, putting an elderly woman into a double crypt. One side contained the remains of her husband who had died long ago. The funeral service itself was held inside the mausoleum since it also doubles as a chapel. When the crowd left, the funeral director helped place the coffin on the elevator and then left.

The men placed the elevator in position and raised the casket up. It was then that they noticed that they were not alone. It seemed as though someone had lingered to watch the burial interment itself take place. It was an old man in an old suit standing in the middle of the mausoleum. He stared at them intently.

Now this in and of itself was not an unusual happening. Many times the family of the deceased will linger after the service to see their loved one laid into their final resting place.

But they had not noticed the old man before when only the funeral director was in the building. They decided to ignore his presence and proceeded with the entombment.

They placed the casket into the crypt and put the cement front piece onto it and finally sealed it with caulking. As they lowered the elevator to raise the granite facing for the tomb they noticed that the old man nodded at them. The supervisor waved back and nodded in response.

Then the old man faded into nothing.

He simply disappeared into the wall behind him.

The supervisor and the helper stood there frozen in fear as the elevator came to a screeching halt. The helper asked his boss what exactly they had just beheld.

The boss had no idea. After a quick look around the building, they still had no explanation.

So they went back to work. Each taking one end, they placed the heavy granite crypt front onto the elevator and raised it to the open hole that held the dead couple. They set it in place, and as they closed it they had the fright of their life.

*The men placed the elevator in position and raised the casket up. It was then that they noticed that they were not alone.*

The crypt plate had pictures of the husband and wife on either side where they were entombed. The husband's and wife's pictures were taken years ago when they had first purchased the crypt. The woman they had just buried looked much younger than the body they had seen at the service. But the husband looked very familiar. It was the man who had been watching them. There was no mistaking it. He was even in the same suit.

It seems that the spirit of the husband wanted to bear witness to their final unity for eternity.

Not all the stories that were related to me by various gravediggers were so touching or heartwarming.

Some were right out of horror movies.

Such as the Mummy with the gray-green fungus.

# OUT OF AFRICA

In September 2001, someone made a ghastly discovery in the River Thames, London, England. Floating in the water was the mutilated torso of a small black boy. His head, arms, and legs had been viciously hacked off.

Investigators of the grisly crime had nothing to work with in their attempt to reveal the young victim's identity. An autopsy yielded little additional information except for an estimate of his age to be around four to seven years.

The detectives were shocked by the crime and maddened that they had no face, fingerprints, or dental records to assist them in their investigation.

Enough of the boy's neck remained to permit a forensic expert to conclude that his throat had been cut and that the body had been deliberately drained of blood.

Scotland Yard called in additional forensic experts from various universities to assist them by using the latest scientific methods to examine the boy's bones, stomach, and intestines for any clues at all.

Ken Pye, a forensic geologist at the University of London, found traces in the victim's bones of strontium, copper, and lead that were two and a half times greater than would be normally expected of a child living in Britain. Pye's meticulous research revealed that the boy had recently arrived from West Africa.

The forensic team, working on the contents of the boy's stomach and intestines, discovered unidentifiable plant material, not at all native to England. In addition, the team attempted to analyze a strange mixture of sandlike material, clay pellets, and flecks of gold. Plant anatomists identified the strange plant material as coming from the calabar bean, a highly toxic vine that could be found in West Africa.

Writer James Owen said that Wade Davis, an anthropologist with the National Geographic Society, immediately noted the use of the calabar bean as a plant that was often used in West Africa to create a variety of poisons, many of which result in total paralysis and a very painful death.

A New Orleans Voodoo altar contains a wide variety of sacred objects to be employed in performing rituals of healing and other magical practices (*art by Ricardo Pustanio*).

A U.K.-based expert on African religions and Voodoo, Richard Hoskins, commented that the calabar bean, in combination with other ingredients in the boy's stomach and intestines, indicated the West African country of Nigeria. Witch doctors commonly used such potions for black magic.

After an exchange of data, the investigators and the forensic experts agreed that the boy had been smuggled into the country for the sole purpose of serving as a human sacrifice.

While Hoskins said that human sacrifices are not common occurrences in contemporary celebrations of Voodoo or Black Magic rites, they still do take place. Animal and fowl sacrifices are regularly practiced, but the ceremonial sacrificial killing of a human is considered a vital element in the most empowering of magical rituals. Special police teams in Southern Africa have estimated that there may be as many as 100 human sacrifices a year—and the most powerful magic of all is created when a child is placed on the altar.

In many parts of Africa, certain witch doctors practice a traditional form of medicine called *muti*. The more unscrupulous of these witch doctors use body parts of children to increase their powers.

According to James Owen, Ken Pye and his forensic team were finally able to trace the murdered black boy's bones to locate his birthplace at a region near Benin City in southwestern Nigeria. According to many authorities, vodun began 350 years ago in Benin. In 1996, vodun, or Voodoo, won state recognition. January 10 was inaugurated as National Voodoo Day, and the religion that is practiced by 65 percent of the 5.4 million Beninese took its place alongside Christianity and Islam.

Voodoo (vodou, vodoun, vudu, or vudun in Benin, Togo, southeastern Ghana, Burkina Faso, and Senegal; also vodou in Haiti) is a name attributed to a traditionally unwritten West African spiritual system of faith and ritual practices. Like most faith systems, the core functions of Voodoo are to explain the forces of the universe, influence those forces, and influence human behavior. Voodoo's oral tradition of faith stories carries genealogy, history, and fables to succeeding generations. Adherents honor deities and venerate ancient and recent ancestors. This faith system is widespread across groups in West Africa. Diaspora spread Voodoo to North and South America and the Caribbean.

On the inauguration of National Voodoo Day, Sossa Guedehoungue, the 86-year-old High Priest of Voodoo, held an audience at his hometown of Doutou, on the Togo border, and scoffed at those who considered Voodoo dangerous. Sossa made a sweeping gesture with an arm to indicate his 24 wives, more than 100 children, and 300 grand-children and declared that if Voodoo were evil, none of them would be there.

Numerous practitioners of Voodoo insist that the practice developed a more sin-ister side only after the slave trade shipped millions of West Africans to Haiti, Cuba, and the Americas. The Old Gods followed their captive people to help them survive and to cast evil spells upon those who enslaved them. At the same time, the people who were carried far from their home villages cleverly began to use the names of Catholic saints to disguise the ancient ones in their pantheon of gods under the names of those whom their captors deemed holy.

### Traditional Tribal Religions

At the center of more traditional African tribal religions is the concept of a universal force of life that finds its expression in all things—human, ani-mal, vegetable, and mineral. The conviction that there is a oneness of all life forms, that both humans and everything else in the environment draw spiritu-al nourishment from the same sacred source is now known to be a common expression of shamanism and the teaching of tribal spirit "doctors." However, when the early European explorers and settlers encountered individuals such as the Swahili *mganga*, the Bantu *nganga*, titles which translated loosely as "doctor," they overlooked the herbal and other healing prac-tices of the tribal doctors to focus upon their commu-nication with the spirits of the oneness of all life. Europeans considered such personifications of the sacred source to be like that of witches and their use of spirit familiars. Hence, the native African shamans and herbal healers became known as "witchdoctors."

Originally, the term "shaman" applied to the spirit doctors and exorcists of the Tungus of Siberia, but in recent years the title applies as well to the medicine men and women of the various North American tribes who also serve as mediums, healers, and visionaries for their people. Shamanic methods are remarkably similar through the world, even for those peoples whose cultures are quite different in many other respects, and who are separated by oceans and continents.

Voodoo (Vodou, Vodoun, Vudu, or Vudun in Benin, Togo, southeastern Ghana, Burkina Faso, and Senegal; also Vodou in Haiti) is a name attrib-uted to a traditionally unwritten West African spiri-tual system of faith and ritual practices (*art by Ricardo Pustanio*).

The anthropologist Ivar Lissner, who spent a great deal of time among the Tungus of Siberia, as well as native peoples in North America, defines a shaman as one "who knows how to deal with spirits and influence them.... The essential characteristic of the shaman is his excitement, his ecstasy and trancelike condition.... [The elements that constitute this ecstasy are] a form of self-severance from mundane existence, a state of heightened sensibility, and spiritual awareness. The shaman loses outward consciousness and becomes inspired or enraptured. While in this state of enthusiasm, he sees dreamlike apparitions, hears voices, and receives visions of truth. More than that, his soul sometimes leaves his body to go wandering."

A crucial element in shamanism is the ability to rise above the constrictions and restraints of linear time, to free oneself from the concept of time as being composed of minutes, hours, and days. Author John Collier opines that at one time everyone possessed such freedom, but the mechanized world took it away from us. "In solitary, mystical experience many of ourselves do enter another time dimension," he writes. But the "frown of clockwork time" demands that we return to chronological time. The shaman, however, recognizes that this other time dimension originated "within the germ plasm [containing hereditary elements] and the organic rhythms ... of eternity."

Achieving a deep trance state appears to be the most effective way that shamans, medicine priests, and Voodoo practitioners regularly abandon linear time restrictions in order to gain entrance to that other dimension of time. Trances permit them to travel with their spirit helpers to a place free of "clockwork time," where they gain the knowledge to predict the future, to heal, and to relay messages of wisdom from the spirit people.

Africans who still follow the old traditional ways have little sense of individualism. From the perspective of those whose worldview is one of complete unity with all things, each individual is simply a member of his or her tribal community. As such, men and women often identify themselves with names that represent tribal affiliation rather than parental heritage. At the same time, reverence toward one's ancestors is extremely important. A tribal member may receive a vision from an ancestor that will dictate a particular course of action and receive preference over any advice offered by a living relative. Some families retain body parts of their departed relatives in containers for prayer rituals, and regular offerings are made at burial sites. Ancestral masks are commonly used in ceremonial rites to honor those in whose bloodline the family recognizes its debt of physical heritage. Since in the traditional tribal cosmology death is not the end, but merely a transition to another form of life, one may frequently encounter the spirit of his or her ancestors.

Many anthropologists and psychiatrists who have spent time studying tribal witchdoctors praise their techniques and abilities. Dr. Raymond Prince of the University of Toronto spent three and a half years with the Nigerian tribe of Yoruba and became quite familiar with the powers of several of their witchdoctors. Dr. Prince observed that Yoruba witchdoctors were men of wisdom whose creative powers had passed down from their ancestors. Various forms of tranquilizing drugs were discovered hundreds of years ago by the Yorubas, who live inland from the Gulf of Guinea.

Dr. Prince found that these native doctors were using vitamins while Americans had only begun to experiment with them. Even more important, the Canadian professor believed, was their treatment of mental patients. Tribes people with a mental illness are treated like human beings; they are not locked away behind iron bars or stone walls, as Americans and Europeans are accustomed to doing.

## Hoodoo

As noted by the staff of Haunted America Tours (http://hauntedamericatours.com), Hoodoo refers to African traditional folk magic. This rich magical tradition was, for thousands of years, indigenous to ancient African botanical, magical-religious practices and folk cultures. Mainly enslaved West Africans brought hoodoo to the Americas.

Hoodoo is a noun and is derived from the Ewe word "hudu" which still exists today. African-American vernacular often uses hoodoo to describe a magic "spell" or potion, the practitioner (hoodoo doctor, hoodoo man or hoodoo woman) who conjures the spell, or as an adjective or verb, depending upon the context in which it is used.

The word can be dated to as early as 1891. Some prefer the term hoodooism, but this has mostly fallen out of use. Some "New Age" non-diaspora practitioners who have taken up Hoodoo as a hobby employ such synonyms as conjuration, conjure, witchcraft, or rootwork. The latter demonstrates the importance of various roots in the making of charms and casting spells.

It is important to note that in traditional African religious culture, the concept of "spells" is not used. Here again, this Afro-botanical practice has been heavily used by the New Age, and Wiccan communities who have little understanding of "hoodoo's" spiritual significance as it is traditionally used in Africa.

An amulet characteristic of hoodoo is the "mojo"—often called a mojo bag, mojo hand, conjure bag, trick bag, or toby—a small sack filled with herbs, roots, coins, sometimes a lodestone, and various other objects of magical power.

Hoodoo refers to African traditional folk magic. This rich magical tradition was for thousands of years indigenous to ancient African botanical, magical-religious practices and folk cultures. Hoodoo was imported to the United States when many West Africans were enslaved and brought to the Americas (**art by Ricardo Pustanio**).

## *Santeria*

Santeria originated in Cuba around 1517 among the slaves who were mostly from West Africa and who were followers of the Yoruba and Bantu religions. The African slaves were at first greatly distressed when they were told by their masters that they could no longer pay homage to the *Orishas*, their spiritual guardians, and that they would be severely punished if they did. But their resourceful and attentive priests quickly noticed a number of parallels between Yoruba religion and Catholicism. While appearing to pay obeisance and homage to various Christian saints, the Africans found that they could simply envision that they were praying to one of their own spirit beings. A secret religion was born—*Regla de Ocha*, "The Rule of the Orisha," or the common and most popular name, Santeria, "the way of the saints."

In Santeria, the supreme deity is referred to as Olorun or Olodumare, "the one who owns heaven." The lesser guardians, the Orisha, were each associated with a different Roman Catholic saint: Babalz Ayi became St. Lazarus; Oggzn became St. Peter; Oshzn became Our Lady of Charity; Elegba became St. Anthony; Obatala became the Resurrected Christ, and so forth. Priests of the faith are called Santeros or Babalochas; priestesses are called Santeras or Lyalochas. The term Olorisha may be applied to either a priest or a priestess.

This sort of religious substitution was also practiced in Europe by followers of the Old Religion, the Witches, when the Pope and his clerical minions began to punish Witches who claimed to interact with their animal "familiars." In those regions where the country folk and rural residents persisted in calling upon their familiars, the church decreed the spirit beings as demons sent by Satan to undermine the work of the clergy. All those accused of possessing a familiar or relying on it for guidance or assistance were forced to recant such a devilish partnership or be in danger of the torture chamber and the stake. In similar manner to the practitioners of Santeria, the Church actually provided saints and their symbols as acceptable substitutes for the ancient practice of asking favors or help from the witches' familiar. Many of the saints of Christendom are identified by an animal symbol: for example, the dog with St. Bernard; the lion with St. Mark; the stag with St. Eustace; the crow with St. Anthony; and the much-loved St. Francis of Assisi was often represented symbolically by a wolf. Perhaps the most remarkable of all, the celebration of the fertility goddess Eostre (Ostare, Eustre) provided the Church with a ready-made festival that commemorated the resurrection of Christ, which was named Easter.

Although the rites of Santeria remain secret and hidden from outsiders, a few churches of that denomination have emerged which provide their members an opportunity to practice their faith freely. The Church of the Lukumi Babalu Aye was formed in southern Florida in the early 1970s and won a landmark decision by the Supreme Court to be allowed to practice animal sacrifice. Each celebration usually begins with an invocation of Olorun, the supreme deity. Dancing to strong African rhythms continues until individuals are possessed by particular Orisha and allow the spirits to speak through them.

Possession in Haitian and New Orleans Vodou and Santeria is described as a god seizing a horse (the human being) who is ridden, sometimes to exhaustion. The all-powerful God is both distant and close, but too great to concern him/herself with humans, instead delegating the mediating task to the spirits (the lwa or loa). There are hundreds of lwa, who may be the protective spirits of clans or tribes from Africa or deified ancestors. Some are conceptualized in human form such as Papa Legba, the old man who guards gates and crossroads and is invoked at the beginning of every service. Others are less tangible like Gran Bwa, who is the spirit of the forest and trees. The lwa are grouped into families, called nations, which are divided by different rituals. Each ritual has distinctive ceremonies, dances, rhythms, and type of offering. The ritual is climaxed with the blood sacrifice, usually a chicken.

While Santeria's rites are controversial in that they may include the sacrifice of small animals, it is essentially a benign religion, and it continues to grow among Hispanics in Florida, New York City, and Los Angeles. Some estimates state that there are over 300,000 practitioners of Santeria in New York alone. Although Santeria was suppressed in Cuba during the 1960s, lessening of restrictions upon religious practices in the 1990s saw its practitioners in that country increase in great numbers.

In April 1989, Santeria was dealt a negative blow to its public image that has been difficult to overcome. At that time, Mexican police officials raiding a drug ring based at Rancho Santa Elena outside of Matamoros discovered a large black cauldron in which a human brain, a turtle shell, a horseshoe, a human spinal column, and an assortment of human bones had been boiled in blood.

Further digging on the grounds of Rancho Santa Elena brought up a dozen human corpses which had all suffered ritual mutilations. When it was learned that the mother of Adolfo de Jesus Constanzo, the leader of the drug ring responsible for the murders, was a practitioner of Santeria, a media frenzy defining the religion as a mixture of Satanism, Voodoo, and demon-worship swept across Mexico and the United States.

Later, investigators would learn that Constanzo had created his own cruel concept of a cult by combining aspects of his own perverse cosmology with Santeria, Voodoo, and an ancient Aztec ritual known as santismo. Constanzo declared himself its High Priest and was joined in the performance of its gory rituals by Sara Maria Aldrete, who led a bizarre double life as a High Priestess and as an honor student at Texas Southmost College in Brownsville.

In June 2009, Bridgeport, Connecticut police conducted a drug raid and found five people suspected of the crimes of selling illegal drugs and firearms in a basement that was splattered with blood. Complaints had been received that ritual sacrifices were being conducted at the address, and from all the initially apparent evidence, the suspicions of those in the neighborhood had been confirmed. What appeared to be satanic writings were scribbled on the walls of the basement, and a beheaded chicken had been placed so its blood drained into a bowl.

From the amount of blood they discovered, the investigators were certain that many animals, probably mostly chickens, had been regularly sacrificed in the basement

The ghede loa is a spirit of the dead who is commanded by the Voodoo Priest or Priestess (*art by Ricardo Pustanio*).

by practitioners of Santeria or some variant of a Voodoo religion. Then one of the officers spotted what appeared to be a skull. It had received a lot of rough use, but it appeared to be human.

On June 10, the medical examiner's office made the official determination: it was a human skull that the officers had brought back from what had begun as a rather routine drug raid.

A disturbing mystery remained. Ten years earlier in Bridgeport, a headless body of an unidentified man had been found. Did the skull that the police found during the raid belong to the headless victim? And had the skull been used in sacrificial rituals ever since its decapitation?

The investigators could only speculate about the grim concept of human sacrifice in Bridgeport, but they had also heard that Santeria groups were growing in the area and they feared that some drug dealers had begun practicing the more grisly possibilities presented by the religion. It is unfortunate that, as in every form of religious expression, there are extremists. It is doubly unfortunate that sometimes those individuals who have contempt for the laws of the gods and of man revert to human sacrifice as a means of securing protection from those who would force them to cease their antisocial and criminal acts.

## *Macumba*

The Macumba religion (also known as Spiritism, Candomblé, and Umbanda) is practiced by a large number of Brazilians who cherish the age-old relationship between a shaman and his or her people. In its outward appearances and in some of its practices, Macumba resembles Voodoo. Trance states among the practitioners are encouraged by dancing and drumming, and the evening ceremony is climaxed with an animal sacrifice.

Macumba was born in the 1550s when the West African tribal priests who sought to serve their people with their old religion were forced to give token obeisance to an array of Christian saints and the God of their masters. As in the cases of Santeria, Voodoo, and other adaptations of original religious expression, the native priests soon realized how complementary the two faiths could be. The African god, Exu, became St. Anthony; Iemanja became Our Lady of the Glory; Oba became St. Joan of Arc; Oxala became Jesus Christ; Oxum became Our Lady of the Conception; and so on. The Africans summoned their the Orishas with the sound of their drums and the rhythm of their dancing. In that regard, the West Africans were more fortunate than those slaves in the States, whose masters forbade them to keep their drums.

During this same period, Roman Catholic missionaries were attempting to convince the aboriginal tribes in Brazil to forsake their old religion and embrace Christianity. In many instances, Macumba provided the same kind of bridge between faiths for the native people as it had for the Africans imported to the country by the slave trade. While they gave lip service to the religious practices of the Europeans, they found that they also could worship their nature spirits and totems in the guise of paying homage to the Christian saints.

The ancient role of the shaman remains central to Macumba. The priest enters into a trancelike state and talks to the spirits in order to gain advice or aid for the supplicant. Before anyone can participate in a Macumba ceremony, he or she must undergo an initiation. The aspirants themselves must enter a trance during the dancing and the drumming and allow a god to possess them. As in Haitian and New Orleans Vodou and Santeria, once the dancer has been taken by the spirit, he or she often dances to a state of exhaustion.

Once the possession has taken place, the shaman must determine which gods are in which initiate so the correct rituals may be performed. The process is empowered by the sacrifice of an animal, whose blood is then smeared over the initiates by the shaman. Once the initiates have been blooded, they take an oath of loyalty to the cult. Later, when the trance state and the possessing god has left them, the initiates, now members of the Macumba cult, usually have no memory of the ritual proceedings.

From the melding of the two religious faiths and the Africans' passion for drumming and dancing, the samba, the rhythm of the saints, was created. The samba became a popular dance, and even today is recognized in Brazil as a symbol of national identity. The dance, synonymous to many as a symbol of Brazil and Carnival, has also become widely accepted throughout the world. One of the samba's derivations is the Bossa Nova.

# VOUDON: HOW TO MAKE A ZOMBIE

Shortly after dictator Manuel Noriega's fall from power in 1989, U.S. intelligence sources revealed that the real ruler of Panama had been a Voodoo practitioner named Maria daSilva Oliveira, a 60-year-old priestess from Brazil who practiced *Candomble* and *Palo Mayombe*.

Witnesses stated that Noriega relied blindly on his Voodoo necklace, a pouch of herbs, and a spell written on a piece of paper to protect him. Journalist John South, writing from Panama City, Panama, said that those close to the dictator were aware that he did not make a single move without first consulting Maria.

When U.S. soldiers searched the house that Noriega had provided for his Voodoo priestess, they found evidence of spells attempted on former Presidents Ronald Reagan and George H.W. Bush. Maria had written out special ritual chants for Noriega to repeat over photographs of his enemies as he burned Voodoo candles and magic powders.

According to U.S. intelligence, Noriega's own spy network had informed him that U.S. forces would invade Panama on December 20, 1989. The dictator ordered Maria to conduct an immediate sacrifice to determine the validity of such intelligence reports.

During a ritual ceremony, Maria sliced open the bellies of frogs in order to study their entrails. Her interpretation of the entrails caused her to predict a U.S. invasion on December 21.

Placing more confidence in his Voodoo Priestess than in his intelligence network, Noriega believed Maria. Consequently, he had not yet moved his troops into position when the U.S. military forces attacked on December 20, a day earlier than Maria's sacrifice had prophesied. Even worse, from the dictator's perspective, he also missed the opportunity to escape in advance of the invading army.

## The Ancient Religion of Voodoo

According to some of its more passionate adherents, Vodun/Vodoun is not a magical tradition, not an animistic tradition, not a spiritistic tradition—neither should it be a pagan religion. The deities of Voodoo are not simply spiritual energies and the path of Voodoo should not be followed for the sake of power over another. Although the Voodoo religion does not demand members proselytize, anyone may join. However, 99 percent of its priesthoods are passed from generation to generation.

The same individuals who esteem their Voodoo religion so highly, insist that it is neither dogmatic nor apocalyptic. Whatever outsiders may make of their faith, the sincere Voodoo follower declares that it has no apocalyptic tradition that prophesizes a doomsday or end-of-the-world scenario.

Although one might suspect that these same true believers are a bit dogmatic when they emphasize that Voodoo was not created as a result of captive West Africans being transported to Roman Catholic countries as slaves, a closer look reveals that Voodoo is not really a blend of African religions and Catholicism, but a clever mask that disguised the ancient deities of the Old Religion.

One point the believers in Voodoo make that cannot be disputed is that the religion did not originate in Haiti. Vodun/Voodoo definitely emerged out of Africa.

Voodoo means "spirit" in the language of the West African Yoruba, and the religion is an assortment of African beliefs and rites that may go back as many as 6,000 to 10,000 years. Slaves, who were snatched from their homes and families on Africa's West Coast, brought their gods with them. Plantation owners in Haiti and other West Indian islands purchased the slaves for rigorous labor and had no interest in their religious beliefs—if they even had any at all. In the minds of their owners, the African slaves were simple savages from the jungle who probably were not even at the level of a culture in which a kind of worship of God would even be comprehended.

In spite of their indifference to any possible theologies that their slaves might hold, the plantation owners in Haiti were compelled by order of the lieutenant-general to baptize them in the Catholic

Some traditional Voodoo Priests and Priestesses will sew closed the eyes and the mouth of the zombie whom they have enslaved (*art by Ricardo Pustanio*).

religion. The slaves were in no position to protest their forced conversion, but by the time the West Africans submitted to mass baptism, the wise priests among them had already discovered simple segues from worshipping the old jungle family of gods and goddesses into bowing and praying to their newly acquired Catholic saints.

As the black population increased and the white demand for slave labor was unceasing, vodun began to take on an anti-white liturgy. Several "messiahs" emerged among the slaves, who were subsequently put to death by the whites in the "big houses." A number of laws began to be passed forbidding any plantation owner to allow "night dances" among his negroes.

In 1791, a slave revolt took place under the leadership of Toussaint L'Ouverture which was to lead to Haiti's independence from France in 1804. Although L'Ouverture died in a Napoleonic prison, his generals had become sufficiently inspired by his example to continue the struggle for freedom until the myth of white supremacy was banished from the island.

After the Concordat of 1860, when relations were reestablished with France, the clergy fulminated against vodun from the pulpits but did not actively campaign against their rival priesthood until 1896 when an impatient monsignor tried without success to organize an anti-vodun league. It wasn't until 1940 that the Catholic church launched a violent campaign of renunciation directed at the adherents of vodun. The priests went about their methodic attack with such zeal that the government was forced to intercede and command them to temper the fires of their campaign.

Today there are over 80 million people who practice vodun worldwide, largely where Haitian emigrants have settled: Benin, Dominican Republic, Ghana, Togo, various cities in the United States (primarily New Orleans), and, of course, Haiti. In South America, there are many religions similar to vodun, such as Umbanda, Quimbanda, or Candomblé.

### *The Practice of Vodun*

A male priest of Vodun, is called a "houngan" or "hungan"; his female counterpart is a "mambo." The place where one practices vodun is a series of buildings called a "humfort" or "hounfou." A "congregation" is called a "hunsi" or "hounsis," and the hungan cures, divines, and cares for them through the good graces of a "loa," his guiding spirit.

The worship of the supernatural "loa" is the central purpose of vodun. They are the old gods of Africa, the local spirits of Haiti, who occupy a position to the fore of God, Christ, the Virgin, and the Saints. From the beginning, the Haitian Voodoo priests adamantly refused to accept the Church's position that the "loa" are the "fallen angels" who rebelled against God. The loa perform good works and guide and protect humankind, the hungans argue. They, like the saints of Roman Catholicism, were once men and women who lived exemplary lives and were given a specific responsibility to

A Voodoo High Priest is called a "houngan" or "hungan" (art by Ricardo Pustanio).

carry out to assist human spirituality. Certainly there are those priests, the bokors, who perform acts of evil sorcery, the left-hand path of vodun, but rarely will a hungan resort to such practices.

The loa communicates with its faithful ones by possessing their bodies during a trance or by appearing to them in dreams. The possession usually takes place during ritual dancing in the humfort. Each participant eventually undergoes a personality change and adapts a trait of his or her particular loa. The adherents of Vodun refer to this phenomenon of the invasion of the body by a supernatural agency as that of the loa "mounting its horse."

There is a great difference, the hungan maintains, between possession by a loa and possession by an evil spirit. An evil spirit would bring chaos to the dancing and perhaps great harm to the one possessed. The traditional dances of vodun are conducted on a serious plane with rhythm and suppleness but not with the orgiastic sensuality depicted in motion pictures about Voodoo or in the displays performed for the tourist trade.

All vodun ceremonies must be climaxed with sacrifice to the loa. Chickens are most commonly offered to the loa, although the wealthy may offer a goat or a bull. The possessed usually drinks of the blood that is collected in a vessel, thereby satisfying the hunger of the loa. Other dancers may also partake of the blood, sometimes adding spices to the vital fluid, but most often drinking it "straight." After the ceremony, the sacrificed animal is usually cooked and eaten.

The traditional belief structure of the Yoruba envisioned a chief god named Olorun, who remains aloof and unknowable to humankind, but who permitted a lesser deity, Obatala, to create the Earth and all its life forms. There are hundreds of minor spirits whose influence may be invoked by humankind, such as Ayza, the protector; Baron Samedi, guardian of the grave; Dambala, the serpent; Ezli, the female spirit of love; Ogou Balanjo, spirit of healing; and Mawu Lisa, spirit of creation. Each follower of vodun has his or her own "met tet," a guardian spirit that corresponds to a Catholic's patron saint.

In Haiti and in New Orleans, Papa Legba is the intermediary between the loa (also referred to as "lwa") and humanity. He stands at a spiritual crossroads and gives (or denies) permission to speak with the spirits of Gine; he translates between the human and "angelic" and all other languages of the spheres.

Papa Legba is also commonly called Eleggua and is depicted as an old man sprinkling water or an old man with a crutch accompanied by dogs. He is also known as

Legba or Legba Ati-Bon in other pantheons. In any vodon ceremony, Legba is the first loa invoked, so that he may "open the gate" for communication between the worlds. The dog is his symbolic animal, moving with him between the worlds and across the waters of the Abyss.

When it comes to the protection of one's domicile, Voodoo practitioners place representations of Papa Legba, similar to those of St. Michael and St. Peter, beside the back and front doors of their homes. Legba will keep evil from entering the home unchecked.

### Trafficking in Zombies during the Civil War

According to the research of historians at Haunted America Tours (http://haunted americatours.com), many Voodoo and Hoodoo Kings and Queens became wealthy during the Civil War in the 1860s by reanimating fallen Confederate and Union soldiers and selling them as zombie slaves. The sorcerers mixed up dead things in a big black stew pot. They ground up corpses and zombie fingers and toes to make special Zombie Brand powders that only the very rich could afford and only the very evil would want to employ.

For some, this was the Golden Era of Zombies. Half white/ half black Creole Queens and Kings plied their special dark swamp medicines, amulets, charms, and "zombified" wares from coast to coast after Uylsses S. Grant became president.

Experts on the history of Voodoo, such as Lisa Lee Harp Waugh, Karen Beals, and the noted New Orleans artist Ricardo Pustanio, have observed that the deep dark secrets of a Voodoo-hoodoo person at the time was always well accepted. These special Creole people were never more sought after and revered than those of the Great White Mamba's whose names are still remembered and honored today.

The old red-bricked, crumbling, white-washed tomb of Marie Laveau is the spot where many say the eternal Voodoo Queen still grants wishes from beyond the grave. However, some say, she will grant your wish only if you promise to come back to the tomb no later than one year and a day. If you do not show at the allotted time then you might just find that you have lost all you gained. Even worse, is the curse that the one you love most will become a real zombie when he or she dies.

Many researchers in certain Voodoo-hoodoo circles believe that real zombification came to America through the teachings of Marie Laveau, the Voodoo Queen of New Orleans. Others believe it was her teacher and mentor Dr. John who first taught Marie. Still others claim that the Great Texan Voodoo Queen Black Cat Mama Couteaux was the ultimate "zombifier."

Black Cat Mama Couteaux, according to Lisa Lee, was the ultimate Voodoo-hoodoo Queen in Marshall, Texas. "The stories of her in the state are often told as far away as Abilene and Fort Worth," she said. "They say she even rode out the Great

Storm of 1900 in a row boat. The woman was said to have been married to her zombie lover. The dead Mamba husband zombie is said to be still around, guarding the treasures she amassed."

Texan Lisa Lee Harp Waugh states that the old spells that they speak of in her part of the United States seem to have originated from Black Cat Mama Couteaux. "But if you listen to most of the old stories," Waugh notes, "they suggest that she was actually taught by a great Voodoo-hoodoo king from New Orleans who had a secret circle of Voodoo-Hoodoo Queens that gave him all their personal attentions as they sat at his knee begging them to teach them more. That great King would, of course, be Dr. John."

## An Abolitionist Zombie Maker

Mary Ellen Pleasant (died January 4, 1904) was a nineteenth-century female entrepreneur of partial African descent who used her fortune to further abolition. She worked on the Underground Railroad helping slaves escape across many states and eventually helped expand the escape route to California during the Gold Rush era. She was a friend and financial supporter of John Brown, the fierce anti-slavery crusader who attacked the Federal Arsenal at Harpers Ferry, West Virginia (then Virginia), on October 16, 1859, and she became well known in abolitionist circles.

After the Civil War, Mary Ellen took her battles to the courts and won several civil rights victories, one of which was cited and upheld in the 1980s and resulted in her being called, "The Mother of Human Rights in California."

But only a few know the great dark secrets she kept and that she was one of Dr. John's greatest pupils. According to researchers at Haunted America Tours (http://hauntedamericatours.com), Mary Ellen Pleasant pried more secrets from him than did any of her contemporaries. The old stories handed down often claim that she was Dr. John's favorite lover, but in spite of their physical passion and admiration for one another, it is supposed that during their affair his zombification book was hidden in the LaLaurie Mansion.

## The Horrors of the LaLaurie Mansion

Local Voodoosants often tell of how Dr. John really trusted no one living but Madame Delphine LaLaurie, the godmother and wet nurse to the infamous Devil baby of New Orleans.

**Mary Ellen Pleasant was a nineteenth-century female entrepreneur of partial African descent who used her fortune to further the abolitionist cause. She worked on the Underground Railroad, aiding escaped slaves and eventually helping to expand routes to California during the Gold Rush Era (*art by Ricardo Pustanio*).**

Madame LaLaurie was thought to have claimed many lives, and, with her diabolical physician husband, tortured dozens of helpless slaves and others in her attic on Governor Nichols Street and Royal Street in New Orleans.

"Recent new discoveries are starting to surface from my research that these poor, gruesome-looking individuals that many witnesses saw with organs outside of their bodies were actually zombies that Madame LaLaurie had hidden away so her husband could experiment on them," Lisa Lee Harp Waugh stated. "As far-fetched as it sounds, it might just be the truth."

On April 10, 1834, the New Orleans fire department, responding to a call that a fire had broken out at the LaLaurie Mansion, discovered a boarded door on the third floor. Forcing the door open to be certain no smoldering fire lurked behind it, the firemen were horrified to find a number of slaves in the room. Some were dead, but some were restrained on operating room tables, their bodies hideously and cruelly cut open. Firemen were shocked as they found human body parts and organs scattered about the room. In a cage they found a slave whose bones had been broken and reset to make her look like a human crab. Other slaves had been the victims of sex change operations. Some had their faces slashed and distorted so that they were transformed into hideous monsters.

While the firemen were dealing with their terrible discovery, Mary Ellen Pleasant is said to have been seen leaving the house carrying some charred papers bound tightly with the skin of a cotton mouth snake. Mama Sallie of Compton, California, a present-day member of Mary Ellen Pleasant's secret society, claims that all Mary Ellen left them regarding zombification is one document that contains three spells that would turn a living man into a zombie on the spot. According to zombie lore, the most famous blackroot magic hex and spell book of Dr. John's zombification techniques is said to have been walled up in a secret place by Mama Mary Ellen.

"One sheet is all that Mama Mary she left us," Mama Sallie said. "If more spells existed and they were in her possession, then they are hidden fast away."

The dark book of powerful Voodoo secrets, "The Pleasant Book of Dark Deeds," is said to be kept under lock and key in a secret vault in Marin County, California. The book is reported to contain spells handed down from generations past, and some on zombification are said to be found therein, including the personal writing of how Mary Ellen Pleasant made an army of zombies help build a city.

In 2007, actor Nicolas Cage bought the legendary LaLaurie Mansion for $3.5 million. Cage was well aware that the LaLaurie Mansion had long been known as the most haunted house in New Orleans—some say, the United States.

Cage sold the house in 2008, admitting that he had never slept there. At any given moment, he said, he was aware of six ghosts in the mansion. He and his family had dinner in the mansion on occasion, but he allowed no one to sleep there. He had respect for the spirits, and he said that he had turned down half-a-dozen requests from parapsychologists to come to the house to research the ghostly inhabitants.

### Zombie Brides for Sale

Zombie brides were the most sought-after creatures throughout the South after the U.S. Civil War. Creole zombie brides were considered the most beautiful; and after men saw Little Sister Sally on Dr. John's arm, every rich man in the city wanted to have a Zombie Bride of his own to show off at the next major social event.

Of all the women who gained Dr. John's special attention, his favorite may have been a very young Voodoo Queen of great beauty. He called her "Little Sister Sally" just because he liked that name, and the way it rolled off his tongue. Sally, whose real name was Alice Slowe Jefferson, was the youngest Voodoo Queen ordained, and she was personally taught by Dr. John, who also zombified her alive.

Though he was advanced in age and she was a mere girl of 12 when he took her into his fold, some believe that it was Little Sister Sally who had taken possession of Dr. John's dark book of all the 100-plus spells on how to zombify someone. Even today, members of the Secret Society of Dr. John believe that Sister Sally is the only complete Zombie Queen who ever existed. Through some dark, mysterious spell that Dr. John perfected in St. Louis Cemetery Number One, the exotic Creole beauty, the daughter of a rich plantation owner, remains alone as the world's most perfect youthful living Zombie Queen. Zombified on her seventeenth birthday, Little Sister Sally has never had to fear the passage of time.

Ricardo Pustanio 2009

## Making Zombie Powder

*Warning: Do not try this. It will not work unless you know the actual chants, prayers, and invocations to the Great Baron Samedi.*

Zombie brides were the most sought after creatures throughout the South after the great Civil War. Creole zombie brides were considered the most beautiful, and every rich man in the city wanted to have a zombie bride of his own to show off at the next major social event (**art by Ricardo Pustanio**).

- One Human Skull
- Assorted Bones from a Water Rat
- A Pure White Cat
- An Iguana Tail
- The Teeth of a Man 19 years dead
- A good dose of pure Vegetable Oil
- A dash or two of Datura
- Two Blue Agama Lizards of the male sex
- One Big Toad called Crapaud Bonga (Bufo Marinus) that must weigh one pound
- One Sea Snake's brain and sex organ
- Several Pods of Itching Pea, "Pois Gratter"
- Two (Preferably Female) Puffer Fish
- Add Tarantulas, Millipedes and White Tree Frogs to taste

The potion should be prepared in June, when the female Puffer fish contains its greatest quantities of Tetrodotoxin. Be careful not to touch the mixture at any time as it can act through skin.

Tie the snake to the Toad's leg. Put them in a jar and bury it.

This is so that the Toad "dies of rage," which increases the concentration of its poison. Place its skull in a fire with Thunderstone and some blessed oil and burn till black.

Roast the animal ingredients and grind with the uncooked plants in a pestle and mortar. Add unheated shaving of the bones.

A few sacred spells (Juju), now grind your mixture to fine powder, place in a jar and bury in the coffin with the rest of your source skeleton if possible for three days.

You now have *coup poudre* or zombie potion. It is traditionally sprinkled in a cross on the threshold of the target. It can only be introduced by touching the skin. If taken internally, death will be final.

Upon the zombie's awakening from the grips of death, one must bite the tip of the tongue—or as some Voodoo-hoodoo practitioners prefer—the entire tongue. The tongue should be kept always in the company of the person who owns the zombie, because the zombie will obey only the one who has it.

If the tongue is swallowed, the zombie is bound only to the "boukur" (bokar), or Voodoosant who created it. The zombie will obey someone else's commands if their master tells them to do so.

### Zombie Stay-Away Powder

Ichintal (chayote root) is used in making Zombie-Stay-Away Powder. The zombies are said to freeze in their tracks and cannot cross over a buried chayote root.

Although most people are familiar only with the fruit itself, the root, stem, seeds, and leaves are all edible. If you feed any part of a chayote (merliton) to a zombie the spell will be broken for nine days. The person will then resume a normal life, but at the end of nine days it will return to being a zombie or die.

The act of feeding of a chayote to a zombie to break the spell will only work once every seven years.

The chayote (*Sechium edule*), also known as sayote, tayota, choko, chocho, chow-chow, christophene, merliton, and vegetable pear, is an edible plant that belongs to the gourd family *Cucurbitaceae,* along with melons, cucumbers and squash. The plant has large leaves that form a canopy over the fruit. The vine is grown on the ground or more commonly on trellises.

Costa Rica is a major exporter of chayotes worldwide. Costa Rican chayotes can be purchased in the European Union, the United States and other places in the world. Chayote is a very important ingredient in the Central American diet.

## *Voodoo Dolls*

Next to the zombie, the so-called Voodoo doll is the most well-known figure associated with Voodoo. Many tourists have brought such souvenirs home from their visits to New Orleans or Haiti where voudun is practiced. Over the years, the portrayal of a Voodoo priest or priestess sticking pins into a doll that represents someone who has incurred their wrath has become so common that such effigies or puppets are known collectively as Voodoo dolls.

Actually, such figures have no role in the religion of Voodoo, and the practice of sticking pins in dolls or poppets (puppets) is a custom of Western European witches, rather than the Haitian, New Orleans, or other Caribbean practitioners of voudun. Perhaps the misunderstanding arose when outsiders who witnessed certain rituals saw the followers of Voodoo sticking pins in the figures of saints or guardian spirits. Such acts are done not to bring harm to anyone, but to keep the good force of magic within the object.

# WITCHCRAFT AND VOODOO

On February 9. 2006, Myrlene Severe was charged with smuggling after federal security screeners found a skull in her luggage at Fort Lauderdale-Hollywood International Airport.

Ms. Severe, a Haitian-born permanent U.S. resident, said that the male skull that she had brought from Haiti would be used in rites that were an important aspect in her Voodoo beliefs.

While members of U.S. Immigration and Customs Enforcement grimaced in disgust, Ms Severe explained how the skull, complete with teeth and hair, would enable her to ward off evil spirits. Attempting to employ their strict discipline as federal security officers, a number of the screeners found themselves recoiling from the skull that still contained organic matter within its shell and was spotted with bits of skin and lots of dirt on its exterior.

Although she was guilty of smuggling because she had not declared a human skull in her luggage, 30-year-old Myrlene Severe was practicing her freedom of religious belief. It is not against the law to practice Voodoo, Witchcraft, or Wicca in the United States—in fact, there are an estimated 800,000 individuals practicing Witchcraft/Wicca/Neo-Paganism in the U.S. Those practicing some form of Voodoo, Voudun, Candomoblé, Macumba, Yoruba, or Santeria number as many as 80 million worldwide.

## Witchcraft—The Ancient Craft of the Wise

Voodoo and Witchcraft are often confused, and both are often incorrectly associated with Satanism, the worship of a malignant deity. Although to the outsider, both religious expressions would seen to give obeisance to a devil, neither Witchcraft nor Voodoo worships the satanic or the demonic.

Witchcraft, the "old religion," or the "ancient craft of the wise," is a nature-based religion, which is thought to have had its genesis in the later Paleolithic period, a time when Stone Age humans had to adapt themselves constantly to changes in the weather, climate, and food supply. Wicca, a more contemporary expression of Witchcraft, has evolved into what its followers term "Neo-Paganism." Voodoo has come to wear many guises, as we shall learn, but its roots are at least 10,000 years old.

Primitive humans were primarily hunters, who needed the meat obtained from their prey, and they needed the animal skins for clothing. When the hunting was bad, their very existence was threatened. Because humans have the gift of reason—and imagination—the more reflective among the early people spent some time wondering why the hunt was successful at times and not at others? Certain members of the group claimed to have visions, and when some of these visions came true, these gifted ones, the shamans, discovered that there was a spirit who decided these things. If certain rules were followed that spirit could be persuaded to allow prey to be slaughtered for subsistence by the human hunters.

> *Certain members of the group claimed to have visions, and when some of these visions came true, these gifted ones, the shamans, discovered that there was a spirit who decided these things.*

The concept of certain spirit beings who assist a magician, a Witch, or a Voodoo sorcerer quite likely hearkens back to the totem animal guides that attended the ancient shamans, for the familiars express themselves most often in animal forms. The black cat, for instance, has become synonymous in popular folklore as the traditional companion of the witch.

The ancient Greeks called upon the *predrii*, spirit beings who were ever at hand to provide assistance to the physicians or magicians. In Rome, the seers and soothsayers asked their familiars or *magistelli* to provide supernatural assistance in their performance of magic and predictions.

Experienced practitioners of Witchcraft may have the ability to manifest a spirit ally or assistant and allow it to assume the physical form of a human being so that it may carry out the Witch's biding, but the supernatural servant is not a person whose will has been taken from him or her. In fact the entity has never been human at all, thus retaining its status as a familiar, rather than a zombie.

In his classic work *The Golden Bough*, Sir James George Frazer points out two factors influencing the nature of primitive religion: (1) the older concept of a "view of nature as a series of events occurring in an invariable order without the intervention of personal agency"; and (2) the later development that the "world is to a great extent worked by supernatural agents, that is, by personal beings acting on impulses and motives."

The earliest rites of primitive religion consisted of sympathetic magic, which is based on the belief that something that resembles something else is able to become or attract that which it resembles, or a given cause always produces a certain effect. It was by such a process that Stone Age humans sought to ensure the success of the hunt. In *Witchcraft from the Inside*, Raymond Buckland writes: "One man would represent the God and supervise the Magick. As a God of Hunting, he was represented as being the animal being hunted. His representative, or priest, would therefore dress in an animal skin and wear a head-dress of horns."

Because of the importance of human and animal fertility, the Horned God was soon joined by a goddess, whose purpose it was to ensure the success of all reproductive activities. She was also the goddess who oversaw the birth of human and animal progeny. At a later date, when primitive religious thought had evolved to the point of belief in some form of continuation after death, the goddess oversaw human and animal death as well.

With the advent of agriculture, the goddess was called upon to extend her powers to ensure fertility of the crops. From this point on, the figure of the goddess began to overshadow that of the Horned God.

The population of medieval Europe descended from the central Asian plateau. Christianity and "civilized" ways were unknown to them and they brought their own gods, customs, and rituals into the land. At the dissolution of the Roman Empire, the civilizing force in Europe was the Roman Catholic church, and even though the ecclesiastical institution made great inroads into the pagan culture, it could not completely abolish the old rituals and nature worship.

**Experienced practitioners of Witchcraft may have the ability to manifest a spirit ally or assistant and allow it to assume the physical form of a human being so that it may carry out the Witch's bidding (*art by Ricardo Pustanio*).**

Surviving the Roman Empire socially in the Middle Ages was the oppressive feudal system. Proud warriors were reduced to the role of serf farmers. Partially because of the frustrations of the common people, the celebration of nature worship and various adaptations of the ancient mystery religions began to be practiced in secret. It was in their enjoyment of the excitement and vigor of the Old Religion that the peasants could allow themselves the luxury of experiencing pleasure without the interference of Mother Church, which sought to control and repress even human emotions.

But it was that same expression of seeing the divine in all of the Creator's works that brought the wrath of the Church down upon the witches in the terrible form of the Holy Inquisition in the fifteenth and sixteenth centuries. On occasions when seasonal nature celebrations were witnessed by members of the Christian clergy, the gatherings were condemned as expressions of witchcraft and were named "Black Sabbats," to distinguish the ceremonies as the complete opposite of the true and Holy Sabbath days. And then, of course, there was the matter of the Horned God, who must certainly be Satan, and the goddess, who was without question, Diana, goddess of the Moon and the hunt.

For the serfs, the observance of nature worship was an expression of their conscious or unconscious yen to throw off the yoke of feudalism. In the Middle Ages, the Christian influence seemed to vanish at night as great groups of people gathered around a statue of the Horned God and began professing their allegiance to the great deities of nature. To staunch Christians, this horned image was an obscene representation of Satan, a black, grotesque figure that was fiendishly lit by the roaring fire in front of it. In the flickering light, the torso of the figure appeared to be human while the head, hands, and feet were shaped like those of a goat and covered with coarse, black hair.

## The Days of Ascendancy

The Sabbat is a day of ascendancy for Witches. In the European countryside during the Middle Ages, the eight festival observances took on immense importance as thousands of peasants, common people, and members of the lesser nobility attended the seasonal celebrations. The Sabbats mark the passage of the year as it moves through its seasons:

Samhain, begins the year for those who follow the ways of Wicca, and it occurs near October 31, Halloween on the Christian calendar. Contrary to numerous misconceptions, however, Halloween is not a witches' holiday, but an old Christian celebration of the dead. Samhain honors the harvest, the time when the crops "die" to become food for the winter and when the veil between worlds becomes very thin.

Yule marks the winter solstice and is celebrated near December 21, the longest, darkest night of the year.

Candlemas, observed on February 2, is the festival of the Goddess Brigid.

The spring equinox occurs around March 21, and for the practitioners of witchcraft, it is a powerful time to practice magic.

Beltane, May 1, celebrates love and oneness.

The summer solstice, occurring around June 21, is also a time of power and a time to pay homage to the strength of the deities of nature.

August 1 recognizes Lammas, a time when fruit ripens and there are signs that harvest is near.

The autumn equinox, near or on September 21, celebrates a balance between light and dark, night and day. It is also a time to prepare to embrace the many mysteries of the Goddess as she oversees the winter months of cold and darkness.

The Sabbat Dance—or, as it is commonly known, the Witches' Round—is performed with the dancers moving in a back-to-back position with their hands clasped and their heads turned so that they might see each other. A wild dance such as this, which was essentially circular in movement, would have needed little help from the supply of plentiful drinks to induce vertigo even in the most hearty of dancers. The celebration lasted the entire night, and the crowd did not disperse until morning.

Reports of regular celebrations of the various Sabbats came from all over Europe. An estimated 25,000 attended such rituals in the countryside of southern France and around the Black Forest region of Germany.

As rumors of even larger gatherings spread throughout the land, the nobility and the churchmen decided to squelch such expressions with the use of the hideous machinery of the Inquisition. Even the most innocent amusements of the serfs were taken away. In the face of such large scale persecutions, the mass meeting celebrations of the Sabbat were made impossible. But even though great pressure was brought to bear on such outward manifestations of the rituals, modified versions of sabbats were still performed in the private fields, orchards, and cellars of the peasants.

The popularity of the pagan celebrations rose to its greatest height in the period 1200 to the Renaissance in the fifteenth and sixteenth centuries. During this period, famines, the ill-fated Crusades, and the Black Death devastated Europe.

## *Traditions of Wicca*

As in the Old Religion, the eight main festival observances or Sabbats remain days of ascendancy for those men and women who follow the modern, innovative schools of Wicca and may, in essence, constitute rather large tribal gatherings of celebration and community. In addition, some Wiccan traditions may also celebrate "esbats," much smaller gatherings that correspond to the phases of the moon. There may also be special purpose gatherings which are limited to the members of a coven who meet to deal with a problem or issue specific to the group or an individual within the coven.

When most Wiccans hold an esbat, they generally meet in a group of thirteen, which comprises the membership of a coven. While some Wiccan traditions permit larger numbers to participate in the esbats, most maintain the old practice that if a coven exceeds more than thirteen, it should split off into another group. During the eight Sabbats, however, many covens may meet together to celebrate the festivities.

While the esbat is considered a sacred event, it does not take place in a building deemed holy. Since there is no dogma within the Wiccan traditions, the esbats primarily occur in an outdoor setting so that the coven members may touch the earth. When a

**An altar combining European Witchcraft symbology with Voodoo-Hoodoo artifacts (*art by Bill Oliver*).**

desirable location has been found, one of the coven members, usually the High Priest or High Priestess, draws a large circle on the ground while walking in a clockwise direction. The instrument used to etch the circle in the earth is generally a wand or the ceremonial "athame" (dagger), and once the circle has been made, the four cardinal directions (and often Above and Below) are invoked by the High Priest or Priestess. Some covens perform this rite of invocation in front of a small portable altar.

Once the parameters of the sacred circle have been drawn, the celebrants usually invoke the names of the Goddess and God and various nature entities to manifest among them in the circle. Some groups conduct this ritual "skyclad" (naked), while others prefer to dress in gowns or other special costumes. The area formed by the circle of celebrants represents a holy space signifying an altered state of consciousness that exists between the material world of time and space and the immaterial world of limitless being. The circle of combined psyches also serves as a receptacle of magical energy that will build its strength until it is released in what is known as the "Cone of Power."

When the Cone of Power has attained the energy deemed necessary for the purposes desired by the coven, it is released and sent out to perform the various tasks assigned to it by the wishes of the celebrants. Once the power has been released, some traditions pass a chalice of wine and small cakes around the circle to be enjoyed by the coven. As the refreshments are passed from member to member, the practitioners pronounce "Blessed Be" to one another. Once the ritual has been completed, the circle opens and members walk around the parameter in a clockwise direction.

If a coven meets for an Esbat at the time of a full moon, it will quite likely engage in the ritual known as "Drawing Down the Moon," in which the spirit of the Goddess and God are "drawn" down into the physical bodies of the High Priestess and priest. During this time, they are considered by the coven members to be the Goddess and God incarnate. While this spiritual possession is taking place, the high priestess and priest relay teachings and knowledge to the coven and may even answer personal questions relevant to the needs of individual members.

### *African Holidays, Voodoo and Santeria Holy Days, Ancient Egyptian Days of Celebration*

To list all of the holy days of African religion, Voodoo, vodun, Santeria, Macumba, and the ancient Egyptian days of empowerment would take up several pages. We list here only some of the more significant, many of which are obviously those of New Orleans Voodoo, reflecting events unique to the United States. Once again, I am indebted to the staff of Haunted America Tours (http://hauntedamericatours.com) for their help in assembling this list.

## January

1: World Peace Day to meditate for peace throughout the world. (Universal Hour of Peace: 7:00–8:00 AM EST.)

Day the Emancipation Proclamation went into effect, freeing the slaves in 1863; a day to mourn African victims of slavery and racism (past and present), to make peace, and celebrate the empowerment of African Americans. (President Abraham Lincoln signed the Emancipation Proclamation on 9/22/1862.)

15: (Observed January 21): Birthday of Rev. Martin Luther King, Jr. (1929–1968), Baptist preacher and non-violent advocate for the rights of African Americans, who died April 4.

17: Yoruba/Santeria feast of Ogun, Orisha of Strength, Endurance, and Perseverance.

20: World Religions Day to contemplate all religions as different paths to the one universal deity of many names and aspects.

24: Old Egyptian festival of Neteret Bastet, the Cat Goddess.

25: Old Egyptian festival of Neteret Amenet-Rait-Mut, the primordial Great Mother.

## February

2: Yoruba/Santeria feast of Oya, Orisha of Death and Rebirth. Yorubas/Santeros worship the One Deity Olodumare and the Orishas—Olodumare's emanations and messengers.

5 to 6: Feast of Old Roman-Egyptian Goddess Isis, the Healer to recall Set (God of Challenges and Chaos) poisoning child God Horus, and Isis intervening, defeating Set, and healing Horus.

24 to 26: Raising Heaven—Old Egyptian Festival honoring the hidden Neteru Amen and Amenet.

25: Old Egyptian feast of Neter Ptah, God of Arts and Creativity.

## March

5: Navigium Isidis—Old Roman-Egyptian festival honoring Goddess Isis as Lady of the Moon and Ruler of the Sea; celebrated with the launching of a boat of offerings.

9: Day slavery was outlawed world-wide (1927); day to mourn slavery's continued existence.

10: Death day of Harriet Tubman (1822–1913), who risked her life to guide slaves to freedom.

19: Yoruba/Santeria feast of Osanyin, Orisha of Deciduous Vegetation.

25: Yoruba/Santeria feast of Oshun, Orisha of Passion and Fertility.

27: Beginning of Old Egyptian Proyet/Emergence month of Paenrenenutet/Pharmouthi, dedicated to Neteret Renenutet and Neter Nepri.

## April

20 to 26: Old Egyptian festival of Neteret Renenutet (Goddess of the Harvest) and Neter Nepri (God of Grain).

23: Yoruba/Santeria feast of Ogun, Orisha of Orisha of Self-reliance and Industrious Labor; Yorubas/Santeros celebrate with drumming, ecstatic dancing, and possession trance.

26: Beginning of Old Egyptian Shomu/Harvest month of Paenkhons/Pakhon.

## May

15: Yoruba/Santeria feast of Ochossi, Orisha of Animals.

26: Beginning of Old Egyptian Shomu/Harvest month of Khentkhety/Paoni.

## June

21: Yoruba/Santeria feast of Orisha Babalu Aye, Guardian of the Disabled.

29: Yoruba/Santeria feast of Orisha Eleggua, Intercessor and Ruler of Destinies; Yorubas/Santeros celebrate with divination and food offerings.

## July

9: Old Egyptian festival of Neteru Amen (God of Transcendent Powers) and Hapi (God of the Nile River); offerings were made to ensure the needed flooding of the Nile River.

18: Day South Africa's apartheid was internationally outlawed (1976); birthday of Nelson Mandela, nonviolent anti-apartheid activist.

24: Old Egyptian feast of Neteret Hathor, Goddess of Love and Fertility

25: Beginning of Old Egyptian Shomu/Summer month of Mesut-Ra/Mesori, dedicated to Neteru Ra and Rait.

## August

2: Feast of the Black Madonna (a.k.a. Feast of the Virgin of the Angels).

6: Day the Voting Rights Act became law (1965)—register to vote! (The Voting Rights Act of 1965 was signed into law by President Lyndon Johnson [Pub. L. 89-110, 79 Stat. 437, 42 U.S.C. 1973 et seq.])

24: Feast of Old Egyptian God Osiris—partner and true love of Isis, and father of Horus, guide of all husbands, fathers, and judges.

25: Old Egyptian birthday feast of Neter Horus the Elder, lover of Neteret Hathor.

26: Old Egyptian birthday feast of Neter Set, God of the Desert.

27: Feast of Egyptian Goddess Isis— partner and true love of Osiris, and mother of Horus, guide of all wives, mothers, healers, advocates, and teachers.

28: Day of Rev. Martin Luther King, Jr.'s peaceful march on Washington, D.C., in 1963, for recognition of the rights of African Americans. (Rev. King made his inspiring "I have a dream" speech at this rally.)

29: Old Egyptian birthday feast of Neteru Ra and Rait, Deities of the Sun.

29 to September 11: Old Egyptian festival marking the return to Egypt of Goddess Isis (as the star of Septet/Sirius) and God Osiris (as the star of Sahu/Orion), and the rains that inundate the Nile River. (Old Egyptian New Year; beginning of Akhet/Inundation month of Tekh/Thout, dedicated to Neter Thoth [God of Time.])

## September

8: Yoruba/Santeria feast of Oshun, Orisha of Love and Compassion.

12: Old Egyptian festival of Neteru Amen (God of Transcendent Powers) and Hapi (God of the Nile River); offerings were made to ensure the needed flooding of the Nile River.

15 to 16: Old Egyptian festival, honoring the dead.

16 to 17: Old Egyptian festival of Neter Thoth, God of Knowledge and Wisdom.

24: Yoruba/Santeria feast of Obatala, Orisha of Peace and Justice.

29: Yoruba/Santeria feast of Orisha Eleggua, Intercessor and Ruler of Destinies.

30: Yoruba/Santeria feast of Shango, Orisha of Passion and Virility.

## October

4: Yoruba/Santeria feast of Orunmila, Orisha of Wise Counsel and Protection.

12 to 22: Old Egyptian Opet Festival, honoring Neteru Amen-Ra-Atem and Amenet-Rait-Mut.

24: Yoruba/Santeria feast of Orisha Erinle, Healer of the Sick and Injured.

28: Beginning of Old Egyptian Akhet/Inundation month of Het-Hert/Athor, dedicated to Neteret Hathor.

## November

1 to 2: Fon/Vodou feast of Ghede, Loa of the Dead; time for honoring ancestral spirits. Fon/Vodouisants believe all Loas (Deities) originate from Co-Creators Goddess-God Mawu-Lisa.

On November 1 and 2 the Fon/Vodou people celebrate the feast of Ghede, Loa of the Dead; it is a time for honoring ancestral spirits. Fon/Vodouisants believe all Loas (Deities) originate from Co-Creators Goddess-God Mawu-Lisa (*art by Ricardo Pustanio*).

3: Christian feast of St. Martin of Porres (d. 1639), healer and advocate of social equality and inter-ethnic harmony, guide of healers and human rights activists.

5: Old Egyptian festival of Neteru Amen-Ra-Atem and Amenet-Rait-Mut.

25: Yoruba/Santeria feast of Oya, Orisha of Death and Rebirth.

27: Old Egyptian feast of Neteret Hathor, Goddess of Fate.

28: Thanksgiving Day—day to give thanks for the abundance of our land and for our food, clothes, shelter, and health.

## December

4: Yoruba/Santeria feast of Orisha Shango, Defender against Evil.

8 to 26: Old Egyptian Sokar Festival/Khoiak Ceremonies commemorates Neteret Isis seeking out and finding the scattered remains of Neter Osiris.

17: Yoruba/Santeria feast of Orisha Babalu Aye, Healer of Deadly Diseases.

21 to 25: Old Romano-Egyptian festival of Goddess Isis giving birth to God Horus.

26 to January 1: Kwanzaa—festival celebrating positive African traditions; emphasizes unity, self-determination, collective work and responsibility, cooperative economics, purpose, creativity, and faith.

31: Yoruba/Santeria festival of Orisha Yemaya, Mother of the Sun and Moon

# VOODOO DEATHS

All the villagers in the Amazonian village of Altamira, Brazil, trusted Valentina Andrade. Not only did the 72-year-old woman have the gifts of clairvoyance and prophecy, but she was kind and generous, loved by all who knew her.

Residents of the area could not have been more horrified when they learned in 2003 that Valentina was the leader of the Voodoo cult of Superior Universal Alignment, which was headquartered in Argentina and had numerous followers in neighboring Paraguay and as far away as Holland. Disclosure that she was the priestess of the satanic-Voodoo group that had been responsible for the murders of as many as nineteen young boys from poor families over the past ten years, transformed the villagers' shock to outrage. The boys had been lured into the jungle where they were killed and their genitals removed for use in Voodoo rituals.

The priestess was placed in custody in early September when she tried to flee the country. Hundreds of area residents gathered outside the jail, and later the courtroom, to maintain a vigil and to pray for justice for the boys whose lives were taken so cruelly. Although the official count of the victims was six young lives snuffed out by Voodoo, an accurate count will probably never be determined, as so many very poor families lived in scattered areas of the jungle.

On trial together with Valentina were five local members of her cult. Among them were Carlos Alberto Santos, a former law enforcement officer, who was sentenced to 35 years for his part in the mutilations and murders. Amailton Gomez, a prosperous businessman and the son of an influential landowner, was given 57-year prison term for his participation in the cult murders, and Antonio Ferriera, a doctor, received a sentence of 77 years.

Court testimonies told of 19 boys, aged between eight and 14, who had been seized by members of the cult of Superior Universal Alignment. Some of the boys were snatched as they herded cattle for their families. Others were grabbed, doused with chloroform, and carried off into the jungle. Boys who worked away from the village

**Some self-styled Voodoo Priests and Priestesses have formed cults that have taken the lives of dozens of victims whom they have kidnapped or tricked into joining their demonic gatherings (*art by Bill Oliver*).**

picking mangoes were easy victims, since they were far away from any adult who might hear their cries for help. Other lads, from poor families, who begged or shined shoes in the village were easily lured by the promise of money for running errands outside the confines of the town.

Over the years, six boys were found dead with their sex organs removed. Although it may never be known for certain how many boys were abducted and murdered by the cult, at least five missing male children remained unaccounted for in the village. Five captured boys had managed to escape from the cult before they had been mutilated, but they had been unable to identify their abductors. And with such a policeman as Santos, a cult member, the investigations did not progress beyond dismissal of a boy's wild story.

Three of the abducted victims of the Voodoo ritual somehow managed to escape from the cult in spite of their painful mutilations. One of them told the court he had been lured into the forest at the age of nine, tied to a tree, then put to sleep with chloroform. When he awakened he felt terrible pain and saw what they had done to him. His injuries had taken much away from his life as a man, but he was glad to see that some of those who had stolen his manhood would be punished.

Those who had crowded into the courtroom cheered when Dr. Ferreira received his sentence of 77 years. He had perverted his skills and his vows as a doctor when he used anesthesia on the young victims and removed their genitals with medical expertise.

Incredibly, after a seventeen-day trial in Belem, Para State, Valentina Andrade was acquitted by a six to one vote. She fainted after the verdict was read.

The decision immediately prompted shouts of protests from those who had lost their sons. The prosecution promised that it would appeal, but many of the villagers were more convinced than ever that Valentina had powerful magic. Everyone expected her to get a sentence of decades of imprisonment after ordering the deaths and mutilations of 19 young boys, but she remained free to move elsewhere and begin a new arm of the Voodoo cult.

## *Did the Dark Magician Conjure a Demon that Slaughtered Him and His Entire Family?*

I often caution individuals who wish to study the Dark Arts that they must not regard such an undertaking lightly. I never encourage people to search the ancient texts for arcane incantations with which to conjure up entities from some other dimension or nether region. Such experimentation—as many have learned to their sorrow—can result in absolute terror, madness, and a grisly kind of death.

Some years ago, a prominent researcher told me of a classic case in the annals of crime detection and the occult, which was a ghastly tale, blood-soaked and one that definitely had a macabre association with the Powers of Darkness. As far as my confidante was aware, the bizarre crime, which occurred over 80 years ago, has never been solved.

It was a little before midnight on July 2, 1929, and in the center of Detroit, Michigan, lights still blazed and music and laughter blared from the city's hot nightspots. But in that part of the city known as Little Italy, most of the inhabitants, who were hardworking folk, had retired early. The day had been a hot one, but a welcomed breeze stirred the trees on St. Aubin Street. The patrolman had just passed down the sidewalk and had turned into the police station on the corner to make his report that all was well.

Dominic Diapolo, who kept the delicatessen on St. Aubin, was always the last tradesman to close his shop. At about 11:30 PM, Diapolo came out of the premises and glanced up and down the street to assure himself that no more customers were approaching. He rather idly observed that lights were still burning at No. 3587 next door; but that was nothing unusual, for his neighbor, Benjamino Evangelista always kept late hours.

Benjamino Evangelista was an enigma not only to Diapolo but many of the other local folk who had known him in Italy before they had immigrated to the States. Evangelista was born in Casino, a rugged mountainous area where peasants still live, in thought and in habit, several generations behind the city dwellers of modern Italy. In 1914—when he was 28—Evangelista left his birthplace for the United States. He rapidly mastered the English language, and soon found work as a carpenter.

Nobody noticed anything unusual about him for several months, when he suddenly revealed himself as a prophet and a healer. Often he would pray fervently in the middle of his work, and one day when one of his workmates seriously cut himself, Evangelista promptly stopped the flow of blood from an artery by saying a few words over it in a language unknown to his companions. It seemed clear to them that he had occult powers.

*Evangelista promptly stopped the flow of blood from an artery by saying a few words over it in a language unknown to his companions.*

Diapolo of the delicatessen didn't believe that his neighbor was so gifted, but when a Mrs. Vaniel Vetrando, who lived nearby, told him that Evangelista had cured her ailing infant by making signs in the air over the child and reading in a strange language from a book, Diapolo began to reconsider the matter.

Later a woman named Santina was carried on a stretcher to Evangelista's house. Doctors alleged that she was dying of consumption. Could Evangelista snatch her from death? "Yes," said the carpenter. "I can cure her, but only if she will marry me." Santina weakly agreed; and although she could not rise from the bed in which he had placed her, they were promptly wedded. As soon as she had become Mrs. Evangelista, Santina began rapidly to recover. As the years passed, she bore him four children, three girls, Angeline, Matilda and Jenny, and a boy, Morrio.

Evangelista flourished and became a master carpenter and a plumber. After work, he attended to his patients—not only the local Italians but also the many individuals who sought him out when their doctors had apparently failed them. Evangelista never turned anyone away. He burned the midnight oil calculating horoscopes, studying occultism, or brewing potions from the herbs that he grew in his garden.

Father Francis Beccherini, a local Catholic priest, tried to persuade him to abandon occultism, but Evangelista refused. The priest warned that the occult was only a path to madness. The Father fumed that it was sad that one so blessed with fine children should be so cursed in other respects.

Thus stood the story until that terrible night of July 2, 1929, when it seemed as if a black cloud of evil descended upon Detroit and lingered over St. Aubin Street. That night Evangelista, having seen his wife and children to bed, returned to his study on the ground floor to check the proofs of a very strange book he had written. One might have called it his bible. It was entitled *The Oldest History of the World Revealed by Occult Sciences*.

Behind him, as he sat at his desk, was an altar, and to left and right were piles of books, astrological charts, and chemical apparatus. He had not locked the front door, but his study door was closed.

While Evangelista sat engrossed in his proof-reading a gust of hot wind blew the lid off Diapolo's dustbin next door. Diapolo, who had gone to bed, heard it as he began to doze.

A woman, living on the opposite side of the street, pulled aside her bedroom curtains to get more air on that sultry night. Just as she was about to turn away, she saw—or thought she saw, for as she later explained, she could not be certain—a vague shadow, like that of an undersized man, cast upon Evangelista's front door. She paid it no special attention and returned to her bed.

Night enveloped the city. Little Italy slept unconscious of the evil on St. Aubin Street. The patrolman leisurely passed by Evangelista's premises. He saw nothing amiss.

Indeed, it was not until about 11:00 AM on July 3, the day following, that the curtain was raised on a crime that stunned and nauseated the whole of the city. It was then that Vincent Elias, an estate agent, called at Evangelista's home at No. 3587. The occultist's dogs in the backyard began to bark as he knocked at the front door. Getting no reply, he entered and listened. All was silent within the house. Elias opened the study door, and called a cheery greeting. His words froze on his lips, for the study resembled a slaughterhouse. Evangelista's body was slumped on his scattered proof sheets. His head was on the floor.

Those who wish to study the Dark Arts must not regard such an undertaking lightly. Caution must be exercised by those who search the ancient texts for arcane incantations with which to conjure up entities from some other dimension or nether region. Such experimentation can result in absolute terror, madness, and a grisly death (*art by Bill Oliver*).

Babbling incoherently, Elias sought Diapolo, who phoned the police.

Patrolmen Costage and Lawrence from Hunt Street Police Station arrived within a few minutes. Immediately they saw what Elias in his horror had missed—a trail of small bloody footprints leading upstairs. They bounded up the staircase, truncheons drawn.

"Don't … don't look," whispered Costage to his partner as he turned from the open doors of the two bedrooms. Mrs. Evangelista and her four children had been decapitated and disemboweled.

A dozen more officers arrived, and then somebody remembered the cellars. Three armed officers descended the stairs, the beams of their flashlights falling upon a heavy green curtain at the foot of a single flight. The scene behind that curtain made them gape with horror and amazement.

Nearly a dozen macabre life-sized waxen figures dangled from the ceiling. Each one had the face of a devil.

Doctors later declared that the murderer must have had considerable strength for his size, for the bloody footprints revealed that he wore size five shoes; yet the mortal wounds found on the Evangelista family had been caused by either a scimitar, a saber, a machete, or some similar weapon. It was also thought that the murderer must have been known to the Evangelistas and to their dogs, which did not bark during the night.

One of the many theories for the crime was that the family had been murdered by the father of one of the two children who had died after being treated by Benjamino Evangelista, but investigation proved this theory without foundation.

The discovery of what appeared to be women's lingerie in the cellar led the police to believe that the murdered occultist had engaged in some sort of devil worship, which included sex rites resulting in the debauching of females; but this theory rapidly exploded when former patients revealed that the healer required a soft, silken garment that had been worn next to the skin when he performed the rites which, in almost all cases, restored them to health.

Every possible trail was followed up by the police. Although many seemed at first to be promising, all proved to be dead ends. Then Inspector Fred Frahm became interested in the script of *The Oldest History of the World*, which Evangelista had written. The detective believed that this bizarre work might be more revealing than any speculations about vendettas and the like. There was a macabre, exalted madness about the script.

Here are a few of the passages that intrigued Inspector Frahm:

> After ninety days they formed a coach of clouds with the strength of the wind and air.... [T]hey opened the coach and in it found a phenomenon in the aspect of a human being. It had arms but no legs, two wings on its arms and one on its back, and a blonde beard; it was seven times the size of a man. The winds named him God and gave him their strength....

> In the Nile the strongest man became king. They wrestled and the winner became king.... In Caion the man who had the longest beard became king.... In Aliel the greatest talker became queen....

The mystery deepened when Frahm remembered that, Angeline, one of the daughters, had one of her arms cut off at the shoulder, for he read in the strange bible the following words:

> If any Caion men would acquaint themselves with Caion or Aliel women they would be cut to pieces and fed to the slaves.

> Berland began to run away from him, but blood came out of her shoulder and she couldn't magnetize the people any more.

Had not the Evangelistas been cut to pieces? Had not little Angeline's arm been severed at the shoulder?

The printer of the "History" was traced. He was Francis Slunder, a Belgian printer, of 3652 Meldrum Avenue, Detroit, but he could throw no light on the mystery or the meaning of the book.

The manufacturer of the devil figures was also traced. He was Fortuna J. Martin of the Johnson Flag and Decorating Co., 3529 Gratiot Avenue, Detroit. Martin said that Evangelista had told him to make the figures as grotesque as possible, as he wanted them for a film that he proposed making. Martin added that his customer seemed sane enough until religion was mentioned.

All the occultists of Detroit were arrested on suspicion. Religious fanatics were questioned for hours. Museums and collectors of weapons were visited, but the murder weapon was never found. No one could reveal anything of value. Utterly baffled, the detectives then decided to consult the occultists themselves for psychic guidance on the problem. They learned nothing that they didn't know before.

James E. Chenot, prosecuting attorney, launched a drive to arrest all the spiritualists and drive them out of Detroit, but when it was revealed that the police were consulting this fraternity the campaign collapsed.

The police were, by that time, so obsessed with the hunt for the murderer that they had almost come to the stage where they might have even believed that Evangelista not only murdered his family, but decapitated himself afterwards and disposed of the weapon by magical means.

"The Evangelista murders," said one of the chief detectives, "constitute one of the most unique cases police were ever called on to handle anywhere. Not only were the murders singularly frightful, but there was an element about them that removed them from the modern world. This is a case in which a murderer from the Dark Ages has baffled a thoroughly modernized police force, though every means known to criminal science was employed to detect him."

Had Benjamino Evangelista conjured up a denizen of some nether region? Some occultists believe that the small shadowy figure seen by one of the witnesses was a demon that Evangelista had managed to summon from some other dimension of time and space. Once, however, Evangelista sought to command the demon, the magician learned to his sorrow and his entire family's slaughter, that playing in the dark side is not for amateurs.

### *Everyone the Voodoo Queen Loved Died*

Anjette Donovan Lyles, a buxom, silver-haired woman with striking features, closed the door of her bedroom, sat down on the edge of her rumpled bed, and carefully opened a package. The first thing she saw was the small, dark bottle with a skull and crossbones printed on the label. Her soft, full mouth did not alter as she read the instructions about the poison. Her blue eyes were undimmed when she opened the bottle and sniffed the arsenic contents.

"I'm going to need a new dress for the funeral," she thought. "Something black. Not too flashy and not cut too low in the neckline. The Voodoo candles didn't work, but this stuff in the bottle ought to be real magic."

Anjette had married Ben F. Lyles, a World War II veteran, in 1947. Ben's father had begun Lyles Restaurant in downtown Macon, Georgia, and after Ben returned from service and married Anjette, the young couple assumed ownership of the place. Anjette loved working at the restaurant. She had never been particularly bright in school, but it seemed that she had a true skill for pleasing the public.

When Anjette learned that Ben was thinking of selling the restaurant, she began burning Voodoo candles to prevent him from doing so. When Ben's health began to fail, he sold the restaurant in 1951 without consulting Anjette. After Anjette learned of Ben's deceitful act of selling the restaurant that she loved so much, without even discussing it with her, she became furious—and Ben's health got a whole lot worse very quickly. He died in January 1952 shortly after he entered the hospital. Puzzled by his sudden demise, the doctors decided upon encephalitis as the cause of death.

Anjette was well-known in Macon, and a large crowd of mourners came to the funeral of her husband, who had passed away of a mysterious malady and left his widow and their two children, Carla Ann and Marcia Elaine.

"Ben's death just left me in real poor circumstances," Anjette drawled to her friends. "I thought he had more insurance, but it was only $3,000. Of course, I'll collect about $190-a-month from his disability from the Veteran's Administration. Every little bit helps when you're a widow with two young girls."

The shapely widow was not the type of person to mourn her husband. She went to work, saved her money, and bought back the restaurant that she thought Ben had stolen from her in 1955. Located in the heart of the business district, the restaurant renamed "Anjette's" became one of the most popular in the city. She had borrowed money to open the place in style, but her congenial personality and astute management brought customers flocking to Anjette's.

She had barely opened for business when a brawny, six-foot, Texan became a steady diner. Joe Neal Gabbert was an airline pilot and he liked Anjette's cooking.

"I could sure use a strong man around here sometimes," Anjette drawled, seductively. "Being a widow just doesn't feel right for a warm-blooded lady like me."

Joe and Anjette were married in June 1955, following a whirlwind courtship that lasted only a few weeks. They returned from their honeymoon and the platinum blonde went to a hiding place and withdrew another deadly bottle of arsenic poison.

Three months after he had become a bridegroom, Joe Neal Gabbert fell ill and took to his bed. His husky body ruptured with running sores. Gabbert's hands had to be tied behind his back to prevent him from scratching. Anjette hired a nurse and, together, the two women fed Mr. Gabbert intravenously.

Gabbert's condition worsened. "You're going to have to take him to a hospital," the nurse informed Anjette. "Unless something is done at once, he's going to die."

Despite hospitalization, Joe Neal Gabbert succumbed to an undiagnosed malady. Anjette brought out her black widow's dress and, once again, Macon's finest citizens trooped to the funeral.

The next to die in Anjette's family was Julia Young Lyles, the mother of her first husband. She died on September 29, 1957, and, about eight months later, Marcia Elaine Lyles, Anjette's beautiful, doe-eyed, nine-year-old daughter, died a terrible death in the Macon hospital.

"There must be some sickness that just strikes down everyone around me," Anjette said, tearfully. "Everyone I love seems to die. It must be the will of God."

Macon law enforcement authorities were also interested in why everyone around Anjette was dying. They performed an autopsy and discovered that arsenic poisoning was responsible for the death of her daughter. When the bodies of Ben Lyles, Joe Neal Gabbert, and Julia Lyles were exhumed, it was determined that all three had died from arsenic poisoning.

"Arsenic poisoning is one of the most dangerous types," explained a pathologist. "A person can be given arsenic over a long period of time. It works in such a way that the effects aren't readily recognized. It doesn't produce an immediate reaction, or convulsions in the victim. Unless a doctor is warned about arsenic poisoning, he will probably be unable to make a correct diagnosis. Arsenic is a great imitator with symptoms that resemble a lot of common ailments."

Detectives rushed to Anjette's home and searched the premises. They turned up six bottles of a virulent rat poison; the main ingredient was arsenic. They also discovered several empty poison bottles.

"There's enough poison here to kill fifteen or twenty people," said a detective.

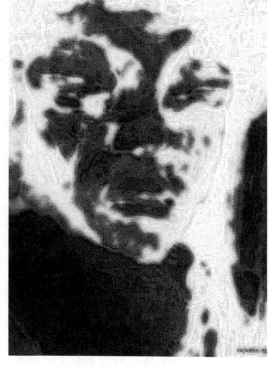

After several members of Anjette Lyles' family died mysteriously of horrifying illnesses, their bodies tested positive for arsenic poisoning (*art by Ricardo Pustanio*).

On May 6, 1958, Anjette Lyles was arrested and arraigned for trial on a charge of murder. She didn't appear to be at all upset by the charge.

"You know there was insurance on my husbands, my mother-in-law, and my daughter," she informed the arresting officer. "Maybe I can collect double indemnity if I get cleared of these charges."

The "Gay Widow" was brought to trial. Dressed in her traditional black dress, composed, serene, Anjette followed the routine in the courtroom as if a stranger was being tried for the heinous crimes.

Each prospective juror was asked: 'Would you sentence a woman to death in the electric chair?"

Anjette tightened her fingers around a white-bound copy of the New Testament in her lap.

As the trial progressed, witnesses painted a fiendish picture of the attractive, ever-smiling Anjette. Besides poisoning her relatives, she had forged a will to collect her mother-in-law's estate. The four deaths had netted the platinum blonde about $47,750.

"She blew every dime of the money on her boyfriends," the state prosecutor explained. "She also purchased a new Cadillac automobile and spent her blood money keeping up with the Macon social whirl that was beyond her means."

There was another obsession that was costing Anjette a small fortune. The serial poisoner was buying everything she could find on Black Magic. She paid dearly for the "blessed" equipment to perform Voodoo rituals. She purchased elaborate concoctions purported to be Voodoo love potions to bring back her erring boyfriends. Anjette didn't deny her belief in Voodoo and the black powers of satanic rituals.

Under Georgia law, a person charged with a felonious crime may testify without taking an oath or being cross-examined.

"I believe in things like black magic and Voodoo," she told the hushed courtroom. "The investigators made fun of me because I messed around with candles. Well, it may be crazy to believe in these things, but I did then and I still do. I have been burning candles for a long time because I know they are supposed to bring luck.

"The candles I used would burn for seven days before they burned out," she continued. "I burned a white candle for peace and an orange candle to keep people from becoming angry at me. I used to light red candles to bring love into my life. I also visited root doctors, old herb ladies, spirit advisers, and I never let a day pass that I didn't see a fortune-teller."

Why did she carry roots with her all of the time? "I never go anywhere without my roots," she explained. "There were roots in my pocketbook on the day I was arrested. They bring luck. I know a certain kind of root that you put in your mouth when you're talking with people. When you do that, they have to do whatever you want them to do. There's even an Adam and Eve root that can be rubbed over your forehead in the morning. You pray and get whatever you ask for in your prayers."

Anjette said she was informed by a fortune-teller that her daughter, Marcia, would die. "I was told this about two years before her death," said the buxom murderess. "I have also been told in advance about all of the other deaths in my family."

Following her testimony, a newsman shook his head in disbelief. He expressed his a horrible suspicion that Anjette's fortune teller created a self-fulfilling prophesy regarding the deaths of her family members, a prophesy that Anjette made come true.

Anjette waited quietly in the courtroom as the jury of 12 men filed out to decide her fate. A short time later, they were back in the jury box with their verdict of "Guilty." The jurors made no recommendation for mercy, and she was sentenced to die in the electric chair.

Anjette Donovan Lyles would have been the first white woman executed in the state of Georgia. A number of politicians weren't pleased that such an execution would occur during their terms. Ultimately, Anjette was committed to a state mental hospital under a Georgia law that prohibits the execution of an insane person. On December 4, 1977, Anjette died of heart failure at the age of 52 in the State Hospital for the Insane in Milledgeville, Georgia.

# DAMBALLAH WEDO
# AND THE AFRICAN PANTHEON

In November 2006, Sheila Coulson of the University of Oslo announced the discovery of 70,000-year-old artifacts that appeared to indicate the worship of a massive snake, thereby revealing the earliest known human religious ritual.

Those who unquestioningly subscribe to conventional wisdom will argue that humankind's intelligence, introspection, or a sense of a power greater than they, did not evolve to the level of group rituals until some 40,000 years ago. Yet here we have—inside a cave in the hills of the Kalahari Desert of Botswana—a representation of a python that was made of stone and was as tall as a man. The area is known to contemporary inhabitants as the "Mountain of the Gods" and local legends tell that humankind descended from the python.

Voodoo is inspired by the worship of the python god, Damballah, who created the world. He stretched out his 7,000 coils to form the stars in the heavens and to mold the hills and valleys of Earth. His mighty lightning bolts cooled to fashion metals, rocks, and stones. When he perceived that water was necessary for life, he shed his skin and allowed it to melt into all the oceans, rivers, lakes, and waters on the planet. As the foam was settling on the life-giving deluge of water, the sun shone through the mist and a lovely rainbow was born. This rainbow was Ayida Wedo. Damballah fell instantly in love with her beauty, and the serpent and the rainbow became one: Damballah Wedo. Damballah Wedo's color is white and his day is Sunday.

Damballah Wedo, a loa (spirit) of peace and purity, speaks only to humans by possessing a follower of Voodoo, Santeria, Macumba or one of the other African religions. This possession most often takes place during the dancing that follows other ritual observances. Damballah's image is that of a very large snake.

Obatala is another name used in Voodoo for the creator god, whose name means "Lord of the White Cloth." His color is white, containing all the colors of the rainbow. He rules the mind and intellect, cosmic equilibrium, male and female. His counterpart in vodoun, the original African religion, Damballah, takes the form of the

Voodoo is inspired by the worship of the python god, Damballah, who created the world. He stretched out his 7,000 coils to form the stars in the heavens and to mold the hills and valleys of Earth (*art Bill Oliver*).

primeval serpent. Although Obatala is considered to be beyond the sphere of direct communication, Damballah possesses his followers in Voodoo rites.

Obatala is the greatest orisha. It is from him that most of the other orisha take their forms. In Voodoo cosmology, Obatala is generally identified with the crucified Christ. He is androgynous, and sometimes depicted as very old, sometimes quite young.

Eleggua (Legba, Exu, Eshu) is the orisha of crossroads, doorways, and gates. He is the messenger of the gods. No orisha can be contacted except through him. Eleggua is also the guardian of the doorway between the earthly and divine realms. In Brazil, he is sometimes equated with Baphomet, and his symbol is a pitchfork. In Santeria, his colors are black and red, and he is associated with St. Martin de Porres. His favorite offering is candy and tobacco and coconuts. Of all the orishas, he has the most aspects (forms), including Pombagira (Candomble), a wantonly sexual prostitute; and Papa Legba (Vodoun) an elderly man. He is considered a trickster, a player of pranks. In some traditions he is malevolent, bringing harm to those who neglect their obligations.

Ogun (Oggun, Ogoun, Ogum) is the chief of the warriors, the God of War, blood, and iron. He is the guardian of the forge, and the patron of civilization and technology. In Candomblé, he is associated with St. George, the dragon slayer; in Lukumi, he is syncretized with St. Peter. Because of his association with blood, Ogun is often petitioned for aid with blood diseases. However, because Ogun enjoys blood offerings, it is considered inadvisable to petition Ogun while menstruating or with a bleeding wound. Ogun is a smith, a soldier, and a politician. In modern times he has come to be known as the patron of truck drivers.

Chango (Xango, Shango) is also a warrior, the orisha of lightning, dance, and passion. He is the epitome of all things masculine, and the dispenser of vengeance on behalf of the wronged. Chango was likely once a Yoruba King. Like Ogun, his colors are red and white, and his best-known symbol is a double-bladed axe. He uses lightning and thunder to enhance the fertility of the earth and of his followers. Legend says that the historic Chango accidentally brought down lightning on his own castle when experimenting with magic, thus destroying many of his wives and children. This lead to a drama of exile, suicide, and rebirth.

Oya (Yansa) is the Goddess of storms, lightning, and cemeteries. She is a warrior, the wife of Chango. Her colors are orange and maroon, and her syncretized saint is Theresa. She epitomizes female power and righteous anger. Legend warns that no one wants to face Oya in battle, for she is as fierce, ruthless, and cunning as any man. She is known to have destroyed towns and villages, uprooting all that was once in its original state. Offer epo pupo (palm oil) to supplicate her and shea butter to calm her. Oya brings sudden change. She is a whirlwind, an amazon, a huntress, and a wild buffalo. Lightning and rainbows are signs of her presence. She also rules communication between the living and the dead.

In vodou, Oya is called Mamman Brigitte, the swaggering, rum drinking wife of Baron Samedi and mother of the Guedde, lords of the dead. Oya watches over both the cemetery and the marketplace. Oya is the guardian of the realm between life and death, and she assists those when they make their final transition. The lungs, bronchial passages, and mucous membranes are associated with her. She can either hold back the spirit of death or call it forth—hence, she is the last breath taken.

Oya is known for using charms and magic and is one of the Great Mothers of the "Elders of the Night (Witches)." Oya has many different faces (masks). Windy days are the most propitious times to pray to Oya, for it is her messenger Afefe (the wind) who will carry your secret longings to her. Oya is associated with the colors maroon, purple, deep dark red, orange, browns, multi-colors, burgundy, and copper.

Yemaya (Yemoja, Iemanja) is associated with manifestations of the Virgin Mary and also of Isis—she is the most beloved female Orisha. Yemaya is the Goddess of the Ocean and the moon, guardian of women, childbirth, fertility, and witchcraft. She rules the subconscious and creative endeavors.

Yemaya's counterpart in Vodoun is called Lasiren, the Mermaid. She is related to Mami Wata (Mamma Water), the African water-spirit beloved by the Dahomey of Benin. Yemaya's symbols are a mirror and comb, powders and perfumes, and other items of female beauty. The holy mother of the world, she rules over the ocean. She is a special intercessor for mothers and gay men. She is one of the great goddesses of Africa and of the African diaspora. In her original homeland, she was the Yoruba goddess of the Ogun river. Blue is her color, and those who worship Yemaya wear a necklace of clear and blue beads. Some who bring adoration to Yemaya wear a blue dress, complete with seven layers to represent the seven seas.

In a Yemaya ceremony everyone dances in a circle, and the altar is in the form of a circle, representing the eternal cycle of life. Both the half moon and a star are symbols of Yemaya, and since she is very vain, she appreciates jewelry, perfume, and flowers. Anything that comes from the sea is a symbol of Yemaya.

There is an old legend that Yemaya chooses her own students. Occasionally someone will disappear, sometimes for seven years, and return with tales of having learned the ways of Magick and healing in Yemaya's undersea kingdom.

> *Yemaya ... She is one of the great goddesses of Africa and of the African diaspora. In her original homeland, she was the Yoruba goddess of the Ogun river.*

The tides represent Yemaya's desires to protect and nurture all her children, by rocking the world as if it were a cradle. Since Yemaya is considered the greatest mother, she is very sexual. The motion of the tides is reflective of her seductive hips, which she moves side to side. Yemaya is very moody and protective. Since nothing can resist water, she is also respected for her strength. Yemaya drowns those who hurt her children.

Oshun (known as Oxum in Brazil) rules the sweet waters— rivers, brooks, and streams. Oshun is closely related to Yemaya, and their aspects sometimes overlap. She is the goddess of love, passion, and sensuality, as well as money and prosperity. Her preferred offerings are honey, copper jewelry or coins (usually in multiples of five). She is most often associated with St. Cecilia, and in Lukumi, she is Our Lady of La Caridad del Cobre, the protectress of Cuba. Her colors are yellow and gold.

Oshun, the Yoruban Goddess of love, delights in the creation of beauty and art, sensual delights and self-adornment. Her symbols are mirrors, jewelry, honey, golden silks and feather fans. Creativity in decorating home and temple is a way of honoring Oshun, who will bless any beautiful space created in her honor. Creativity in dress and self-adornment please her as well, and when Oshun is pleased, her blessings know no limits.

In Vodoun, Oshun is known as Erzulie. Erzulie's colors are shades of pink. While Erzulie and Oshun are very much alike, Erzulie has a vengeful, implacable aspect when angered, similar to that of her sister and rival Erzulie Dantor. In this dark, vengeful aspect, Dantor is a fierce protector of women, especially single mothers, and a powerful avenger of domestic violence.

Her colors are royal blue, red and gold, and her offerings include spicy fried pork, cinnamon candies, and libations of rum mixed with storm water. Oshun likes to heal hurt with love, and she plants seeds of change in people.

In her African homeland, Oshun mated with the god Chango, with whom she had human children. Their descendents, who still live along her waters, are forbidden to eat snails or beans, or to drink beer made from sorghum.

Oshun is still honored in Nigeria with an annual ceremony called Ibo-Oshun. A feast of yams begins the evening, then women dance for the goddess, hoping to be chosen as one of her favorites. Those who are selected are granted new names which include that of the goddess: Oshun Leye, "gift of Oshun," or Oshun Tola, "treasure of Oshun." Once selected in this way, the woman serves her community as advisor, particularly assisting with family problems and illnesses. Oshun is especially consulted by those who wish to have children, for she encourages this womanly activity.

Oshun is the primary divinity of Oshogbo, an African orisha religion, where she is honored with brass objects, as well as jewels and yellow copper. Her chief festival there celebrates the arrival of the ancestral family on the banks of Oshun's river.

In the African diaspora, Oshun gained new names and titles: Oxum in Brazil, Ochun in Cuba, Erzulie-Freda-Dahomey in Haiti. When she possesses dancers, their movements are those of a woman who loves to swim, who makes her arm bracelets jangle and who admires herself in a mirror.

Oshun's appearance at ritual dancing is greeted with welcoming shouts of "Ore Yeye o!" In Brazilian Macumba, Oshun is goddess of waters; she is depicted wearing jewels, holding a mirror, and wafting a fan. Altars to her hold copper bracelets and fans, as well as dishes of Omuluku (onions, beans and salt). In Santeria, Oshun is revered as "Our Lady of La Caridad," patron of the island of Cuba.

### *Remembering the Serpent Kings*

The serpent is universally recognized as a symbol of the wave form of energy, a sperm-symbol representative of life. Nearly every ancient culture has its legends of wise Serpent Kings who came from the sky to advance the beneficent and civilizing rule of the good spirits on Earth—e.g., Quetzalcoatl, the "feathered serpent" of the Incas, who descended from heaven in a silver egg. The awesome respect that our ancestors had for these wise serpent-like humanoids could surely have been retained in the collective unconscious of our species today.

Let us suppose that a highly advanced reptilian species with an astonishing technology has been interacting with developing life forms on Earth for millions of years. These Serpent People have been so well known in so many cultures that they are believed to be involved in the very act of creation.

Let us suppose, further, that, upon the emergence of humankind's earliest ancestral relative, they made a decision to interfere with the gradual evolutionary process of *Homo sapiens* and to initiate a program of genetic engineering whereby they could accelerate the physical and intellectual development of certain of the bipedal creatures.

Exceedingly patient, detached, almost emotionless in its approach to scientific projects, the reptilian race experimented with skin pigmentation, facial and body hair, height, weight, and intelligence in its efforts to improve developing humankind.

The serpent is universally recognized as a symbol of the waveform of energy, a sperm-symbol representative of life. Nearly every ancient culture has its legends of wise Serpent Kings—e.g., Quetzalcoatl, the "feathered serpent" of the Incas, who descended from heaven in a silver egg (*art by Ricardo Pustanio*).

At the same time, the evolutionary process of selection and survival was taking place on the planet, so that by the time the serpentine scientists had created cities of rather sophisticated inhabitants about 200,000 years ago, Neanderthal man was just beginning to huddle together in caves.

Since the Serpent People had elected to accelerate the natural evolutionary pace of humankind and had, in essence, created beings without spiritual awareness, the more compassionate and more responsible of their leaders felt that they had no moral or ethical choice other than to interact with both the developing primitives and the members of the advanced *Homo* cultures and to provide them with the spiritual teachings that the more material and detached reptilian extraterrestrials had little interest in providing. The Bible's references to God's anger at the serpent's interference with the natural flow of things in the Garden of Eden may have been the ancient people's understanding of the Serpent People's leaders' disgust with the reptilian genetic engineers' failure to instill spiritual teachings along with material knowledge. The "missionaries," "the Angels," among the reptilians, may have believed that their scientists were very wrong to have interfered with the natural evolutionary processes on this planet. Perhaps they understood that, to some of the reptilian people, developing humankind was nothing more than a scientific project. *Homo sapiens* was merely a laboratory experiment.

The great metaphysician Rudolf Steiner theorized that the people of our prehistory had been largely guided and directed by a higher order of beings who interacted and communicated with certain humans—the smartest, the strongest, the most intellectually flexible. Eventually, these select humans produced what might be called demigods, divine human beings, who, in turn, could relay instructions from higher intelligences. In effect, Steiner may have given us another definition of the progeny that the ancient Hebrews named "Nephilim," which does, in fact, mean demigod, people of "great renown."

Steiner went on to speculate that within the larger evolving human race were the descendents of those divine-human hybrid beings, men and women who are animated by higher ideals, who regard themselves as children of a divine, universal power. It need not be overemphasized that the larger body of humankind appears to be devoted to the service of egotism, materialism, and selfish, personal interests.

Steiner believed that within what he termed the emerging "Sixth Post-Atlantean Race" would be children of the divine universal power who would be able to initiate those men and women who have developed their faculty of thought so that they might better unite themselves with the divine. The children of the divine universal power, those who have the "seed" within them, will be able to initiate the more advanced members of humankind. People so initiated will be able to receive revelations and perform what others will consider miracles. The initiates will go on to become the mediators between humankind and the higher intelligences.

The whole point of the efforts of these higher intelligences is to enable humankind to become more independent, more able to stand on its own feet without having to rely on the higher order of beings that directed us in ancient times.

## A Supernova and Serpent Beings Create Our World

If such a scenario is bit too far-out for you, consider a second theory to suggest why the people of every culture have at one time worshiped the snake or recognized it as a powerful totem of wisdom. Every single aspect of the technology with which humankind surrounds itself today was initiated when a star died in a dramatic, brilliant explosion about 6,000 years ago. Astronomers recognize that the nearest and brightest supernova ever witnessed by humankind was Vela X, now a faintly flashing pulsar about 1,300 light-years from our solar system.

The psychological and cultural impact of the supernova on the inhabitants of Sumer was overwhelming. Literally "overnight" in evolutionary terms, the Sumerians gave the world a law code, the first love song, the first school system, the first parliament, and the first directory of pharmaceutical concoctions. The origins of contemporary Western culture were nursed in Sumer, the cradle of civilization. The roots of the Judeo-Christian religious beliefs grew from the "tree of knowledge," the Garden of Eden, which tradition places in that same area.

George Michanowsky, a specialist in Mesopotamian astronomy, saw how the very first and most fundamental symbol of Sumerian script was one which represented "star." He went on to show how the first word ever written by a human soon became linked with the symbol for "deity," thus communicating "star god." Michanowsky saw the death-blaze of Vela X to have been such a profound sky show that it became a "cultural organizing principle" that forced human knowledge to take a dramatic leap forward.

But was there something more that took place at that time? The priest-historian Berossus chronicled the account of Oannes, a half-man, half-fish serpentine creature who surfaced from the Persian Gulf to instruct the early inhabitants of Mesopotamia in the arts of civilization. Oannes was said to be one who was possessed of an insight into letters, sciences, and every kind of art. Oannes was but an ancient Greek form of Ea, the star god of the Sumerians.

Were the Sumerians so overwhelmingly inspired by the starburst that they were stimulated into creating writing, law, education, and many of the essential concepts of modern science?

Or had they received some overt physical assistance and instruction from survivors who might have been escaping the supernova, the death of their sun?

The so-called reptilian Star Gods may have been inhabitants of a planet that had been in the process of a vibrational transition from matter to energy. About 12,000 years before, shortly before their Sun was about to become a supernova, certain of their kind chose to leave their planet on a mission to seek out a cousin species to whom they might bequeath their concepts of spirituality, of morality, of aesthetic appreciation of the fruits of the Source, and their penchant for structure and self-discipline.

When they discovered Earth on their quest for heirs, they found primitive, but vitally emerging, *Homo sapiens*, who were beginning to establish the rudiments of culture in certain pockets scattered about the globe. Their collective unconscious would revere the snake and even build religions in memory of the gods who came from the sky to teach and assist the human species.

In Voodoo, the most important concept is to revere one's ancestors and to remember with respect those who have walked this Earth before us. By embodying the concept of a creator god as a serpent, the followers of Voodoo may unconsciously be remembering and honoring the Serpent People who came from the sky.

# KING AND QUEEN OF THE ZOMBIES

*When my friend Chad looks back on his bizarre meeting with a Voodoo Queen that strange night in the hot tub, he is uncertain if she had come to take his blood or to "zombify" him. She claimed that she had come to teach him and to save him from a sinister occult group with incredible powers.*

*In Chad's own words:*

During my late teens, certain of my friends and I discovered gaming conventions. There was one in particular called "Necronomicon" that we attended regularly. This convention at heart was more of a literary convention dedicated to the works of H.P. Lovecraft than it was for gaming, and the two worlds found a comfortable meeting ground.

It wasn't long before we began to host our own live-action game there which we ran nonstop from sundown Friday night till sunrise Sunday morning. The game was based largely on the concept that vampires had taken over a hotel, and it was up to the players to identify who the vampires were and figure out how to destroy them—but ultimately the goal was to survive for the weekend. It was a blast terrorizing players, and for years it was a highly successfully event.

To some, the game was more of an interactive bit of theater that was enacted to terrify the players. For others, it was a challenge to survive. Most of the "vampire" cast and crew were from the local bay area Renaissance Festival, and in the off-season when they weren't fighting with swords they donned the pale make up, prosthetic teeth, and were denizens of the damned Undead for one weekend of the year. I would find myself in an interesting category, caught between both worlds (which is my usual lot in life). I was friends with the cast of the game, as well as serving as the main guide to the players. I never officially had a name, but the running joke was that I was "The Van Helsing-Like Character," the vampire hunter from the classic novel and film, *Dracula*.

On this one particular year, it seems that I was also unwittingly drawing the attention of another group amid the conventioneers— a group with a much more sinister agenda than we had.

Although the game ran nonstop, traditionally we'd wind down around three or four in the morning and enjoy a truce while soaking in one of the greatest hot tubs that I have seen to this day. By the time I found my way to the hot tub, there were about eight or so people I didn't recognize. I wound up seated next to a woman whose name was Rona. I really didn't know too much about her at the time, but I was told that she was a rather gifted psychic.

Everyone was enjoying themselves. Rona was captivating, warm, and charming. She greeted me up by saying, "You're later than you should have been, mister. Your hunters are fewer in number now, but plot changes and twists can have better outcomes than you realize at first."

I thought her comments to be a bit peculiar, because to the best of my knowledge she had nothing to do with the game, and I was right. She did get my attention though.

Steam rose from the hot tub; it was an October evening inside a large atrium at the hotel where we were all staying. The hot tub was considered both indoors and outdoors, because there wasn't an actual ceiling enclosure. There must have been ten of us in the hot tub, and room for more.

Strangely, I began to *feel* a voice in my ear more than hear it. The voice was very melodious, laden with either a Jamaican or Haitian accent, very Islandish either way. "We have much to discuss, Lost One," the voice told me. "You think this all an accident? No sir, guided it was, much energy spent in the timing."

I wasn't entirely sure where the voice was coming from, but then I saw that Rona was looking and speaking directly to me.

I shook my head a bit as I came back into focus. Rona smiled and winked and continued to entertain the others who were indulging in the soothing hot waters.

Everyone was laughing and having a great time. She was a natural entertainer. You couldn't help but love her. The more she talked on, the more mesmerized I was becoming. There was something about the way she was waving her hands and arms around. And she seemed to exude an enthralling accent.

Just as I was about to get lost in her personal appeal and magnetism, I got hit with another internal "hiss" and a "ah ah ah." Then: "No, child, pay attention. Watch, don't follow."

The voice startled me, but as I looked at Rona, she was already turning her head back to the guests.

Then I was aware that the laughter had ceased, and the eight others with us in the hot tub were chanting and swaying back and forth. Rona had moved into the center of the tub, removed her bathing suit top, and had begun a similar chant. I found it no longer entertaining.

I seemed to be the only one aware of what was going on, even though I was completely without a clue as to what was happening. Rona shot me a warning look, and I would swear that with a brief flash her eyes glowed as she smiled at me.

"Child, you have much to learn, and little time to learn it," she said. "I've been watching you for some time. They know of you because you know of them. There is no turning back from this point."

Watching the bodies sway back and forth and this woman looking straight at me, I was about to speak—but inside my head I got blasted with another "Hiss."

"Quiet," I was commanded. "We'll have our time, but first I must handle something, Lost One."

Rona's hands and arms sank beneath the water, then she spun onto the redheaded guy who was swaying behind her. She rose up, her ample breasts firmly planted into his face. It was then that I saw the vial, which must have had a needle at its tip. The guy was still mesmerized as Rona caressed him with her breasts. Again her hands with the vial went beneath the water. A few seconds later, she pulled back away from the redhead, spun around in the center of the hot tub again. In her hands held high above her head was the vial. It was now filled with blood.

I was so stunned by all of this that I didn't know what to do.

I heard a strange sound from the distance. Once again, Rona submerged under the heated waters. When she surfaced, her bathing suit top was back in place and there was no sign of the vial. She returned to her seat next to me, and I tried to flee, but the internal voice returned, "Be still, Lost One!" And still I was.

Queen Bianca has been the reigning Voodoo Queen of New Orleans since 1983, when she received the title from Liga Foley, her aunt by marriage, who claimed to be a granddaughter of Marie Laveau. (*art by Ricardo Pustanio*).

Rona reached behind me, picked up her margarita glass, returned the smile to her face, snapped her fingers, and said the punch line to a joke. She roared in laughter—and everyone else in the tub laughed as if they had heard the entire joke.

Taking a sip from the margarita, she turned and faced me with a wide smile, and gave me a wink. Everything and everyone returned to normal.

Whatever spell was woven had come to an end. "Your time is almost here," she told me. "Please stay while I finish my margarita. I promise you, child, you are safe in my presence, and I wish you to remain that way."

I wasn't sure if she meant remain safe or remain by her side. Images of such historical succubi as Lilith were quickly rising to my mind. I had no idea what I was witnessing or with whom I was dealing. I cursed myself for my insatiable curiosity. I had always figured that it would one day be the death of me, and I wasn't entirely sure that day hadn't arrived.

With a round of yawns coming from everyone in the hot tub except Rona and me, everyone began making their excuses and bidding their farewells.

The redheaded man who had enjoyed Rona's breasts in his face lingered a moment. He had an odd look to him. He smiled and exited the hot tub. While he was drying off, he kept pulling at his crotch. Finally he stuck his hand in his bathing suit to scratch a more deeply personal itch.

It was obvious that on some level of consciousness he was aware that something had happened to him.

My mind was already dismissing everything I witnessed—or thought I had witnessed. And then, there we were left alone.

"Chad, you don't know what you have locked inside of you," she said. "It will come when it's ready. Do not destroy yourself pursuing it. All things in time. I brought you here to make you aware that there are things beyond our reality, things you can tap into."

She caught my attention mostly by using my first name. I listened with curiosity and sat on my right hand with my fingers bent inward, an action I did instinctively. If I felt any sign that I was falling into a trance it was my intention to put weight on my hand in hopes the minor pain would distract me enough to keep me aware. Where or why I came up with that notion to this day remains a mystery.

My subtle action did not go by unnoticed. Rona cocked her head, smiling wildly. "You already know when to let your instincts take over," she said. "I will teach you to turn those instincts into intuition, and that intuition into something you have only ever dreamed of, child."

A traditional symbol of Voodoo/Hoodoo/Voudun (*art by Ricardo Pustanio*).

This time she definitely spoke in an Island accent. "There is a group you need to be aware of," she warned. "You made the unfortunate mistake of noticing them at some point, and even worse they took note of you as well. Great troubles they will cause you. Only what lies beyond your intuition can save you … or make you understand. Don't pretend you understand their motives, because you can't. They are beyond the sum of your experiences."

I was incensed by this limiting of my ability to comprehend, but my hostess could tell this as well and responded quickly.

"That's your arrogance getting the best of you, child. Your grandfather Emerson took it down a few notches for you once already as he crossed over. You will thank him one day."

At this I was blown away for more than one reason. My grandfather had recently passed away. I was going through such a dark occult fascination phase that I was pretty much exiled from my family in Indiana. I hadn't seen them since I was a child and we moved to Florida. Now it was my teenage years. I didn't have a typical angst-style rebellious streak, but I did go the dark-strange route. I found little recourse but to stare into a pond for the couple of weeks my parents and I tended to matters in Indiana. In that time, a lot of what was dark within me became light. I began a transition from accumulating knowledge of the occult to exploring metaphysics, and I began to ponder connections on quantum levels. I was fifteen. Now from what I was hearing from Rona, it seems it was my grandfather who compelled me to sit pondside like I did. And yes, his name was Emerson.

Rona continued: "These individuals who are as yet beyond your comprehension are not members of a cult that you can read about or learn about. Only by experience will any light be shed on them. In your curiosity, you judge too quickly. You seat yourself upon a throne of right or wrong, good versus evil, it is the human way. Just as you judged what you witnessed tonight as bad or wrong, well before you had any clue as to why it was happening."

Rona pulled out the vial concealed in her bathing suit top and slid it back in. "Once you know how to talk to the blood, the blood listens."

Rona went on to explain in more detail: "The man you think I violated made a few poor choices for which too many others would have to pay the price. Yes, I took something from him, and you'd be wise to be grateful for it, child! Rarely is anything as it seems. The man doesn't even know it, but he was just given a second chance. He was given a different path to choose, but I fear that he's a fool. He will find his way back to the road he was traveling. I simply provided a detour. Hopefully a few lives will be saved because of this detour."

I had no idea what she was talking about, but I felt a truth to her words even though they were beyond my comprehension.

This was the most bizarre woman I had ever met in my life. I had so many questions, the least of which being why I felt safe in her presence when by all rational thought I should have bolted screaming, never looking back.

Suddenly, Rona seemed to become anxious. It was as if a blast of cold air had just struck her.

"Something I wasn't expecting this weekend has begun," she said. "They just found me. You need to be aware of Angels and Demons and other creatures. They are a species as real as any other. They're just on different frequencies. Some are as clueless as people can be; others more powerful and dangerous, just as people can be. They don't see time linearly as you do. Ponder this and ponder it often. Can you think of a direction that you cannot go? Or a way in which to walk between the rain drops without getting wet?"

Even I felt something on the air. I knew our time had ended.

We both turned at the same time to face a man who appeared at the top of the steps that led down into the hot tub area. Underneath the water Rona touched my thigh. Waves of images flew through my head, and the internal voice returned, "Child, make no move. This is the most dangerous moment you've had. Learn this, 'Jordon' up there isn't human. Now you will be drunk, and our paths will cross again, in Sedona or Tempe, Arizona. I am about to find out the fate of my daughter."

Prince Ke'eyma, known popularly as "Chicken Man," was said by some authorities to have founded one of the largest secret sosyetes since the one created by the legendary Voodoo Queen Marie Laveau. The Cult of the Chicken Man, according to many, survives today. Although Chicken Man died just a few days before Christmas in 1998, a full Voodoo burial and New Orleans jazz funeral was held for him in January 1999 (*art by Ricardo Pustanio*).

A buzz came over me. At the time I really hadn't discovered that divine nectar of the gods known as "tequila." I hadn't been drunk before, but somehow I knew the feeling.

"Rona, is that you?" the man said from the top of the steps. "Imagine, after all these years. How have you been?"

"Jordon, good to see you," Rona said as she took hold of the rail and began to exit the hot tub.

Jordon came down the steps, but it seemed more like he floated, for he descended with such grace. There was an aura to him that I hadn't felt before.

Jordon shot a glance at me. I hiccupped. My stomach lurched like it never had before. I spun around to the hot tub's edge, leaned over, and threw up all over the deck.

"Jordon, leave him alone," Rona said. "He's just a drunk kid who was flirting with me."

The world was spinning. I was losing consciousness, but fighting it with a strength that I didn't have. I no longer cared about what was going on near me. I wanted desperately to be dry, in a bed, and wrapped up in two comforts of reality—a warm blanket and a remote control.

The two of them began talking. I managed to stagger out of the hot tub and get to my towel. I again threw up in the bushes. The two "adults" politely looked away.

Whatever Rona did to me was effective at shutting me down for a time, that is for certain. I grabbed the Pepsi that I had forgotten about and washed out my mouth. As far as I was concerned, that Pepsi was the Ark of the Covenant, a priceless treasure that I would have protected with my life at that particular moment. My head felt like it was a globe that a child had just thrown with all his might, seeing how fast he could get it to spin. I staggered to the steps, not entirely confident that I was capable of ascending them at the moment.

I nodded at Jordon and attempted to say goodnight to Rona when she came in for a hug. As she hugged me she whispered, "Get to the door straight ahead. When the door closes your head will clear up."

Although I stumbled at first, I managed to make it without further embarrassing myself. The door seemed to glow. I made a beeline for it. I just wanted to get back to my hotel room. The glowing door was the long way, but I did what I was told.

The minute I walked through it and it closed behind me, my head and stomach cleared up. I felt fine. I was about to turn around and make an attempt at a more eloquent departure, but my head was suddenly filled with the tales of Sodom and Gomorrah and Lot's wedded pillar of salt. I left things as they were.

In the morning, I only had one thing on my agenda and that was to track down Rona. I managed to find her hotel room. Housekeeping was nearby, but I faked them into letting me in. Rona's stuff was still there, but there was no sign of her in the room or anywhere else in the hotel. I poked around a bit but wasn't invasive. I did notice an opened hotel issued tampon wrapper in the bathroom wastebasket.

As I walked the halls, trying to figure out my next move in finding Rona, I encountered the redheaded fellow from whom Rona had taken a blood sample. On his arms were two of the ladies who were in the hot tub with us.

We exchanged pleasantries, and I asked if they had seen Rona. Amazingly, they all looked at me, puzzled at first. Then it dawned on them, "Oh, that black lady who was so funny last night?"

I nodded in agreement, thinking how peculiar it was that they remembered Rona as someone who had entertained them. Then I remembered that when Rona brought them out of trance after she had taken a vial of blood from the redhead, everyone in the tub began to laugh, as if Rona had just told a hilarious joke.

After a moment or two of recollection, one of the girls spoke up and said, "She wasn't black, though. She was Spanish."

The other girl shook her head and said, "No, she wasn't either black or Hispanic. She may have had a deep tan—how I wish I could tan like that. She must really work on it, especially with that blonde hair of hers. No way was she black or Spanish, guys. She was a blonde lady with a neat tan."

Listening to their responses to Rona completely threw me off balance. It seemed everyone had a different memory on what she looked like.

I never saw Rona again. I have only the vaguest of recollections of her encounter with Jordon, because of the whammy that I got out of the deal.

I suddenly connected that whammy and the sample of blood taken from the redhead in the hot tub. Like rocket man, I flew back to my hotel room in a panic, jumped into the bathroom, stripped off all my clothing, and searched for any signs of a puncture wound.

There was none to be found. And then the voice echoed in my head for what-to-date has been the last time. "Child, don't be silly, you knew you were safe."

And I did, too. Why? I couldn't tell you.

After searching for Rona well after the convention had come to an end, I found a lady at the hotel who said that she had seen Rona getting into a nice car with some guy; but, now, a few hours later, she was unable to describe him.

Later, I managed to discover some ladies who said that Rona was a High Priestess of a Voodoo cult, and that she had a thing for blood. One woman told me that she had been to Rona's home in St. Petersburg. Around the perimeter of the living room in strange jars on high shelves, Rona had saved every one of her menstrual cycles. The lady asked Rona about them, and with a smile, Rona had answered, "Blood we live by; blood we live through, and in blood we can live again and again."

Then the woman told me something else that Rona had said that she found strange: "Losing blood leaves a trail that the creatures can find you through."

The woman continued: "That stuck in my head, because the entire setting was strange. I was completely disarmed by her. While I was there with her, the entire scenario seemed totally natural and normal, as if every woman did this. But what she meant about creatures finding you seemed ludicrous. I kind of got away from her after that. She was a bit over the top for me."

"Sounds like it." I replied, feeling as if I needed to say something. Truth was, I wanted to find out as much as I could about Rona and what had happened to her.

Rona had seemed as though she was in so much control of the scene that I couldn't figure out how this "Jordon" thing caught her by surprise and obviously interrupted something important taking place.

That's when I thought of the wrapper I saw in the hotel room. It was hotel issue. Rona's menstrual cycle must have begun or got triggered somehow. She seemed very convinced that leaving blood around would leave a scent or trail that these beings could track. Over time I became convinced that was what she meant in the hot tub by something unexpected having occurred that night.

As for the saving of lives, we're going back to the mid-eighties when this encounter took place. Our society was just starting to accept AIDS as a real disease and not just a gay cancer. Rona demonstrated some tremendous abilities. I wonder if she "spoke" to the blood in the redheaded man in the hot tub and removed a virus from him that was unknown by the majority of the masses at the time. She did say that she had given him a second chance at life.

As I recall the entire scene in the hot tub, I can even now remember feeling drums constantly beating while the whole trance session was going on. The drums were being "broadcast" on an alternate channel than our physical reality, but Rona was able to tune everyone into it.

I do think of her often, and I wonder about the fate of her daughter. Destiny being what it is, I hope our paths will cross again. One thing is certain—there is always something more going on in this world than is apparent to the naked eye, and rarely is anything ever really just as it seems.

## Baron Samedi and Maman Brigitte, King and Queen of the Zombies

Voodoo deities, or loas, are among the most feared divine beings in the world. Wild, short-tempered and immensely powerful, these spirits communicate with humans by possessing those attending Voodoo rituals. Those who obey the loa are granted their wishes and good health, but those who do not can meet a terrifying fate at the hands of their gods. There seems a sense in Chad's story of his encounter with Rona, an alleged Voodoo Queen, that she must somehow have run afoul of a loa and that she was being monitored by such spirit beings as "Jordon," who so mysteriously appeared as Rona was beginning to convey certain metaphysical truths and secrets to Chad.

On the other hand, if Chad had been selected to become a member of Rona's Voodoo cult, he may soon have had the dubious pleasure of meeting Baron Samedi and Maman Brigitte, the King and Queen of the zombies.

Baron Samedi is the most famous and the most frightening of the loa spirits. The Baron is the infamous master of the dead who escorts souls from the graveyard to the underworld.

However, the Baron does not concern himself with only with the dead— he can enter the realm of the living and force people to do his terrible bidding.

**Baron Samedi is one of the loa of Haitian Vodou. Samedi is usually depicted with a white top hat, black tuxedo, dark glasses, and cotton plugs in the nostrils, as if to resemble a corpse dressed and prepared for burial in the Haitian style (*art by Ricardo Pustanio*).**

Baron Samedi (Baron Saturday, also Bawon Samedi, or Bawon Sanmdi) is one of the loa of Haitian Vodou. Samedi is usually depicted with a white top hat, black tuxedo, dark glasses, and cotton plugs in the nostrils, as if to resemble a corpse dressed and prepared for burial in the Haitian style. He has a white, frequently skull-like face (or actually has a skull for a face). He is the head of the Guádé (also Ghede; pronounced GAY-day) family of loa, those gods concerned with death and resurrection.

Many call Baron Samedi the ruling loa or god of New Orleans. He and his bride the Great Maman Brigitte are sometimes referred to as the King and Queen of the Zombies. Voodooists believe that only through his power can a soul be forced from a living body and placed between life and death.

On Halloween night, Baron Samedi stands at the Crossroads, where the souls of dead humans pass on their way to the gate to Guinee, the astral counterpart of the ancient homeland in Africa. Samedi is a sexual loa, frequently represented by phallic symbols, and he is also noted for disruption, obscenity, debauchery, and having a particular fondness for tobacco and rum. As he is the loa of sex and resurrection, he is often called upon for healing by those near or approaching death. It is only the Baron who can accept an individual into the realm of the dead. Samedi is considered a wise judge and a powerful magician.

He, as well as Ghede, the most benevolent loa of the dead, often possesses individuals whether they are practicing Voodoo-Hoodoos or not. Many have documented and experienced such possession.

Lisa Lee Harp Waugh, "The Great American Necromancer," reports to having been in the company of the Baron Samedi many times. She suggests that many people in the paranormal field fear or have not investigated the sacred rites of Voodoo and the many spirit and ghost contacts that occur.

Waugh, a Voodoo reactionary herself, was called upon to help discover if a young Haitian woman in Miami, Florida, was actually possessed. Her case drew a lot of local attention in early 2009. The young woman had been held— or "ridden"— by the spirit since Halloween 2008. The case has been documented and will be featured in a forthcoming documentary on Voodoo-Hoodoo possession and exorcism.

As well as being master of the dead, Baron Samedi is also a giver of life. He can cure any mortal of any disease or wound—if he thinks it is worth his time to do so. His powers are especially great when it comes to Voodoo curses and black magic. Even if somebody has been inflicted by a hex which brings them to the verge of death, they will not die if the Baron refuses to dig their grave. So long as this mighty spirit keeps them out of the ground they are safe. What he demands in return depends on his mood. Sometimes he is content with his followers wearing black, white, or purple clothes, and offering a small gift of cigars, rum, black coffee, grilled peanuts or bread. On other occasions, the Baron will ask for a Voodoo ceremony in his honor. If he is in a bad mood, he may dig the grave of his supplicant, bury him alive, or bring him back as a mindless zombie.

The spiritual children of Baron and Maman Brigitte are the Ghede loa, the protectors of the dead. A New World loa, Maman Brigitte is probably traceable back to the Irish Saint Brigid. The Ghedes are powerful, and will prophesy the future, heal the sick, give advice, or perform magic of all descriptions. They also exert control over those who become zombies.

At Voodoo ceremonies, the Ghede possess the Voodooists and dance the banda, which is a wildly suggestive dance miming sexual intercourse. And in the midst of all this winding and grinding, these loa keep perfectly straight faces. They have reached such a deep trance state that it is as if they are cadavers and feel nothing.

Papa Legba (also Papa Ghede) is considered the counterpart to Baron Samedi. If a child is dying, it is Papa Legba to whom the parents pray.

The spiritual children of Baron and Maman Brigitte are the Ghede loa, the protectors of the dead. A New World loa, Maman Brigitte is probably traceable back to the Irish Saint Brigid (*art by Ricardo Pustanio*).

It is believed that he will not take a life before its time, and that he will protect the little ones.

Papa Ghede is supposed to be the corpse of the first man who ever died. He is recognized as a short, dark man with a high hat on his head, a cigar in his mouth, and an apple in his left hand. Papa Ghede is a psychopomp who waits at the crossroads to take souls into the afterlife.

Although he was one of the most revered loa in Haitian Voudun, he was eventually transformed into the figure of a gentle and loving old man, who stands at the Guardian of the Centerpost, the Opener of the Gates, to any who communicate with the loa.

Ghede Nibo is a "psychopomp," an intermediary between the living and the dead. He gives voice to the dead spirits that have not been reclaimed from "below the waters."

Ghede Masaka assists Ghede Nibo. He is an androgynous male or transgendered gravedigger and spirit of the dead, recognized by his black shirt, white jacket, and white head scarf.

November 2, All Soul's Day, is also The Feast of the Ancestors, commonly called Fet Ghede. New Orleans' Catholics attend mass in the morning, then go to the cemetery, where they pray at family grave sites and make repairs to family tombs. The majority of New Orleans Catholics are also said to be Vodouisants, and *vice versa*, so on the way to the cemetery many people change clothes from the white they wore to church to the purple and black of the loa Ghede, the spirits of the departed ancestors.

Fet Ghede, is considered the end of the old year and the beginning of the new, much as in the European Wiccan tradition. Any debts to Baron Samedi, Maman Brigitte, or Ghede must be paid at this time.

# MARIE LAVEAU, VOODOO QUEEN ETERNAL

My friend and colleague Paul Dale Roberts interviewed Julie, who told him that she had encountered a zombie while she was visiting friends in Biloxi, Mississippi, in March 2009.

Julie was driving down the road towards her friend's house, when she saw a dark-haired woman in a white flowing gown walking alongside the road. She looked through her rearview mirror and saw that this lady had no pupils and her skin was ash white. Finally the woman faded away into nothingness.

Paul said that the mysterious woman at the side of the road sounded to him to be more like a ghost than a zombie.

Julie agreed, but then proceeded to tell him the story of Xara the Zombris. Yes, she knew there was no such word as "zombris," but that's what the locals called the entity.

Julie said that she did her own investigating and started talking to people on the streets about her encounter. Jeff, 52, told her that back in the early 1980s, Xara, who was originally from Nicaragua, was practicing Santeria. The story goes that she traveled to New Orleans to obtain various ointments and potions from a Voodoo priest. The Voodoo priest and Xara became entangled in an affair.

When the Voodoo priest discovered that Xara was cheating on him with his own brother, he poisoned her with toxins from the puffer fish. With various rituals, he was able to turn her into a zombie.

Xara became a zombie prostitute on the streets on New Orleans. Her mind was under the complete control of the Voodoo priest turned pimp. Eventually the Voodoo priest released Xara, and she returned to Biloxi.

Xara was never the same again. She always seemed like she was in a daze. The last time anyone saw Xara is when she was picked up by a trucker in a Mack truck. Xara was never seen or heard from again. Many people thought she was killed by a trucker serial killer.

Julie was driving down the road towards her friend's house when she saw a dark-haired woman in a white flowing gown walking alongside the road. Later, she learned the story of Xara the Zombris (*photo by Shannon McCabe*).

One year later, Xara was seen walking the road side, staring blankly ahead—and if anyone watched her long enough, she would dissipate into nothingness.

Xara learned to her everlasting sorrow that it can be extremely detrimental to one's health to anger a Voodoo Priest—perhaps especially in New Orleans, the center of Voodoo practice in the United States.

### The Life and Legend of Marie Laveau

I doubt many would disagree when I write that no one single person is more associated with the legends and folklore of zombies and Voodoo than Marie Laveau.

Each year, the reportedly haunted wishing tomb of Voodoo Queen Marie Laveau is visited by thousands of people from around the world. Located in St. Louis Cemetery Number 1 in New Orleans, people capture ghost photos with their cameras. Others hear messages from beyond the grave on their tape recorders as they attempt to pick up some EVPs (Electronic Voice Phenomena). Almost daily, someone conducts a Voodoo-Hoodoo ritual in Mama Marie's honor. Not too many tourists stay too long after dark, however, for the cemetery has a reputation of being haunted. And, then, of course, there is the restless spirit of Marie herself, who may manifest at any time, seeking someone to zombify.

Mama Sanite Dede was in her time the most powerful of all the Voodoo Queens. As a young woman from Santo Domingo, she bought her secret hexes and Hoodoo-Voodoo to New Orleans. She often would hold rituals in her brick-lined courtyard on Dumaine and Chartres Streets, just walking distance away from the St. Louis Cathedral.

Marie Laveau succeeded Sanite Dede as the Voodoo Queen (High Priestess) of New Orleans sometime around 1830. No one in the hierarchy of Voodoo Priests and priestesses disputed Marie's rise to that prestigious position, for it was widely known that she was gifted with remarkable powers of sorcery.

Marie was a Creole freewoman and a hair dresser by profession. Her prestige among the white establishment was assured when the son of a wealthy New Orleans merchant was arrested for a crime of which he was innocent, although there was much false evidence against him. His father appealed to the Voodoo high priestess to put a spell on the judge to cause him to find the young man "not guilty."

Marie took three Guinea peppers and placed them in her mouth before she went to the cathedral to pray. Although she was the recognized Voodoo Priestess of New Orleans, she did not find her beliefs incompatible with Catholicism and Christian charity, and she attended Mass daily. On that particular day, she knelt at the altar for several hours, praying for the young man to be found innocent.

Then, later, by a ruse, she managed to enter the courtroom and place the peppers under the judge's seat. The judge found the prisoner not guilty, and Marie Laveau was handsomely rewarded by the wealthy merchant.

Marie Laveau was the reigning Voodoo priestess of the nineteenth century. New Orleans Voodoo as a social phenomenon came into its heyday during the early 1800s. The population of the city doubled in the 1830s, and, by 1840, New Orleans had become the wealthiest and third most populous city in the nation. The Union captured New Orleans early in the American Civil War, an action which spared the city the destruction suffered by many other cities of the American South.

As a principal port, New Orleans had a leading role in the slave trade. At the same time, the city had the most prosperous community of free persons of color in the South. The touch of Voodoo-Hoodoo got a firm grasp on the city. Voodooists such as Sainte Dede, Dr. John, and Marie Laveau prospered.

New Orleans developed its distinctive variety of Voodoo, due in part to syncretism with Roman Catholic beliefs, the fame of High Priestess Marie Laveau, and New Orleans' distinctly Caribbean cultural influences. Under Mama Marie's guidance, Voodoo thrived as a business, served as a form of political influence, provided a source of spectacle and entertainment, and was a means of altruism.

Marie greatly popularized Voodoo by revising some of the rituals until they became her unique mixture of West Indian and African tribal religions and Roman Catholicism. She was certain to invite politicians and police officials to the public ceremonies that she conducted on the banks of Bayou St. John on the night of June 23, St. John's Eve. On other occasions, she would hold Voodoo rituals on the shore of Lake Pontchartrain and at her cottage, Maison Blanche.

Hundreds of the best families in New Orleans would be present at these public celebrations of Voodoo, hoping to get a glimpse of Marie Laveau herself dancing with her large snake, Zombi, draped over her shoulders. For the white onlookers, the music and the dance provided exciting entertain-

Marie Laveau succeeded Sanite Dede as the Voodoo Queen (High Priestess) of New Orleans sometime around 1830. No one in the hierarchy of Voodoo priests and priestesses disputed Marie's rise to that prestigious position, for it was widely known that she was gifted with remarkable powers of sorcery (*art by Ricardo Pustanio*).

ment. For Marie Laveau's fellow worshippers, the rites were spiritual celebrations, and even Zombi was an agent of great Voodoo powers, a physical embodiment of Damballah Wedo. On other occasions, in private places, the High Priestess celebrated the authentic rites of Voodoo for her devoted congregation, far from the critical eyes of the white establishment and clergy.

Madame Delphine LaLaurie and her third husband, Leonard LaLaurie, took up residence in the mansion at 1140 Royal Street sometime in the 1830s. The pair immediately became the darlings of the New Orleans social scene which at that time was experiencing the birth of ragtime, the slave dances, the Voodoo rituals of Congo Square, the reign of the great Marie Laveau, and the advent of the bittersweet Creole Balls. Madame LaLaurie hosted fantastic events in her beautiful home that were talked about months afterward. She was described as sweet and endearing in her ways, and her husband was nothing if not highly respected within the community.

At the same time, it is said that Madame's friendship with the infamous Voodoo Queen, Marie Laveau, began to grow. Laveau lived not far from LaLaurie's Royal Street home, and the two women became acquainted when Laveau occasionally did Madame's hair. Under Laveau's tutelage, Madame LaLaurie began to act upon her latent interest in the occult, learning the secrets of Voodoo and witchcraft at the hands of the mistress of the craft.

Madame LaLaurie and her husband had horrid ways that extended far beyond Voodoo. They began to practice hideous experiments on slaves in a secret room in their attic. Unfortunate black men and women were placed on an operating table where their vital organs were removed while they were still living or their faces were turned into grotesque masks by Dr. LaLaurie's savage scalpel.

Many locals say this is when Madame LaLaurie became the wet nurse or the nanny to the infamous Devil Baby of Bourbon Street.

It is said Madame LaLaurie fled with the cursed creature after it had killed many people and took refuge at the pilot house located on the shores of Bayou St. John. Some say she left the Devil Baby there, and that later she boarded a merchant schooner and escaped to France.

According to one version of the Devil Baby legend, Marie Laveau strangled the horned and murderous demon after it began biting her and her children.

Voodoo lore says that zombie children taken straight from the womb never age as mere mortals do. They may take over 30 years to grow into what appears to be a beautiful girl or a handsome boy in their teens. Many Voodoo cultists insist that Marie Laveau never grew old because she was of zombie birth. The great High Priest, Dr. John himself had performed her zombification one the day that she was born in September 1801.

Although Baron Samedi, the powerful loa of the dead, spends most of his time in the invisible realm of Voodoo spirits, he is notorious for his outrageous behavior, swearing continuously and making filthy jokes to the other loa and Voodooists. He is married to another powerful spirit known as Maman Brigitte, but he often chases after mortal women. It would surprise no one to learn that the Baron soon developed an unbearable desire for Marie Laveau.

In exchange for the hope of one brief romantic liaison, Baron Samedi is said to have revealed the secret of The Zombie Trance to Marie Laveau and her followers in a late night necromantic ritual in the 1840s. With this power, Mama Marie was able to instantly "zombify" anyone of her choosing.

For many years, legend had it that Marie Laveau had discovered the secrets of immortality and that she lived to be nearly 200 years old. Some speak in hushed whispers that she is still alive, conducting Voodoo rituals in the secret shadows of New Orleans.

Such a legend quite likely began when Marie cleverly passed the position of High Priestess to her daughter, who greatly resembled her, at a strategic time when she had just begun to age. Marie retired from public appearances to continue to conduct the intricate network of spies and informants she had built up while her daughter, Marie II assumed the public persona of Marie Laveau, Voodoo Queen of New Orleans. Because she now appeared ageless and could sometimes be seen in more than one place at a time, her power and mystery grew ever stronger among her Voodoo worshippers and the elite white community, as well. As far as it can be determined, Marie Laveau I died in New Orleans on June 15, 1881.

Or maybe not.

It is said that Marie Laveau I is the only person who is able to cross over, back and forth, between the two worlds because she was so powerful a Voodoo Queen. But she is only allowed to be in our world on five or six days of the year. Those days are Christmas Day, New Year's Day, Fat Tuesday, Carnival or New Orleans Mardi Gras day, All Saints' Day, or All Souls' Day, St. Johns Eve, and her birthday, September 10.

BLACK CAT MAMA COUTEAUX ZOMBIE WAR

or the following account of
he Zombie War of (circa)
nder of the Sorcerers Guild
and conducting rituals for

ecame involved with the
re revealed to her regard-
ptized and trained in the
New Orleans. Lisa Lee
as much as possible about

e Ebenezer Baptist Church-
ed grave of Black Cat Mama
d to those blessed beings who
loodoo, all say … *keep away.*

t Mama's hidden grave lies
le unmarked grave detected
lessed and dressed offerings.

in an all-white cemetery—
bie husband who is buried

I
reall

behi
only

and t
with

Ceme                                           if you went to Whetstone
real z                                          at 3:00 AM, you can hear a
ly waiting his time for someone to dig him up.                scratching from the hard ground, impatient-

**Lisa Lee Harp Waugh is a professional necromancer and founder of the Sorcerers Guild of greater Houston, Texas. She has been practicing and conducting rituals for over 20 years (*art by Ricardo Pustanio*).**

Many say that Black Cat Mama Couteaux was buried with an axe in her brain, a Bowie knife in heart, with her legs and arms burnt to ashes and scattered in the great Caddo lake.

"Be glad she's still buried," others add, "*Because you're standing on her unholy cursed head!*"

In spite of the hard times and its many woes, a great Voodoo prophecy of a Zombie War was fulfilled. An old New World Creole Voodoo woman named Black Cat Mama Couteaux (or Couteau) arrived in New Orleans on a dark and stormy day, a High Holy Day, Good Friday the 13th, 1838, to be exact. No one really knew how old she was, but she was old.

Those who knew her well talked of her being the great-grandmother or even the great-great-grandmother of the New Orleans Voodoo Hoodoo Queen, the great Marie Laveau. Others said that she was an evil black cat magic hexin' woman from the swamps, who went to war with all the Voodoos and Hoodoos in New Orleans at the time to seize complete control of the city.

What is known for certain is that she was eventually banished from the Old French Quarter for her evil deeds and that she left for Texas with an army of zombies that followed Black Cat Mama Couteaux alone and that only she could control.

Black Cat Mama and her army had descended on New Orleans from the yellow fever and mosquito-ridden Jefferson, Louisiana, dark swamps. Black Cat Mama and her zombie hoard arrived ready to battle the Voodoo Kings and Queens over Voodoo-Hoodoo territory in New Orleans.

"How to Make and Control a Real Zombie" is often disputed. In the first step of zombification, special powders are made and the person is cursed before his or her death. Then the corpse is dug from its grave on a moonless night. A ritual of indescribable infernal actions takes place in the graveyard. The soul of the person is called out, then imprisoned in a bottle or large clay human-shaped pot. As the body becomes animated by that of the Ghede and the powers set forth by Baron Samedi, it is held down in its coffin by several strong white-hooded men. The Voodoo Priestess alone must bite out the tongue of the zombie-to-be to gain power over the soulless creature. By this action, the zombie will always do the bidding of the last person who had its tongue in his or her mouth.

Many Voodoo Queens or Kings who own zombies keep the dried tongues in jars so that when the zombie is sold to its new master, he or she must put the tongue in his or her mouth to gain the complete power to totally control the zombie's actions.

In order to raise a Voodoo army that no one else can command, all the tongues of the dead at the reanimation process must be swallowed whole by the original zombie maker. Such action insures complete control over all the zombies he or she made. The zombies will only be set free when the zombie maker dies or the tongue is cut from the belly.

Black Cat Mama Couteaux was said to wear a belt and a long necklace under her clothes with over 1,600 dried tongues attached. These tongues taken from the members of her zombie army compelled the creatures to follow only her control. Voodoo historians advise that we must consider that Mama Couteaux's army may have been larger than 1,600 zombies, for it is not really known how many tongues she actually had bitten off and swallowed over the years.

The Voodoo-Hoodoo war first took place in the open area of Congo Square. It began at sunset and lasted 32 days and nights. Over 100 zombies of Black Cat Mama's army were killed and sent back to hell through the Gates of Guinee. It is estimated several hundred zombies fighting at the command of the New Orleans Voodoo royalty were killed as well.

Black Cat Mama Couteaux was winning in the beginning, sending great hordes of zombies to kill the followers of lesser Queens of New Orleans. The other Queens are said to have countered with many spells, because they never really knew where Black Cat Mama Couteaux would strike next. Finally, with the help of several other Voodoo-Hoodoo Kings and Queens from across the great South—including the forces of Marie Laveau—Black Cat Mama was finally defeated.

As time in the Voodoo zombie war went on, Black Cat Mama Couteaux never grew weak. One often heard that the woman used to like to mix things up with her fists, and she was known to beat grown men and women, including judges and politicians to the ground.

To say that she lost the war to the power of Marie Laveau's secret "Black Magic Zombie Voodoo Dust" is incorrect. Most people say that it was because her husband-to-be, the handsome and dashing Rudolph Couteaux, was killed over a bet he lost at a local cock or dog fight. This is what made her stop the war cold.

After his untimely death, she resurrected him to become her husband. She knew he had died from a real Voodoo-Hoodoo curse. What mattered most was bringing him back from the dead.

With the help of Dr. John and Marie Laveau, she dug up his body on a rainy night when a full hurricane was tossing the city around like a cockroach

**An impression of Mama Courteaux in her younger days (art by Ricardo Pustanio).**

on an old stick in a puddle. On the weed-filled shores of the black Bayou St. John at the foot of the Great Spanish Fort, she bit out his dead, rotting tongue and made him into her zombie lover forever.

She fled the city that night, swearing unholy revenge on those who had defeated her. Many say that is where the curse of the New Orleans Devil Baby began.

Black Cat Mama and Rudolph arrived in Texas with the remnants of the zombie army. Rudolph was said to be a handsome, but skinny and overly lanky fellow. He was always well-dressed with a tall top hat and a beard like the good President Lincoln's. Black Cat Mama's Creole man was at least 45 to 50 years her junior in appearance, but he cared for her and caressed her publicly as if she were a mere girl of marrying age. Many frowned on these actions, for such public displays were not the norm of the period. However, no one uttered an open word or spoke even in hushed circles for fear of what magic retaliation Black Cat Mama would put upon them.

*"I knew a woman who had a real Zombie baby once. But I swore to tell no one anything, and by that I said too much."*

"He took her out on his bended arm with white cotton gloved hands and showed her off day and night like an expensive gem glittering in the light," my Grandma said. "They say that he never looked at another woman. His fine store-bought clothes were always just too finely pressed for any a live freeman of color. He never spoke a word or made a sound or blinked his eyes. No one ever saw him eat or drink. And many more around say they never saw him sleep. He would stand in the front yard, guarding his Queen rain or shine, 102 degree heat or the cold of winter's icy deep freeze, night and day. And always he smelled of lavender and rose so sweet."

The clue was always the sweet smelling lavender and rose smell, my old Grandma said. She would stop her story and tell me, oh, so low, as if God or the Devil would not or should not hear her: "That sweet sickening smell! That cursed black blood and cat gut stench perfume."

She would go on to say: "That's to cover it up! You knows. To cover up if someone be dead for a real long time. Everyone around knew that Rudolph there was a full cuss-ed real Texas zombie."

Often Grandma would tell me with her half-Louisiana, half-East Texas drawl: "I knew a woman who had a real zombie baby once. But I swore to tell no one anything, and by that I said too much." And with this she would chuckle.

After repeated attempts to establish a county seat on the Sabine River since the county was established in 1839, the city of Marshall, founded in 1841 as the seat of Harrison County, was incorporated in 1843. The Republic of Texas had decided to choose the site of land granted by Peter Whetstone and Isaac Van Zandt after Whetstone proved that the hilly location had a good water source. Marshall quickly became a major city in the state because of its position as a gateway to Texas on several major stagecoach lines. The establishment of several "colleges" (i.e., schools offering little more than secondary education) earned Marshall the nickname "the Athens of Texas," in reference to the ancient Greek city-state. The city's growing importance was confirmed when Marshall was linked by a telegraph line to New Orleans, becoming the first city in Texas to have a telegraph service.

The county had more slaves than any other in the state, making it a hotbed of Voodoo-Hoodoo anti-Union sentiment. At the time the faithful Voodooists cried out to New Orleans to send them a Queen to rule their band of devotees. From the practices of conjuring the spirits and the dead, the followers of Voodoo were told that soon a great priestess would be delivered to them.

Marshall became the seat of civil authority and headquarters of the Trans-Mississippi Postal Department after the fall of Vicksburg. Toward the end of the War Between the States, the Confederate States government had $9 million in Treasury notes and $3 million in postage stamps shipped to Marshall, possibly indicating that Marshall was the intended destination of a government preparing to flee from advancing armies.

Marshall's Railroad Era began in the early 1870s. Harrison County citizens voted to offer $300,000 bond subsidy, and the City of Marshall offered to donate land north of the downtown to the Texas and Pacific Railway if the company would move to Marshall. Black Cat Mama Couteauxes' magic spell is said to have made T&P President Jay Gould accept the offer which at first he refused six times. By Mama's insistence and black magic, he finally located the T&P's workshops and general offices for Texas in Marshall.

African-Americans came to the city seeking opportunities and protection until 1878, when the Citizens Party, led by former Confederate General Walter P. Lane and his brother George, took control of the city and county governments and ran Unionists, Republicans, and many African-Americans out of town. The Lanes ultimately declared Marshall and Harrison County "redeemed" from Union and African-American control. Despite this the African-American community would continue to progress with the establishment of Bishop College in 1881 and the Freedman's Aid Society in 1882.

The city benefited immediately from a population explosion. And so did Black Cat Mama Couteaux. She sold her Voodoo-Hoodoo wares—tall black Texas-style zombies, powders, and snake-poisoned teas. She would sell chicory-flavored love potions and "Hate Me Not" liquorices flavored juice to all who wanted them. She made woman bear children, and men more virile. She ruled the city with the strong grip that only she could.

Mama Couteaux would embroider special *Veves* on her red silk-laced multiple petticoats and on the skirts or blouses of those young women who came to her for help. A Veve, or *Vévá* (also spelled as Beybey and Vever), is a religious symbol commonly used in all of Voodoo. It acts as a "beacon" for the loa (also spelled lwa)— a type of spirit or ghost—and will serve as a loa's representative during rituals. In the past, it was believed that the veve was derived from the beliefs of the native Tainos, but more recent scholarship has demonstrated a close link between the Veve and the cosmogram of the Kongo people.

According to Milo Rigaud's book *Secrets of Voodoo* (1969), "The Veves represent figures of the astral forces.... In the course of Voodoo ceremonies, the reproduction of the astral forces represented by the Veves obliges the loas ... to descend to earth." And wearing one on your under garments helps protect you from all that could harm you.

Every Loa has his or her own unique Veve, although regional differences have led to different Veves for the same loa in a few cases. Sacrifices and offerings are usually placed upon them, and they must be specially made and hand done on a dark night while sitting in cemetery atop a fresh grave of a virgin.

A Veve is usually drawn on the floor by strewing a powder-like substance, commonly salt, baking soda, rice, cornmeal, wheat flour, bark, red brick powder, or gunpowder, though the material depends entirely upon the ritual. In Haitian Vodou, a mixture of cornmeal and wood ash is used. In Texas Voodoo they use salt, rat's blood, and white flowers from a grave.

If you had the money, Mama Couteaux would sell you her secret black magic spell to kill a man quick or to make a woman your eternal love or sex slave.

By 1880 the city was one of the South's largest cotton markets. And so Black Cat Mama Couteaux went into the fine dress- and petticoat-making business. She began to make and sell handmade Voodoo wedding dresses for all the fine rich ladies who needed to marry quick. These gowns and undergarments with handmade fine white-lace trim are still hidden away in someone's attic today. These haunted wedding gowns are said to make a man marry you when he sets his eyes on you. They are embroidered with white stitched Veves.

The city's new prosperity became apparent with the opening of J. Weisman and Co., the first department store in Texas. With the installation of a single light bulb in the Texas and Pacific Depot, Marshall became the first city in Texas to have electricity. Black Cat Mama Couteaux was said to be the first woman of color to have electricity in her fine home. A supposed gift from a wealthy client or maybe from Weisman himself.

During this period of wealth, many of the city's now historic homes were constructed. Black Cat Mama Couteaux's was a finely built mansion, and it is said to have been given to her by a man she saved from hanging. As well as gathering a mass fortune of her own, she is said to have made many a man a millionaire. Legend has it that her treasure is buried in the ground of her old estate, guarded by no less than 50 zombies. Although all that is left of the great house is a blood-stained Voodoo-cursed memory of where the evil Black Cat Mama Couteaux once lived. No one would ever dare to dig on the property.

The city's most prominent industry, pottery manufacturing, began with the establishment of Marshall Pottery in 1895. They say Black Cat Mama Couteaux had a secret hand in that and was

*Ricardo Pustanio 2009*

An elderly New World Creole Voodoo woman named Black Cat Mama Couteaux (or Couteau) arrived in New Orleans on a dark and stormy day, High Holy Day, Good Friday the 13th, 1838. It would not be long before she began a Zombie War with Marie Laveau (**art by Ricardo Pustanio**).

given many stone clay jars to keep her many captive souls locked away. Mama Couteaux's house was said to contain over 1,000 small zombie bottle human-shaped jars made especially for her. Each of the jars or small human-shaped bottles were said to contain the spirit of someone who died in Marshall. Many families would come to Mama Couteaux and ask that their loved ones' ghosts be put in the clay bottle jars so they would not come back as zombies.

Black Cat Mama Couteaux never used Voodoo-Hoodoo dolls except for very important matters. Her spells were usually magic potions and strange-colored powders. Red, blue, yellow orange or black—and all the colors of God's rainbow twirled into one. Some gris-gris were for making a man love you, while still others to cure the curse of gout. There was even a special powder to make a black baby white or a white baby black while still in a mama's belly. And this spell came with a steep price.

I am privileged to have in my private collection a leather Voodoo-Hoodoo gris-gris bag said to have been made by Black Cat Mama Couteaux in the late 1800s in Marshall, Texas. The small deer hide bag contains many things: a wad of red hair tied tight with a yellow faded bow; a string of purple embroidery thread with 199 knots in it; and many other small crockery, metals, ju-ju cat bone dirt, and strange Voodoo bead items of the time.

Many stories of the time say that Mama Couteaux made zombies of whole families—from infants to the elderly. She would sometimes threaten to zombify a person, and their only salvation would be to pay her a large monthly or weekly fee.

Despite the prosperity of Black Cat Mama Couteaux and Marshall in the industrious railroad era, poverty continued to be a big problem in the city among all the races. Tensions between whites and African-Americans continued to worsen. Black Cat Mama Couteaux was an exception to all the rules. She was rich, affluent and said to be the only woman who could hold her head higher than all the fine ladies in Texas, be they black or white. And it was because everyone feared her wrath.

The rural areas of Harrison County saw greater interaction between white people and African-Americans. Whites and blacks living as neighbors was commonplace. And Black Cat Mama Couteaux's great two-story house sat in the middle.

Many tell that she had an army of zombies numbering 150 strong—all of them made from the wealthy sons of those who died in the war. It is said that she received a fine payment every month from their grieving families.

Black Cat Mama Couteaux was said to go dig up the fresh corpses on black moonless nights. From even the not-so-fresh dead she made her ju-jus and death powders and made them all into zombies. She would then extort large amounts of monies from the families. This she did by turning up at the door with the family's dead relative completely zombified. Mama would bargain with them, drawing up contracts to allow their enslaved loved ones go free and be buried in peace.

For those families who would did not pay what she demanded, she sent the zombies far north where they worked for nothing and would eventually turn to dust as their bodies wore away.

According to my great grandma, when Black Cat Mama Couteaux died sometime in the late 1890s, her followers asked Marie Laveau to come to Marshall to free

Black Cat Mama's dead body from her zombie husband's grip. You see, she died old and sickly in his arms, and at her death he grabbed her and held her so tight that parts of her burst from the pressure. No one could break his mighty hold. So Voodoo Queen Laveau was summoned to Texas to see what could be done.

Her decision was simple. She said bury them both standing on their heads, and they will never rise from the grave to bother anyone.

If you never have heard of a real Voodoo funeral for a Queen, then you do not know the visual horrors that are set before the innocent. The Couteauxes' funeral took six days to prepare. With Marie Laveau presiding as mortician, clergy, and Voodoo Queen all in one, she dressed the couple both in their finery. Then, with love and care, the two were placed in a special coffin made large enough to hold them both. The funeral was set, and the corpse and living zombie were lowered head first into a deep pit, possibly an old dried-out well.

From all over the United States the news of Black Cat Mama's demise was mourned. On the day of her Voodoo burial rites, it is said to have thundered and lightning and rained from midnight to midnight.

Many say it was the tears of the lost inconsolable Voodoo-Hoodoo Gods crying for her soul.

Others say it was God in heaven crying tears of great joy and relief because Black Cat Mama Couteaux was finally dead.

Many hundreds of zombies across the nation were said to have just frozen and fallen, destroyed on the very spot where they stood. When Black Cat Mama died, her great curse of curses was forever broken.

Nights at the old Ezel's Bar-B-Que in Marshall, folks sometimes get hushed and frightened when talking about Black Cat Mama. No one denies that she once walked the dusty streets of old Marshall, Texas. Some say that her ghost still haunts the place where her great zombie house once stood.

When you live in Marshall, Texas, some say that you can call her name on a full moon night to help you with your problems. The catch is, if Black Cat Mama doesn't like you, you could be dead by dawn. Or so the Texas Voodoo legend goes.

# CURSES, SPELLS, AND HEXES

"The average person may say that curses, spells, and hexes are all a bunch of hogwash," said my friend Laura Lee Mistycah. "That person will change his or her mind after a close encounter with these taboo dark forces!"

Mistycah is the author of such books as *Living in an Indigo House—The Heartaches & Victories of First Wave Indigos* and the popular *Got Ghosts??? The Bizarre but True Tales of the Ghostbuster Gals*, co-authored with her ghostbuster partner, Ronnie Rennae Foster. She has no reluctance in admitting that, among other things, she is a solitary practitioner of Wicca.

"Actually, I have recently morphed into more of a sorceress," she said. "I practice practical Magick, and I have witnessed wonderful miracles through the use of Magick. I have also witnessed, personally and vicariously, the diabolical hostility and deliberate devastation of what I call 'mean magic,' more commonly referred to as curses, spells, and hexes."

As a researcher and practitioner in so called "fringe" sciences for over three decades, Laura Lee has seen and experienced things that defy logic and the laws of physics. Her biggest education has come through personal experience.

"One such personal encounter with the dark side of Magick came toward the end of 2001," she said. "I became entangled with some of the foulest of the foul on this planet as I attempted to free a young man from the clutches of his family ... a family that was immersed in what I termed, 'The Leather Cult.' The young man's father was the leader of this creepy international sect, and he had been well educated in the ways of Black Magick and Voodoo. My blatant interference in these family affairs caused me to be the target of a massive retaliation for five hellish years. I experienced a myriad of events that caused devastation and extreme personal suffering as well as energetic attempts on my life.

"Curses, hexes, and Voodoo.... I was the target of all of these at once. No one can understand these attacks fully unless they have experienced them. People get sick

Laura Lee Mistycah is a solitary practitioner in Wicca and the author of such books as the popular *Got Ghosts??? The Bizarre but True Tales of the Ghostbuster Gals.*

and/or die every day from this stuff ... and the sad fact is, the perpetrators go undetected. No court of law would dare try a case that claimed, 'John Doe put a curse on my client and now he/she is dead.' So people are quietly murdered all the time, and no one is ever prosecuted for it. When a powerful High Priest or Sorcerer kills someone, there are no fingerprints, no guns, no knives—no evidence that our court system would acknowledge."

"I hope that some of my insights and personal experiences shared for this book will be of value for those unfortunate recipients of cures, hexes, and spells who are trying to get relief from these dark energies."

### The Leather Cult

*In Laura Lee Mysticah's own words:*

At the time of my entanglement with "The Leather Cult," I had previously acquired a diverse education in the Dark Arts both through what I had researched and also by personal experiences. I was not naive. As the evil energies prevailed upon me and this young man (I will refer to him as "L.Q.") escalated, I started to show my own teeth and stand up to them. At one point, I was so upset with the manipulation of him by his family that I aggressively proceeded psychically to shut them down and take back what was lost and stolen. I also attempted to get into his mother's head and make her go to her bank, draw out the amount of money she had stolen from L.Q., and send it to him. (She was using financial tyranny to make him come back home to the family.) This was "the right thing to do" as far as I was concerned.

Well, as I tell my clients "the strongest force wins," and I obviously was not the strongest force at that point in time because I had just activated what I call a personal "class action energy assault" that darned near killed me.

The next morning, I felt some stinging on the right side of my chest. This persisted, and after a few days, I could feel distinct pains of what I can only describe as stab wounds in five different places on my chest. (I later realized that it was in the shape of an upside down pentagram!)

The pain never let up and continued to get worse. Every movement in my upper torso caused pain. It stung just like a cut, and my ribs felt bruised. Sleeping was difficult, because it felt like I was getting constant fresh wounds. I could not even drive alone and had to have my daughter, Ma'Lady, accompany me in my car to help me turn the steering wheel!

I would periodically check the skin on my chest, fully expecting to see cuts or bruises, but there was *nothing* visible. As the days went on it started to get hard to breathe, and I knew that I was in deep trouble.

I tried everything physically and metaphysically that I could think of to heal this pain. I tried herbs, vitamins, minerals, homeopathy, reflexology, acupressure, energy-work, positive thinking, and even doing the New Age thing of sending love and forgiveness to the perpetrators. This only seemed to make it worse!

I was at a loss, and I could feel my life force depleting. I knew I was in deep trouble but tried to keep my courage up so depression couldn't take over.

At this time I was staying in my girlfriend Ronnie Foster's basement because I had also become "homeless." Ronnie and I had been partners in our new venture as professional ghostbusters for about a year.

One evening we were in her basement chatting about some of the bizarre things we had experienced and she said something really funny that made me laugh hard. I said, "Ouch, stop it … don't make me laugh … it hurts to laugh … (which only made both of us laugh even more!) I tried to contain myself, but it was difficult to maintain my composure. All of a sudden the light went on inside my head and I thought … wow … maybe this is it … maybe this is the hidden answer I have been searching for!

To fully understand what I just said, you need to be introduced to one of my spirit guides named "Hal" (how is that for exotic and spiritual sounding?) I call him "the cosmic jokester" because he is always telling me jokes and showing me the funny side of life. Hal has helped me out of a lot of pickles, so I have learned to trust him, even though his tactics are a little off the wall and nonsensical at times. He is constantly harping on me to maintain my "laughter quota," so that I won't get stuck in "energetic goo" and get trapped there.

After this laughter epiphany, I was hearing Hal in my head tell me funny things, and even though it hurt like the dickens, I let myself go and laugh. I repeated these jokes to Ronnie and she laughed, too. As we laughed, we started making fun of everything, including the "Voodoo-kaka" and all the other stuff that had been plaguing me. It all seemed so surreal, and I could really truly see the humor in it all.

As I did, I began to feel the pain, suffering, and death energy which had filled my body and magnetic fields start to rip, split, and crumble. The more we laughed, the more it fell away.

When we finally calmed down and Ronnie went to bed, I scanned myself and found that I was nearly 70% better! Each day my pains improved, and within a week I was completely healed! We had literally reversed the death grip of these curses/spells/hexes with intense, sustained laughter.

Remember when I said earlier that "the strongest force wins"? Well, during this "laugh fest" our energy infiltrated the dark Magick and became the dominant force. It literally neutralized the opposition as we fearlessly took over its turf and locked into the superior position. The high frequencies of our energy fields and the endorphins we created had overridden the darkness.

I would like to say that it all stopped there, but that is not how it happened. I had overcome this particular death assault, but many more were to follow. With the aid of numerous spirit/etheric supporters and also Aulmauracite, the Magickal Stone of Truth and Justice, I now have a grand education on how to address all sorts of dark forces.

I had four more years of hell before I developed "The Spiral Curse Reversal Ceremony" which brought it all to an end and removed L.Q. from my life. The Spiral Ceremony was revealed to me in one of my darkest hours of desperation and can be found on my website www.FirstWaveIndigos.com. This site was created to assist and support all the first wavers or real life "X-Men & Women" on this planet, many of whom are baby boomers.

It is my experience that when dealing with "mean Magick" that there is no "one size fits all cure." I learned that you have to do two things: You have to fearlessly face it and stand up to it, and then you have to be persistent in finding the right energetic recipes (some of which have to be done with exact precision) in order to overcome and be victorious.

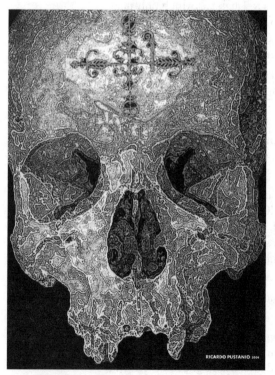

Voodoo death has been assessed by medical doctors as a real phenomenon set in motion by shocking emotional stress to obvious or repressed terror (*art by Ricardo Pustanio*).

I can attest that humor and laughter are key ingredients in managing these energies. Fear is the mind killer. When you are authentically and heartily laughing, fear cannot hold you, bind you, and possess you. You literally slip through its fingers and set yourself free!

## Voodoo Death and Fear

Anthropologist Walter Cannon spent several years collecting examples of "Voodoo death," instances in which men and women died as a result of being the recipient of a curse, an alleged supernatural visitation, or the breaking of some tribal or cultural taboo. The question that Cannon sought to answer was, "How can an ominous and persistent state of fear end the life of a human?"

Fear, one of the most powerful and deep-rooted of the emotions, has its effects mediated through the nervous system and the endocrine apparatus, the "sympathetic-adrenal system." Cannon has hypothesized that, "if these powerful emotions prevail and the bodily forces are fully mobilized for action, and if this state of extreme perturbation continues for an uncontrolled possession of the organism for a considerable period … dire results may ensue."

Cannon has suggested, then, that Voodoo death may result from a state of shock due to a persistent and continuous outpouring of adrenalin and a depletion of the adrenal corticosteroid hormones. Such a constant agitation caused by an abiding sense of fear could consequently induce a fatal reduction in blood pressure. Cannon assessed Voodoo death as a real phenomenon set in motion by "shocking emotional stress-to obvious or repressed terror."

Dr. J.C. Barker, in his collection of case histories of individuals who had willed others, or themselves, to death (*Scared to Death*, 1969), saw Voodoo like death as resulting, "purely from extreme fear and exhaustion … essentially a psychosomatic phenomenon."

## The Curse that Followed a Family for 100 Years

Curses, spells, and hexes are to be found among all cultures, and sometimes an entire family can suffer a malediction unto the second and third generations.

To the peaceful Navajo who made their home in the rugged mountain country of Arizona centuries ago, few things were to be feared more than the countless devils that might overtake a man were he not faithful to his friends and to the good life prescribed by his religion. Ruthless *chindis*, or devils, were known to bring down a man who profited by crafty dealings with simpler friends or who did injury to another when he might have done good.

Navajo legend tells of countless encounters between evil men and *chindis*, in which eye-for-an-eye justice was meted out to the malefactor—almost always a punishment the victim had brought upon himself by his erring ways.

But among the Navajo legends that deal with man and the devil, none is so bizarre as the strange fate that overtook an entire family and followed them down through the years until revenge was exacted upon the sole remaining member of the family the *chindi* had been called upon to punish more than 100 years earlier.

It is one of the few legends of the Navajo in which the demonic intelligence seemed intent not only upon punishing the original transgressor, but to ruthlessly snuff out even those members of the clan who were unborn when the offense was committed.

The curse of the *chindi* was believed to have fallen upon the peaceful and industrious Long Salt family sometime in the mid 1820s when a rascally tribe member, unknown to the others, decided to cheat a medicine man he had summoned to drive out evil spirits from his camp.

The shaman who came to exorcize the Long Salt hogan was blind, but known to have great powers in such undertakings. As part of his price, the medicine man asked for five butchered sheep.

But the crafty Long Salt cousin, reluctant to part with valuable herd stock, felt the blind shaman would not know the difference between the carcass of the slaughtered sheep and the dressed-out flesh of wild antelope, much easier to obtain, and much similar in taste to the rangy sheep who scrounged for forage in the harsh north central Arizona ranges where the Long Salts had settled many generations earlier.

The deceitful Long Salt member was vastly amused when the blind medicine man apparently fell for the slippery switch, but kept the secret of his swindle for fear of how other respectable members of the clan might react.

It was not long, however, before the Long Salt family knew that some terrible wrong was being revenged upon them. Once strong sheepherders, their family began falling strangely ill. Children became afflicted with illnesses that had never plagued the healthy Navajos before.

Frightened by what was taking place, the Long Salt family met in council and listened in wild fright as the offending tribesman confessed the deceit that he had played on the blind medicine man.

At once the Long Salts knew the cause of the wrath that was being visiting them: The old man had discovered the swindle and had set a terrible *chindi* upon the family to exact revenge for the shabby ruse that had been attempted.

After much worried consultation, a delegation of Long Salts was given the frightening commission of visiting the aged priest to make certain that what they feared had really happened and to determine if there might be a way to appease the old one's anger.

It was in fear that the Long Salts made the journey, but they had been honest men, and known for it, and hoped the shaman would take into account the sad fact that any family might find in its number one who was stupidly negligent. But certainly, they hoped, the medicine man would not call the whole family to suffer for the misdeeds of one misguided member.

His face a wrinkled mask, the old medicine man listened to the entreaty of the Long Salts. Yes, a terrible wrong had been done, he said in tight-lipped anger, but perhaps there was some way the wrong could be righted.

It would be, however, a matter for great study, for the *chindi* that had been released was the grandfather of all *chindis*, known only to the blind medicine man; and when that particular devil had been given a task to perform, one could rest assured that it would be done with unmatched ferocity.

"Return to me in ten days and I will tell you what must be done," the old one told the worried Long Salt delegation, who left then to spend a very uncomfortable ten days before daring to return to the shaman's presence.

When the days had passed and the Long Salts returned to the medicine man's village, horror of a new kind awaited them: the old man had died while they were gone!

No, he had not left any final message for the Long Salts. His death had been as sudden as the rain. No, they were sorry, no one else knew the old one's secrets or knew the sacred name of the *chindi* that he had unleashed for vengeance.

Numbed, the Long Salts made their way in sorrow back to their home. New illnesses had raged while they were gone. There had been more untimely deaths for which one could fathom no reason, save the anger of the *chindi* now among them.

In desperation, the Long Salts summoned great medicine men from all corners of the Navajo world to release their land from the old man's curse.

The medicine men came and heard the story, and exacted large fees for their services, making certain to watch as the sheep were butchered, but most of them confessed they had no power to expunge the powerful spell the wronged medicine man had lain upon the Long Salts.

The once-proud family became a weakened band of near-ghosts, who jumped at sudden noises and watched over their shoulders in constant terror for the *chindi*'s next attack.

In the early 1920s only one member of that original family still remained, and she, too, seemed to have been marked for untimely death by the *chindi*.

With the early passing of her own parents, young Alice Long Salt was taken in by relatives through marriage of the family, who were considered immune to the ancient curse.

Among them, an uncle vowed that the *chindi* would never claim the girl as long as he had strength in his body. The curse could be broken, the uncle reasoned, and somehow, he would break it.

The uncle became convinced that a friendly owl had taken Alice Long Salt under its wing and that its sudden hootings near the camp were a warning to the family that the *chindi* was approaching to claim the girl.

When the owl's lyrical hooting reached the campsite, Alice's adoptive family would bundle the girl into a wagon to which fresh horses were kept constantly hitched.

Then, as though the terrified horses could see the fire-breathing *chindi*, the uncle would set out across country at mad gallop, carrying Alice out of the demon's reach.

For a while it seemed as though the *chindi*'s curse had indeed been broken. Alice seemed to recover her vigor, and there was cause for celebration once more among the remnants of the Long Salts.

It was during a bitter winter in 1928 that the Long Salt family felt most secure in Alice's safety from the ancient devil. They had camped in an isolated place where they had never stayed before. The hoot of the owl had not been heard for several days. Then, even more comfortingly, a heavy snow fell, obliterating whatever tracks the cautious uncle might have left leading to the new camp.

Ricardo Pustanio 2009

In Navajo legend, the *chindis* are devils that in a way are actually good, because their victims are wicked men who take advantage of other people (*art by Ricardo Pustanio*).

It was Alice Long Salt's aunt who found her dead that night, cold and lifeless among the heavy robes in which the loving family had tucked her before retiring.

The *chindi* had taken his last victim when he claimed 13-year-old Alice Long Salt, the last of the family to suffer from a curse placed more than 100 years before.

The bitter winter did not permit the burial of the frail young Navajo girl, and it was much later before an Indian agent, at the behest of still-frightened tribal members, went to the site with a rude pine box in which to bury Alice Long Salt.

The white men found the Indian girl's body remarkably preserved in the heavy robes that had shielded her from the elements. Upon her small face they observed a peaceful smile.

Alice Long Salt had joined her family at last, in a place where the *chindi* curse could not touch them. The Navajo understood the smile.

## How the Kahunas of Hawaii
## Dealt with the Horrid Things of Darkness

In 1968, I was contacted by Max Freedom Long, a scholar who had spent over 30 years researching the philosophy and the secrets of the kahuna, the magician-priests of Hawaii. He believed that these traditional shamans had discovered the secret science behind all miracles in all religions—including those miraculous feats performed by Jesus. Max feared that his work was too scholarly for the masses, and he wished to see a popular synthesis of his work before he died. To help me make up my mind to undertake such a task for him, he sent me package after package of books, tapes, and notes. We entered into a heavy correspondence through letters and telephone calls, and in 1971, *Kahuna Magic* was published.

Max called me to tell me how pleased he was with my presentation and interpretation of his work. A few days later, Max Freedom Long was dead at the age of 81. It was as if his spiritual guides allowed him to stay around just long enough to see that his monumental research would be perpetuated.

In discussing such matters as curses, spells, and hexes, Max Freedom Long issued this warning:

> There are horrid things which belong in the realm of darkness, but which we are powerless to combat because we have become too civilized to realize that they are there. Doctors know nothing of them. Priests and ministers have such a garbled idea of devils that their advice is useless. Psychic sensitives and mediums know only enough to be afraid, to warn dabblers to be careful.

Modern occultists have guessed at a whole plethora of evil things and have written gravely about "black" Magick, spells, and enchantments. They draw their magic circles and retreat within them to escape the Dark Forces, not sure that such forces are present. They hark back to the Middle Ages and employ the talisman and the charm.

The practitioners of mental healing recognized these forces as "malicious animal magnetism," little understanding their nature, but waging frequent war on them when their activities were suspected.

All so-called primitive people know something of them, and among the priceless gifts which the kahunas have given to the world is a clear and comprehensive knowledge of the horrid things of darkness and an effective way of fighting them.

The kahunas believed that each person had three "selves:" 1) the Low Spirit (*unihipili*) or in more contemporary terms, the subconscious, the shadowy body; 2) the Middle Self (*uhane*), the conscious mind, a separate spirit from the Low Self; 3) the High Self or spirit (*Aumakua*), the superconscious mind, a kind of "overself," a parental guardian spirit.

When we die and cross into the afterlife in the shadowy bodies, the things we have believed here on the Earth-plane become almost fixations, and may haunt us there.

Long believed that when sentient beings die and take up life in the invisible world in the shadowy body, the beings make their own level or gravitate to it through their thinking. If the shadowy body thinks of familiar surroundings on earth, it makes such surroundings in the afterlife. The kahunas say that the spirit makes everything out of the shadowy stuff of dreams.

The afterlife, then, is made up of the manifestation (in image form) of the memories and desires of its inhabitants, including their repressed or unconscious memories and desires. It might be every bit as detailed, as vivid, and as complex as this present perceptible world which we experience now. We may note that it might well contain a vivid and persistent image of its previous Earth body. The surviving personality, according to this conception of survival, is in actual fact, an immaterial entity. But if one habitually *thinks* of oneself as embodied (as one well might, at least for a considerable time), an image of one's own body might be as it were the persistent center of one's image world, much as the perceived physical body is the persistent center of one's perceptible world in this present life.

"There is a definite going on for those who know the afterlife conditions for what they are and who are thus enabled to escape being caught there and held back," Long says. "The goal is not that of reincarnation. Only a few come back to inhabit other bodies. The low selves come back as the middle selves of individuals being born on this physical level, but the middle selves, at least those from fairly civilized people, eventually go on to the level next higher.

"The uninitiated," Long continued, "stay on for a very long time in the dream-surroundings, frequently coming back to contact the earth and loved ones here. Only now and then do they make trouble."

In the Huna view, the troublemakers are the low selves who get separated from their middle selves after death. They are the poltergeists that haunt houses and often molest the living. They are without the ability to reason, for they have lost contact with

Horrible curses can be set in motion by invoking demonic intelligence not only to punish the original transgressor, but to ruthlessly attack even members of the transgressor's family who were unborn when the offense was committed (*art by Ricardo Pustanio*).

their middle selves and have become the spirits that obsess the living and sometimes render them insane.

The kahunas also believe that there are other low-self spirits who stay near the living by choice and who learn to touch the shadowy bodies of the living and steal vital force (*mana*). If they can steal enough *mana* from the living, they can solidify their shadowy bodies sufficiently to enable them to move solid objects.

The kahunas hold that, for the most part, these low selves are fairly harmless, but they never lose sight of the fact that these low selves may become the horrid and darkly evil entities that stalk the living and prey upon them, stealing their vital force, often to the point of complete exhaustion and mysterious death, or of seizing their bodies and rendering them insane.

"Thousands of the living are silently and invisibly haunted in this way, by low selves which appear as secondary or multiple personalities," Long stated. "They are not 'split off' parts of the resident selves of a body, as is the popular belief today of our psychologists. They are individuals in their own right."

Not only do the low selves, separated from their middle selves, fasten themselves on the living as parasite personalities, but middle selves separated from their low selves do the same to a lesser degree, and now and again a normal ghostly spirit composed of both low and middle selves is guilty of taking up its abode in the shadowy body of a living victim.

"It is not for nothing that the living have an instinctive fear of ghosts," Max Long cautioned. "Dreadful things are done constantly to the living, with none to recognize the invisibles who are taking their life forces and, even worse, are implanting thought forms as suggestions into their low selves to cause endless erratic behavior, crimes, mischiefs, and sometimes utterly vile and evil acts."

The kahunas were also ever mindful of the danger of a purposeful attack by a spirit upon a living person in order to punish him for his acts against others in the flesh or to work revenge for acts perpetrated against the spirit when it was in flesh. The kahunas believed that the departed spirit could also use suggestion, especially if it could get a supply of *mana* from a living person and could acquire the thought form that had been used as the suggestion.

"A kahuna, in explaining this to me a long time ago in Hawaii, stressed the danger of thinking and voicing any thought which might be used as a suggestion by a normal ghost (a normal ghost is called *kinowailua*, or body of two waters, water being the kahuna symbol of vital force. If a ghost had two kinds of vital force, it was composed of a low and middle self living in their interblended shadowy bodies)," Max Freedom Long recalled. "I was warned never to say, even in jest, 'He ought to be shot,' or 'I hope he chokes,' lest this thought be taken and given as a potent suggestion by some spirit enemy."

In Honolulu, Max Freedom Long studied a case of spirit attack involving the brother of a Chinese-Hawaiian friend of his.

As Long told it:

The young man had a pretty Hawaiian sweetheart. While he had not proposed to her, it was taken for granted that he would do so as soon as his financial affairs were in such condition that he could marry.

When his new business of salt making was established, his father stepped into the situation and demanded the customary right of the Chinese father to select a bride for his son, The son loved and respected his father and, although much embarrassed by his predicament, agreed to stop courting the Hawaiian girl and give time for a parental choice to be made. He knew that the Hawaiian girl would be deeply hurt when he broke off seeing her, but he was so filled with a sense of guilt and shame that he did not try to go to her and explain what had happened. Undoubtedly he developed a guilt complex which lodged in his low self and which was shared by the middle self in its conviction that he had done the girl a wrong.

The girl was heartbroken for a time, then fiercely angry at the treatment accorded her without a word of explanation. Following the tradition of her people, she began "grumbling," calling on the spirit of a beloved grandmother to avenge the wrong.

Soon the young man was overtaken by a strange malady. He would faint at unexpected times and without warning. He fainted and fell into a fire, burning himself painfully. He fainted while driving to his salt works and wrecked his car, narrowly escaping severe injury. He fainted and fell on his bed while smoking, setting fire to the bed and again burning himself. Three doctors were consulted, but none of them could diagnose the cause of the trouble. Almost from the first his Hawaiian mother had urged him to go to a kahuna, but the son was very modern and had been taught at school that the kahunas were superstitious charlatans and nothing more.

When all treatment failed, however, he did as his mother suggested. The kahuna, then a man well advanced in years, listened to his story, sat for a time in silence with his eyes closed, then raised his head and announced that he had sensed the spirit of an old Hawaiian woman near him, and that from her he had learned that the young man had been guilty of one of the worst sins of all—that of hurting one who loved and trusted him. The spirit of the grandmother had been doing her best to avenge the injury.

The young man was amazed. He admitted his guilt and asked what he should do. The kahuna explained to him the ancient rule of the Hawaiians that no one should hurt another, bodily, or through theft of goods or injury to feelings. These were the only sins, and for them there was but one remedy. The guilty one had to make amends and get the forgiveness of the injured party.

Taking his leave, the young man went directly to the girl. He was met by anger and disdain, but he persisted doggedly in his effort to make her understand his position in the matter. Scornfully, she refused to be pacified.

The spirit of the young Hawaiian woman's grandmother cursed the suitor who had jilted her descendant by giving him a strange malady which could not be cured until he asked for forgiveness (*art by Ricardo Pustanio*).

The next day he returned with gifts and more apologies, and the next day and the next. At last his pleas broke down the girl's anger and aroused her sympathy. She forgave him and agreed to go with him to the old kahuna to acknowledge her forgiveness.

The kahuna seemed to be expecting them. He praised the girl for her kindness, called to the spirit of the grandmother to observe that the wrong had been righted and forgiveness obtained. He thanked the spirit for having done so well in forcing justice to be done, and asked her to cease her attack.

When she agreed to his request, he took a sprig of leaves and some sea water, sprinkled the girl and the air where the spirit stood, and spoke the words of the *kala*. Then dismissing the girl and the spirit, he turned to the young man, explaining that the *kala* (to bring back the "light") or cleansing for him was a more difficult matter.

Because he had been guilty and because his sense of guilt had made it possible for the spirit to place thoughts of fainting in his mind when she pleased, the punishment might even now be continued by his own low self (*unihipili*) unless it was well cleansed.

For the cleansing or forgiving ceremony he would have to use a very powerful and effective ritual—one which could not fail to cure the fainting forever. He brought an egg, holding it long in both hands and chanting a little as he commanded healing and forgiving power to enter the egg.

When the work of filling the egg with vital force was finished, he stood the young man before him and ordered him to hold his breath as long as he could. When he could hold it no longer, he was to put out his hand. In his hand would be placed a china cup into which the kahuna would have broken the raw egg while the breath was being held. Without drawing breath the young man was to gulp down the egg. At the same time the words of forgiveness would be spoken and, reinforced by the egg and the power in it, would affect the complete cleansing and cure.

The instructions were followed to the letter. The kahuna gave the suggestion of forgiving and of dispelling the guilt and fainting attacks. He continued the suggestions, rubbing the young man's stomach briskly after he had swallowed the egg and begun once more to breathe. The kahuna announced the complete success of the cure, warned the patient to forget the whole affair as soon as possible, and accepted graciously his fee for his work.

Max Freedom Long investigated this case and checked all the details of the healing treatment. He also kept in touch with his young friend for several years following. Never once did the fainting attacks return.

## *Objects to Ward Off Evil*

A black candle formed in the shape of a skull was often used in ceremonial magic to dispel curses. The skull-candle was to be burned at midnight, and a proclamation, which had been formally written on paper, was to be read above the flame, demanding the removal of any curse that had been set against the victim. The candle was to be anointed with oil and was to be burned precisely at midnight.

It was believed that power and success might be gained through the ritual burning of a candle formed to the shape of a mummy's sarcophagus. One first anointed the candle with oil and set before it an incense offering of sandalwood or myrrh. The candle was lighted, and the magician concentrated on a mental image of the goal that he or she most wished to attain.

The gris-gris of Voodoo is a small cloth bag filled with items from herbs to cloth to animal parts, created in a ritualistic practice and intended to bring money, love, or good health to the wearer.

According to some authorities, the widespread notion that the spilling of salt produces evil consequences is supposed to have originated in the tradition that Judas overturned a salt shaker at the Last Supper as portrayed in Leonardo da Vinci's painting. But it appears more probable that the belief is due to the sacred character of salt in early times.

*Bells have been associated with mystical occurrences and the spirit world since very ancient times. Goddess images were frequently cast in the shape of bells.*

At one time salt was regarded as being almost as valuable as gold, and soldiers, officials, and working people in Greece and Rome received all or part of their pay in salt. Money paid for labor or service was termed "salarium," the origin of our word "salary," meaning money paid for services rendered. From this custom of paying with salt also comes the popular phrase "to earn one's salt."

In many Asian countries salt was offered to guests as a token of hospitality, and if any particles fell to the ground while being presented it was accounted an omen of ill luck. The belief was that a quarrel or a dispute would follow.

Among the Germans there is the old saying, "Whoever spills salt arouses enmity." The ancient Romans believed that to spill salt was to cause quarrels or disputes, and when salt was spilled it was the custom to exclaim, "May the gods avert the omen!" Another old tradition says that if salt is thrown over the left shoulder, it will appease the devil, who will otherwise make enemies of friends whenever salt is spilled.

And then, of course, as we have stated previously in this book we have the tradition of using salt to ward off zombies.

Bells have been associated with mystical occurrences and the spirit world since very ancient times. Goddess images were frequently cast in the shape of bells. Ancient Jews wore bells tied to their clothing to ward off evil.

The ringing of bells or death knells for the deceased is a very old custom. Some authorities believe that the ringing of bells at times of death originated in the practice of seeking to frighten away the evil spirits that lurk beside a corpse, waiting the opportunity to seize the newly released soul. In ancient times bells were rung only when important people died, but with the advent of Christianity it became the custom to ring death bells "for all good Christians."

In medieval times, church bells were rung during epidemics with the hopes of clearing the air of disease. It was generally believed that church bells had special magical or spiritual powers, especially because of their position, suspended between heaven and earth, guarding the passageway between the material and nonmaterial worlds, frightening away demons.

The sacred bell of the Buddhists, the *ghanta*, serves that spiritual expression in a similar manner, driving away the negative entities and encouraging the positive spirits to manifest. The very sound of a bell is a symbol of creative power.

People along the west coast of Africa tie a bell to the foot of an ill child to ward off evil, and food was placed nearby to lure those spirits away.

In contemporary times, bells above the door of a shop alert the shopkeeper that customers have entered. That practical function is predated by the use of bells over doors to keep evil spirits from entering into a home or shop.

Prehistoric amulets representing fertility and animals have been found near some of the oldest known human remains. Archaeologists have also unearthed shells, claws, teeth, and crystalline solids dating to 25,000 B.C.E.; engraved with symbols and sporting small holes, the objects were probably worn as necklaces.

By the time the Roman Empire was established in the first centuries B.C.E., however, amulets had a long history of being worn for luck and protection. Egyptians considered amulets necessary for protection of the living and the dead. Likenesses of scarabs (a kind of beetle) were also prominent. A scarab encloses an egg in mud or dung and rolls it along to a spot where it can be warm and safe. That act was considered by Egyptians as a metaphor for the journey of the sun each day. The scarab amulet became a common emblem for regeneration and was placed with the dead.

Sumerians, who inhabited Mesopotamia (present-day Iraq) and were contemporaries of the Egyptians, had amulets inscribed with images of animals and gods. They also inscribed such images on seals for everything from pottery to vaults to doors; the emblem on the seal represented a guardian spirit that would bring bad luck to those who opened the sealed compartment without permission of the owner.

Ancient Jews wore amulets around their necks that contained slips of parchment on which the laws of God were written. The Torah, comprising five books of the Old Testament of the Bible, is among the copies of holy books including the Bible (Christians), Vedas (Hindu), the Qu'ran (Muslims), and the Avestar (Zoroastrians) believed by the faithful to bring good luck and to ward off evil.

Amulets are frequently mentioned in Talmudic literature where they are called *kemiya* and often consist of a written parchment or root of herbs worn on a small chain, a ring, or a tube. Many such amulets had healing purposes: they were considered legitimate only after having worked successfully in healing on three different occasions.

Another kind of parchment amulet was the *mezuzah*, a Hebrew word for door post. Moses commanded Israelites to inscribe the words, "Hear O Israel, the Lord Our God Is One God" on the doorposts of their homes to protect them from plague in Egypt. An amulet with those words continues to be attached to doors in many modern Jewish households, or worn as a gold chain around neck for good luck.

Early Christians inscribed the word *ichthys* (Greek for "fish") on their amulets because the word contained in Greek the initials for Jesus Christ, Son of God, Savior. The fish symbol has been important to Christians ever since.

# THE DEVIL BABY
# OF BOURBON STREET

The most popular version of the Bourbon Street Devil Baby legend began in the early 1800s, when a young Creole woman married a plantation owner, a very wealthy man who wanted a male heir to continue the Louisiana family name he had established. He already had three daughters from his first wife, so the new wife was kept continually pregnant. After bearing six healthy female children, she was dismayed to find herself pregnant with her seventh child. She knew this child had better be a boy, or she would be likely to find herself abandoned and a new wife would be selected to bear a male heir. The anxious mother-to-be is said to have gone to a Voodoo-Hoodoo Queen and asked her to use her powers to help her deliver a boy child.

Unbeknownst to the desperate mother-to-be, the Voodoo Queen hated the plantation owner because of his past actions against her, so under the guise of manifesting a healthy male heir for the woman to deliver to her husband, the Voodoo Queen cursed the unborn child, making certain that the woman would bear the Devil's son. The Voodoo Queen's magic was strong, for the boy child was delivered from the womb with horns, red eyes, cloven hooves, claws, and a tail. The Devil Baby's birthday was said to be on a Mardi Gras Day.

The horrific newborn proceeded to eat the neighbors' children, bear its teeth at its terrified siblings, and was locked away in the attic garret room. It was here that his parents held him captive before he escaped to begin his reign of terror on New Orleans citizens.

The legend of a Devil Baby invites a number of accounts of its origin. Rather than the desperate wife of a plantation owner insistent upon the birth of a male heir, certain versions of the lore have the monster born of a slave girl who was raped by a plantation owner. Still others state that the horrid abomination was born of a French aristocrat's daughter who was addicted to absinthe. As the lurid story goes she was drunk to the very hour that she gave birth, and she abandoned the grotesque infant in Pirates Alley. His demonic cries are said to have disturbed the Ash Wednesday Mass.

St. Anthony's Garden, sometimes called the Devil Baby's Playpen or simply the Devil's Garden, is said by some to be the place where the Devil Baby hides at night to attack unsuspecting passersby (*art by Ricardo Pustanio*).

St. Anthony's Garden, sometimes called the Devil Baby's Playpen or simply the Devil's Garden, is said by some to be the place where the Devil Baby hides at night to attack unsuspecting passersby. The garden is thought by some locals to be one of the very seven gates of Hell.

Another old New Orleans oral tradition tells that the Devil Baby was born in that very garden. According to this version of the creature's birth, its mother took refuge here in the late hours of her labor just before dawn on a Mardi Gras Day. As dawn approached and the long early morning hours turned to day, some churchgoers at early Mass later testified that they had seen a bloodied young woman, staggering from the garden, just as a scream from Hell could be heard coming from the low hedges. The woman managed to walk toward the church and leave the newborn devil infant on the back door steps before she died.

The large open garden behind the eighteenth century St. Louis Cathedral is said to be the best spot to sight the Devil Baby today. A history of duels fought and much bloodshed on the grounds is said to be the reason that he haunts the spot.

An often-told story has it that the Devil Baby was given to the priest of the Grand Cathedral to guard. Held captive by the parish priest, the Devil Baby would often escape and run wild in the streets, wreaking havoc and frightening those who crossed his path.

The Devil Baby is less than three feet high, about the size of a four-year-old child. He is bald-headed with pointed ears and has arms and hands like a raccoon. His face is somewhat like a goat's in appearance, but still recognizably human-like. The Devil Baby has split hooves for feet and a long ratlike hairy tail.

Others who fall under his spell say that he has the face of the most innocent child one would ever wish to see, and they stare at its beautiful countenance, falling into a trance or a spell. Many have reported seeing this innocent lost infant crawling through the streets as if abandoned by its mother. However, when they reach down to help the child, they find to their terror that the Devil's spawn is upon them, trying its best to kill them. Some say he has superhuman strength and is able to leap to the roof tops of the tallest building in New Orleans in one bound.

The Devil Baby is known to drink blood and to eat human organs from the living and the dead. Many old Voodoo-Hoodoo tales say his urine and feces is used to make zombie powder. On the other side of the supernatural coin, a lock of hair from him is said to cure blindness. If the Devil Baby attacks you and only kisses you, it means that you will become a ghost when you die and have to do his bidding.

The Devil Baby is said to be able to climb like a squirrel, swim like a fish, and run faster than a greyhound. He only attacks from dusk until dawn, because he cannot exist in daylight, much like a vampire. Many say holy water boils on its own when he is near. Crosses fall off the wall, and a blessed rosary will break in your hands if you should attempt to ward him off by holding it in front of you.

A few old legends insist that he also has the power to see the future. On Mardi Gras Day, he takes on the guise of a normal man. If you find him then and guess his true identity, you may ask him any question and he will answer it with the whole truth. At midnight he will return to his original form.

Many New Orleans women have claimed over the years that they were brutally raped by the Devil Baby. The unholy children grew up to be murderers, vampires, werewolves, or evil, mindless grunch. The grunch is the New Orleans version of the chupacabras. Many believe that the Devil Baby is the forefather to all the grunch and that he commands the hideous creatures to go out and steal babies and cats and dogs for him to eat.

To find urine, excrement or vomit from the Devil Baby on or near your front doorstep in the New Orleans French Quarter or any other area is not a good sign. How can you tell if the disgusting deposit is from him? Locals say that when you see it you will know!

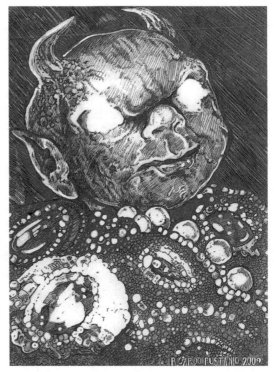

Some say that the Devil Baby of Bourbon Street is less then three feet high, about the size of a four-year-old child. He is bald-headed with pointed ears and has arms and hands like a raccoon. He has split hooves for feet and a long ratlike hairy tail (*art by Ricardo Pustanio*).

In New Orleans' Ninth Ward, old legends say that Baron Samedi, the loa of the dead and sexuality, the ultimate suave and sophisticated spirit of Death, is the father of the Devil Baby. He is also said to be the savior of the Devil Baby, and he will open the gates of Guinee for him to enter if he is ever on the brink of being captured. (Guinee is an astral paradise modeled after the lands in Africa from which so many slaves were taken.)

According to this Old New Orleans Devil Baby lore, Baron Samedi lusted for of a young Creole girl of exceptional beauty. On All Saint's day, as she visited the grave of her mother, the Baron seized her and made her pregnant as he savagely raped her in the shadows of the old tombs. Eventually, Maman Brigitte (a death loa) found out about the affair and turned the poor young Creole girl into a zombie before the child could be born. Her child was born not human, but as the Devil Baby.

Some Voodoo lore has named the infamous Madame Delphine LaLaurie as the Devil Baby's wet nurse or nanny. After a portion of the LaLaurie mansion burned, it is said Madame LaLaurie took refuge at the Pilot House located on the shores of Bayou

St. John. Some say she left the Devil Baby there, and that later she boarded a merchant schooner and escaped under cover of darkness. Though many hold that she escaped to France, others insist that she took refuge with the Devil Baby on the North shore of Lake Pontchartrain and lived in secret for a time at Claiborne Cottage in what is now Old Covington. Still other accounts have her escaping to Lacombe, Louisiana, also on the North shore, where she is said to have reclaimed some of her wealth and station—and more than a little of her old habits of serial murder and terrible experiments on unfortunate captives. The Devil Baby was said to roam the city at night looking for unfortunate homeless people to bring to Madame LaLaurie to satisfy her bloodlust.

After she had lived deep in the verdant darkness of the piney North shore woods, it is said Madame's anger at those who had stripped her of her previous grand life in the Mansion (now said to be among the most haunted in the United States) grew stronger and she pursued her interest in the Dark Arts that she had learned under Marie Laveau's tutelage. Soon tales began to spread through the rural community of the "witch woman," the "devil's wife," living among them, whose strange rituals filled the dark woods with fire and smoke and otherworldly chanting. An atmosphere of dread pervaded the little community, and there were whispered stories of animal sacrifices and torture, of curses falling upon land and livestock, of children falling sick and wasting away. Soon the name of Madame Delphine LaLaurie began to be uttered once again with fear and loathing—yet none moved against her, fearing that the Devil Child would kill them in their sleep.

There are those who tell that the Devil Baby of New Orleans was captured one night in 1881 and poisoned with laudanum, an opium-based painkiller. In his stupor, he was taken to St. Louis Cathedral where long nails were driven through his eyes, hands, and his black heart. After these nails or spikes had been pounded into him, the Devil Baby was impaled on the altar before God.

Those citizens and clergy who were involved in this assassination of the demonic creature were certain that he was dead. Seven days later, after the first morning Mass of Easter Sunday, the Devil Baby's body was taken to Slidell, Louisiana, where it was buried in a deep pit. Local folklore states that purple blood stained the beautiful marble floor of St. Louis Cathedral and that spots can still be seen to this day as one approaches the altar.

But it is no simple matter to kill a Devil Baby. Many old stories say that he feigned his death and crawled out from the foot of Marie Laveau's tomb where they had buried him. After the Devil Baby's resurrection, he wreaked havoc on those individuals who had tried to dispose of him and managed to kill a number of them.

Another account tells that the Devil Baby was struck by lightning one stormy night after he had been cornered by an angry mob outside of the St. Louis Cathedral. He had scaled the spire of the cathedral, seeking to escape the wrath of the citizenry, and God struck him dead with a thunderbolt.

There seems to be a great variety of accounts of the Devil Baby's birth and his death. One tale tells that a old Catholic nun who was walking on Bayou St. John in the 1860s beat the Devil Baby to death with a umbrella. He then sank into the waters of the bayou near where Holy Rosary Church stands today. Many say that no one swims in the bayou to this day, because at one time the bayou was crystal clear, but when the Devil Baby died in it, the clear water turned black and murky.

A favorite story of the Devil Baby's demise among Voodoo practitioners is that Voodoo Queen Marie Laveau herself strangled him with her bare hands one night when he was teething. According to the legend, the little monster drove her crazy, biting her and her many children.

The Devil Baby will stay a child for the rest of his life, because the first time he was destroyed was on holy ground and on holy ground he was born. It is also believed that because of this the Devil Baby has a chance at redemption and some day might actually go to heaven.

A very stern caution is always issued to those who seek the Devil Baby of Bourbon Street: never hunt for the Devil Baby unless you want him to hunt for you!

# VOODOO CHILDREN

*Angela Thomas, also known as Oct13baby, is known world-wide for her accurate psychic readings, and her advice is widely sought by those who need honest and ethical insight into their physical, emotional, and spiritual problems. In addition to being a world renowned psychic reader, Angela Thomas is also co-host of "P.O.R.T.A.L. Paranormal Talk Radio," a weekly paranormal radio show devoted to bringing its audience the most fascinating information in the paranormal world.*

*Especially for this book, Angela Thomas has shared an account from her own experience with Voodoo and real zombies:*

### Mama Cee and the Swamp Child, Richard

I do not recall the last time I saw Mama Cee alive, but I do remember the last time I heard her voice calling for me.

"It's Richard. Come right away," her voice sounded desperate on the telephone. Cee's tone was serious and laced with fear.

"What's wrong, Mama?"

No answer. A hard click followed the last words I would ever hear from her.

A gripping feeling came over me as I made my way across Jackson Square and to the Pontalba where Mama Cee lived. Something was terribly wrong. Mama Cee was not the type of person who would reach out to others, but rather one that many

**Well known for her accurate psychic readings, Angela Thomas has had some personal encounters with Voodoo and zombies.**

people went to for help. She was a known root woman who practiced the old ways of folk magic, a healer to many who lived along the rivers and swamps of Louisiana and Mississippi. Some claimed she was a High Priestess, whose rituals encompassed both the good and evil sides of Voodoo, the Rada and the Petro, who wanted nothing more than to cater to the tourists and the locals looking for spells, but I never witnessed it. Mama Cee had left her life on the river and opted to live in the heart of the French Quarter. She never discussed why the sudden move other than to say that the river had become "too dark." I never pressed for any other answer. I knew better.

As I made my way to the Pontalba, I could see people milling outside her apartment. The door was wide open. The apartment was filled with Louis XIV antiques, a collection she had inherited from the old Frenchman, Antoine, whose latter years were spent with Mama Cee. At first glance, the place appeared pristine, but then I noticed droplets of blood and broken glass on the wooden floor. A New Orleans policeman was questioning a woman who sat crying on the sofa.

"Ma'am," the policeman said. "I'm going to ask you one more time. What happened here tonight?"

The woman became hysterical and answered, "I could hear Mama Cee yelling at someone. Then I heard a loud crash and the sound of something breaking. Maybe it was that boy of hers."

The policeman shook his head and asked, "What boy of hers?"

"Sir, a boy Mama raised from the swamp," she continued. "Richard, the crazy one. I think he was here tonight."

From the corner of my eye, I could see a tall, slender woman coming toward me. She was wearing a long white dress covered with beads and scarves. She was a Creole woman whose beauty was hard to deny. Her skin was the color of mocha. She motioned for me to come toward her.

"Aren't you Mama's friend?" she asked. "That boy child of hers took her away. He was dragging her kicking and screaming. I tried to help her, but she said to stay away from him. He was wild-eyed and scary-looking. Something isn't right with him. He looked like the devil himself."

Relieved that she was still alive, I asked, "Did you tell this to the police? Do you know where he might have taken her?"

"I'm not telling a thing to NOPD", she said with suspicion. "You know how they are. I don't know where he was going, but I know that he lives on Bayou LaCroix. No one is going to go in there looking for him or Mama on this kind of night. Don't go getting any ideas about going there yourself. It's All Soul's Night and things have a way of disappearing there this time of year."

*Jesus!* I thought to myself. *Bayou LaCroix. Of all places to be.*

I shivered with the thought of Mama Cee being there. It would be just the kind of place a person like Richard would live. Bayou LaCroix is wrapped beside a dark pine forest along the Gulf Coast of Mississippi some 30 miles away. I had to help Mama.

I slipped away before I was noticed by the police. Now was not the time to answer questions. It was a time to search for Mama Cee. I kept hearing her voice over and over in my head.

Driving on the back roads along the Mississippi bayou looked no different than the swamp of St. Tammy Parish where I first met Mama. She was summoned to comfort the young widow Mary whose son had been missing for hours. As a search party was formed to scour the veins of the swamp, loud screams of the young child could be heard echoing in the distance.

By the time they had found the boy, he was nearly dead. He had been tied to a cypress stump and left in the elements to die. His body was covered by flies and mosquitoes and two large gashes formed an X on his forehead. No one knew for sure who would do such a thing. Rumor had it that the child's birth brought bad luck and certain evil to the swamp.

Mama Cee took pity on the boy, and after his mother died, she raised him. That child was Richard.

It would be my love for Mama that would take me into parts unknown on Bayou LaCroix—and on All Soul's night, the bayou became a different world.

I drove on the narrow road which wound and curved around tall grasses. I had a feeling that the grasses harbored another life on the other side of it. The sounds of alligators chirping and bellowing let me know I was deep into the bayou. Paths that were paved with old oyster shells splintered off into parts unknown and could be seen from my headlights.

To break the sounds of the bayou, I turned on the radio only to hear some report of a missing child. I turned it to music, not wanting to hear anymore than I could deal with.

In the distance, a glimpse of a lighted grave yard caught my eye. As I neared it, I could see candles lining the graves and some people dancing around them. It was a typical ritual to dance around the graves while chanting prayers for the lost souls of the dead.

Mama Cee was known in these parts. She had led many prayers on All Soul's night—prayers for the dead. I once watched her sprinkle milk and holy water on the graves speaking in a language that was foreign to me.

I decided to approach the people in the graveyard. Perhaps they had seen Mama or Richard. I spotted an elder among the group and approached her, hoping my appeal for information would lead me to Mama.

Slowly I approached the elder and asked, "Do you know Mama Cee? I'm a friend of hers from New Orleans. I believe she's in trouble. Have you seen her tonight? She's with Richard."

"I've been looking for Mama myself," replied the elder. "She was supposed to be here earlier tonight to lead the prayers with me. I haven't seen hide nor hair of her. You say she may be in some kind of trouble? What kind of trouble?"

"Richard LeBlanc was seen taking Mama by force out of the Pontalba tonight," I explained. "A neighbor says he lives on the bayou and he may have brought her back here somewhere."

"Richard LeBlanc! I saw him earlier," she exclaimed. "He was acting strange, but I didn't see Mama with him. He was headed for the old Cassabon fishing camp. That's where he's been staying."

She gestured to a younger man who looked to be in his twenties and said to him, "Anthony, show her where the Cassabon camp is. Don't come back until you know something about Mama Cee."

*Anthony lifted up a candle and held it high toward the ceiling. Hanging from an old clothes line that stretched across the room were dead birds.*

As I followed Anthony to the camp, I said prayers for Mama Cee. I petitioned all the saints in my own prayers for protection. I had a feeling I was going to need it.

Tagging behind rear lights into the unknown was daunting, and as Anthony turned off onto a long, gravel drive lined with oak trees, I grew more fearful. I could see a house in the distance. It sat on pilings, characteristic of houses along a body of water. Lights shining from the house illuminated the drive as we got closer to it. A string of lights tacked along the length of a pier could be seen at the edge of the camp. I knew Richard was there. I could feel his presence.

Anthony jumped out of his truck with a gun in hand and quickly started up the stairs of the house.

"Wait," I said in a harsh whisper. "Let's stay together."

I grabbed a flashlight from the car and tucked it into my pocket. Anthony nodded, and we slowly crept up the steps and found an open door. As we walked inside, we could see several candles burning on the far side of the room, giving off just enough light to see the room in full disarray. A peculiar odor hung in the air despite the breezes blowing through the screened windows.

Something dark above me moved, and I jumped back quickly and screamed.

Anthony lifted up a candle and held it high toward the ceiling. Hanging from an old clothes line that stretched across the room were dead birds—all black birds dangling upside down with one leg tied to the line by string and swaying from the wind in the house.

"Something evil lives here," I said. I fought back the nausea that came without warning.

"Let's find Mama and leave. I don't want to stay here longer than I have to," Anthony responded.

"Richard," Anthony shouted. "You answer me! Richard, where are you?"

No response. Like a madman, Anthony stormed through the house, but he did not find Richard. "He's not here. Let's go," he urged.

"He's somewhere around here. I can feel him," I whispered. "He's hiding."

Anthony cocked the hammer of the gun back. "If he's here, I'll find him," he said.

I do not know if I was more afraid of Anthony's gun and what he would do with it if he found Richard, or what had happened to Mama Cee. My anxiety grew with each passing second. Suddenly, I spotted something moving near the door.

It was Richard! He froze at the sight of us. There was something that looked different about him. His eyes were strangely fixed, and his face seemed distorted. With his back against the wall, he began to slowly slither his way to the door. Water dripped from his clothes, and I could see blood trickling down his arms.

"What have you done with Mama?" I asked.

Richard kept moving.

"Richard, tell me," I pleaded, but there was no reaction.

"Hold it right there," Anthony demanded as he pointed the gun at Richard. Richard began twisting and jerking as he made his way through the door.

Anthony raced outside and fired a shot over Richard's head, but that did not stop him. He ran into a nearby tree grove.

As I caught up to Anthony, I could hear the faint sounds of crying. It was coming from the pier.

Mama Cee! I thought as I rushed in the direction of the pier. The cries became louder as I got close to the end of the planks. I shuddered at the sight before me. A small boy was tied to the far post of the pier with his body almost entirely covered by water. The boy's cries escalated as I tried to release the ropes from his body.

"Anthony!" I yelled as loud as I could.

Silence.

"Anthony! Help me!"

I struggled to pull the boy from the water and onto the pier. The child was bleeding and covered by mosquito bites. As I turned his face toward mine, I could not believe my eyes. There on his forehead was a large X slashed into his skin. It was the same thing that had happened to Richard in the swamp.

Scooping the boy in my arms, I hurried to the car.

"Anthony! Where are you?" I screamed.

The sound of gun shots could be heard in the distance. I lay the boy down in the back seat of the car and ran into the grove. Something was thrashing in the moonlight against a large tree in front of me.

Grabbing the flashlight from my pocket, I turned the light to the base of the tree only to find Richard convulsing on the ground. His body contorted and moved strangely in front of my eyes. All of a sudden his body stopped moving.

I thought he was dead, but to my surprise he stood up. I could not move. I was paralyzed with fear. Richard lunged at me and then I heard a gunshot. Richard fell at the base of my feet.

Realizing how close I had come to harm, my body began violently shaking. Anthony held onto me as we walked through the tree grove, reassuring me that everything was going to be all right.

The sounds of police sirens could be heard coming up the drive, and by the time we reached the house, several police cars had arrived, along with an ambulance. Apparently, someone had heard the gunshots and called the police to the Cassabon camp.

I led a medic to the young boy in the car while Anthony talked to the police. He guided them back into the tree grove to retrieve Richard.

All at once a policeman came running to his car and got on the radio. He looked pale. Anthony soon followed.

"They found Mama Cee," Anthony said, barely able to speak.

I ran into the tree grove, not knowing whether she was dead or alive. All I knew was that I had to see her. A police officer stood beside a large oak tree with a flashlight in his hand.

"Where is she?" I asked.

The officer held his hands up to discourage me from coming closer and said, "Ma'am, stay there. You don't want to see this. We'll take care of her. Go on back to the house."

I did not listen. As I rounded the tree what I saw I will never forget. Mama Cee was standing dead inside the hollow of the tree with Spanish moss wrapped around her body. I do not remember much after that.

It would be later on that I would hear that Richard's body was not recovered. When the police went into the tree grove to retrieve him, he was nowhere to be found.

Some say he is still living somewhere on the bayou, while others claim that he has returned to the swamp. Legend has it that an evil spirit or loa had possessed Richard and he is now part of the unseen—the undead—a zombie, who lurks in the dark waters waiting to find another victim.

### The Darklings

Since the late 1800s they have been aptly called "The Darklings." In New Orleans Voodoo, darklings are creatures that prowl the city looking for innocents to possess. They will take possession of people and make them act like someone they are not. In extreme cases, those who are possessed by a darkling have been known to kill or to hurt their family members.

The great Voodoo Queen Marie Laveau described them as the evil thoughts come to life that good church people have that they do not act upon.

Some believe that a darkling enters an individual through his or her mouth. The victim is like a zombified demon. Marie Laveau is said to have used ground up monkey and cock statue powder, red brick, and a secret ingredient to chase them off.

Small children between the ages of three to nine are more apt to encounter these beings and see them clearly. Darklings have been known to hide at the sign of any type of light. Their favorite spots to hide are in dark cracks or inside a child's toys, such as dolls and stuffed animals or in closets.

Those who have psychic powers have been known to see them as sparkling dark shapes in the blackness.

### Their Son Became Possessed by the Darklings

*Claire Lee's eight-year-old son was possessed by the darklings while the family was on a vacation trip in New Orleans in the late summer of 1998. Mrs. Lee kept a journal of their six-month ordeal, which I have rewritten for inclusion in this book.*

The nightmare began for the Lee family from the Chicago area when they went to New Orleans on their annual vacation. Ethan Lee had always declared that he was descended from the great General Robert E. Lee and that he had always wanted to visit New Orleans and other great cities in the South. His wife, Claire, would laugh at his claim and remind him that his great-grandfather had come from Sweden long after the Civil War had ended and he could not possibly be related to the hero of the Confederacy. She had always wanted to see the grand old southern city and had expressed her wish that their eight-year-old son, Timothy, be exposed to as many historical sites as possible. "Travel is one of the greatest educations," her father had always said, and Claire agreed.

Earlier that afternoon the Lee family had visited the tomb of the legendary Voodoo Queen Marie Laveau. They were walking down Bourbon Street, with Timothy between them holding on to their hands. They had been talking about how great it would be to visit during Mardi Gras when Claire caught a glimpse out of the corner of her eye of two young boys who seemed to appear out of nowhere, knock Timothy out of their hands and send him sprawling to the street.

Ethan snatched his son from the street and into his arms. Timothy began to cough violently, as if he had swallowed something and had the wind knocked out of him when the two boys struck him.

Claire turned to shout her anger at the two little hoodlums, but they were nowhere to be seen.

Ethan wondered who she was shouting at. "What boys?" he asked, seeing only two elderly couples, obvious tourists who had turned to watch them with concern.

Each year—sometimes twice a year—Queen Bianca hosts a ritual in which the monkey and cock statues, created in honor of Marie Laveau, are blessed and charged. In this ritual Queen Bianca invokes the spirit of Marie Laveau, who used ground up monkey and cock statue powder, red brick, and a secret ingredient to chase off Darklings (*art by Ricardo Pustanio*).

"Did your son trip on something?" one of the women, an obvious motherly type asked. "Oh, dear," she exclaimed. "He's bleeding."

Choking back a cry of fear, Claire examined her son cradled in Ethan's arms. Timothy seemed barely conscious. He had evidently brought his head down hard on the sidewalk. A thin trickle of blood oozed from his forehead.

Later, at the emergency room of the nearest hospital, the doctor assured Claire and Ethan that Timothy was fine, just a little shaken. One of the nurses in the ER who had also examined Timothy chuckled that he had kept complaining that he had swallowed something that tasted "awful."

"But there is no sign that his throat was injured in anyway," she said in a comforting tone. "He might have swallowed a little of that ol' Bourbon Street dust when he fell."

Two days later, after they had returned to their home in a suburb of Chicago, Claire and Ethan agreed to keep Timothy as quiet as they could, just in case he should show signs of more serious injury. The ER doctor had promised them that Tim had not suffered a concussion, but he seemed to be not quite himself. He seemed to be afraid to sleep in his own room, and he insisted upon sleeping between the two of them at night.

After they had been home for less than a week, Ethan received word that his aunt in Springfield had passed away. Although Ethan had been very close to his aunt when he was growing up, both he and Claire were concerned about taking Timothy on an overnight trip so soon after his accident in New Orleans. At the same time, they were reluctant to leave him with friends when he was behaving so strangely. Timothy would cling to them as if he were an infant, whimpering and sometimes crying if they left him alone. With school starting in just a few weeks, they were becoming increasingly concerned about his behavior.

Nicole Miller, Claire's best friend, who lived next door to them in the apartment complex with her husband Mark and their two kids, Brady and Autumn, urged them to leave Timmy with her and her family.

"Ethan, will never forgive himself if he isn't there for his aunt's funeral," Nicole advised them. "I will take care of Tim. You know he loves it here with Brady and Autumn. We'll promise to keep an extra close eye on him because of his head."

Reluctantly, albeit gratefully, the Lees agreed to leave to attend Ethan's aunt's funeral.

When the Lees returned to Chicago on a Sunday night, Nicole gave her husband Mark a "let me handle this" look when the Lees arrived at their front door.

Claire immediately detected the discomfort in her friend's manner. "Is … is it Timmy?"

Nicole nodded. "It's Tim. But it's not what you might be thinking. I mean, well, I think you'd better get him to a doctor as soon as possible."

Claire felt her knees tremble, and she chewed nervously on her lower lip. She leaned heavily against her husband.

Ethan could see that Claire was doing her best to fight back hysteria. "Good God, Nicole, Mark? What's going on here?"

Mark said that they should see for themselves. Nicole nodded her agreement. "Timothy, would you please come here?"

Although Timothy walked into the room as soon as Nicole called his name, Claire could see at a glance that something was terribly wrong with her son.

He stared disinterestedly at his parents, then directed his attention to Nicole. "Yes, Mrs. Miller? You called me?"

"Timothy," she smiled weakly. "Your parents are here."

Not a spark of recognition shone in his eyes as he glanced briefly at Claire and Ethan Lee.

"My parents, you say? These two? I am sorry, but I am quite certain that I don't know them."

The voice that came from their son was polite, a bit stuffy, more like a somewhat cultured man of 50 rather than a little boy of eight. To be more precise, he spoke with a soft Southern drawl, like a well-educated gentleman from New Orleans.

Ethan and Claire stared openmouthed at each other, completely at a loss for words.

Confused, not really knowing what else to do, Claire dropped to one knee and hugged her son.

Seeming to be shocked by such a display of affection, Timothy struggled out of his mother's arms and stared at her coldly.

"Maybe we had better go into the kitchen for a cup of coffee," Nicole quickly suggested.

"I'd rather have iced tea, if you don't mind," requested the voice issuing forth from the eight-year-old Timothy. "And perhaps with a few drops of good quality sippin' whiskey mixed in."

"I wonder if you would please look after Autumn," Nicole asked him. "Now that her brother has gone to bed, she needs someone with her."

"Be glad to, madam. I have always loved children."

The reply would have been ludicrous coming from an eight-year-old boy if all four adults in the room had not realized that something far from ludicrous and quite alien to their normal concept of reality was taking place in front of their astonished eyes and ears.

As they sat huddled around the kitchen table, talking in hushed tones, Nicole explained that Timothy had begun exhibiting the bizarre behavior almost as soon as the Lees had dropped him off at the Millers' apartment. At first both they and the children had thought that Timothy was playing some strange sort of game with them, perhaps imitating an accent that he might have heard during their trip to New Orleans, but it soon became obvious that something much more eerie and unusual was occurring.

"It's really weird," Mark commented, shaking his head in wonder. "You know, after the first few hours of his talking in that kind of Southern Colonel accent and acting so differently from the little eight-year-old kid I know, I found it difficult to treat him as a child. It's truly as though Timothy is a totally different person. Last night he discussed business with me! I never expected to find myself discussing mergers with an eight-year-old!"

Nicole hastened to interject that Timothy was not like that all the time. "There are times when he is just fine. I mean, he's the little Timothy that we all know and love so much."

The four continued their baffled table talk until Ethan turned to his wife and reminded her of the time. "Whatever is going on, we've prevailed on these kind folks and their patience long enough. We'll take Timothy to the doctor first thing tomorrow. Let's get him and take him home now, so Nicole and Mark can get some sleep. I have a feeling they didn't get too much shut-eye this weekend."

When the Lees stepped into Autumn's room to collect their son, he let out a small whoop of joy, and his wide smile beamed his happiness.

"Mommy, Daddy, when did you get here?"

He rushed over to them and gave each of them a big hug.

The next morning Timothy was scheduled for a complete physical examination with their regular family physician, Dr. Morgan. Although the Lees did not know their doctor well, they had always perceived that he was an extremely well-educated and very broad-minded individual. They would later be exceedingly grateful that Dr. Morgan was even more open-minded toward the endless wonder of the universe than they could even have guessed.

Although the examination began with Timothy, it was not long before Dr. Morgan found himself conversing with a very polite Southern gentleman.

"Extraordinary," the doctor exclaimed after he had chatted with the personality for a few minutes.

Claire nervously wrung her hands, and Ethan asked Dr. Morgan if their son could be suffering from some kind of split personality caused by the blow to the head.

Dr. Morgan carefully considered the question before he responded. "It seems likely that the blow to Timothy's head was the catalyst that set all this in motion, but this other personality speaks from a frame of reference that is far older and more knowledgeable than an eight-year-old boy's."

"But *who* or *what* is it that speaks through my son?" Claire wanted to know.

The Darklings favorite spots to hide are in dark cracks or inside children's toys, such as dolls and stuffed animals, or in closets. Small children between the ages of three to nine are more apt to encounter these beings (*art by Bill Oliver*).

Dr. Morgan, clearly understanding the mother's concern, said that he would try to ask the personality some pointed questions in an effort to determine more about the alleged Southern gentleman.

But when Dr. Morgan returned his attention to Timothy, he was dealt a shocking surprise. Timothy stiffened sharply and the voice and mannerisms changed remarkably. Now, instead of conversing with a small boy or a polite man, he was speaking with a woman who addressed him in a frightened manner—a woman who was terrified that she was being buried alive, that she would be a slave, that some evil sorcerer had her soul in a bottle.

Ethan Lee clasped the forearm of the ashen-faced doctor. "What is happening here? How can a woman's voice be coming from our little boy's mouth?"

Dr. Morgan shook his head and drew Ethan and Claire aside from Timothy and the newly arrived communicating entity.

Before the doctor could speak, another voice, that of a man with a deep Southern accent, cried out that he had been Hoodooed and taken away from his wife and children.

In less than 30 seconds, the accent changed to that of a pleasant-voiced woman.

Dr. Morgan was stunned: "It—the voice—claims to be Mrs. Loretta Sheldon, a patient of mine whom I recently treated," Dr. Morgan told them. "I don't know what to say. I mean, it sounds just like her. And she's referring to matters that only the real Mrs. Sheldon could possibly know."

Ethan crinkled his forehead in disbelief. "But this Mrs. Sheldon, where is she?"

Dr. Morgan lowered his eyes. "She died a few weeks ago. She died of burns that she suffered in a fire."

Overhearing the doctor's comments, the personality presently inhabiting Timothy began to speak of the pain that she had endured before she passed away.

Claire slumped into a chair, mumbling weakly that she felt faint.

Dr. Morgan had a nurse bring her a paper cup of cold water, then pulled a chair next to hers and indicated that Ethan join them for a conference.

"I cannot find anything wrong with Timothy physically," he told the Lees.

"But mentally?" Ethan asked, interrupting the doctor. "He must have multiple personalities or something. Can you recommend a good psychiatrist? We've got to help our son get his own self back."

Dr. Morgan shook his head. 'We're not talking about some bizarre kind of mental illness here. I cannot vouch for the unidentified Southern gentleman or the other two voices, but that was Mrs. Sheldon's voice and personality speaking through Timothy."

"Just what are you saying, Doctor?" Claire asked.

"If it didn't take so long to arrange, I would suggest an exorcism."

"Come on, Doctor!" Ethan scowled in disbelief. "For one thing, we're not Catholics. Besides, it's not the Middle Ages, and you're supposed to be a man of science, not some witch doctor who believes in evil spirits!"

"You believe Timothy is possessed by evil spirits?" Claire asked incredulously. "This is all getting too much for me to handle."

"I said nothing about *evil* spirits," Dr. Morgan clarified. "But I do believe that Timothy is being invaded by spirits of the deceased."

Ethan got to his feet. "Let's go, Claire. Get Timothy. This is the 1990s, not the 1690s. Next he'll be prescribing garlic and wolfbane to wear around Timothy's neck."

Dr. Morgan asked Ethan to please be seated. He admitted that much of what he had just said would be considered highly unorthodox by most medical professionals and the great majority of laypersons.

"Very quietly, over the past 20 years or so, I have developed a strong interest in psychical research, in parapsychology," he explained. "I have been working with a number of other scientists and doctors here in Chicago who believe that man and mind are something other than physical things."

Ethan admitted that he believed in the soul. And so did Claire. But exorcism? Possession? Those, he felt, were very much different matters.

Dr. Morgan continued. "We've been conducting rigorous experiments with matters that often appear to contradict known physical laws, and we have examined phenomena—such as that which now afflicts Timothy—that do not fit into recognized bodies of knowledge."

Claire stiffened. "Are you dealing with the supernatural?"

Dr. Morgan explained that both he and his colleagues firmly believed that these currently unexplainable events would someday be found to fit into the total scheme of nature.

"We recognize that there do exist phenomena that lie beyond the five senses and the reach of the physical sciences. We deal with phenomena in which effect often precedes cause, where mind often influences matter, where individuals communicate over great distances without physical aids and yes, where it sometimes seems as though the living can communicate with the dead."

> *We deal with phenomena in which effect often precedes cause, where mind often influences matter, where individuals communicate over great distances without physical aids....*

Claire and Ethan wanted to know exactly what course of action Dr. Morgan was suggesting that they follow in an attempt to solve their incredible dilemma.

"Chicago is blessed with many fine, responsible, ethical mediums and healers," Dr. Morgan told them. "I'm giving you the name and address of a spiritual healer named Xavier Foster, who is one of the best. Please make an appointment with him and ask him to examine Timothy. I don't really know what else to do."

Claire Lee managed a weak smile. "You are really quite serious about this, aren't you, Dr. Morgan? You really think that Timothy may be possessed by spirits of the dead."

The doctor shrugged his shoulders as though he were not completely comfortable in his role as spiritual diagnostician. "I believe that it is a possible answer that fits all of the symptoms."

That night Ethan and Claire sat around the kitchen table for a long time, discussing Dr. Morgan's unexpected advice.

"I never thought I would hear a doctor in the 1990s talking about possessing spirits," Ethan said, "but you know, if he's willing to stick his neck out like that, he must really believe that there is something to what he is saying. Hell, I've sat and talked with Timothy, and I know that I am not always talking to him. I mean, I know my own son."

"Then you're willing to give this Xavier Foster a try?" Claire asked, wanting to be certain of her husband's position on the bizarre matter.

"I guess so. What do we have to lose?"

The next day Claire called Xavier Foster's office and found that the spiritual healer was quite busy. It would be nearly two weeks before he could see Timothy.

In the meantime Timothy continued to behave erratically. The Southern gentleman eventually disappeared. The woman who had died from burns, who had manifested in Dr. Morgan's office, never communicated again.

But in place of those two entities, several others appeared. Some spoke only once through the channel of the eight-year-old Timothy and were gone for good. Others continued to manifest for quite some time. Nearly all of them appeared to be frightened souls who told of bizarre rites of Voodoo. Some spoke in what the Lees could only guess were African languages. Before the strange series of occurrences would be over, Timothy would manifest more than 40 personalities over a period of six months.

In the two weeks before their appointment with Xavier Foster, Claire and Ethan kept a careful record of the individual persons who spoke through their son. They also maintained an account of the happenings and events that the entitles claimed to have witnessed.

The Lees noticed that Timothy's "receiving set" seemed most often to attract those persons who had died in accidents, those who had committed suicide, or those who had been murdered in very mysterious ways.

Many of the spirits possessing the boy claimed to have been buried alive and, as a consequence, Timothy became terribly frightened of the dark or of small enclosed spaces.

On many occasions Claire would become quite chilled by harrowing accounts of fatal crashes that Timothy would describe as they would be driving over the actual scenes of the accidents.

Another consequence of the violent blow to Timothy's head was his sudden apparent acquisition of clairvoyant abilities.

One morning the boy ran down the halls of their apartment complex, shouting for help. "They're drowning!" he cried hysterically. "Somebody save them. Their boat is capsizing and they're drowning!"

Claire managed to quiet him and to ask for further details. Timothy described four people who had been fishing off the Gulf Coast of Florida in a small boat.

Out of curiosity, Claire checked the daily newspaper, but she could find no account of such a mishap.

Later that day, however, she searched the Internet and found a report of the boating accident.

At last the day of the Lees' first appointment with the spiritual healer, Xavier Foster, arrived. Later, Claire would tell Nicole Miller how impressed they were with the man's initial reading. He correctly described many of the various spirit entities that had been possessing Timothy, and he went on to make a number of interesting comments concerning the case.

Xavier, a tall African-American, seemed versed in everything from the passion of a Baptist revival to the ecstasy of a Voodoo ritual. After he had sat observing Timothy for a few moments, he spoke in what seemed to the Lees to be an African dialect.

At the sound of the words, which Xavier soon made a kind of chant, Timothy blinked his eyes and answered back in a strange jumble of words.

"This boy received more than a blow to his head that jarred some things out of place," Xavier Foster said. "He was touched by some rowdy kind of entities. If he were a different kind of boy, he might have become a vicious little monster. Because you've done a good job teaching him morals and the need to walk a pure path, he has become like an open door to the spirit world."

Ethan Lee wanted to be certain that he understood the man correctly. "Do you mean to say that our son has become some kind of receiving set for spirits of the dead?"

Xavier nodded in confirmation. "Especially for those who have only recently crossed over, those who are confused over their deaths. These troubled spirits see Timothy as a portal through which they can reenter the physical world. Most of these spirits died violently or in a great deal of pain, and they do not yet understand that they are dead."

Timothy walked over to Xavier and took one of his hands in his. "Those mean boys shoved something in my mouth," Timothy said. "Then they knocked me down and ran away."

Claire thought back to that day in Bourbon Street when she thought she saw two shadowy figures push her son to the ground.

Xavier nodded. "Yes, the darklings. They just love to pick on boys and girls about your age."

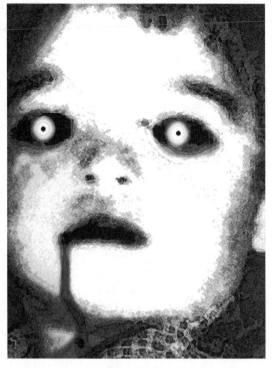

Timothy was knocked down by two Darklings and sent sprawling to the street after visiting the tomb of Marie Laveau in New Orleans. The Darklings entered his mouth and possessed him for weeks, until his family found a practitioner familiar with Voodoo (*art by Ricardo Pustanio*).

The healer's method for dealing with the confused spirits was to place himself in a light trance and urge the possessing entities to come forward. When he could perceive that they had heeded his entreaties, he would converse with them and attempt to help them understand that they had lost their own bodies through physical death and that it was wrong to use the small boy's body to maintain a hold on the Earth plane.

Claire and Ethan were astounded as they listened to the bizarre conversations. Often, after a spirit had been apprised of its condition and the wrong that it was doing to Timothy, it would express contrition, beg forgiveness, and promise to leave the child at once.

Xavier prayed earnestly for the souls of the entities, comforting them and bidding them to go in peace and into the Light.

At the conclusion of their first session, the healer spoke honestly with Claire and Ethan. "The doorway in Timothy's head is still open, and I do not know exactly what it will take to close it. The power of Voodoo in him is very strong. Many of the entities who cry out through him are men and women whom some dark Voodoo priest or priestess has made a zombie slave."

Claire could not suppress a small cry of distress.

"Do you mean that he will always be like this? He … We … we will all go crazy!"

Xavier shook his head reassuringly. "I have every confidence that it will close naturally in time."

Ethan wanted to know how long a time.

"I honestly do not know," Xavier repeated. "But until it does close, Timothy will continue to attract restless spirits. The evil darklings forced their energy down his throat. This is a strong energy to fight."

Claire reminded her that they had heard some of the spirits agreeing to leave the boy.

"Yes," Xavier agreed. "I feel confident that those with whom we spoke this evening will not return."

"Thank God," Claire said, closing her eyes as if in prayer.

"*But*," Xavier emphasized, "I cannot guarantee that other new spirits will not slip into Timothy in their places."

Ethan leaned down to place a supportive arm around Claire's trembling shoulders.

"Each time your son is near the scene of a fatal accident, his mind will act like a magnet, drawing toward him those poor unfortunate entities who hover around the scenes of their deaths, waiting for someone to tell them what to do, waiting for someone to help them toward the Light," Xavier explained. "These spirits are lost, lonely, and terribly confused. As I said before, they do not realize that they are dead, and they become very frustrated when they find that they cannot alert anyone to their presence. They seize desperately and thankfully upon the opportunity that Timothy offers them."

Ethan's own shoulders began to sag under the enormity of their dilemma. "What can we do to help our son?"

Xavier's eyes misted with tears in empathy. He could feel the anguish of the troubled parents as if it were his own. "You can continue to bring Timothy to me, and I will continue to assist the spirits on their way to a higher vibratory plane."

Ethan lowered his eyes, avoiding the direct gaze of the medium. 'We would like to be able to do that, but I'm afraid that we really can't afford to...."

Xavier held up his hand to stop him and to erase discomfort over discussing finances. "My dear people, do not concern yourselves over my fee. I charge people for readings, seances, and healings, as that is my profession and my only source of income. Timothy's case, though, is something different. How can one demand monetary payment for the privilege of setting souls back on the path of their spiritual odyssey to the Creator?"

Claire smiled warmly at the spiritual healer. "Thank you. Thank you so much."

Ethan protested that they did not wish to take unfair advantage of his generosity.

Xavier clarified his position. "I would be most happy if you continue to bring Timothy to me, as I would appreciate the opportunity of being able to help these unfortunate souls in whatever way I can. Look upon it as a facet of my ministry."

The Lees indicated that they thought they understood his spiritual motivation, and they were grateful for his high moral principles.

"Please understand further," Xavier told them, "that you can continue bringing your son to me and I will repeatedly assist the tormented spirits on their way, but at no time will I be able to return Timothy to you and say that I have cured him. Only time and the Great Spirit of the Light can do that."

The Lees continued to take Timothy to see Xavier Foster on a regular basis for the next six months. Each time the boy saw the healer, he had picked up another entourage of lost souls, which Xavier dispatched as best he could.

At last there came the evening when Xavier was able to announce to the happy parents that the "door" had closed and little Timothy would no longer be an unwilling host to possessing spirits.

"You might keep an eye on him, though," Xavier advised them. "He has all the makings of a great natural spirit medium."

Timothy made a grimace of distaste. "No way are those creepy boys going to make me swallow any more of their nasty tasting New Orleans soda pop. I'll be watching out for them if we ever go back to that city."

Xavier agreed. "The darklings won't bother you again. Once they have been defeated, they will never bother you again."

# LITTLE VIOLETTE, THE ZOMBIE CHILD

Folklorist and occultist Alyne Pustanio is a New Orleans native whose roots go deep into the local culture, and it is from that proverbial "gumbo" that she draws her inspiration for most of her tales of terror and fascination.

A descendant of Portuguese and Sicilian immigrant families who trace their ancestry to European gypsies, Alyne was exposed to the mysteries of the occult at an early age. Two great-grandmothers were gifted and sought-after mediums, and another relative is a verified psychic. However, Alyne credits her mother—an avid spiritualist—with inspiring her lifelong interest in the supernatural and unexplained.

These interests, combined with her avocations in folklore and history, result in a validity and passion that is immediately obvious in all her writings. Some of her most colorful pieces, "The Zombie Child of New Orleans" among them, owe much to the rich supernatural heritage that steeps New Orleans; others, such as her essay on "Psychic Vampires" published in Doorways Magazine, are the product of harrowing real-life experiences. Essays such as her "Defense of Demons" are breaking new ground in the realm of paranormal investigation, changing preset notions and concepts about the real dangers of the supernatural realm.

## The Zombie Child of New Orleans: A Frightening Tale of the Living Dead in Old New Orleans

There are hundreds of fascinating and frightening tales that come down to us from the days of Old New Orleans and though they all puzzle us, only a few of them

**Folklorist, occultist, and New Orleans native Alyne Pustanio is a descendant of other gifted mediums and psychics.**

actually reach out and touch our present-day lives in a real way. Among these tales one of the most tragically gruesome is that of Little Violette, whose name is forever associated with the epithet "The Zombie Child."

Here, then, is her story, as told in the legends, said to be set down by Madame Popleuse herself, a grand old dame of the secret Voodoo *sosyete* founded by the legendary Voodoo Queen Marie Laveau. Some say she heard it firsthand from her old aunt Josephine Mosebury, alleged to be one of the famous "Seven Sisters of New Orleans." According to other sources, Madame Popleuse claimed to have personally experienced the entire event while still a child immersed in the mysterious arts of her African and Creole ancestors in the old Quarter.

It is said that the "zombie child" was born into one of the wealthiest families in Old New Orleans; although the surname has been obscured by the passage of time (perhaps deliberately so), the given names of her parents never change in the telling. They were known as Laurent and Mathilde among both the Europeans and the Creoles whose society, before these tragic events, they often kept.

Most contend the couple once lived in a beautiful home on the edge of the Old Quarter on lands then owned by members of the great Marigny family. Their marriage, while both were still quite young, had been a joyous occasion and the source of celebration among all the extended members of their families. But though they were wealthy and rich in love, for several years the greatest blessing—that of a healthy child—seemed to elude them.

On the advice of an elderly aunt, Laurent sought the help of one of the most famous physicians then practicing in New Orleans, Dr. Joseph Victor Gottschalk, known to all as "Physician, Surgeon, Occultist and Accoucheur." In these last two capacities, particularly, Dr. Gottschalk was to serve his clients only too well, for when his advice as a physician helped produce the desired result—pregnancy in Mathilde—his services as an *accoucheur,* the French name for male midwife, were then also required. However, in a tragic twist of fate, his dabbling in the occult, and his association with others who practiced the forbidden arts, would secure a place in infamy for Mathilde's poor child.

The beautiful little child, it is said, came into the world in one of those vibrant New Orleans springs that make a person happy to simply be alive. In the courtyards and alcoves of the old Quarter the foliage was growing lush and every breeze smelled like mimosa and honeysuckle in the day while in the evenings the scent of jasmine hung heavy on the air. Across the Marigny estates the native azaleas were budding in splashes of pinks and purples and the dogwoods bursting into bloom. It seemed that the entire landscape had been painted by some unseen hand to be a gift in celebration of the arrival of little Violette.

Relieved of her nine-month burden, the young mother, Mathilde, held socials in her home where the landed and the wealthy came bearing tokens of welcome for the little girl whom the doting parents had named Violette because her eyes were the color of pure amethyst. The doctor himself presented little Violette with a pair of beautiful amethyst earrings—only a pale reflection of the color of her eyes—that had been sent as a gift from his sister Adelaide in Philadelphia. While the women cooed over the gorgeous child, the men heaped congratulations on the proud father, Laurent. Now at last, the couple felt their married life was complete.

For the first year of Violette's life this feeling of joy and contentment reigned over the little family. The child thrived under the care of Dr. Gottschalk, who had secured a mulatto woman to provide constant care for the beautiful little girl. Violette's life was one of pampered elegance because her parents had so longed for a child, the baby lacked for nothing.

Laurent's business often took him to more distant areas of the estates where he is supposed to have acted on behalf of Count Marigny in the capacity of manager of the estate overseers. Little Violette would watch wide-eyed when her father rode away to work and would wait patiently in her nursery, sometimes for several days, for his return. Eventually, as she grew, she made her discontent with Laurent's absence well known, throwing a tantrum every time he prepared to depart and insisting that he take her with him. Mathilde, however, always objected to the mere suggestion that Laurent might take Violette into the swampy lowlands and woods of the unoccupied estates where she might be exposed, so Mathilde assumed, to all sorts of dangers.

But even the most doting mother cannot be at hand all the time and one day Mathilde received a message that her mother was ill and had asked for her daughter to come and nurse her. Reportedly, Mathilde's mother lived a sizeable distance outside New Orleans, among the Acadiens of St. John Parish, and Mathilde was adamant that Violette should not make the rigorous trip, again because she feared to expose the child to the dangers of the road and to possible illness. On Mathilde's strict orders, Violette was to remain at home in the care of her mulatto nurse while her mother was away.

Now, it was said that the nurse always spoiled the now five-year-old Violette, giving in to her whims and letting her have almost anything she asked for, even, so they say, despite the disapproval of the child's mother. So it was that on a day when Laurent was departing and Violette was embroiled in another of her violent tantrums, the well-meaning nurse gave in to Violette's demands to accompany her father, and Laurent, seeing no harm in it, agreed to take the little girl along, just this once.

They were gone for almost five days when in the dusk of the fifth day the mulatto woman watched from the porch as Laurent's surrey heaved into view. It seemed that the little trap was hurrying more than usual and the nurse could hear the rapid beat of the horse's hooves as it drew nearer. A sudden fear fell over the nurse as she ran down the porch steps to meet her master's carriage and her heart nearly burst when she saw Laurent hunched over and carrying a small bundle. It was little Violette, lying limp and feverish in her father's arms.

"Send for Dr. Gottschalk!" Laurent barked as he ran upstairs to place his little burden in her nursery bed. "Take the trap!" came his order and at this two strong house servants jumped into the little surrey and disappeared in a cloud of dust, heading for the Old Quarter.

After what seemed like a lifetime, the surrey once again came into view, this time accompanied by a man on horseback. Laurent recognized the tall figure of Dr. Gottschalk. The two men met at the front door and as they ascended the stairs, two at a time, Laurent provided Dr. Gottschalk with all the information he could about little Violette's condition.

The physician came to Violette's bedside and examined her with an expression of grave fear on his face—the flaccidity of her little white arms and legs, the languid, almost lifeless expression except where the fever burned, like two clown spots, one on each little cheek. The child's breathing was shallow and every few minutes she shivered as if a chill wracked through her little body.

Dr. Gottschalk took Laurent aside. The news was grave. Violette had contracted a delirium, possibly scarlet fever or malaria, and it had so drained her tiny body that there was little hope of her survival. "We can make her comfortable, insofar as that is possible," he said as Laurent fell to his knees beside the little girl's bed. "But I do not expect that she will be with us tomorrow."

Nearby the mulatto nurse wept quietly, but Laurent, already wracked with guilt at having taken Violette against his wife's constant wishes, now cried out miserably, "My child! My little child!"

Though he could do nothing to stave off the illness, Dr. Gottschalk did not leave the child's side that night, ministering to her as best he could as the fever ran its course.

Just before dawn, with the birds beginning their morning song outside, the beautiful little angel with the haunting violet eyes passed from this life. The doctor, looking out into the morning, remembered a spring five years before, when the little innocent had come into the world. He sighed and was grieved that he should also be in attendance at her passing.

Indeed, it was Gottschalk who made the funeral arrangements for Violette as her father Laurent succumbed to his grief and could not be comforted. The next visitor to the elegant Marigny home was a New Orleans undertaker who came to prepare the little body for its last presentation.

Word was sent to St. John Parish to tell Mathilde that her dearest child was no more. Only gargantuan efforts on the part of the patient undertaker and Dr. Gottschalk convinced Laurent to allow Violette to be removed from the family home to the doctor's surgery, where all the mortuary arts available would be employed to preserve the precious little body until the arrival of Mathilde could allow the funeral and interment to proceed.

When the dark day came, the funeral procession to St. Louis Cathedral was a long river of black following the cortege and the little copper casket that held Violette. Afterwards, led by the priests, the river changed course and flowed to the Bayou Cemetery on the city's outskirts, where Laurent's family had donated a picturesque spot for the interment of their jewel. They laid Violette in one of the brick and mortar "oven" vaults that yawned like a black maw as it consumed the little casket into darkness. When the time came to leave and let the caretakers do their grim work, both Laurent and Mathilde were inconsolable, loath to leave their precious child so alone.

Laurent's guilt and grief were only exacerbated by the grief of his young wife and the blame she could not help but place on him; nor did the mulatto nurse escape her sharp rebuke. It soon became obvious that Mathilde's mourning had taken on tragic proportions and that her mind had suffered a blow from which it could not recover. Such was the lamentation and grief that accompanied the end of this child's life that many who saw it could hardly believe the reality of the situation. Indeed, some family friends and servants who had last seen the child vibrantly alive refused to believe that she could possibly have died. An almost surreal, non-reality seemed to prevail.

The once-beautiful and bright home on the Marigny estate was now encased in a strange, almost impenetrable darkness and no one—not the well-meaning visitors nor the prayerful religious, nor the caring Dr. Gottschalk—could stem the tide of mourning and bereavement. No prescription seemed to work and the mere suggestion that there might be other children yet to come produced angry outbursts from both parents.

**Marie Laveau refused to grant a mourning father's wish to bring his beautiful little daughter back from the grave, but enough money can buy anything, and the father found a darkside Voodoo priest to perform a ceremony to return lovely Violette to life as a zombie (*art by Ricardo Pustanio*).**

All business, all domestic obligations seemed to come to a complete halt and had it not been for the reliable servants, the home and lands might have gone derelict. There seemed to be nothing that could bring back the light that Death had snuffed out when He took Violette.

Thus it was a surprise to Dr. Gottschalk when one rainy day nearly four weeks after Violette's death, when he was locking up his surgery for the evening, none other than Laurent himself accosted him in the gloomy street. Gottschalk looked at him: the man seemed strangely animated, his movements furtive and nervous, as if he were wearing his tortured mind for all to see. It was with no small amount of shock and consternation then that Gottschalk recoiled from Laurent even more after he had taken him inside to hear out the madman's ravings.

"It is said that you know about these things," Laurent rambled wildly. "Then you must know something of what I am asking you."

"What you are asking is blasphemous in the eyes of God and man, Laurent!" Gottschalk is said to have responded. "I will not do it. Not for all the money in the world," he added quickly as Laurent produced a copious amount of gold and paper money.

"Then tell me who will!" Laurent demanded, but Gottschalk was adamant. "Very well," Laurent growled. "I will find someone who has the courage to do the deed!"

Gottschalk watched as Laurent rushed out into the rainy street. "The child has been dead a month, Laurent!" he called after him. "In the name of the saints, let her rest in peace!"

It is said that in the old New Orleans of those days money might buy anything, even the name of a person of power who could do extraordinary things. This is just the person Laurent now sought.

Whether in league with God or the Devil, he did not care: he would find the man or woman who would help him put an end to his pain and give him back the life he had known. Thus one night soon after his confrontation with Gottschalk, lurking outside the gates of Congo Square in the wild torchlight of one of the great Vodou "bamboulas," Laurent finally found a link in the chain he had been dredging through the darkness of his thoughts.

To hear Madame Popleuse tell one version of the tale, she stood with Marie Laveau and her mavens the night the great Voodoo Queen refused to enter the hellish pact that Laurent presented to them. She also remembers seeing the dejected Laurent leaving the square only to be accosted by a shadowy group of men known among the "vodusi" as black magic hoodoo workers.

Popleuse watched until her Aunt Josephine called to her, "Yo come back here, girl or I'm gwon to box yo ears! Don't yo be watchin' after that man! The dead gwon to eat him up soon! Dey'll git yo, too!" Little Madame Popleuse quickly rejoined her aunt.

What Laurent and Mathilde desired has been the heart's wish of bereaved parents since time immemorial; it was only a rare few, however, who attempted what he was about to allow. Because what Laurent had done that night in the wild heat of the bamboula was to make a pact with the dark vodusi sorcerers: for money, they had agreed to attempt to bring his beloved Little Violette back to the world of the living.

By methods best kept secret and which even Popleuse in her retelling would not reveal, the decaying corpse of Little Violette was removed from its resting place and taken to a secret location where for one full cycle of the moon it was subjected to the most powerful hoodoo magic the dark Devil's minions could muster. In bargains with the Guede, the keepers of the Dead, and even perhaps with Death himself, the root doctors were attempting something that was only whispered of in dark legends straight from the black heart of Haiti.

Brooding in their Marigny home, Laurent and Mathilde waited for the appointed time to pass. As the passage of the moon brought it again to full, one night there came a knock at the front door. The couple rushed to open it and was puzzled to see an old vodusi matron standing there, seemingly alone.

Imagine, then, the joy that overcame them as the old black woman stepped aside and moved the folds of her skirt to reveal none other than the dear, departed—but now very much alive—Violette holding tightly to her dark hand!

The couple burst into tears of joy and happiness. Mathilde scooped the little girl into her trembling arms. With violet eyes once again burning with life, the little girl said in a familiar voice like the sound of tinkling glass: "Mama!"

With that, the couple's joy seemed once again complete.

Though they urged her to come into the house, the old vodusi would not enter the couple's home where servants were eyeing her suspiciously. But the matron did not hesitate to take the cash that Laurent now happily forked over. With that, the couple was left to their joy.

And joyful it was, at least for a time. Although, when the servants learned of the child's return, they immediately recoiled from the little girl. Loathe to leave the couple, and not certain how the child was reanimated, most of the house servants remained loyal; some—those who had never believed Violette to be dead—felt vindicated.

The mulatto nurse was the most frightened of all the house servants, not the least because the care of the child was returned to her once "Violette" had miraculously reappeared. Fear kept them all in place: fear for their master and his wife, fear of what this little jewel might now be capable.

The house took on a dreamlike quality immediately after Violette returned. It was clear, even to the most slow-minded of the servants, that Laurent and Mathilde had now finally lost their sanity. Not only this, but the once beautiful and vibrant Violette was now somehow different; something about her was never quite "right" and none of the servants liked being in her presence very long. Where they had previously seen untainted innocence, they now sensed a brooding presence, something entirely "other" had come to live with them.

It wasn't long before their worst fears and superstitions seemed to be coming true. Deep inside the house, pattering footsteps troubled the watchful servants late in the night; grunting and scratching sounds or the sounds of furtive eating could be heard in the darkness outside, but no one had the nerve to investigate.

Small animals were frequently found dead, hidden under the outside bushes; even the boldest of the field hands would not touch these little victims, marked unmistakably with the biting and tearing of human teeth.

Yet while all these activities accelerated around them, Laurent and Mathilde, living in a perpetual dream state, seemed only to see Violette.

Knowing they were trapped and fiercely loyal to the degenerating Laurent and Mathilde, some of the house servants, led by the zombie child's nurse, visited Dr. Gottschalk.

He listened intently to what they had to say, and though most would dismiss what he heard as the ramblings of the servile or ignorant, Dr. Gottschalk had complete faith that what he was hearing was true. He recalled the night the desperate Laurent came to see him, the look in the grieving father's eyes as he ran off into the darkness of what now appeared to be his longest night.

"We know the chile must be destroyed," said the old nurse. "But it would tear my heart out to have to be the one to do that thing!"

"You could not even attempt it," Dr. Gottschalk said consolingly, "Nor shall I. We need the aid of someone powerful in the ways of Voodoo, someone without fear who can command the spirits of the dead."

This is how the case came again before the great Marie Laveau. Not surprisingly, recalling the desperation in the eyes of Laurent the night she turned him away, Madame Marie was sympathetic for the grieving parents. She saw the horrible act of reanimation for what it was: an affront to all the realm of Spirit that went against the practices of Vodou and its respect for the sanctity of life and death. What angered her more was that the act had been committed for money.

On the night that Dr. Gottschalk brought the servants to her, Madame Marie said to them: "For the child, I will give you strength to do this thing. For Violette."

Of all people it was the faithful mulatto nurse who found the courage and the strength to face the little creature that had taken the place of her beloved Violette. Alone with the zombie child in the grim nursery, the mulatto woman was able to overcome her worst fears and trap the horrible creature in a bed sheet. Tying it tightly in knots and praying in the Kreyol language words Marie Laveau had taught her, the nurse rushed to a wagon that waited to take her to a rendezvous with the Voodoo Queen herself.

When she arrived at the appointed place, the nurse found that Madame Marie was not alone. With her were some of her closest followers such as her daughter, Marie II, and the loyal Josephine Mosebury; even the children, Fanny Mosebury and Little Madame Popleuse were there. Two burly black men held tight to the very same old matron who had deposited the zombified Violette in the waiting arms of Laurent and Mathilde. The old woman looked in great distress and shook whenever Marie Laveau turned her fierce dark eyes upon her.

Thinking at first that she had been betrayed, the nurse was reluctant to turn over the kicking bundle that contained the zombie baby. But a gentle smile from Marie Laveau reassured her, and she handed the bundle over to the powerful mambo.

As soon as Madame Marie took hold of her, the zombie Violette burst into a horrific tantrum, not unlike those she threw in the days when she begged to be taken about with her father. This tantrum, however, sounded more like the ravings of a caged animal; there were even bloody marks from the zombie child's fingernails as she began to claw her way out of the bed sheets.

Madame Marie shouted a word of command and the tantrum stopped; she then turned to the nurse. "Go home," she told her, "and perform the house cleansing ritual just as I taught you earlier. Turn your back on this child immediately and forget her. She is in my charge now."

Violette the zombie child never did return to the house of her parents, who, once she had been removed, seemed to return as if from a dream world; even their grieving had ceased. The loyal servants never mentioned anything about the horrible visitation of the zombie child, nor did the nurse ever reveal what she had done with it. A year and a day from the moment the nurse relinquished the child to Marie Laveau, the young couple was blessed with another child: this time a strong, healthy son.

What happened to little Violette, the Zombie Child?

According to Madame Popleuse, who told the tale while she yet lived, what is already dead cannot be killed again, and such was the anger of Marie Laveau that, it is said, the old vodusi matron could not resist when commanded to take the zombie child into her care.

"You brought the men that made this thing," said Madame Marie, referring to the woman's sons, the black hoodoo workers. "You keep it, until the dead come back for their own!"

Legend has it the old matron kept the zombie Violette confined, but when Death did come to find the old woman there was no trace to be found of the child. No one ever knew for certain, but most assumed that the old woman had finally found a way to destroy the creature and thus discharge her burden.

Madame Popleuse never knew for sure.

\* \* \*

Who could guess that the tale of the Zombie Child would be revived in the aftermath of Hurricane Katrina? But that is just what happened.

A couple renovating a cottage in the old Rampart section of New Orleans are said to have been hard at work scraping years of plaster from the gabled ceiling of what was once the old kitchen when suddenly what appeared to be a small door was revealed.

Assuming it went into the attic, the owners put some elbow grease into the work and by the time they wrapped up that evening they could both see the outline of a little trap door. It had been painted shut under a heavy plaster coating and had all the appearances of having been sealed for generations.

Leaving off their work for the night, the owners cleaned up and enjoyed a well-deserved dinner before relaxing and going to bed. Late in the night, however, they were awakened by what sounded at first like cats yowling. Thinking that perhaps a stray had wandered in during the day while the doors were wide open, the owners got up and searched but found nothing.

The sounds continued for the next several nights and soon were compounded by small grunts and scratchings. The owners became convinced that they had somehow disturbed a family of rats lurking in the old frame house.

When at last the weekend arrived and the renovating work could be resumed, the owners decided to investigate the little door again, thinking it might hold the secret to some of the unusual night noises. Together they chipped at the paint and plaster holding the trap door in place and finally were able to pry it open. A gust of unwholesome air, full of dust and the passage of years, wafted into their faces; when the dust cleared the owners took a flashlight in hand.

Peering into the darkness of the attic gable, pushing aside the bones of dead pigeons and rats, sorting through a rusty pile of antique toys, metal plates, and tattered rags, they came upon what appeared at first glance to be an old doll. It was the size of a young child, but it appeared for all intents and purposes to be a doll wrapped in layers of tattered cloth—like a mummy, there was even a kind of gauze around the face. What caught their eyes though, even in the dim light of the attic, was the dazzling purple flash of a pair of amethyst earrings, still brilliant—and still attached—even after all the intervening years.

Something about the discovery greatly disturbed the homeowners and they debated for days about what to do with their find. Soon, however, a decision was about to be made for them.

As Hurricane Katrina was poised in the Gulf of Mexico to strike New Orleans, massive evacuations were called. So disturbed by their attic find were the young couple that even in the midst of the evacuation mayhem, they took the time to replace and nail shut the trap door to the attic. Their house secured, they joined the mass of humanity fleeing the storm of the century.

When they were finally allowed to return to their home after the storm they discovered that although their home had not flooded, there was minor damage to one side where a collapsed Chinaberry tree had pierced the roof. Their hearts fell when they saw this and not just because of the horror of insurance claims and Federal Emergency Management Agency (FEMA) paperwork. It was as if, they said, they "knew" the broken roof meant trouble.

Reluctantly, they moved aside the branches of the fallen tree and went to the little attic door. With a feeble flashlight they peered inside.

Horror and dismay overcame them when they saw that the mummified "doll"—which they now fully believed was really the body of a dead child—was nowhere to be found. There was nothing in the attic but the bones, the rusting toys and plates, and swatches of the decaying rags that had once encased the awful little body. It was gone.

\* \* \*

I can think of nothing now except the words of Madame Popleuse saying, "You can't kill what's already dead!"

Where, I wondered, in all of Katrina-ravaged New Orleans, would such a thing go? Where would it hide now that the whole landscape was as surreal as the world it was called back from? I shudder to think, to this day, that somewhere, in the tattered remains of Old New Orleans, Little Violette the Zombie Child is bewitching someone, even now, with violet eyes to—quite literally—die for!

# THE SIN EATERS

Most people who have heard of the concept of "sin eating" associate the custom with England, Scotland, or Wales. The 2007 motion picture *The Last Sin Eater*, based on the novel by Francine Waters, was set in a small rural community of Welsh immigrants in the Appalachia region during the 1850s. As we shall see in this chapter, the "last" of the Sin Eaters did not cease their unusual occupation in the mid-nineteenth century, and the task of consuming another's sins was not limited to the British Isles or its settlements abroad.

Basically, sin eating is a form of religious magic in which someone who is selected for the ritual eats food set at the bedside of a dying person and thereby absolves that individual of his or her sins by figuratively eating them. Of course, those who believe in the validity of such rites believe the Sin Eater to have literally taken the deceased's misdeed into his own body.

Generally, the Sin Eater was someone down on his luck who had no better choice than to accept the coins that he might receive for performing such an act. However, in some villages (we are led to believe from historical documents) members of one congregation or another might call upon a particularly devout man to serve as a Sin Eater.

The Sin Eater would be brought to the bedside of a man or woman whose family sought him out to perform the absolution of sins. A member of the family would place a piece of bread upon their relative's chest, and another would hand the Sin Eater a bowl of ale to help wash down the bread and the sins.

After reciting prayers and elements of an ancient ritual, the Sin Eater and the family members who had gathered at their relative's bedside would wait quietly until he or she died. At that time, the Sin Eater removed the piece of bread from the deceased's chest and ate it. Some people believed that as the person lay breathing his or her last, the bread would absorb the accumulated sins of that individual's lifetime. The Sin Eater would swallow the bread, wash it down with the ale, and the ritual was completed.

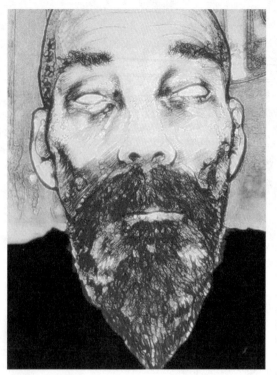

Sin Eaters consume the sins of the dying so that they may enter the afterlife without the burden of their life's misdeeds (*art by Ricardo Pustanio*).

Some village customs preferred that the proceedings be conducted outside of the house. The deceased would be placed on a bier and carried to the lawn or the flower garden. Here, the Sin Eater would accept a small loaf of bread to consume over the corpse while the family reverently encircled the proceedings. The Sin Eater would then request a large bowl or chalice of ale to quaff. Once all the bread had been eaten and all the ale drunk, the family was joyful that their beloved had been freed of sins. The Sin Eater was paid his wages and went on this way, pleased with the way he had conducted the ceremony.

While some villages held the Sin Eater in rather high esteem, such was not always the case. In *Funeral Customs* (1926), Bertram S. Puckle includes an account from 1825 in which the townspeople regarded the Sin Eater as a "thing unclean." Although the man had chosen such a path for himself, his fellow villagers regarded him as they might a leper, and he was cut off from all social contact. Only when they needed him to absolve the sins of their dearly departed did they seek his favor. At all other times, he was regarded to be an "associate of evil spirits," a practitioner of witchcraft and unholy practices. When he had completed the ritual, everything he had touched was burned.

### Sin Eating Voodoo-Hoodoo Style

My friend Lisa Lee Harp Waugh, an expert on so many aspects of the paranormal, necromancy, and Voodoo, grew up in Marshall, Texas, and went to school with a daughter of a well-known local Sin Eater.

"At the ripe old age of 14," Lisa Lee said, "I witnessed her father practicing the Sin Eater's trade on her grandmother before the mortuary hearse came to retrieve her body."

According to Waugh: "The body was laid naked on the kitchen table, and all the food in the house had been prepared and set out along side and on top of this 69-year-old woman's nude corpse. It was explained to me that in Texas Voodoo-Hoodoo Sin Eaters had a redemptive role in the religious practices of the American civilization. At the end of an individual's life, he was allowed to confess his misdeeds to this Soul Eater, and according to legend the Soul Eater would cleanse their dirty soul by 'eating its filth.'"

Waugh learned that while many believed the old custom to be abandoned, "in many parts of Louisiana and southern Texas, it is still a common practice that occurs regularly."

As she grew up, she discovered that Marshall alone was home to many Sin Eaters and that there were no less than 22 adept Sin Eaters across the United States who ate the awful and many assorted sins of those who could not rightfully go to heaven unless their evil sins were gone.

Waugh has met a wide variety of paranormalists in her life, but she says, "Actual Sin Eaters are very much more interesting than the average ghost enthusiast. And many times during the process of the actual eating of the sins, it is said that the ghost of the deceased is seen and witnessed, moving and crying around the room. I will tell you that this has been witnessed by many besides myself."

### Lisa Lee Waugh Talks about Voodoo-Hoodoo Sin Eaters

*The following is according to Waugh:*

Voodoo-Hoodoo Sin Eaters seem to be the outcast of the group of religious practitioners, making up five percent of the more devout individuals in the U.S.A. Their sin-eating ritual differs in many ways from those of the nineteenth century. It has been related to me over the years that Marie Laveau was visited by a Sin Eater several years before she died—and she was one of the few individuals who had their sins eaten while still alive. This is why many say she turned pious and renounced Voodoo.

Displaced by hurricanes Katrina and Ike, several of these individuals who eat their meals off of the bodies of the dead now live throughout Texas. As a result many have been noticeably in the spotlight in recent months. I happened to meet the King of all the Voodoo-Hoodoo Sin Eaters just recently.

A Sin Eater known as Papa Jaxmano, a former New Orleans resident, is revered by many as the lord of all Hoodoo-Voodoo Sin Eaters. This man has been eating sins since the age of seven when he had to eat the sins of his father after his untimely death. Now 68 years of age, Papa Jaxmano lives in Dallas, Texas, where he applies the ancient art for individuals all races, faiths and social strata. He does charge a fee for his services, but the price depends on the amount of sins carried by the individual who has passed on.

At one time Papa Jaxmano was a close friend of the Voodoo King Chickenman, and he is said to have eaten the sins of the Witch Queen of New Orleans Mary Oneida Toups.

Papa Jaxmano also tells of eating sins publicly and privately for many well-known celebrities and politicians around the world.

Public ceremonies, he relates, often consist of laying cakes or candies in the coffin with the deceased prior to viewing of the corpse. They are then removed and given out, or placed in a bowl at the door of the funeral home or the coffee room.

Voodoo-Hoodoo Sin Eaters had a redemptive role in the religious practices of the faithful. At the end of an individual's life, he was allowed to confess his misdeeds to this Soul Eater (*art by Ricardo Pustanio*).

Relatives and friends are then told to take a candy and eat it before the corpse is buried. This custom is still widely practiced today. Many use donuts and even packets of sugar instead of candy. Many of the funeral goers are not aware that they are eating the sins of the deceased, and Papa Jaxmano says this is more of a sin than one might imagine. In Texas, cupcakes, brownies, pastries, tacos, burritos and even store-bought canned goods are placed alongside the body inside the coffin during the wake or funeral and later taken home and offered guests.

"I charge no fee for what I do for the poor," says Papa Jaxmano. "I do it because … I do it. Others charge a fee all the time. If someone is poor, I might just ask for a ride or a friendly handshake."

Then he added with an expression of distaste, "Still, there or others that you could not pay me to eat their sins."

Papa Jaxmano next stated an important afterthought: "If you are the one who contacts a Sin Eater to eat someone's sins, then you need your sins ate too, or you is going to hell also!"

In the past week, I have watched Papa Jax, as I call him, eat the sins of over 40 dead individuals. He often brings food home with him to offer to others.

In his brand of Voodoo-Hoodoo, there is a group of individuals who gather each week to eat the sins of others. Papa Jax's group has over 50 members who assemble in a Dallas suburb to eat the food and sins of the dead. These Sin Banquets are very trendy and only rarely are individuals like myself invited.

In doing research, I discovered that such "Sin Eating parties" go back to the late 1700s in New Orleans. A Voodoo congregation would gather each Saturday night and eat the sins of others, then go to Mass first thing Sunday morning and go to Confession. Thus their savory sins were forgiven.

## The Terrible Secret of the Soul Eaters

In 1968, a British anthropologist named Boltan Simmons claimed to be the first tribal outsider to have witnessed the awesome powers of the Mayaxa Tochlan cult of "soul eating" Guatemalan Indians.

The Mayaxa Tochlan are the object of mind-rotting fear among the jungle dwellers upon whom they prey. Their power stems from the legend that they have discovered the secret of life eternal and may not be harmed by mortals, who live only to serve their wills.

Translated roughly, Mayaxa Tochlan means "Take Soul Life," and to the Guatemalans, this is exactly the power with which the cult has been endowed.

The Tochlan live in dense jungles surrounding villages; there natives steal a precarious living from the ungenerous earth. In each cult there are 13 men, many of them reported to be more than 100 years old, who are kept youthful through that incredible span of life by draining the vital forces from a ritual victim each year.

Through the power of fear they have instilled in the natives, the cults extract one child each year from the nearby tribes to be the victim of their psychic cannibalism. The frightened village children must draw lots each year to determine who among them will go to the camp of the Tochlan, never to return.

While for years stories of the soul-eating clan had circulated among Europeans who lived along the coastline cities, few ever took the stories seriously, until the summer of 1968 when Simmons was able to persuade a native acquaintance to take him to the camp of a Tochlan cult.

> *When the cult reached the site where the ceremony was to be held the whimpering child was stripped naked and bound with small ropes to a mat woven of jungle palms.*

Wishing to put the cult members on notice that he had strange powers of his own, Simmons injected morphine into the arms of several Tochlan leaders. When the astonishing numbness crept through their limbs, Simmons told them that he could take all the spirit from their body if he so wished.

Convinced they were dealing with a magician every bit as powerful as themselves, the Tochlan offered to permit Simmons to witness the strange ritual of eating souls—if he would, in turn, tell them more of his powers.

Delighted to strike the bargain, Simmons spent the next several days making notes, as the Tochlan prepared for their ceremony. Later, he would wish he had never been a part of what took place.

The ritual opened with the choosing of the victim who would lose his soul to the cult. The scientist began to grow uneasy when he saw the real terror that churned through the small girl the tribe had selected to accompany the Tochlan to their secret place.

When the cult reached the site where the ceremony was to be held, the whimpering child was stripped naked and bound with small ropes to a mat woven of jungle palms. Though the child pleaded to be allowed to return home, her tears were greeted by a sharp slap from the clan leader to remind her that it was the way of her tribe that brought her there and that such things were inevitable.

While the child moaned her fears, the Tochlan chief cut quickly across her arm with a razor edged knife he had taken from inside a white ceremonial robe. The cut was not deep, but blood flowed from the wound, and it was caught up in a polished bowl that seemed to contain some ritual herb. To it was added the juice of a berry the jungle shaman said had been taken from the "Tree of Life."

Then began the strange chant that convinced Simmons he was witnessing no sham illusion, but rather a starkly terrifying ritual that would lead to the death of the helpless little victim.

"With your blood we call forth the blood of your soul," the 13 white-robed Tochlans chanted in eerie unison. The child paled and passed into a trance-like state.

For 13 days the macabre ritual continued as Simmons looked on in growing alarm. Each day the chant was repeated. And each day the child grew obviously closer to death.

The child's eyes spoke a terror too deep to have a name.

Bound hand and foot, totally unclothed, she thrashed upon the woven mat of jungle leaves with what strength her bonds would permit.

Then, she saw them coming again, and with a scream dying in her small throat, slumped into some merciful, unconscious corner of her mind.

Toward her, 13 white-robed men approached for the climax of a bizarre and almost unbelievable ritual in which they would draw the force of life from the child and gather it into their own aging bodies in order to have life eternal.

The Tochlan dipped their fingers into the blood-herb bowl and marked their bodies 13 times.

Again the chant: "With your blood, we call forth the blood of your soul."

The repeated symbolic use of the number 13, Simmons learned, stemmed from the Tochlan's conception that all life, like the signs of the zodiac, centered on the number 12. Add to it the number required to make 13, the cult believed, and the cycle of life and death was broken, and one might live forever.

Throughout the 13 days of ritual soul eating, the child who was being consumed was fed more than enough to sustain life, but each day the emptiness grew in her eyes, and each day there seemed to be less life in the frail body that lay inside the circle.

The child was never left alone at any moment as the ritual dragged toward its inevitable end. Some member of the cult was constantly at her side, repeating the terrible chant that told of her soul's departing, flowing into the bodies of the ancient ones who were her captors.

On the thirteenth day, Simmons was horrified to observe the child in what seemed to be a nearly lifeless condition, while the cult members seemed to have been infused with some demonic vitality, belying their obvious age.

Again the ritual began, and this time, the anthropologist knew with terrifying certainty what the outcome would be. Once again the white-robed Tochlans emerged from the jungle toward the dying child.

For a moment she opened her eyes and watched them slowly advance. Then the trancelike state passed over her again, and Simmons hoped it would protect her from the ordeal that remained.

Taking up the chant once more, the cult members varied the ritual this time. Over small charcoal braziers they placed torn pieces of turtle flesh, revered because of the turtle's longevity.

Symbolically they placed the roasted flesh to their lips. Once again they spoke to the fear-numbed child.

"Now we shall eat your flesh and your life shall become our life," they said.

Simmons watched in horror as spasms shook the child's body, and he saw the grimace of terrified death brutalize her once innocent face.

The ritual had ended.

Simmons felt the child's pulse, then her heart. The child was dead.

The old men sang a song of celebration. Their voices had the mellow bell sound of youth. Simmons felt suddenly old. Perhaps, he feared, they had eaten his soul, too. Perhaps, indeed, they had.

The child's body was dragged into the jungle to be eaten by wild animals, and a much shaken Simmons made a hasty retreat from the secret camp of the Tochlan.

In later studies, the anthropologist learned that the natives who obeyed the cult out of fear were convinced that the soul-eating ritual really did give them life eternal.

The oldest members of some of the tribes said they could not remember a time when all of the Tochlan had not been among them, exactly as they had been when they were children. The Tochlan were young always, never dying, sustained by the life of a child given in fear each year.

Scientists who have studied the reports Simmons made in 1968 have some very good explanations for what happened in that steaming jungle clearing.

Accustomed from youth to believe that the soul could be drawn from the body by strange forces, the child would naturally die because of her own superstitious beliefs.

The long life attributed to the Tochlan members might also be explained by their strict life style, in which meat is not taken and a strict vegetarian rule is observed.

And perhaps that is how the old ones go on living while generations pass away.

But then, perhaps it is not.

# WENDIGOS CRAVE HUMAN FLESH

Throughout the tribes of the Native American people there are numerous stories of shamans, sorcerers, and witches with shape-shifting abilities. Even when the power to transform is used for evil by those who have chosen the dark side, there are few accounts of people being attacked, mutilated, or killed by the shape-shifter. A savage exception is the cannibalistic, werewolf-like monster known as the Wendigo (also Windigo, Windago, Witko, and other variants), a creature that hungers for human flesh.

According to the Chippewa-Ojibwa people and many other tribes, the Wendigo was once a brave warrior, respected by his people. Then, after a fierce battle against tribal enemies, he showed his contempt for the fallen foes by cutting off a piece of flesh and eating it.

Unfortunately, the once-esteemed warrior developed a taste for human flesh, and his fellow warriors were horrified when they discovered him several days later roasting another portion of a fallen enemy. Warnings by shamans and chiefs had no effect on the warrior, who ceased hunting game and began to prey upon the people of other tribes for sustenance.

After a time, the Master of Life decreed that if the warrior chose to live like a savage beast, he should appear as a monstrous creature, a vicious giant—and the Great Spirit Being transformed him into the Wendigo. Driven away from the fires of all tribes, the Wendigo prowls the desolate forests and frozen wastes of northern America, always starving for human flesh.

## Cheeka, the Wendigo of Sproat Lake

It is a pleasant place today, but time was, and not so long ago, that the tribal people and the white settlers knew with a certain dread that beautiful Sproat Lake belonged to a devil, a Wendigo whose calling card read "Cheeka."

Today, tourists marvel at the placid beauty of the silver-hammered lake near Vancouver, British Columbia, and send home picture postcards that cannot quite fully capture its loveliness.

The unspoiled beauty of Sproat Lake began attracting white settlers to the Canadian paradise in the early 1880s when the American West was beginning to close and the great northland frontier was only beginning to open its majestic doors.

According to the Chippewa-Ojibwa people and many other tribes, the Wendigo was once a brave warrior, respected by his people. Then, after a fierce battle against tribal enemies, he showed his contempt for the fallen foes by cutting off a piece of flesh and eating it (*art by Ricardo Pustanio*).

While the settlers could barely contain their excitement when first glimpsing the towering woodlands and rich soil that banked the lake, the tribes, such as the Cree, Cowichan, and Kutenai, who had made the Alberni region their home for generations shunned Sproat Lake, warning the pioneers that it was ruled over by a particularly malevolent devil to whom the Indians had given the name Cheeka.

Until they had given up trying to ply the lake and take its rich harvest of fish, the tribal people said they had been beset by unending calamities caused by the wrathful Cheeka, who apparently had no intention of sharing his sacred domain.

While such warnings seemed to the settlers to be the frightened gibbering of the primitive mind, the Native Americans repeated their advice that the white man would be wiser to move on and leave Sproat Lake to the Wendigo. The north was endless, they told the pioneers. Go find someplace where demons had not declared a previous claim.

With true pioneer disdain for the advice of those who had lived on the land for centuries, the warnings of the tribes went unheeded and a succession of settlers took up temporary lodging on the lake where a monster was the landlord.

Early accounts relate that a Kentucky family named Cooper first attempted to settle the land near the lake somewhere around 1885. Landing with a wife, two children, and the kind of spirit that had tamed the Ohio Valley, Cooper set about building a cabin and clearing the wilderness for seed.

No sooner had Cooper set camp then a series of disastrous fires began roaring through the encircling timber. Time and again the family fought through suffocating smoke to save their belongings, but each time a little more was lost.

Finally, with little more than their clothing left, the Coopers yielded their claim to Cheeka and left. The fires stopped soon after.

No sooner had the devil squelched his flames than another pioneer, of sorts, came to claim Sprout Lake's shoreline. He said his name was Watkins, and rumor had it that he had jumped ship to find the peaceful life he was certain awaited him in the Canadian wilderness.

Watkins had scarcely completed his cabin when an unusual flood poured its way out over the rich valley, forcing several pioneer families to seek shelter at the former sailor's new digs. When food scarcities threatened the group, the obliging Watkins set off by canoe to obtain more provender. During the night, his cries for help were heard, and the next morning, Watkins was found drowned, his canoe bobbing quite safely near a log. Apparently, the sailor thought he had struck a sand bar and got out to investigate—and found himself in deep water over his head.

Only Cheeka could so confuse a sailor, the tribespeople said—and the settlers began to wonder if they might not be right.

In the years that ensued, there followed to Sprout Lake quite a number of confident immigrants, lured by the beauty of the place. In a very brief time, large numbers of them were quite dead, under circumstances that sometimes passed credibility. Some had their throats slashed. Others appeared half-eaten by mountain lions or bears.

While the settlers blamed the large predators for such attacks, the tribes people argued that bears or mountain lions would not leave their future meals lying carelessly about the forest. The carnivorous killers would drag their prey back to their cave for safe storage from carrion eaters. The tribes people all agreed that the murdered victims had been claimed by the Wendigo.

A German settler named Fraust canoed across the lake one day and vanished forever. His canoe was found, nicely beached on a bank, but only Cheeka knew whatever became of Mr. Fraust.

A multiple tragedy on the lake was also laid to the bloody hands of the Wendigo. Unafraid of the legends, to which even the white settlers were now willing to add their accounts, a prosperous engineer named Fabre brought a considerable tract fronting the lake, built a fine home for his wife and daughter, and extended an invitation to a pair of young nieces to join them for a summer holiday.

It was on a particularly stifling summer afternoon that the nieces and Fabre's daughter hung their clothes to a hickory limb and dived into the lake for a refreshing swim. When night fell and they had not returned, searchers paddled from the shore to find their lifeless bodies, bobbing in the moonlight. Fabre carved a small cemetery from the vast wilderness that surrounded his grief-stricken home and buried the chil-

The Cree, Cowichan, and Kutenai trubes, who had made the Alberni region near present-day Vancouver, British Columbia, their home for generations, shunned Sproat Lake, warning the early pioneers that it was ruled by a particularly malevolent devil known to the Indians as the Cheeka (*art by Ricardo Pustanio*).

dren there. Later, he was laid to rest at their side, and sleeps there yet, for Cheeka demanded no further indemnity from the dead.

Perhaps the most dramatic devilment attributed to Lake Sproat's evil spirit was the thunderous fate that overtook a settler named Weiner who took up residence on the ill-omened shores in 1910.

For a time, it seemed that Weiner was about to snap the jinx that plagued that clouded place until, one night, neighbors heard a horrendous series of explosions that seemed to come from the new homestead.

Rushing to the scene, the neighbors found Cheeka had struck again, this time with unparalleled fury. Weiner's home had been flattened by a terrific explosion, leveled as though some mad mammoth had stomped an angry foot on the substantial cabin. The outbuildings that surrounded the home had burned to the ground, although there seemed no rational explanation for either the explosion or the fires.

Worried friends sifted through the ashes and combed the flattened wreckage of the cabin, but no trace of Weiner was ever found.

The heavy waves of migration that followed poor Mr. Weiner's ascension seemed to cause Cheeka to withdraw farther back into the forest, for soon after, the curse of Sproat Lake seemed to lift itself and the area's idyllic setting soon made it a popular tourist attraction where vacationers from both Canada and the United States flocked without ever being molested by the devil that once owned the lake.

The Native peoples, however, hold to the belief that Cheeka is probably just off on a vacation of his own and that he'll be back some day, with an eye toward collecting some overdue rent.

### The Spirit of a Wendigo Turned a Bus into a Place of Bloody Death

The Greyhound bus was nearing Portage la Prairie, Manitoba, on its route from Edmonton, Alberta, to Winnipeg on July 30, 2008. There were 37 passengers on board, plus the driver, and the trip had been uneventful—until the spirit of the Wendigo suddenly possessed one of the passengers, Vince Weiguang Li. With a bloodcurdling scream, Li began viciously stabbing the passenger in front of him, a young man named Tim McLean. McLean's seatmate, Cody Olmstead, 21, said there was no provocation for the attack. McLean was simply sitting quietly, dozing with his earphones on.

Garnet Caton, who was seated in front of McLean, said that Li must have stabbed his victim 50 or 60 times in the chest.

Olmstead said that Li, wielding a huge "Rambo-type" knife, stabbed McLean everywhere—the chest, arms, legs, neck, stomach—everywhere he could reach with his blade.

Olmstead managed to push his way out of the carnage and began running up the aisle of the bus, slapping other passengers awake and shouting that there was a madman attacking his seatmate with a large knife. The bus driver pulled over to the side of the road and opened the door so the pushing, shoving, panicked passengers could exit the bus.

A truck driver seeing the bus parked at the roadside sensed serious problems, and he pulled over to ask what was happening and if he could help in any way.

As Caton, the truck driver, and the bus driver looked in the windows of the bus, they could see Li hacking away at McLean, whom they assumed was dead. As they watched in horror, they could see that the madman had nearly gutted his victim and was now hacking at his neck, apparently seeking to decapitate him.

The three men decided to enter the bus and try to disarm Li, but when they started down the aisle toward him, Li brandished his large knife and ran toward them. The men hastily retreated from the bus and held the door closed as the blood-stained murderer tried to push it open and claim more victims.

Li left the bus door, slashing his knife menacingly in the air. Next, he sat in the driver's seat and started the bus in an attempt to flee the scene.

The bus driver managed to disable the bus while Caton and the truck driver kept pressure on the door.

Leaving the driver's seat, Li walked back to the door, holding McLean's head aloft as if it were some trophy won in battle. Then, in a gesture of contempt, he dropped the head right in front of the men who were imprisoning him in the bus.

Less than 10 minutes after the horrible attack had begun, police cruisers pulled up alongside the

**Could it have been the spirit of a Wendigo that possessed a passenger on a Greyhound bus that was nearing Portage la Prairie, Manitoba, on its route from Edmonton, Alberta, to Winnipeg on July 30, 2008? The driver and 37 passengers witnessed the sudden transformation of a passenger who emitted a bloodcurdling scream and then began viciously stabbing the passenger in front of him without provocation (art by Ricardo Pustanio).**

bus, followed by a couple of school buses that would take the shocked passengers to a hotel in nearby Brandon.

Caton later told members of the media that as they pulled away in the school buses, they could see Li taunting the police with the head of the unfortunate young passenger in his hands.

Over a year later, on September 2, 2009, ethno-historian Nathan Carlson of Edmonton, one of the world's leading experts on the Wendigo phenomenon, said that he had barely had a solid night's sleep since the incident aboard the bus. Carlson admitted that even though such terrible encounters with the "Wendigo psychosis" were within the realm of his expertise, he hadn't been able to get the horror of the attack out of his mind.

The Wendigo psychosis refers to a mental condition in which the afflicted develops an insatiable desire to eat human flesh. Western psychologists largely identify the psychosis as a culture-bound syndrome, though many members of various Native American tribes believe that the victims of the curse literally turn into Wendigos.

## *A Stranger Took a Bite Out of His Arm*

About 2:00 PM on April 4, 2009, Joseph Lancellotti, 67, of Metairie, Louisiana, was gardening at his home, enjoying the serenity of the day.

Suddenly, he saw a man approaching, shouting angrily. Lancellotti couldn't understand a word the man was saying to him, and he was completely unprepared for the blow that the stranger landed on his head as soon as he had approached within striking distance.

Lancellotti attempted to defend himself with a rake, but as the two men wrestled with the rake between them, the stranger bit Lancellotti on his forearm, ripping away a large chunk of flesh. Then, to Lancellotti's horror, his attacker chewed the piece of his forearm and swallowed it.

Completely stunned by the attack, Lancellotti fell to the ground, his assailant on top of him. As he struggled to escape the man's savage clutches, the stranger began to choke him.

Lancellotti's neighbor, Chantal Lorio, director of the Wound Center at East Jefferson General Hospital, came out to investigate what was happening on Lancellotti's front yard. At first, she thought Joseph was having a heart attack and a passerby had come to his aid. Then she saw the pool of blood and the blood issuing from Lancellotti's forearm.

Lorio grabbed her medicine bag and ran out to begin dressing Lancellotti's arm. She told the stranger to step back, but he wouldn't release his grip on her neighbor's shirt.

When he caught his breath, Lancellotti told Lorio that the man had bitten his arm, chewed his flesh, and swallowed it as they struggled. The bite mark measured almost 3 by 1.5 inches and was about a quarter of an inch deep.

The stranger finally released his hold on Lancellotti's shirt and calmly walked away to an empty lot where a police car was parked. He was still standing there when the deputies returned to their car and took him into custody.

The man who experienced the bizarre Wendigo-type seizure was later identified as Mario Vargas, 48, of New Orleans. Although officials refused to release any details, it was learned that just 45 minutes before he attacked Joseph Lancellotti, Vargas had been treated for a finger injury at East Jefferson General Hospital.

Vargas was booked for second-degree battery, but Mrs. Bonnie Lancellotti wondered if the hospital staff had not noticed anything peculiar when they treated him. She ventured her opinion that a person who goes around eating people's skin cannot be in complete control of their senses.

## The Rugarou, Werebeast of the Swamp Indians

*Perhaps the man with the incredible rage who attacked a stranger and tore out a chunk of his flesh was possessed by the Rugarou, a type of Wendigo or werewolf known to the tribal people who inhabit the swamps of Louisiana. In this account folklorist and occultist Alyne A. Pustanio, whose roots go deep into the local culture, shares the legend of this frightening creature.*

*According to Alyne A. Pustanio:*

Once there was a swamp trapper who used to parade about in the skins of the animals he had caught, terrifying neighbors and friends by pretending to be the Loup Garou (werewolf). When the disrespectful trapper fell under the eye of a Louisiana Indian shaman, it is said that the man danced a different dance thereafter—as a real Loup Garou under the yellow swampland moon.

The heritage of Louisiana's Native American peoples is rich with tall tales and legends and among these the tale of the werewolf looms large. The Indians know the werewolf as the shape-shifting "Rugarou," a variation of the Cajun French "Loup Garou." But the name matters little—Rugarou, Loup Garou, shape-shifter or skin-walker—these deadly, half-human beasts have been part of the legacy of terror that has haunted the Louisiana swamps for generations. One of the most chilling tales told among the Indian tribes of South Louisiana concerns a warrior tribe of cannibals and how they came to be known—and feared—as Wolf Walking man-eaters. This is that tale.

Where modern-day parish boundaries now exist there were once the mutable limits of the tribal nations of the Opelousas and the Chitimacha, and there exists in the oral tradition of all these tribes a shared memory of vicious and powerful warriors who once held sway over large areas of native lands, using their powers to instill fear among their own people and to manipulate or control their rivals.

This was the Attakapas tribe, and they were the source of much fear and loathing among the swamp Indians who shunned them for their reputation as a nation that cannibalized its enemies. But many Louisiana Indian legends hint at something even more sinister at work among the Attakapas. Many believe this dark secret to be evidence of a skin-walking tradition that, if true, would mark the Attakapas as something unique in the annals of lycanthropy: an entire tribe of werewolves.

Only a very few of those who have studied the history of Native Americans in this area of Louisiana are not familiar with the story of these cannibalistic warmongers, whose name, "Attakapa," in Choctaw means "Man-Eater." The Chitimacha and Opelousas tribes were the traditional enemies of the Attakapas, and it was an unstated fact that any conflict with them (the Attakapas) simply had to be won because the Attakapas were long in the habit of eating their captives.

In one such battle in the 1700s the three tribes went to war in a low country six miles outside of what is today St. Martinville. The Chitimacha and Opelousas won the day and decimated the Attakapas tribe. Only a half dozen or so were said to have survived the conflict, fleeing to refuge in the area around what is now Indian Bend. Fearing retribution from the victorious tribes, the local people—mostly Cajuns and Spaniards—the Attakapas ran away into the unforgiving swamps.

These swamplands were described by early explorers as "embracing such half-solid, half-fluid areas of no agricultural value, but supporting a forest growth so dense with cypress, tupelo, gum, water oaks, ferns, palmettos, and a network of ancient vines, that the appearance is similar to that of the Mayan jungles." The swamps were then (and for the most part still are) only sparsely inhabited by hunters, trappers, and fishermen who lived in palmetto tents and small frame houses or houseboats along the interior bayous.

The renegade Attakapas were unwelcome interlopers in this strange country. None less than Alvar Núñez Cabeza de Vaca, who encountered them on his travels, reported that after the great battle the few surviving Attakapas lived for a while in this environment, subsisting on roots and fish. Some bravely appeared as beggars in the settlements along the edge of the swamplands. But soon they were discovered by members of their fierce rival tribes who chased them back to the swamps—if they could not kill them. In the harsh winter following the great battle, the remnant Attakapas were forced to find a way to survive in the unforgiving environment they now called home.

Some traditions, including Spanish accounts of that time, suggest that the Attakapas, exhausted as subjects of fear and hatred, turned to their shamans for answers. It is said that these elders, once servants of the Great Spirit, now turned aside from the enlightened path and, in desperate search of help and sustenance for their people, began to feel out the heart of darkness for answers. According to all accounts, something responded.

It is said that dark spirits came down and entered into the starving Attakapas. In desperation they had obtained a unique gift: the power of shape-shifting at will. Once notorious as cannibals in conquest, the Attakapas, so other Indian wise men taught, gave over entirely to their animal nature and had somehow transcended the deprived state of their humanity, crossing over into the realm of the animals. Not only this, their numbers were once again growing. They were now predatory hunters, and humans were their prey.

Not surprisingly, winter was the time when the shape-shifting Attakapas were most feared. In the summer, it was said, they seemed to live as other human beings, content with small harvests and the food sources provided to them by their environment. Only the most brutal-natured of them remained in their animal forms all the time. But when the bare winter months came on, bringing in the damp Louisiana chill, sending fish to the bayou bottoms and making other animals scarce, it was believed that all Attakapas—men, women, and even children—lived constantly in their animal forms and were most to be feared.

As the short winter days gave on to long, moonlit nights, so the legends say, the Attakapas "Rugarou"—driven to frenzy with memories of starvation—would leave the swamp and traverse the low country nearby in search of humans to devour. More frightening still was the knowledge—especially among the Chitimacha and the Opelousas—that the beasts were not driven by fear alone; revenge, too, was ever-present in their hearts.

The Rugarou, a type of Wendigo or werewolf, is well known to the tribal people who inhabit the swamps of Louisiana (**art by Ricardo Pustanio**).

Today the Chitimacha are the only tribe left who prosper in the area, though the Opelousas endure in lesser numbers. This, however, has done nothing to lull these ancient peoples into complacency, especially where the Rugarou is concerned. Fear still lingers among them, particularly when a cold, hard winter sets in and the dampness chills the bones. Then their thoughts turn to their long enemy, the man-eaters, the Attakapas, and they wonder if—or when—the Wolf Walkers will strike again.

Recently, the discovery of the grisly remains of mutilated farm animals and sightings of ghostly figures lurching close to the ground near darkened roadsides have been reported from the Chitamacha reservation near Charenton, Louisiana. Many believe that the Rugarou are once again active. Tribal elders have blamed the strange activity on the series of devastating storms—first Hurricanes Katrina and Rita, and more recently Hurricane Gustav—that have struck the area in the last few years. They say the fragile eco-system of the nearby swamplands was impacted and may have affected the resources on which the Rugarou have long been dependent. Many fear these natural disasters may have turned the Wolf Walkers back to their predatory ways.

Once again the Native Americans who live on the edge of the noisome Louisiana swamps are speaking in nervous whispers and the tale of the killer Attakapas is being retold to a new generation. These tribes know, and must let others know, that as the fortune of the land goes, so goes the vengeance of the dreaded Rugarou.

## *The Werewolf Tribe of Eagle Creek, Ohio*

Is it possible that there was once a tribe of Native Americans who, in a time long ago, worshipped the werewolf—or truly believed that they were werewolves? And, as Alyne A. Pustanio questions, do members of the tribe survive today as the Rugarou?

On a pleasant fall afternoon in 1949, Kentucky farmer A.C. Ayres was digging postholes in a field on his small bottomland acreage when a metal glint suddenly caught his eye. He bent down to examine what appeared to be an old copper wrist band among the wet clay.

While finds like the one Ayres made that afternoon were not uncommon in an area that had once been the home of many Native American tribal cultures and where artifacts were regularly turned up by a farmer's plow, something about the small copper bracelet Ayres had found along Eagle Creek told the canny hill man that it was no ordinary find he had made.

A.C. Ayres was right in that feeling. He had found the first clue pointing the direction to one of the most macabre archeological finds ever made in North America. The Kentucky farmer had unearthed the first evidence of a bizarre wolf-worshipping Indian cult that had practiced strange rites when the field in which he was standing had been a wilderness.

Turning the ancient copper bracelet over and over in his rough hands, Ayres decided to call archeologists at the University of Kentucky, who had made known to farmers in Owen County their deep interest in artifacts from the Ohio Valley moundbuilder Indians who had once flourished there in prehistoric times.

The field team that arrived at Ayres' farm became greatly excited when they examined the bracelet, and when the farmer took them to the site where the object had been found, they observed at once that Ayres had been digging his new posthole on an ancient burial mound built perhaps 1,500 years earlier by a group of people, which anthropologists refer to as the Adena Culture.

Carefully staking out the mounds for digging in the spring of 1950, archeologists began probing the areas which the farmer's excavations had not already damaged, with only the slight hope that any further significant finds might be made.

But then digging tools encountered shreds of what appeared to be the decomposing fiber of some organic material, suspected to be leather. Proceeding with great care from the small corner of the material that had been exposed, the archeologists began moving with excited swiftness when portions of a human skeleton began to emerge.

Within hours the scientists had uncovered the skeletal remains of what had been a large man, who had apparently died or been killed at the prime of his life in some remote era.

The body had been encased in tightly bound leather and had been laid to rest in the mound on a pallet of bark. A second covering of bark had been placed over the corpse. Curiously, the skull of the ancient man had been violently crushed in some manner, and the team decided to take a large portion of the surrounding earth back to the university where the painstaking work of reassembling those pieces could be accomplished under laboratory conditions.

As scientists labored to put all the pieces back together, an amazing discovery was made. Among the bone shards, a skeletal fragment that was not of human origin was found.

Examination showed the alien bone to be the intricately cut jaw of a wolf, carved from the total skull of the animal in such a fashion that a rear, handle-like portion extended forward to a point where the front teeth of the animal still protruded from the upper palate structure.

An object identical to the cut wolf jaw on the Ayres farm had been found almost 10 years earlier at another archeological dig in nearby Montgomery County, Kentucky, by scientists sifting another mound grouping.

Archeologists had conjectured that the strange wolf tooth artifact had been significant to some ancient Adena religious ceremony, but it remained for the scientists assembling the Ayres skull to discover the macabre use to which the prehistoric tribe had put the sacred instrument.

A reconstruction of the skeletal remains indicated that the man buried in the mound had been no more than 30 years old at death. Piecing together the skull, scientists found the man's four front teeth missing, although the remaining teeth were in perfect condition. Healed portions of the jaw showed that the four missing teeth had been deliberately taken out at some time during the man's life.

When the archeologists once more picked up the wolf jaw carving they could not help observing that it fit perfectly into the space where the teeth of the prehistoric Indian had been removed.

The bloodcurdling composite that emerged was one in which a full set of wolf fangs protruded from the skeletal mouth of the Ayres man, giving him, even in death, an appearance that frayed the nerves. How much more frightening the wolf man

**Is it possible that an ancient American Indian tribe in Ohio once worshipped werewolves and, indeed, performed surgery on themselves to make them look more wolflike? (*iStock*)**

of Eagle Creek must have appeared on the moonless nights when he stalked the primeval forests of Kentucky.

The spine-tingling discovery set off a flurry of scientific speculation about the meaning of the wolf tooth artifact in the daily life of the ancient culture.

Was there a special wolf cult among the Adena? What might their ceremonies have been to require the use of the raw, keen wolves' teeth inserted into the mouths of their priests?

Anthropologists were certain that the body found buried in lonely splendor in the Ayres mound must have been that of a tribal leader, or a man of some other great importance. Few Adena people were given the honor of single mound burial, a practice reserved for persons of high rank.

Some knowledgeable observers believed the Ayres man may have given his life in a sacred ceremony designed to propitiate a god, most likely the wolf. Several Indian cultures were known to place victims inside a leather bag, allowing the material to slowly contract and squeeze the life from the body. Often the skull was crushed when this method was employed.

While science still ponders the full significance of the werewolf cult of Kentucky and the Ohio Valley, the find substantiates, in part, a number of tribal legends previously thought to be baseless, in which terrible stories of men who became wolves are told.

Sometimes when the moon is full, those legends say, strange forms stalk the deep woods of the Ohio Valley and sharp, piercing howls reach toward the sky. These may only be legends, of course, but they are worth considering from time to time—especially during those confident hours when we are certain that we know everything there is to know.

# RECIPES TO FEED HUNGRY GHOSTS

Because early humankind so feared the evil spirits that caused death and believed that these entities continued to dwell in the corpse of their beloved, awaiting new victims, it is not surprising that cremation, the burning of the body, became one of the earliest methods of disposing of the dead. Cremation appears to have been practiced widely in the ancient world, except in Egypt, in China, and among the Hebrews.

In ancient Greece only suicides, infants who had not yet grown teeth, and persons who had been struck by lightning were denied the privilege of cremation and were buried. When cremation was conducted, the ceremonies were elaborate and solemn and the ashes of the deceased were placed in urns of burned clay and buried. Later, when burial became the custom in Greece, the bodies were enclosed in elaborate stone caskets, similar to the Roman sarcophagi.

In the Danish colony of Greenland, the Vikings who settled on its shores believed that there was danger of pollution from the evil spirits that lurked around the corpse until the smell of death had passed away. They burned the dead body almost before it became cold and tried to avoid inhaling any of the fumes from the fire. They also burned every object in the dead person's house.

The Zulu tribe of Africa always burns the property of the dead to prevent evil spirits from remaining in the person's home. Many Native American tribes followed the same custom of burning the possessions of the deceased, and it is not uncommon to hear of contemporary men and women who, after the funeral of a relative, superstitiously burn the individual's clothes and other belongings.

Buddhists, Hindus, and Sikhs employ cremation as a standard method of disposing of the dead. In India the body is cremated on a funeral pyre whenever possible, and in ancient times widows were sacrificed alive on the burning pyres with their husbands.

## Early Efforts to Preserve the Dead

As early religions began to teach that there was a spirit within each person that might someday wish to return to its earthly abode, it became increasingly important that efforts be made to preserve the body. Burial ceremonies, which had at first been intended solely as a means of disposing of the dead, came to be a method of preserving the physical body as a home for the spirit when it returned for a time of rebirth or judgment.

Embalming the body of the deceased was practiced in ancient Egypt where the warm, dry climate assured its success. The Egyptians anointed, embalmed, and buried their dead, and made mummies of the men and women of power, rank, and importance.

> *To mummify, the Egyptians extracted the brain and the intestines, cleaned out the body through an incision in the side, and filled the body cavities with spices.*

To mummify, the Egyptians extracted the brain and the intestines, cleaned out the body through an incision in the side, and filled the body cavities with spices. The body was then sewn up and set aside to lie in salt for a period of 70 days. Then it was placed in gummed mummy cloth and fastened into its ornamental case. The poorer classes were not mummified but merely salted.

In Africa, many native people smoke their corpses to preserve them. In the Congo, tribes build fires above the graves of the dead and keep the fires burning for a month. After that period, the bodies are unearthed, smoked, and wound in great swaths of cloth. The smoked corpse is placed upright in the hut where the person died and remains there for years.

## The Evolution of the Coffin

The coffin has taken many shapes and forms in its evolution as a final resting place for the deceased. Many authorities attribute the presence of trees in the churchyard or cemetery to ancient notions concerning a hollowed out tree as a dwelling place for the spirits of the dead. In Babylonia, great boxes of clay were baked to form a kind of coffin in which the dead were buried.

The first actual coffins, as we know them today, probably originated in ancient Egypt where the people believed that the body of the deceased must be kept safe until a future time of resurrection. The Egyptian word for "coffin" is from *Kas* which means "to bury." Another form of the word became *Kast*, indicating the receptacle into which the body is placed, the coffin.

In the Hindu faith, the deceased are given a ceremonial washing, then the body is wrapped in a burial cloth and placed in a coffin. If at all possible, within one day of death, the coffin is to be carried to a place of cremation by six male relatives. The coffin is placed on a stack of wood and covered with flowers. Melted butter is poured over the coffin to help it to burn, and the eldest son or nearest male relative of the deceased lights the funeral pyre.

Traditionally, the cremation takes place outdoors and the ashes are collected and scattered in the waters of a holy river, such as the Ganges. In other countries, Hindu dead are taken to a crematorium. Followers of the Hindu religion believe that the soul, the *Atman* of each individual is reborn many times in a cycle of spiritual evolution before it can become one with God.

Those who follow the path of Judaism bury their dead in a plain coffin after the body has been washed and dressed. If possible, the funeral takes place on the day after the death has occurred. The coffin containing the deceased is taken first to the synagogue and then to the place of burial.

At the grave site, the rabbi says a few words of remembrance about the deceased, and the coffin is placed in the grave. The closest male relative of the deceased says a prayer called the *Kaddish* to help the soul travel to the *Olam Ha'ba*, the world to come, and the family of the dead person fills in the grave with earth.

Muslims prefer not to use coffins for their dead unless they are residing in a country that requires such containment for the deceased. If it is possible to do so, the dead are buried on the day following their death. The deceased is washed, perfumed, and wrapped in three cotton burial cloths.

Those who follow the religion of Islam believe that the soul of the deceased is guarded by the angel of death in a place called *Barzakh* until the Day of Judgment. If at all possible, friends and relatives gather around a dying person and read verses from the Qur'an. With his or her last breath, the dying person always tries to say the *Shahadah*: "There is no God but Allah, and Muhammad is his messenger."

Large graves and headstones are not permitted to mark a Muslim burial site, but the grave itself is to be raised above ground level. As the body is being taken to the burial ground, the *Salatul Janazah*, a prayer for the deceased is read. The body is buried facing Mecca, the sacred city toward which all Muslims turn when they pray.

### Honoring the Dead through Funerals

For those Buddhists who believe in reincarnation funerals are happy occasions. Death in the present life frees the soul from Dukkha (worldly existence) and returns it to the path that leads to Nirvana, where all misery and karma cease. The coffin of one who has died in the Buddhist belief system is taken to the funeral hall in a brightly decorated carriage. The coffin is carried three times around the Buddhist temple or funeral hall and then brought inside, where it is set down in the midst of the flowers and gifts which friends and family of the deceased have placed around it.

A Buddhist monk leads the people in a prayer known as the Three Jewels that helps the soul find refuge in the Buddha, the Dharma (the true way of life that a devout Buddhist seeks to lead), and the Sangha (the unified faith of the Buddhist monks). Together with the people in the funeral hall, the monk recites the Five Precepts, the rules by which Buddhist strive to live.

Throughout the ceremony, food is served and music is played. There are few tears of mourning, for the family and friends are reminded by the monk that the soul will be reborn many times in many bodies. After the service, the body is cremated, and the ashes are buried or kept in the temple in a small urn.

The followers of Tao envision the soul of the deceased crossing a bridge to the next life. Ten courts of judgment await the new soul, and if it passes this series of trials, it may continue on the path to heaven. If it fails because of bad deeds during the person's lifetime, the soul must be punished before it is allowed to go to a better place.

The family and friends of the deceased place the body in a wooden coffin and carry it to the graveyard. They pound drums, clang cymbals, and shoot off fireworks to frighten away any evils spirits that might attempt to catch the soul even before it reaches the 10 courts of judgment. Beside the grave as the coffin is being lowered into the ground, paper representations of houses, money, and other material objects are burned, symbolically providing the soul of the deceased with property which to pay the judges who await the spirit in the afterlife.

After 10 years have passed, the coffin is dug up, and the remains are cleaned and placed in an urn, which is then sealed. A Taoist priest assesses the home of the person's immediate family and decides the most harmonious spot for the urn of bones to be placed. It is of utmost importance that the priest find a place where the spirit of the deceased will be happy among its surviving family members, or the spirit may return to punish those it deems disrespectful of its physical remains.

### August: The Month of the Hungry Ghost

*Lisa Lee Harp Waugh relates the following:*

The Ghost Festival is a traditional Chinese festival and holiday, which is celebrated by Chinese in many countries. In the Chinese calendar (a lunisolar calendar), the Ghost Festival is on the fifteenth night of the seventh lunar month.

In Chinese tradition, the thirteenth day of the seventh month in the lunar calendar is called Ghost Day, and the seventh month in general is regarded as the Ghost

Month, in which ghosts and spirits, including those of the deceased ancestors, come out from the lower realm. During the Qingming Festival the living descendants pay homage to their ancestors and on Ghost Day, the deceased visit the living.

On the thirteenth day the three realms of Heaven, Hell, and the realm of the living are open, and both Taoists and Buddhists perform rituals to transmute and absolve the sufferings of the deceased. Intrinsic to the Ghost Month is ancestor worship, where traditional filial piety of descendants extends to their ancestors even after their deaths. Activities during the month would include preparing ritualistic food offerings, burning incense, and burning joss paper, a papier-mâché form of material items such as clothes, gold and other fine goods for the visiting spirits of the ancestors. Elaborate meals would be served with empty seats for each of the deceased in the family. The deceased were treated as if they are still living.

Ancestor worship is what distinguishes Qingming Festival from Ghost Festival because the former includes paying respects to all deceased, including the same and younger generations, while the latter only includes older generations. Other festivities may include burying and releasing miniature paper boats and lanterns on water, which signifies giving directions to the lost ghosts and spirits of the ancestors and other deities.

In Chinese tradition, the thirteenth day of the seventh month in the lunar calendar is called Ghost Day, and the seventh month in general is regarded as the Ghost Month, in which ghosts and spirits, including those of the deceased ancestors, come out from the lower realm (*art by Ricardo Pustanio*).

The Ghost Festival shares some similarities with the predominantly Mexican observance of El Día de los Muertos. Due to its theme of ghosts and spirits, the festival is sometimes also known as the Chinese Halloween, though many have debated the difference between the two.

## Taboos during the Month of the Hungry Ghosts

Those who fervently believe in the taboos that many bad things may happen to people during the most cursed month of the year do their utmost not to give birth during this month—nor to renovate their homes, take trips, go swimming, buy real estate or get a haircut.

Never look into a mirror during August between the hours of 8:00 P.M. to 8:00 A.M. Do not wear borrowed clothes or those items that belonged to the deceased in any way. Tradition says that if you do so, angry spirits will come and claim you (**art by Ricardo Pustanio**).

Never look into a mirror this month of the year during the hours of 8:00 PM to 8:00 AM. Do not wear borrowed clothes or those items that belonged to the deceased in any way. Tradition says that if you do so, the angry spirits will come and claim you.

Avoid looking into water upon which the moon reflects its light. If you see the moon's reflection during this month, your firstborn child will be struck down.

## Buddhists Emphasize the Joy of Feeding the Ghosts

To Buddhists, the seventh lunar month is a month of joy. This is because the fifteenth day of the seventh month is often known as the Buddha's joyful day and the day of rejoicing for monks. The origins of the Buddha's joyful day can be found in various scriptures. When the Buddha was alive, his disciples meditated in the forests of India during the rainy season of summer. Three months later, on the fifteen day of the seventh month, they would emerge from the forests to celebrate the completion of their meditation and report their progress to the Buddha.

In the *Ullambana Sutra*, the Buddha instructs his disciple Maudgalyayana on how to obtain liberation for his mother, who had been reborn into a lower realm, by making food offerings to the sangha on the fifteenth day of the seventh month. Because the number of monks who attained enlightenment during that period was high, the Buddha was very pleased.

The Buddhist origins of the festival can be traced back to a story that originally came from India, but later took on culturally Chinese overtones. In the *Ullambana Sutra*, there is a descriptive account of a Buddhist monk named Mahamaudgalyayana, originally a Brahmin youth who was later ordained, and became one of the Buddha's chief disciples. Mahamaudgalyayana was also known for having clairvoyant powers, an uncommon trait amongst monks.

After he attained arhatship (one who has attained the goal of nirvana), he began to think deeply of his parents, and wondered what happened to them. He used his clairvoyance to see where they were reborn and found his father in the heavenly realms (i.e., the realm of the gods). However, his mother had been reborn in a lower realm, known as the Realm of Hungry Ghosts. His mother took on the form of a hungry ghost—so called because it could not eat due to its highly thin and fragile throat yet it was always hungry because it had a fat belly. His mother had been greedy with the money he left her. He had instructed her to kindly host any Buddhist monks that ever came her way, but instead she withheld her kindness and her money. It was for this reason she was reborn in the realm of hungry ghosts.

Mahamaudgalyayana eased his mother's suffering by receiving the instructions of feeding pretas from the Buddha. The Buddha instructed Mahamaudgalyayana to place pieces of food on a clean plate, reciting a mantra seven times, snap his fingers then tip the food on clean ground. By doing so, the preta's hunger was relieved and through these merits, his mother was reborn as a dog under the care of a noble family.

Mahamaudgalyayana also sought the Buddha's advice to help his mother gain a human birth. The Buddha established a day after the traditional summer retreat (the fifteenth day of the seventh month in the lunar calendar, usually mid-to-late August) on which Mahamaudgalyayana was to offer food and robes to 500 bhikkhus (monks). Through the merits created, Mahamaudgalyayana's mother finally gained a human birth.

Due to Confucian influences, the offering became directed toward ancestors rather than the Sangha and ancestor worship has replaced the simple ritual of relieving the hunger of pretas. However, most Buddhist temples still continue the ancient practice of donating to the Sangha as well as performing rituals for the hungry ghosts.

Chinese Buddhists often state that there is a difference between Ullambana festival and the traditional Chinese Zhongyuan Jie, usually saying people have mixed superstitions (such as burning joss paper items) and delusional thoughts, rather than believing that Ullambana is actually a time of happiness.

## O-Bon, The Japanese Ghost Festival

O-bon, or simply Bon, is the Japanese version of the Ghost Festival. It has been transformed over time into a family reunion holiday during which people from the big cities return to their hometowns and visit and clean their ancestors' graves.

Traditionally including a dance festival, O-bon has existed in Japan for more than 500 years. It is held from July 13 to 16 ("Welcoming Obon" and "Farewell Obon," respectively) in the eastern part of Japan (Kanto), and in August in the western part (Kansai). The festival offers the opportunity for pardoning guilty ghosts that are homeless and not taken care of by benevolent beings. People worship ghosts and liberate animals, such as birds or fish.

Influenced by Buddhism, this holiday is also the Vu Lan festival, the Vietnamese transliteration for Ullambana. The festival is also considered Mother's Day. People with living mothers would be thankful, while people with dead mothers would pray for their souls. In the city of New Orleans, the Vietnamese population has also incorporated this into its Hoodoo-Voodoo traditions.

## Ghost Festival in Malaysia: Beware the Red Chairs

Ghost Festival in Malaysia has its own characteristics, and it has been modernized by concert-like live performances by groups of singers, dancers and entertainers, known as *Koh-tai* by the Hokkien-speaking peoples. The performances take place on a temporary stage setup within the residential district. Several empty red seats are reserved just for the dead. Spectators are warned not to sit in these chairs for they will be cursed and haunted for life.

## Hungry Ghost Month Recipes in New Orleans

Always prepare a special table in your house to seat the dead. Feed them specially prepared dishes of red beans and rice each Monday of the month. The Recipe for Ghost Month Red Beans and rice differs from the norm.

The quintessential New Orleans dish for the dead:

- 4 1/3 cups water, divided
- 1 1/2 cups brown basmati rice
- 1/2 teaspoon salt
- 1 tablespoon extra-virgin olive oil
- 1 cup diced onion
- 2 teaspoons minced garlic
- 2 15-ounce cans red kidney beans or pink beans, rinsed
- 6 ounces sliced Canadian bacon, chopped
- 1/2 cup chopped celery plus 1 tablespoon finely chopped celery leaves
- 1/2 cup diced green bell pepper
- 1/4-1 teaspoon ground chipotle pepper (see Note) or cayenne pepper
- 1 cup of red wine
- A real Catholic blessed rosary cross or crucifix

### Cooking Instructions

1. Combine cross, and 3 1/3 cups water, rice and salt in a large saucepan. Bring to a simmer; reduce heat to low, cover and cook until all the water has been absorbed, about 45 minutes.

2. About 10 minutes before the rice is ready, heat oil in a large skillet over medium-high heat. Add onion and garlic and cook, stirring, until the onion is lightly colored and tender, about three minutes.

3. Place 1 cup beans in a small bowl and mash with a fork. Add the mashed and whole beans, the remaining cup water, Canadian bacon, celery, celery leaves, bell pepper and ground chipotle (or cayenne) to the pan. Simmer, stirring occasionally, until the liquid has thickened into a gravy and the vegetables are crisp-tender, about six minutes. Serve in shallow bowls, spooned over the rice.

*Note:* Chipotle peppers are dried, smoked jalapeno peppers. They are often used to add heat and a smoky flavor to foods. Ground chipotle can be found in the specialty spice section of most supermarkets.

*Caution:* This is not to be eaten by the living. This is only for the dead. Tradition says that if you eat this dish, you, too, will leave for the other world when the ghosts leave at the end of the month. The dish should then be brought in a new pot to the cemetery on September first and left at your family's graves.

# EATING HUMAN FLESH AS A RELIGIOUS EXPERIENCE

*Because of the enormous popularity of the current cinematic zombie mythos that the undead rise from their graves to cannibalize the living, real zombies are believed to be blood-hungry creatures who seek only to devour the flesh of their victims. As we have clarified throughout this book, the real zombies are not cannibals, but mindless human automatons, who are slaves to their masters and suffer a miserable existence under a Voodoo practitioner's control. Although real zombies are not cannibalistic, all too often real humans are.*

### The Body He Dug from the Grave Was "Very Tasty"

When Sumanto, an Indonesian farmer in rural Central Java, was about to be released from prison in July 2009, he promised his neighbors in his home village that he was no longer going to be eating people. His cannibal days were over, he assured them. He was now going to eat only spinach and vitamins. His old neighbors rejected his request to come home. The memories of Sumanto digging up an old lady and eating her was far too fresh in their minds.

In his room at a Muslim mental rehabilitation center, Sumanto said that he loved meat and that the corpse of the elderly woman that he had dug out of her grave was very tasty. Even though eating the deceased made for inexpensive meals, Sumanto argued, he would restrain himself from ever again stealing another body to put into his stew pot.

Neighbors in the village rejected Sumanto's plea for understanding. A woman who had been his next-door neighbor had had the unpleasant experience of investigating a terrible smell coming from Sumanto's house. She said that she would never forget the stench of death and the sight of a Sumanto eating from a bowl of whitish-yellow human flesh dripping with soy sauce.

## Sexual Confusion Caused Him to Make a Meal Out of His Former Lover

In April 2008, Anthony Morley, 36, a handsome chef from Leeds who had won the Mr. Gay UK title in 1993, killed Damian Oldfield, 33, a former lover, then carved flesh from his body and made a meal of it. Morley, it could be argued, was sexually confused, for at the time that he won the Mr. Gay UK title he also had a steady girlfriend. There seems nothing at all to indicate why he suddenly became a murderer and a cannibal.

On the day of the murder, Morley and Oldfield went to the chef's apartment where they had sex, then cuddled in bed to watch the film *Brokeback Mountain*, a 2005 film about two men who find they are attracted to each other.

Suddenly, it seemed, without any provocation, Morley slashed Oldfield's throat and stabbed him several times. When his sometime lover was dead, Morley sliced sections of his thigh and chest and set about making a meal of the cuts. Police, investigating a complaint from neighboring apartments, found six pieces of human flesh on a chopping board, cooked so they were raw in the middle and browned on the edges. Some olive oil and seeds were found on the kitchen's work surface and a frying pan was waiting on the stove. Morley was chewing a piece of flesh when the police apprehended him.

Morley told the Leeds Crown Court in October 2008 that he had no memory of killing Damian Oldfield. His barrister argued not guilty on the grounds of diminished capacity. It took the jury two hours and 20 minutes to find Anthony Morley guilty of murder.

Such cannibals as Anthony Morley, who was found guilty of a solitary slaying, are hardly worthy of mention when compared to Fritz Haarman (1879–1925). The famous Hanover Vampire bit and slashed his victims to death, then ate their flesh. What he didn't eat himself, Haarman sold as fresh meat in his butcher shop.

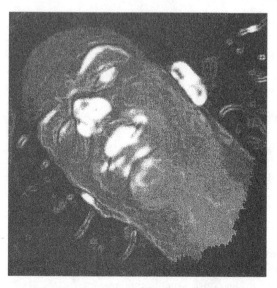

**After entering Jeffrey Dahmer's home, police found nine severed heads (*art by Ricardo Pustanio*).**

Jeffrey Dahmer (1960–1994) killed, dismembered, butchered and ate portions of at least 18 of his human victims. When police entered his apartment, they discovered nine severed heads—seven in various stages of being boiled—two kept fresh in the refrigerator—four male torsos stuffed into a barrel, and several assorted sections of male genitalia stored in a pot. At his trial, Dahmer described how he cooked the biceps of one of his victims and seasoned it with salt and pepper and steak sauce.

## The Bloody Revenge of Liver-eating Johnson

John Garrison had flaming red hair and beard, stood over six feet tall, and weighed a solid 240 pounds. Born near Little York, New Jersey, around 1824, Garrison joined the Union Army. After he struck an officer, he deserted, changed his name to John Johnson, and decided that he was better suited to life as a mountain man out in the West where there was little or no law officers to interfere with a man's life.

In 1847, Johnson married Swan, a girl from the Flathead tribe, and took her with him to his cabin on the Little Snake River in northwestern Colorado. After making certain that Swan was comfortable and had plenty of food and firewood, Johnson left for his winter trapping grounds with his .30 caliber Hawken rifle, his tomahawk, knife, and back pack. He was unaware that Swan was pregnant with his child.

When he returned as soon as the spring thaws permitted, he was horrified to see vultures circling over his cabin. Inside he found the bones of Swan scattered by birds and animals. Beside her lay the skull of an unborn baby. The markings on a feather lying among the skeletal remains told him that the murderers had been members of the Crow tribe. At that same moment of recognition and rage, Johnson vowed a vendetta to the death—a personal feud that according to the legends of the mountains would take the lives of 300 Crow braves.

Whenever he triumphed over a Crow warrior, he would slash open the fallen brave's chest with his knife, rip out the warm liver from within, and eat it raw. Thus the mountain man earned the sobriquet of "Liver-Eating Johnson."

The rugged lad from New Jersey had peeled away centuries of civilization and allowed the unbridled lycanthrope within his psyche to assume control. Such savagery inspired great terror among the Crow tribe, for it seemed as though they were dealing with a wild beast, something much more terrible than a mere man.

Once, it is said, Johnson was captured by a group of Blackfeet who saw a chance to sell him to the Crow and receive a rich reward. Bound with leather thongs and placed under guard in a teepee, Johnson managed to gnaw through the straps, disarm one of his captors and amputate one of his legs. Fleeing into the deep snows and freezing cold of winter, it required superhuman strength and endurance to survive. But he had food in the form of the Blackfoot brave's leg to sustain him until he reached the cabin of a fellow trapper.

During all the years of Johnson's one-man war against the Crow, they never once managed to catch him unaware. Johnson finally made peace with the Crow, and in 1864, he joined the Union Army and served in Company H, Second Colorado Cavalry. During the 1880s, he was appointed deputy sheriff in Coulson, Montana. He built a home outside of Red Lodge, Montana, and lived to a ripe old age, passing away in a Los Angeles veterans' hospital in 1899.

In 1972, Robert Redford starred as Johnson in *Jeremiah Johnson*, a beautifully filmed tribute to the mountain man. While the plot of the movie was built on the feud between Johnson and the Crow, the motion picture chose not to portray the liver-eating part of his revenge, perhaps deciding that a lot of shooting and tomahawk chopping was blood enough.

Some historians theorize that Johnson only cut out the livers of his victims and pretended to eat them to increase the horror that would spread among the Crow that a madman was stalking them. Others suggest that he may have done it once or twice early on in his revenge killings. To eat the liver of a victim is a symbolic act of revenge and an ancient act of assuming the strength and prowess of one's victims.

And then there are those students of the Old West who maintain that Liver-Eating Johnson cannibalized every one of his victims to avenge the murder of his wife and unborn child.

*Although the Aztecs were well-known for their ritual cannibalism, only the Karankawa tribe of southeast Texas was accused of practicing ritual cannibalism on their defeated enemies. None of the other 1,200 Native American tribes engaged in the eating of human flesh—ritual or otherwise. Of course, as happens on occasion in contemporary times, there may have been times when groups of individuals were stranded in snow storms or other situations of enforced isolation when cannibalism was prompted by necessity. Other than such extraordinary situations, cannibalism was not a culturally approved practiced by any tribe and those who were caught in such a perversity were put to death. The Mohawk tribe was called the "man-eaters," but contemporary tribal leaders insist that was due to their ferocity as warriors, not their dietary preference.*

## Our Species Has a Long History of Cannibalism

Although it may seem difficult and stomach-churning for us to acknowledge, our species has a long history of becoming cannibals for purpose of seeking revenge, staving off hunger, or worshipping a god. Even more difficult to swallow (pun intended) is the growing evidence that humans and Neanderthals may have considered one another as viable food sources.

In both human and Neanderthal cave dwellings, a large number of the bones of the cousin species have been found with tell-tale signs of scraping, gnawing, and cutting. Some scholars have argued that throughout the Proto-Neolithic and Neolithic periods of time, rather than an occasional act of consuming human flesh being the exception when game was scarce, all of our predecessors practiced cannibalism. At the Honne caves in Germany, Emil Carthaus and Dr. Bruno Bernhard discovered 1,891 signs of cannibalism.

Cannibalism was recorded in ancient Egypt (1073–1064 B.C.E.) during eight years of famine when the Nile failed to flood the delta.

There are many reports of cannibalism during the Great Famine of 1315 to 1317, which swept nearly all of Europe.

During periods of isolation from their larger units and facing starvation, there are historical records of soldiers on both sides of a war having to resort to cannibalism—from the Crusades to the Civil War, from World War II to the Korean War.

## *Blood Sacrifice for an Angry God*

**B**lood sacrifice, whether of humans or animals, is the oldest and most universal propitiatory act of the pious seeking favor from a benevolent or a wrathful god. An ancient Hittite cylinder seal from the Second Millennium B.C.E. depicts a human sacrifice in intricate detail.

The Abrahamic God strictly prohibited his followers from imitating their neighbors in the offering of human sacrifices (Lev. 20:25; Deut. 18:10). The one God placed a high value on human life and forbade this practice (Lev. 20:2–5; Jer. 32:35).

The Old Testament book of Leviticus acknowledges (17:14) that blood is "the life of all flesh, the blood of it is the life thereof," but the children of Israel are instructed that they "shall not eat of the blood of no manner of flesh; for the life of all flesh is the blood thereof: whosoever eateth it shall be cut off."

Again, in Deuteronomy (12:20–24), the Lord warns, "… thou mayest eat flesh, whatsoever thy soul lusteth after.… Only be sure that thou eat not the blood: for the blood is the life; and thou mayest not eat the life with the flesh."

While the Hebrew God on the one hand repeatedly emphasized that He, as Spirit, did not need or require food and that the true gift that He required was that of man's love, commitment, and service, the Laws of Moses did require the blood of animals and the sacrifice of grain to God. These sacrifices were conducted for three basic reasons: Consecration, to dedicate oneself; Expiation, to cover one's sin or guilt; Propitiation, to satisfy Divine anger.

Consecration sacrifices were vegetable or grain offerings, but they could not be brought to God unless they had been preceded by an expiatory offering of a blood sac-

Bloody sacrifices of animals or even humans to appease a god or gods has a long history in human civilization (*iStock*).

rifice. There was no consecration or commitment to God apart from expiation. According to the law, man could not approach God and be right with Him without the shedding of blood—that of a bull, a lamb, an ox, and so forth. The sacrifice itself could only be carried out by a High Priest under the strictest obedience to the law. The High Priest himself had to be consecrated before entering the innermost part of the temple or Holy of Holies where the sacrifice was offered to God.

## Cannibalism in the Old Testament

Sam Vaknin, Ph.D., has pointed out that while human sacrifice is denounced numerous times in the Old Testament, the eating of human flesh goes virtually unmentioned. "The major monotheistic religious are curiously mute when it comes to cannibalism," noted Dr. Vaknin.

Cannibalism is mentioned several times in the Old Testament, but in all fairness it must be pointed out that a number of the passages are said to be prophetic predictions of what may come to pass unless the children of Israel obey the Lord. Some contemporary theologians believe the curse upon the Jews made by Moses in Deuteronomy 28:53–57 foresees the Roman Siege of Jerusalem in 70 C.E.. Others believe that the passages indicate the siege against the people of Judah when King Nebuchadnezzar of Babylonia conquered them in 586 B.C.E.:

> Because of the suffering that your enemy will inflict upon you during the siege, you will eat the fruit of the womb, the flesh of the sons and daughters the Lord your God has given you. Even the most gentle and sensitive man among you will have no compassion on his own brother or the wife he loves or his surviving children, and he will not give to one of them any of the flesh of his children that he is eating. It will be all he has left because of the suffering your enemy will inflict upon you during the siege of all your cities. The most gentle and sensitive woman among you will begrudge the husband she loves and her own son or daughter the afterbirth from her womb and the children she bears. For she intends to eat them secretly during the siege and in the distress that your enemy will inflict upon you in your cities.

Other famous passages occur in 2 Kings 6:26–30 when the massive Syrian army has attacked Samaria and continued the attack "until there was nothing to eat."

One day as the king of Israel was walking along the top of the city wall, a woman shouted at him: "Please, your Majesty, help me!"

"Let the Lord help you!" the king said. "Do you think I have any grain or wine to give you … What's the matter?"

The woman answered: "Another woman and I were so hungry that we agreed to eat our sons. She said if we ate my son one day, we could eat hers the next day. So yesterday we cooked my son and ate him. But today when I went to her house to eat her son, she had hidden him."

The king tore off his clothes in sorrow, and since he was on top of the city wall, the people saw that he was wearing sackcloth underneath.

In Ezekiel 7–10, the Lord has become so angry with the people of Jerusalem, that he instructs Ezekiel to present them with the following warning:

"Now all the nations will watch as I turn against you and punish you for your sins. Your punishment will be more horrible than anything that I have ever done or ever will do again. Parents will be so desperate for food that they will eat their own children and children will eat their parents. Those who survive this horror will be scattered in every direction."

### *Flesh Eating as Religious Ritual*

When it comes to the religious or ritual aspects of eating human flesh, some readers will be certain to think of the words of Jesus during the Last Supper before his crucifixion:

Unless you eat the flesh of the Son of Man and drink his blood, you have no life in you. Whoever eats my flesh and drinks my blood has eternal life, and I will raise him up at the last day. For my flesh is real food and my blood is real drink. Whoever eats my flesh and drinks my blood remains in me, and I in him. (John 6: 53–56)

While many devout Christians interpret the words of Jesus as symbolical and regard their participation in the Eucharist as an act of spiritual restoration, such scholars as Dr. Vaknin argue that Holy Communion is nothing more than "an act of undisguised cannibalism."

The *Catholic Encyclopedia* states firmly that the act of Transubstantiation converts the bread and the wine into the actual body and blood of Christ.

Canon II warns that those who deny the "wonderful and singular conversion of the whole substance of the bread into the Body and of the whole substance of the wine into the Blood" should be declared anathema (cursed and consigned to damnation).

Canon VIII emphasizes that anyone who suggests that the Eucharist is a spiritual, rather than a physical act, a sacrament only, shall be anathema.

Most Protestant Christians consider the Lord's Supper to be a holy sacrament, but they do not insist that their congregants believe that they are partaking of the actual body and blood of Christ. However one wishes to interpret the words spoken by Jesus establishing the Eucharist, it must be acknowledged, state some students of religion, that one of Christianity's most important rituals does have its roots in cannibalistic sacrifice.

"Far from being a Christian invention, the ritual of the Eucharist has been practice for millennia by various cults and sects around the globe," states Acharya S in her essay, "Is Cannibalism a Religious Experience?" Thousands of years before the Christian faith was established, Acharya S writes, "An actual human being, acting as proxy for the deity worshipped, was sacrificed and eaten by the cult's followers."

Although a good number of contemporary Christians have studied enough anthropology to concede that ancient peoples often ate the body of their deceased leaders to gain their strength, power, and wisdom, it seems appropriate to state that in the Christian cosmology, the surrender of Jesus to submit to the will of the Father and to accept the ignoble death of crucifixion as the Lamb of God was to serve as the final sacrifice and was forever to put the issue of blood sacrifice to rest.

And we can only hope that this chapter puts to rest the cinematic contention that cannibalistic zombies are driven only by the unholy impulse to eat our brains and our flesh. Some Voodoo groups do require blood sacrifice of a small animal—usually a chicken. None of the practitioners requires the consumption of human flesh.

# HITLER'S QUEST TO ZOMBIFY THE WORLD

*Paranormal investigator Paul Dale Roberts has indicated that he met a zombie up-close-and-very-personal when he was working undercover narcotics with CID (Criminal Investigation Division)—DST (Drug Suppression Team) in Bremerhaven, Germany.*

*According to Roberts:*

In 1974 while serving in Germany, I was dating a lovely blonde Fraulein by the name of Gabriela. I met Gabriela at a discotheque that I was staking out. You might find this to be an odd story, or a story that is unbelievable. But what I will tell you is the truth.

Gabriela and I dated for some time. When we became intimate, I noticed a large circular hole on the right side of her buttocks. It was as if someone had taken a spoon and dug out a hunk of her flesh. I asked her how this hole was created. Her story was horrifying: She had been a former zombie—a former sexual servant zombie.

She told me that she had been vacationing with her girlfriend in Munich and that they befriended two Middle-Eastern boys. They decided to go out dancing with these boys. It was a fun night of disco music, throbbing lights, and drinking.

At some point of time, they both blacked out, and when they both awoke, they were in a strange bedroom with strange men looking at them. Eventually, they discovered that they were in the Middle East. Every day and every night they were given hallucinogenics. Men were having sexual liaisons with both of them and there was nothing they could do to stop it.

At some point in time, Gabriela tried to escape and that is when a chunk of her flesh was cut out as punishment. It was only during this one incident that she felt as if she was somewhat in control of her mind. Otherwise, during her full stay there, she had no will of her own. She felt like her mind was under the constant control of her captives.

Paranormal investigator Paul Dale Roberts says that he met a zombie up-close-and-very-personal when he was working undercover narcotics with CID (Criminal Investigation Division)—DST (Drug Suppression Team) Bremerhaven, Germany, In 1974 (*photo by Shannon McCabe*).

She gave herself willingly to the strange men that visited her bedside. She tells me that she was a zombie.

It would appear that her captives controlled her mind and her body. She was truly a zombie slave. She was given drugs to make her a willing participant during her enslavement.

Gabriela told me that it was her father, a former Nazi officer, who was able to hire a small mercenary team to rescue her and bring her back home safely.

## Did Hitler Create a Zombie Army to Serve the Third Reich?

Paul Dale Roberts' bizarre story reminded me of a number of strange accounts that I heard as a boy from G.I.s who had served on the European front and had participated in the final vicious days of fighting during World War II as the Allies pushed toward Berlin. Later, I heard similar stories when I went to college: old war stories passed along from uncles, brothers, fathers, and cousins to wide-eyed youngsters. Although I was nine at the closing days of the war, I can clearly remember stories of the desperate struggle of the Wehrmacht to defend the last stronghold of their Führer in his underground bunker. I also have clear memories of the newsreels of the Allied victory that we cheered in our little small town theater.

Often I heard eerie stories about both veteran German soldiers and members of the Hitler Youth who were hit by machine gun or rifle fire who just kept marching toward the overwhelming tide of Allied soldiers. Some said that the men had been so indoctrinated by the Nazi propaganda of the majestic Third Reich that would dawn under Hitler's leadership that they sustained bullet after bullet ripping through them, ignoring the pain to reach their own special Valhalla.

Some who were there said that not only were the German soldiers marching to their death as if they were zombies, some G.I.s swore that the men—especially those in the S.S. and the Hitler Youth—were zombies. Some of the charging troops, it was said, revealed faces that had been half-blown away in earlier conflicts. Some of the zombie-like troops had a number of old unclosed or unhealed bullet wounds that had left gaping wounds before they were finally struck down for the final count.

While some of their buddies laughed at the wild war stories and stated that the Nazi troops were fanatics and bore terrible wounds to fight on for their Fuhrer, others would insist that Hitler's scientists had begun to produce an army of zombies.

One veteran of such an encounter told me that when he searched for a fallen German's identification papers, he was repelled by the stench of death. "People were dying all around us," he said, "but some of these SS guys smelled like they had been dead for days and decomposition was setting in."

### The Quest to Create Frankenstein Monsters

Although zombies are considered more indigenous to Africa, Haiti, and New Orleans, the most famous of all reanimated creatures brought back from the silence of the grave is to be found in the novel *Frankenstein: The Modern Prometheus* (1818). In this well-known story the daring scientist Dr. Victor Frankenstein pieces together a monster made of human parts that he brings to life. In other words, he creates a zombie. The gruesome tale has inspired over 100 motion pictures, and the character of the lumbering undead monster has appeared in dozens more stage plays, television shows, and, today, video games.

Many fans of the motion pictures are surprised to learn that the author whose work has become one of the great classics of horror was a teenaged girl. Mary Wollstonecraft Godwin (1797–1851) was 16 when she met the poet Percy Bysshe Shelley (1792–1822), a devotee of her father, the political philosopher William Godwin (1756–1836). Mary ran off to Europe with Shelley in 1816, and they spent the summer with Lord George Gordon Byron (1788–1824) and his friend and personal physician Dr. John Polidori (1795–1821) in Geneva. To pass the time during a dreary summer, Lord Byron suggested that each of them should write a ghost story. The 18-year-old Mary was the only one of the four who actually fulfilled the assignment, publishing her novel two years after she married Shelley in December 1816.

While the novel has been hailed as a masterpiece and a work of genius, scholars have long debated the source of Mary Shelley's inspiration. What—or who—suggested the character of Dr. Victor Frankenstein, who became the prototype of the mad or obsessed scientist?

Many researchers argue that Dr. Polidori is the obvious source for the medical and scientific concepts that fired Mary's imagination. Mary wrote in her diaries that she and her sister, who had accompanied her when she and Shelley left England, found Polidori both attractive and interesting. He regaled the group with accounts of strange medical phenomena, such as experiments in reviving corpses. Polidori also wrote a horror novel that summer, *The Vampyre* (1819), that many scholars claim contains the seeds of inspiration for both *Frankenstein* and Bram Stoker's *Dracula* (1897).

In 2002, while researching the influence of science upon the poetry of Percy Shelley, Chris Goulding, a doctoral student at Newcastle University, found historical documents that indicated the model for Victor Frankenstein was Dr. James Lind (1736–1812), Shelley's scientific mentor at Eton in 1809–1810. Lind had become fascinated with the ability of electrical impulses to provoke muscle movement in the legs of dead frogs, and he was quite likely the first scientist in England to conduct galvanic experiments similar to those which enabled Dr. Frankenstein to focus electricity from lightning and bring his monster to life. Percy Shelley was greatly interested in science, and Goulding points out passages in Mary Shelley's unfinished biography of her husband wherein she commented that Percy often spoke of the great intellectual debt that he owed to Dr. Lind.

## Nazi Experiments to Resurrect the Dead

Such experiments in reviving the dead through the use of electrical stimulation was not lost upon Nazi scientists. We do know that the doctors in the various concentration camps were under orders from the Fuhrer to conduct experiments on reviving the dead and to learn anything about the human body that could aid the German people in becoming superior examples of the species.

In Auschwitz, experiments were conducted on prisoners to see how long it would take to lower the body temperature until death came. Next, several methods were employed to see if it were possible to bring the victims back to life. Such tests were deemed important because of the German troops suffering the terrible cold of the Eastern front in the invasion of Russia.

Other prisoners, selected largely from groups of Jews or Gypsies, were submerged in water and timed to determine how long a person could survive under such conditions. This was deemed an important experiment that could aid Nazi aviators shot down over oceans, rivers, and lakes and keep them alive after ditching. Experienced aviators were becoming scarce as the war progressed, and every effort must be made to keep them afloat and alive in the water.

Dr. Josef Mengele, the infamous Angel of Death, conducted his horrible experiments primarily to learn if the Master Race could be improved genetically. For example, blue eye color was preferred, so he sought a means of altering eye color by injecting various dyes. Unfortunately, such procedures resulted only in painful infections and blindness in his test subjects.

Mengele also infected healthy individuals with numerous viruses to see how long they might live untreated. Cruelly, he removed prisoners' limbs without anesthesia to see how long they would survive unattended.

Mengele often selected his victims by deciding that they possessed "satanic bloodlines." Many hapless individuals for his experiments were selected because they came from orphanages, foster care homes, or incestuous families and were pronounced as "expendable," meaning, if any of them should die during the experiments, they would not be likely to be missed. They were fulfilling their destiny as the chosen ones, those who had been selected to give their lives so the Third Reich could achieve perfection. This cold-hearted dismissal of "accidents" which resulted from the consequences of harsh experiments is said to have been coined by Mengele at Auschwitz.

All of these cruel and sadistic experiments were conducted in order to help keep the Nazi soldier healthy and strong. Even such single-minded madmen as Hitler and his inner circle did not want to lose any more fine examples of the Master Race than necessary. Early on in their master plan for world dominance, the hierarchy of the Third Reich had decided that it would be far less risky to find some means of enslaving the minds of those opposed to their politics and their treacherous invasions rather than having to endanger members of the stalwart German youth by fighting bloody wars.

Doctors in various Nazi concentration camps were under orders from the Fuhrer to conduct experiments on reviving the dead and to learn anything about the human body that could aid the German people in becoming superior examples of the species (*art by Ricardo Pustanio*).

## Hitler's Dream of Creating a Master Race Worthy of the Ancient Ones

It is seldom understood today that Nazism had as much to do with the dark side of the occult as it did with politics and the conquering of other nations.

In 1871, occultist Edward Bulwer-Lytton wrote *The Coming Race*, a novel about a small group of German mystics who had discovered a race of supermen living within the Earth's interior. The super race had built a paradise based on The Vril Force, a form of energy so powerful that the older beings had outlawed its use as a potential weapon. The Vril was derived from the Black Sun, a large ball of "Prima Materia" that provided light and radiation to the inhabitants of the inner Earth.

In 1919, Karl Haushofer founded the Brothers of the Light Society in Berlin, and soon changed its name to the Vril Society. As Haushofer's Vril grew in prominence, it united three major occult societies, the Lords of the Black Stone, the Black Knights of the Thule Society, and the Black Sun and chose the swastika, the hooked cross, as its symbol of the worship of the Black Sun. As with many secret groups, there appears to have been more than one order—those who followed the Golden Sun and those

who followed the Black Sun. The Black Sun, like the Swastika, is a very ancient symbol. While the Swastika represents the eternal fountain of creation, the Black Sun is even older, suggesting the very void of creation itself. The symbol on the Nazi flag is the Thule *Sonnenrad* (Sun Wheel), not a reversed good luck Swastika. The Black Sun can be seen in many ancient Babylonian and Assyrian places of worship.

These societies placed special emphasis on the innate mystical powers of the Aryan race. The Vril and its fellow societies maintained that the Germanic/Nordic/Teutonic people were of Aryan origin, and that Christianity had destroyed the power of the Teutonic civilization.

The secret societies formed in Germany wanted desperately to prove themselves worthy of the superhumans that lived beneath the surface of the planet, and they wished to be able to control the incredibly powerful Vril force. This ancient force had been known among the alchemists and magicians as the Chi, the Odic force, the Orgone, the Astral Light, and they were well aware of its transformative powers to create supermen of ordinary mortals.

The Vril Lodge believed that those who learned control of the Vril would become masters of themselves, those around them, and the world itself, if they should so choose. Such members of the Lodge as Adolf Hitler, Heinrich Himmler, Hermann Goring, Dr. Theodor Morell (Hitler's personal

**The German culture relates in many ways to the Norse and their heroic ideals of superhumans such as the Valkyries. Hitler was clearly influenced by this notion in his quest to create a Master Race (art by Dan "Wolfman" Allen).**

physician), and other top Nazi leaders, became obsessed with preparing German youth to become a Master Race so the Lords of the Inner Earth would find them worthy above all others when they emerged to evaluate the people of Earth's nations.

In 1921, Maria Orsic (Orsitch), a medium in the society, now renamed the Vril Gesellschaft, began claiming spirit messages originating from Aryan aliens on Alpha Tauri in the Aldeberan star system. Orsic and another medium named Sigrun, learned that the aliens spoke of two classes of people on their world—the Aryan, or master race, and a subservient planetary race that had evolved through mutation and climate changes. A half billion years ago, the Aryans, also known as the Elohim or Elder Race, began to colonize our solar system. On Earth, the Aryans were identified as the Sumerians until they elected to carve out an empire for themselves in the hollow of the planet.

In April, 1942, Nazi Germany sent out an expedition composed of a number of its most visionary scientists to seek a military vantage point in the hollow earth. Although the expedition of leading scientists left at a time when the Third Reich was putting maximum effort in their drive against the Allies, Goering, Himmler, and Hitler are said to have enthusiastically endorsed the project. Steeped in the more esoteric teachings of metaphysics, the Führer had long been convinced that Earth was concave and that a master race lived on the inside of the planet.

The Nazi scientists who left for the island of Rugen had complete confidence in the validity of their quest. In their minds, such a coup as discovering the opening to the Inner World would not only provide them with a military advantage, but it would go a long way in convincing the Masters who lived there that the German people truly deserved to mix their blood with them in the creation of a hybrid master race to occupy the surface world, truly a New World Order.

## Hitler's Plan to Turn All Europeans into Zombies

In the early 1930s, certain of Hitler's scientists learned of some experiments with fluoride that had been conducted in England in which infinitesimal doses of fluoride in drinking water would in time reduce an individual's power to resist domination. Since the dosages would be small, the victims would unknowingly be slowly poisoned and a certain area of the brain would be narcotized, thereby making the victims submissive to the will of those who wish to govern them. The Nazi masterminds envisioned worldwide domination through mass medication of drinking water supplies.

The first of the Nazi's secret zombie-making potions was demonstrated by mixing fluoride in the drinking water in Nazi prison camps in order to subdue the more unruly inmates into calm submission. Repeated experiments indicated that the addition of fluoride appeared to produce excellent results in calming the most troublesome of the prisoners.

Nazi scientists confidently projected that their early experiments enabled them to predict that entire cities could be made submissive to the Hitler gospel. Rebellious regions could be made passive and be commanded to enter work programs as if they were zombies. And, as a marvelous bonus, entire regiments of soldiers could become a zombie army, never questioning their officers, never resisting any order, never complaining about lack of comfortable living conditions.

Sodium fluoride is a hazardous waste by-product of the manufacturing process of aluminum. The fluoride contamination of the environment comes from the following things: coal combustion, cigarette smoke, pesticides such as cockroach and rat poison, animal feeds, fertilizer, plastics, nonstick cookware, soft drinks, juices and other drinks (both canned and bottled), and unfathomably, in an astounding number of pharmaceutical products, including anesthetics, vitamins, antidepressants, hypnotics, psychiatric drugs, and of course, military nerve gas.

A prominent German chemist who worked in the massive I.G. Farben chemical company testified after the war that when the Nazis under Hitler decided to go into Poland, the German General Staff planned to accomplish mass control through the process of water medication.

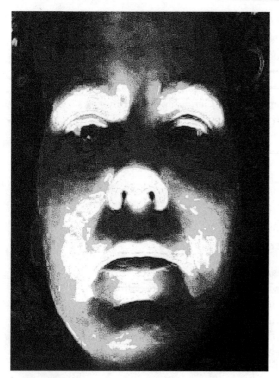

The first of the Nazi's secret zombie-making potions was demonstrated by mixing fluoride in the drinking water in prison camps in order to subdue the more unruly inmates into calm submission. Repeated experiments indicated that the addition of fluoride appeared to produce excellent results in calming the most troublesome of the prisoners (*art by Ricardo Pustanio*).

German scientists boldly declared that any person who drank artificially fluorinated water for a period of one year or more would never again be the same person mentally or physically. Large numbers of German soldiers had fluoride introduced into their daily supply of drinking water. It is quite possible that the slavish devotion that so many Nazi troops had to their Fuhrer was due to the submissiveness induced by fluoride.

After fluoride had been used on the German people for a number of years, researchers, scientists, doctors, neurosurgeons and other professionals began to notice during autopsies a rise in the presence of the chemical within the human brain. Since fluoride was known to have effects on the right temporal lobe, hippocampus and the pineal gland, some of the professionals began to ask similar questions: Was the fanatical rise in the worship of the Fuhrer due to the fluoride placed in the water? Had a combination of the chemical and the Fuhrer's fiery speeches that emphasized the German people being the true Master Race begun to take great effect on large numbers of the mass public? Had he truly achieved his goal of submissive, compliant, zombies with no true will of their own?

One cannot resist pointing out that in 1945 fluoride was introduced into the public water supply and drinking water of select cities across the United States. Eventually, most cities across North America followed suit, believing it was the healthy thing to do. The "wonder-working" benefits of fluoride were taught to dentists and dental/hygienists and to children in elementary school health classes. Soon, families across the United States spent extra money and time making dental appointments for their children and themselves, in an effort to have strong, healthy and hopefully, cavity-free teeth. As early as 1954, some doctors have suspected and reported fluoride to be harmful. Dr. George L. Waldbott, M.D., observed that his fluoridation patients became forgetful, drowsy, lethargic, and incoherent. Comparable cases of "impaired cognition and memory" have been reported to the government by many other dental professionals. Government reports themselves indicate similar findings of "impaired cognition and memory." Contrary to popular belief, fluoride has never been approved by the FDA for ingestion, only for topical use.

Mixing fluoride with drinking water remains controversial. On December 18, 2009, Graham Demeny, who had served 15 years at the Glenmore Water Treatment Plant in Rockhampton, Queensland, Australia, resigned his position because he questioned the safety of adding flouride to the city's water supply. Graham told reporter

Allan Reinikkaar that until that time all processes adopted by the city council had made the water clean or safe to consume. "Flouride addition does neither," he said, "and questionably compromises the safety aspect."

## Seeking a Failproof Method of Loosening Tongues

After their success with fluoride, the Nazi scientists wanted to discover some kind of drug that could achieve effective interrogations. They had already experimented with barbiturates, peyote, marijuana, and hypnosis in an effort to find something that really worked immediately to loosen tongues.

On May 2, 1938, Dr. Albert Hoffman of the Sandoz Research Laboratories in Basle, Switzerland, first synthesized Lyserg-Saeure-Diaethylamid (LSD). On April 19, 1943, five years after synthesizing the drug, Hoffman accidentally inhaled a minute quantity while working with other ergot derivatives, and experienced a kind of pleasant feeling of inebriation, which consisted of hallucinations that lasted for several hours. Lysergic acid is found naturally in ergot, a fungus that grows on rye and other grains, and throughout history it has been used in various medications. Some researchers have even attributed ingestion of ergot to hallucinations which in the Middle Ages may have caused people to believe that they could fly through the air like witches or transform themselves into werewolves.

LSD was found to create such primary effects as the following:

1. A feeling of being one with the universe

2. Recognition of two identities

3. A change in the usual concept of self

4. New perceptions of space and time

5. Heightened sensory perceptions

6. A feeling that one has been touched by a profound understanding of religion or philosophy

7. A gamut of rapidly changing emotions

8. Increased sensitivity for the feelings of others

9. Psychotic changes, such as illusions, hallucinations, paranoid delusions, severe anxiety

The concentration camp at Dachau was less than 200 miles from Hoffman's laboratory, where scientists experimented with mescaline as a truth serum under the demanding eyes of the Gestapo and the SS. After the war, Walter Neff testified that the secret police wanted use of a drug that could erode the will of the person being interrogated. The experiments, conducted at Dachau by Dr. Kurt Plotner were not deemed satisfactory because mescaline basically brought out the paranoia and fears already seething within by the prisoners who were selected as subjects. Instead of revealing information the Gestapo could use, the prisoners confessed to childhood pranks and screamed in terror at their hallucinations.

Experiments with LSD were even more unsuccessful. When a group of German soldiers' drinking water was spiked with the chemical without their knowledge, the troops were sent on a march to investigate suspicious activity in a forested area. They did not emerge as the fearless fighting men that Hitler envisioned for his unconquerable army. Some men began to giggle; others collapsed in fear of their terrifying hallucinations; and others began to climb trees, wanting to fly as if they were birds.

The Nazi scientists concluded that such drugs as mescaline from the peyote cactus, the so-called "magic mushrooms," and LSD were "psychedelic." They caused people to hallucinate, to see and hear things that were not really there. The hallucinogenic might be useful in causing chaos if added in large amounts to a city's drinking water, but otherwise such drugs were useless in creating fearless, zombie armies.

## Were Nazi Mind Control Methods Used to Transform Sirhan Sirhan into a Killer Zombie?

The smoke from the fires of World War II still hung heavily in the air over a destroyed Berlin and shattered Third Reich to nightmares whose would horrify for decades to come, when many German doctors who were masters of mind control were snatched by the Office of Strategic Services (OSS), laterthe CIA, to work on a number of insidious projects. Hitler's Chief of Intelligence against the Russians, General Reinhard Gehlen, arrived in Washington in 1945 and spent months working with William "Wild Bill" Donovan, Director of the OSS and Allen Dulles to reorganize the American intelligence program into the Central Intelligence Group in 1946, then, in 1947, the Central Intelligence Agency led by Dulles. General Gehlen shared the behavior modification research of Dr. Josef Mengele at Auschwitz and the brain-washing experiments conducted at Dachau with hypnosis and mescaline.

While serious medical researchers in the late 1940s and early 1950s focused on psychedelics for purposes of learning more about the human brain, relieving pain, finding antidotes to drug overdoses, and other medical applications, the Central Intelligence Agency could not care less about those high-minded purposes. One of their most sought-after projects was to create "sleeper assassins," in the style of a "Manchurian Candidate," an assassin who has been programmed to kill upon receiving a key word or phrase while in a post-hypnotic trance.

Drawing upon their own background with occult secret societies, the Nazi doctors conducted a satanic ritual while they were programming a subject to become an assassin. The goal of the ritual was to attach a demon or a group of demons to the entranced subject. The skeptic might say that the programmers were compartmentalizing the subject's mind into multiple personalities to reinforce the command to kill. In either event, the programmed assassin would believe that he was possessed by demon or by a spirit who was guiding him and ordering him to kill.

Moments after he had fired the last of eight bullets from a .22 revolver and Senator Robert F. Kennedy lay dying at his feet, Sirhan Sirhan appeared to be in a state of tranquility. The enormity of the deed seemed to fail to penetrate his consciousness.

Author George Plimpton was one of those people in the Ambassador kitchen on the night of June 5, 1968, struggling to disarm Sirhan. Plimpton recalled, as did so many other witnesses to the shooting, that Sirhan had "enormously peaceful eyes" (William Klaber and Philip H. Melanson, *Shadow Play: The Murder of Robert F. Kennedy, the Trial of Sirhan Sirhan, and the Failure of American Justice*). Others wondered if the assassin had been hypnotized or drugged.

After his arraignment at the police station, Sirhan calmly asked his jailers to bring him a copy of Madame Helena Blavatsky's *Secret Doctrine*.

Soon enough, the authorities learned that the murderer was Sirhan Bishara Sirhan, an Arab Christian, who was born in Jerusalem on March 19, 1944. Before the Sirhan family immigrated first to New York, then California in 1956, the 12-year-old boy had already seen a great deal of bloodshed and witnessed bodies torn about by bombs in the guerilla war between Israel and Palestine.

**Did Sirhan Sirhan knowingly kill presidential candidate Robert Kennedy in 1968, or was he the victim of a zombification plot? (*Library of Congress*)**

As an Arab Christian, Sirhan found no appeal in Islamic militancy, but he was devastated when one of his heroes, Gamal Abdal Nasser, and the armies of Egypt were so easily defeated by Israel in the war that began on June 5, 1967 and ended on June 10.

It is at this time that Sirhan found solace in the occult. He managed to get a part-time job at a Pasadena occult bookstore and while there read all the books on self-hypnotism, astral projection, and mind control that were on the musty shelves. In May 1968, he joined the Rosicrucians, an occult order that claims to be connected to the ancient priests of Egypt and the mystical society formed by Christian Rosencreutz in Germany, circa 1460.

Strangely enough, Sirhan began to write in his journal that he wanted to kill Robert F. Kennedy and that his death had become an obsession with him. Apparently, his motive was to assassinate RFK before he could become president and send bombers and other assistance to Israel.

Sirhan's defense team, all of whom took the case *pro bono*, was headed by Grant Cooper and Russell Parsons. Emile Zola Berman was added the day before trial began, because Cooper felt having a Jew join the team might deflect some of the political overtones. Sirhan was not pleased with his attorneys pleading a defense of "diminished mental capacity."

When Sirhan took the stand, he told the courtroom how much he had loved President John Kennedy. Furthermore, he said that he had absolutely no memory of killing JFK's brother, Robert, but he remembered that he had been angry with the younger Kennedy for breaking his promise to give the Arabs back their home in Israel. Questioned repeatedly, Sirhan denied ever wanting to kill Robert Kennedy. He said that he did not recognize the journal that the prosecution claimed was his or remember writing about a plan to kill RFK. As the prosecution continued its case, Sirhan conceded that he must have killed Robert Kennedy, but he had no knowledge of doing so.

A parade of psychiatrists pronounced Sirhan suffering from "paranoid psychosis," acting in a dissociated state of mind. Dr. Bernard Diamond testified that he had hypnotized Sirhan several times, and he concluded that Sirhan had likely hypnotized himself and created self-induced trances that led to the assassination. During Sirhan's Rosicrucian and self-hypnosis experiments, he had gradually been programming himself to kill RFK.

Norma Lee Browning of the *Chicago Tribune* learned that before Sirhan Sirhan's trial began, his defense team had considered arguing that he had been possessed by the spirit of an Arab terrorist. On April 17, 1969, Sirhan was found guilty of first-degree murder and sentenced to death in the gas chamber. In 1972, California abolished the death penalty, and Sirhan is now in California's Corcoran State Prison, where he still insists that he was but a dupe for mysterious individuals who hypnotized, drugged, and programmed him to kill the senator.

*Some conspiracy theorists have made much out of a brief conversation that Sirhan had with a ghostlike girl in a polka-dot dress shortly before he shot Kennedy....*

Some conspiracy theorists have made much out of a brief conversation that Sirhan had with a ghostlike girl in a polka-dot dress shortly before he shot Kennedy, suggesting that she may have served as a kind of physical stimulus mechanism that reinforced his orders to kill. Others have constructed elaborate plots involving several shooters in addition to Sirhan. And, then, of course, some theorists contend that organized crime was behind the assassination. As Senate Rackets Committee attorney, RFK had certainly infuriated plenty of Mob bosses. And then there are theories that Arab terrorists conditioned Sirhan to be their hit man in getting revenge against Kennedy for his indifference to the Palestinians' plight.

Or could the CIA have exploited Sirhan's fascination with the occult and incorporated mysticism with one of their mind-control experiments? Could Sirhan have been a victim of members of the occult societies of Nazi Germany and the early techniques of mind control developed by secret societies?

Overlooked in the horror of Senator Kennedy's death was a familiar ritualistic element. A few feet from where Senator Kennedy fell after being struck by the bullets from Sirhan's revolver was a large ice cabinet. Scrawled in crayon upon the front of the box was the inscription: *The Once and Future King*. Although the phrase was never publicly explained, such shibboleths have been used along with certain ritualistic symbols in other occult motivated murders. The words do not refer to King Arthur and his magical days at Camelot or JFK and his appropriation of Camelot to describe his modern court. Rather, the inscription heralds the handiwork of Satan, who, in the eyes of his minions both mortal and immortal, is the "once and future king" of Earth, the God worshipped by secret occult societies.

As Sirhan went through his Rosicrucian programming and worked at the occult bookstore, it would have been a simple matter for undercover agents to have contacted him, made friends with him, and invited him to participate in their metaphysical studies. Once Sirhan had attended a number of meetings and been conditioned to assassinate Kennedy, all memory of his having attended the meetings would be erased from his mind.

During satanic rituals employed with the process of hypnotic conditioning and the occasional use of LSD, Sirhan would have come to consider himself to be the slave of the programmer, who would have the status of "master" or "god." During his interrogation by the police, Sirhan mentioned the Illuminati three times and referred to "Master Kuthumi (Koot Hoomi)." Kuthumi was Madame Blavatsky's spirit teacher, but Sirhan's programmer may also have assumed this identity during the conditioning process.

Some investigators theorize that the key or "trigger" word for Sirhan may have been "port wine," since these words are scrawled numerous times in his journal along with the repetition, "RFK must be assassinated," written over and over until it fills the page. It was learned that Sirhan used candles and mirrors during his personal experiments with self-hypnosis.

On the fateful night of June 5, 1968, Sirhan would have crossed the lobby of the Ambassador Hotel, with its bright lights and mirrors, entered the kitchen, heard an agent, perhaps disguised as a waiter, shout, "Port wine!" and pulled the trigger of his .22 revolver eight times, assassinating Robert F. Kennedy precisely as planned.

# CIA EXPERIMENTS TO CREATE A ZOMBIE NATION

Many Nazi psychologists who were masters of mind control were smuggled out of Germany at the end of World War II by the Office of Strategic Services (OSS). Hitler's Chief of Intelligence against the Russians, General Reinhard Gehlen, arrived in Washington in 1945 and worked with William "Wild Bill" Donovan, Director of the OSS, and Allen Dulles to restructure the American intelligence program into the Central Intelligence Agency under Dulles's leadership.

Rumors and half-truths about new mind-control techniques being used by Soviet, Chinese, and North Korean interrogators on U.S. prisoners of war panicked the CIA into a search for its own method of sure-fire successful questioning of captives. In 1947, the U.S. Navy developed Project CHATTER in response to the Soviet's supposed success with "truth drugs." In 1950, Allen Dulles approved Project BLUEBIRD to discover mind-control methods; in 1951, BLUEBIRD was renamed ARTICHOKE and assigned the problem of utilizing hypnosis and drugs to resist interrogation. The CIA conducted hundreds of experiments with hypnosis, mescaline, peyote, and other hallucinogenic drugs, before they had some success with LSD.

A new program, MK-ULTRA, initiated on the order of CIA chief Allen Dulles on April 13, 1953 and conducted by Dr. Sidney Gottlieb, had mind control as its principal objective. The "MK" in MK-ULTRA stood for "Mind Kontrolle," a German spelling of the English word "control," because there were many Nazi doctors who were supposedly masters of mind control; they were recruited by the Office of Strategic Services (OSS; now the CIA), to work on a number of insidious projects in the United States.

At first, "acid" seemed to fill the bill. Dr. Gottlieb used himself as a frequent LSD guinea pig. In order to rush the studies of how effective LSD might be on a wide variety of individuals with vastly differing personalities, Dr. Gottlieb ordered experiments on mostly unsuspecting CIA agents, military personnel, prostitutes, mental patients, and members of the general public.

Further research by Dr. Gottlieb became quite sadistic. Perhaps his own use of the drug released his inner-sadist, for some of the experiments with LSD seem more like torture than scientific inquiry. On occasion, Dr. Gottlieb would lock volunteers in sensory deprivation chambers while they were on LSD. In one extreme case, volunteers were given LSD for 77 days straight. MK-ULTRA's records were destroyed, no document exists that reveals how many of these unfortunate individuals were driven insane.

## Testing LSD on Their Own Agents

CIA Director Richard Helms saw the potential in LSD to induce temporary insanity in target individuals, causing them to behave in a manner that would discredit them and any information that they might wish to disseminate. To be certain of the drug's effectiveness, Dr. Sidney Gottlieb ordered agents to test LSD on themselves and surreptitiously slip the drug into each other's drinks (*photo by Caitlyn Yankee from "Judd the Zombie"*).

In the 1950s and '60s, with LSD being hailed by some individuals as "mind-expanding" and by others as a recreational drug that could be exploited for fast "trips" to "far-out" places, the CIA now possessed a chemical that was more effective than hypnosis, marijuana, peyote, or other drugs. But it was not so much as a drug of interrogation as it was humiliation.

In their *Acid Dreams: The CIA, LSD, and the Sixties Rebellion*, Martin A. Lee and Bruce Shlain write that CIA Director Richard Helms saw in LSD the potential to induce temporary insanity in target individuals, causing them to behave in a manner that would discredit them and any information that they might wish to disseminate. To be certain of the drug's effectiveness, Dr. Sidney Gottlieb ordered agents to test LSD on themselves. According to Lee and Shlain, agents would surreptitiously slip the drug into each other's drinks. As soon as the target ingested the LSD, his colleague would inform him so he would take the rest of the day "to turn on, tune in, and drop out" (an expression made famous by Dr. Timothy Leary [1920–1996], an educator and outspoken proponent of the drug in the 1960s).

Frank Olson worked for the CIA at Fort Detrick, Maryland, studying the use of LSD to enhance interrogations. In the autumn of 1953, Olson went to Europe to observe the interrogation of former Nazis and Soviet citizens at a secret U.S. base. In late November, Olson joined a group of government officials at a conference at Deep Creek Lodge in western Maryland. It was here that someone slipped LSD into his drink.

Olson began acting strangely withdrawn and told his wife and son that he was going to quit his job. Early in the morning of November 29, Olson crashed through the window of his room at the Statler Hotel in New York and died on the street below.

## *Testing Hallucinogenics on an Unsuspecting U.S. Public*

Many of the early tests focused on drugs that might become "truth serums" and might be used for successful interrogations of prisoners and were performed with volunteers, very often military personnel, government agents, and CIA employees. When experiments with LSD seemed productive, Dr. Gottlieb exercised the *carte blanche* authority given to him by Dulles and began to experiment with the effects of LSD on unsuspecting individuals.

At first CIA agents would infiltrate large outdoor gatherings, such as ballgames and concerts in the park, and clandestinely spray private citizens with LSD in containers labeled as insect repellent. Later, agents would infiltrate private cocktail parties and spray the unsuspecting guests with LSD in containers marked as deodorant and perfume.

Curiosity about the drug's effectiveness as an aid in sexual entrapment in covert operations led to the development of Operation Midnight Climax, known officially as MK-ULTRA SUBPROJECT-3.

With the expressed mission of learning more about sexual behavior under LSD, Operation Midnight Climax set up a number of apartments to be used as rooms for sexual encounters. Prostitutes in the employ of the agency would solicit unsuspecting men and slip LSD in their drinks before returning with them to the apartments and having sex. Two-way mirrors allowed the researchers to observe the responses and reactions of the men while under the influence of the drug.

After a period of interpreting the one-on-one drug reactions of the prostitutes' clients, Midnight Climax established several brothels in Greenwich Village and San Francisco in order to study the drug-induced sexual behavior of a larger cross section of men. Two-way mirrors once again permitted the CIA researchers to film the prostitutes and their LSD-dosed clients for later interpretation.

## *Zombifying New York and San Francisco*

It was such effects as those listed above that convinced Major General William Creasy, chief officer of the Army Chemical Corps, that LSD and other psychoactive drugs

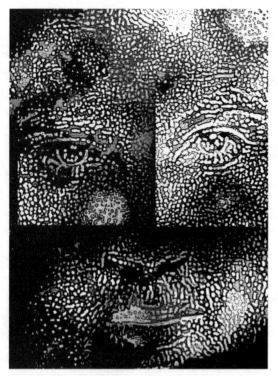

In 1957 operatives released a biological effects gas on the Golden Gate Bridge in San Francisco. The intent of the experiment was to blanket the entire city with the gas and then monitor how powerfully the disorienting properties of the substance would affect the population (*art by Ricardo Pustanio*).

would be the weapons of the future. If CIA agents or Special Forces units spiked a city's water supply with LSD, the enemies within would offer no resistance.

Among the assignments given to Dr. Sidney Gottlieb by CIA chief Allen Dulles was to create a method of producing large scale aberrant mental states on an unsuspecting population. A substance was sought that could be used by the U.S. military when engaging an enemy that they could spray over a city and render both civilians and military opponents relatively helpless and unable to resist. The substance should be able to "cause illogical thinking" or "produce shock and confusion over extended periods of time" or "produce physical disablement, such as paralysis of the legs" or "cause mental confusion." In essence, to create a population of zombies.

It would have been awkward at the time to experiment on foreign populations, so MK-ULTRA created Operation Big City in the United States. Agents modified a 1953 Mercury so its exhaust pipe extended 18 inches beyond its normal length. A gas concocted to cause hallucinations was then emitted through the automobile's exhaust as the agents drove the Mercury for 80 miles around New York City, making note of the effects on pedestrians.

In another test, operatives equipped with nasal filters boarded the New York subway with battery-powered emissions equipment fitted into suitcases to test the effect of LSD on people in confined areas.

An ambitious project was conducted in 1957 when operatives released a biological effects gas on the Golden Gate Bridge in San Francisco. The intent of the experiment was to blanket the entire city with the gas and then monitor how powerfully the disorienting properties of the substance would affect the population. The agents were dismayed when a sudden wind arose and blew the gas away before it could cause any harm.

It should also be noted that in an experiment to determine how susceptible an American city would be to biological attack, the U.S. Navy sprayed a cloud of bacteria from ships over San Francisco in 1950. Many residents become ill with pneumonia and other illnesses.

In 1951, the U.S. Department of Defense began open air tests over many U.S. cities, using disease-producing bacteria and viruses.

Senate hearings on Health and Scientific Research in 1977 confirmed that 239 populated areas in the United States had been contaminated with biological agents between 1949 and 1969. Some of the cities included San Francisco, Key West, Panama City, Minneapolis, and St. Louis.

## *The Nazis' "Angel of Death"*
## *Participates in Making Zombies in the U.S.*

The infamous Dr. Josef Mengele himself, under the assumed name of "Dr. Green," participated in the formulation of many MK-ULTRA programs. Dr. Mengele had come to be known as the "Angel of Death" when he had conducted his infamous experiments with hypnosis and mescaline on countless numbers of victims at the Auschwitz concentration camp. While Mengele's presence could not be acknowledged by the CIA, his unprecedented research on thousands of unwilling victims provided valuable data on mental programming, mind control, and many other areas of great interest to MK-ULTRA.

Dr. Green was known to work often with Dr. White, the pseudonym of Dr. Donald Ewen Cameron, the former head of the Canadian, American, and World Psychiatric Associations. A personal friend of CIA Director Allen Dulles, White/Cameron was given millions of dollars by MK-ULTRA to conduct a series of mind-control experiments and to serve as a resource for other subprojects of the secret program.

Dr. Cameron had begun his career in psychology assisting the Office of Special Services (OSS, the forerunner of the CIA) in interrogating Nazi prisoners during World War II. Dr. Cameron, a Canadian, became intrigued by the experiments conducted on concentration camp prisoners by German doctors, and he contracted to work for the OSS, then the CIA, in the field of behavior manipulation. He continued this specialty in Projects BLUEBIRD and ARTICHOKE, which became MK-ULTRA in 1953.

According to those who knew Dr. Cameron, he was a man driven by a need to understand the workings of human behavior and a obsession to find the methods to modify and control it. He conducted numerous experiments in sensory deprivation, sensory overload, and drug inducement. He also performed a great number of pre-frontal lobotomies and oversaw electro-convulsive shock treatments.

Dr. Cameron's favorite experiment seems to have been what he called "psychic driving," in which subjects were kept in drug-induced comas for weeks, then administered electroshocks through electronic helmets strapped to their heads. Many of the subjects were abused children who had been passed on to him through the Roman Catholic orphanage system.

Some of the behavior modifications achieved by Dr. Cameron seemed to tread into the world of the supernatural. When Cameron worked for MK-ULTRA, the secret group had 150 subprograms, ranging from biology, drugs, psychology, sexual activities, and even motion pictures. Many of the Hollywood films of the 1950s were influenced by MK-ULTRA operatives who suggested storylines about the threat of Communism, brainwashing, or invasion from monstrous aliens from outer space.

In 1957, when Dr. Cameron's experiments in effectively creating potential *Manchurian Candidate*-type assassins became known, he relocated his work to the

Allen Memorial Psychiatric Institute in Montreal, Canada, with the help of his friend, CIA Director Allen Dulles and the Canadian government. The Allen Institute soon became known as "the brain butchery," due to Dr. Cameron's excessively harsh experiments with electro-shock, LSD, bright lights, sounds, lobotomies, and drug-induced comas that sometimes lasted for months. Many of his experiments proved far too extreme for his "patients" and many of them died.

## Mind Control—Top Secret!

In 1957, CIA Inspector General Lyman Kirkpatrick issued an internal memo that cautioned operatives to use utmost secrecy to protect the operation not only from enemy intelligence, but also the American public. If the American people should learn that the CIA was engaging in activities that were unethical and illicit, such knowledge could become detrimental to the accomplishment of the agency's mission. People in large cities would surely have been outraged if they had learned that secret experiments were being conducted with them as unwilling, unknowing guinea pigs— experiments that could have turned victims into zombie-like individuals who could walk into traffic, drive into other cars, or fall off bridges.

When the CIA was denied their plan to send clouds of psychochemical weapons over major U.S. cities to test their effectiveness, they settled for making as much LSD as possible available to the youth counterculture. In the late 1960s, the growing use of psychedelics by the "hippies," and those who felt alienated from mainstream American society because of their anti-Vietnam war sentiments, contributed to a growing traffic in illegal distribution of the drugs on the street corners and dark alleys of cities throughout the United States.

## Project Monarch

Project MONARCH was officially begun by the U.S. Army in the early 1960s, and it is still classified as "Top Secret" for reasons of National Security. Some researchers are quite certain that MONARCH likely evolved from such MK-ULTRA subprojects as SPELLBINDER, established to create "Manchurian Candidate" assassins, and OFTEN, which explored black magic and the occult. Conspiracy researchers assert that the process of choosing the type of subjects to be used in the early MONARCH experiments was reminiscent of the rationale of Dr. Mengele, who often selected his victims by determining that they possessed "satanic bloodlines." Many hapless individuals for the MONARCH experiments had been selected because they came from orphanages, foster care homes, or incestuous families and were pronounced as "expendable"—meaning, if any of them should die during the experiments, they would not likely be missed. "They are fulfilling their destiny as the chosen ones." This cold-hearted dismissal of "accidents" which resulted from the consequences of harsh experiments is said to have been coined by Dr. Mengele at Auschwitz, and it was repeated often by the MONARCH personnel.

Researcher Ron Patton theorizes that "MONARCH" had nothing to do with royalty, but to the Monarch butterfly and "the feeling of light-headedness" as if one is "floating or fluttering like a butterfly" after undergoing the trauma induced by electroshock. One may also think of the common occult symbolism of the butterfly for the soul or the mind and an ancient belief that human souls become butterflies while they are between lives awaiting reincarnation.

Patton states that MONARCH was essentially about programming the mind, modifying human behavior, and placing its subjects into a "Marionette Syndrome." A marionette is a puppet whose actions are determined by a puppeteer pulling its strings, hence the analogy concerning the psychologist and the programmed subject. Conventional psychologists might use the term "conditioned stimulus response sequences," but the MONARCH experimenters called the process, "Imperial conditioning." MONARCH also diverged greatly from traditional psychological conditioning exercises by including Satanic rituals in order to enhance the trauma experienced by the subject. The programmer might choose to intensify the rituals by having the hypnotized or drugged subject "image" (envision) ancient archetypal symbols of mysticism and the occult, such as spiders, bats, snakes, masks, castles, mazes, demons, and monsters.

> *Patton states that Monarch was essentially about programming the mind, modifying human behavior, and placing its subjects into a "Marionette Syndrome."*

MONARCH programming had six levels:

- ALPHA: General conditioning designed to improve memory retention, visual acuity, and physical strength. Exercises were employed that would deliberately subdivide the subject's personality and emphasize left-brain/right-brain division.

- BETA: Sexual programming that would eliminate all moral values and remove all inhibitions.

- DELTA: Deadly force programming for special agents and elite forces of the military. Subjects were conditioned to have no fear and subliminal instructions were implanted to instruct the agent to commit suicide if captured.

- THETA: Psychic programming through various electronic mind-control systems, brain implants, and telemetry devices. The implants were used with highly advanced computers and satellite tracking systems.

- OMEGA: Also known as "Code Green," this level was a self-destruct programming that would cause the subject/agent to commit suicide if too much memory was being retrieved by interrogation.

• GAMMA: This level activates itself within a subject/agent when an opportunity arises wherein misinformation and deception may be disseminated to great advantage.

## Wiring the Brain to Kill

In April 1961, Dr. Gottlieb decided the animal experiments, which he had been conducting with electrode implants in their brains, were successful and that it was time to experiment with human brains. Information has leaked out concerning experiments with three Viet-Cong prisoners in July 1968.

A team of "behaviorists" flew into Saigon and traveled to the hospital at Bien Hoa where the prisoners were being confined. The agents from Subproject 94 set up their equipment in an enclosed compound, and the team's neurosurgeon and neurologist inserted miniscule electrodes into the brains of the three VC prisoners.

After a brief recovery period, the prisoners were armed with knives and direct electrical stimulation was applied to their brains. The goal of the experiment was to determine if individuals with such electrodes implanted in their brains could be incited to attack and to kill one another. Once again, the Agency was seeking a perfect sleeper assassin, a true "Manchurian Candidate," who could be electronically directed to kill a subject.

After a week of enduring electrical shocks to their brains, the prisoners still refused to attack one another. They were summarily executed and their bodies burned.

## Seeking the Perfect "Manchurian Candidate"

In 1964, a subproject MKSEARCH, began a refined search for the perfect truth serum. Based on some of the initial research of Dr. Donald Ewen Cameron and Dr. Sydney Gottlieb, the head of MK-ULTRA, the project required "expendables," subjects that might die during the course of the experiments, but whose disappearance was unlikely to arouse suspicion.

The experiments were carried out at CIA safe houses in such cities as Washington, New York, Chicago, and Los Angeles. The experiments focused on the exploitation of human weaknesses and the destabilization of the human personality. The subjects of the experiments would be exposed to tests designed to create disturbances of behavior, alterations of sex patterns, and stimulations of aberrations, which could all be used in the process of interrogations and obtaining information.

When Richard Helms became the Director of the Central Intelligence Agency on June 30, 1966, he began to push hard for more effective results in the mind-control projects. The few cautions regarding working with "expendables" were discarded. The researchers were informed that they would be receiving a steady arrival of Viet Cong captives on which to experiment. The prisoners of war were to be considered expendable, already listed as missing in action or killed in Vietnam.

The special mission of Operation Spellbinder was to create an effective sleeper killer, a "Manchurian Candidate," who would be assigned to assassinate political figures. The programmed assassin would be hypnotized, drugged, or conditioned through a combination of mind-control techniques to kill without being aware of his or her lethal programming. The assassin would be "triggered" into entering a trance state and committing the murder by a key word, phrase, or symbol. Once the target victim (in this case, Fidel Castro) had been assassinated, the programmed subject would have no memory of his or her role in the murder—and quite likely would be killed by Castro's bodyguards or arrested, convicted, and sentenced, unaware that he or she was programmed to kill by the mind manipulators of Operation Spellbinder.

The special mission of Operation Spellbinder was to create an effective sleeper killer, a "Manchurian Candidate," who would be assigned to assassinate political figures (*art by Ricardo Pustanio*).

A hypnotist was selected from among candidates from the American Society of Clinical and Experimental Hypnosis, an individual who expressed no qualms about being involved in experiments with subjects who might die during the series of drug, hypnosis, and behavior modification techniques.

After numerous unsuccessful attempts to program potential assassins—and no records of how many "expendables" were lost—Operation Spellbinder was halted and declared a complete failure. Or at least that is what they would like us to believe.

## Operation Resurrection—Apes First, Humans Next

In this secret project, implemented from 1965 to 1966, the CIA replicated the isolation chamber that had been constructed earlier by Dr. Donald Ewen Cameron, the "brain butcher," at the Allen Memorial Institute in Montreal and rebuilt it at the

National Institutes of Health. In Operation Resurrection, the experiments would not be with humans, but with apes.

The apes were first lobotomized, then placed in total isolation. After a time, the experimenters, adapting the radio telemetry techniques developed by Leonard Rubenstein, directed radio frequency into the brains of the apes. Those apes that appeared to receive the frequencies were decapitated and their heads transplanted to another ape's body to see if the radio frequency energy could bring them back to life—thus, Operation Resurrection. The apes that were not selected for possible resurrection from the dead were bombarded with radio waves until they collapsed and became unconscious. Autopsies yielded the information that the apes' brain tissue appeared to have been literally fried.

It is difficult to see how Operation Resurrection could possibly have produced information of any value to any study of behavior control, behavior modification, or mind control. Researchers will probably never know the rationale behind the belief that dead apes could be resurrected if you switched heads and bodies, though the experiment seems another step toward the creation of human zombies.

### The Unabomber—the Experiment that Failed

In 1957, a 37-year-old Ph.D. in psychology named Timothy Leary read an article by R. Gordon Wasson on entheogens in indigenous Mexican religious ceremonies and made the decision to travel to Mexico and experiment with psilocybin mushrooms. It was a decision that altered Leary's life and the lives of millions of others. Upon Leary's return to Harvard, he began the Harvard Psilocybin Project with Dr. Richard Alpert (who would later be known as Ram Das) and other colleagues. Leary went on to experiment with LSD, and he became convinced that properly administered dosages could alter behavior in many beneficial ways, including profound mystical and spiritual experiences.

Another of Leary's colleagues at Harvard who was soliciting volunteers among the students for experiments was Dr. Henry A. Murray, a psychiatrist, who had been a lieutenant colonel in World War II and had devised special tests that the Office of Strategic Services (OSS) used in selecting agents.

Among those students who volunteered for Dr. Murray's series of experiments was a brilliant young man named Theodore Kaczynski, who had entered Harvard when he was not quite 16. Kaczynski earned his Ph.D. by solving in less than a year a problem in mathematics that his professors had been unable to crack. Maxwell O. Reade, a mathematics professor who had served on Kaczynski's dissertation committee, speculated that there were probably only 10 to 12 people in the United States who could understand Kaczynski's specialty, a branch of complex analysis known as geometric function theory. Had he not volunteered for experiments in mind control at Harvard, he might not have become the infamous "Unabomber."

Dr. Henry A. Murray had become convinced that he had a special mission to transform individuals from their nationalistic indoctrination as National Man into World Man. Murray's famous system, used by the OSS to select agents who could withstand torture and interrogation, involved a test that in many trials left the applicants crying and broken.

The experiments in which Kaczynski participated were even more elaborate than the ones devised by Murray for the OSS in wartime. The subjects were bound to chairs, wired with electrodes and various monitoring devices, and subjected to total darkness, blinding lights, highly personal verbal attacks—and probably, unknowingly, doses of LSD.

The entire program was under the direction of Dr. Sydney Gottlieb, who was also the leader of the CIA's MK-ULTRA project in mind control.

After receiving his Ph.D. from the University of Michigan and being recognized as a gifted mathematician, Kaczynski obtained a position as assistant professor of mathematics at the University of California, Berkeley, in the fall of 1967. He had few friends among the faculty and his aloof and reserved manner caused students to give him poor ranking as a teacher. Unexpectedly, in 1969, Ted resigned without explanation.

In 1971, he moved to Great Falls, Montana, and began building a cabin near Lincoln, 80 miles southwest of Great Falls, on some land that he and his brother David had acquired. Like so many intellectuals before him, Kaczynski sought personal transformation in nature. He would be another Henry David Thoreau, living alone in his own version of Waldon Pond. In his solitude, he also had time to reflect upon the evils of contemporary society and how the Industrial Revolution had destroyed forever humankind's link with the rural lifestyle that had nurtured it for centuries. He also had plenty of time to consider Dr. Murray's fears about living in a nuclear age and surviving as World Man, rather than as National Man.

Kaczynski mailed the first bomb to Professor Buckley Crist at Northwestern University in May 1978. A campus police officer sustained minor injury when he opened the package.

The FBI became involved when the second bomb was found smoking in the cargo hold of a commercial airplane before it could explode. A faulty timing mechanism prevented the bomb from detonating, but investigators said that it contained enough explosives to have blown the plane to bits—along with its passengers and crew. FBI agents began a search for a disgruntled airline employee, but John Douglas, the father of the FBI's "profiling" of criminals, assessed the sophistication of the device as the work of a "disgruntled academic," rather than a airline mechanic seeking revenge against a former employer.

The third bomb caused the first serious injury. In 1985, a Berkeley graduate student, who had just been accepted for astronaut training, lost four fingers and vision in one eye because of the blast.

The first death resulted from the fourth bomb, which exploded in the parking lot of a California computer store in 1985, killing the owner with nail and splinter projectiles. In Salt Lake City, Utah, on February 20, 1987, a similar bomb detonated near a computer store, but no one was injured. Each of these bombs bore the inscription,

"FC," which investigators first interpreted as "F—k Computers," but which was later revealed to stand for "Freedom Club."

There were no more bombs until 1993, when Kaczynski mailed another potentially fatal package to David Gelernter, a computer science professor at Yale, who escaped injury. Later, in 1993, geneticist Charles Epstein was maimed by the bomb that he received.

Kaczynski wrote to the *New York Times*, claiming to be the leader of an anarchist group called the "Freedom Club," and accepting responsibility for the bombings. Within a few months, in 1994, an advertising executive was killed by a mail bomb, and a subsequent letter by Kaczynski justified the assassination by condemning the public relations field for manipulating people to obey the wills of the advertisers and to buy things that they didn't really need.

In 1995, shortly after the murder of Gilbert Murray, California Forestry Association president, the Unabomber demanded that newspapers print his 35,000-word manifesto, *Industrial Society and Its Future*. The Unabomber threatened to send more bombs unless his manifesto appeared in print. He promised to cease his campaign of terror if his philosophy could be made known to the general public.

In September 1995, the *New York Times* and the *Washington Post* published the Unabomber's thesis word for word as he had written it. The authorities encouraged the newspapers to present it as the Unabomber had written not only to appease him, but in the hopes that someone would recognize his writing style and phraseology.

Among Kaczynski's main points were the following:

- The Industrial Revolution and its technological legacy have proven to be a disaster for the human race.
- Modern technology is undesirable, and it should be halted so that people can return to a simpler, happier lifestyle living next to nature.
- A collapse of the technological society is inevitable at some future time, so it would be best to bring about a "social crash" as soon as possible before it can get any worse.
- There should be no illusions about creating an ideal society; the goal should be only to destroy the existing form of society.
- If revolutionaries do not destroy the present form of society, the future will see the common people surviving as "house pets" or slaves to an elite class of humans or to intelligent machines.

Kaczynski was arrested outside his remote Montana cabin on April 3, 1996. His younger brother David had recognized his writing style and notified the authorities. Ted managed to avoid the sentence of death by pleading guilty on January 22, 1998, and he was delivered to the Federal ADX supermax prison in Florence, Colorado to serve a life sentence without the possibility of parole.

When we reflect upon the brilliant, barely 16-year-old, shy and sensitive Harvard student who volunteered for mind-control experiments under the direction of Dr. Henry Murray and Dr. Sydney Gottlieb of the infamous MK-ULTRA, we can only wonder exactly what programming was directed toward Theodore Kaczynski and hundreds of others. We know today that Murray and Gottlieb conducted mind-control tests that flagrantly violated medical ethics. What we don't know, is how many other "Zombie Unabombers" might be triggered some day by an insidious posthypnotic suggestion that was planted in a student's psyche 45 or 50 years ago.

## Biochip Implants—Creating the Ultimate Zombie Nation

In the 1950s and '60s, a large number of experiments in behavior modification were conducted in the United States, and it is well known that electrical implants were inserted into the brains of animals and humans. Later, when new techniques in influencing brain functions became a priority to military and intelligence services, secret experiments were conducted with such unwilling guinea pigs as inmates of prisons, soldiers, mental patients, handicapped children, the elderly, and any group of people considered expendable.

Rauni-Leena Luukanen-Kilde, M.D., Former Chief Medical Officer of Finland, has stated that mysterious brain implants the size of one centimeter began showing up in X-rays in the 1980s. In a few years, implants were found the size of a grain of rice. Dr. Luukanen-Kilde stated that the implants were made of silicon, later of gallium arsenide. Today such implants are small enough that it is nearly impossible to detect or remove them. They can easily be inserted into the neck or back during surgical operations, with or without the consent of the subject.

> *Today ... implants are small enough so it is nearly impossible to detect or remove them. They can easily be inserted into the neck or back during surgical operations....*

It has been stated that within a few years all Americans will be forced to receive a programmable biochip implant somewhere in their body. The biochip is most likely to be implanted on the back of the right or the left hand so it will be easy to scan at stores. The biochip implant will also be used as a universal type of identification card. A number will be assigned at birth and will follow that person throughout life. Eventually, every newborn will be injected with a microchip, which will identify the person for the rest of his or her life.

Initially, people will be informed that the biochip will be used largely for purposes of identification. The reality is that the implant will be linked to a massive supercomputer system that will make it possible for government agencies to maintain a surveillance of all citizens by ground sensors and satellites. Today's microchips operate by means of low-frequency radio waves that target them. With the help of satellites, the implanted person can be followed anywhere. Their brain functions can be remotely monitored by supercomputers and even altered through the changing of frequencies. Even worse, say the alarmists, once the surveillance system is in place, the biochips will be implemented to transform every man, woman, and child into a controlled slave, for these devices will make it possible for outside intelligences to influence a person's brain cell conversations and to talk directly with the individual's brain neurons. Through cybernetic biochip brain implants, people can be forced to think and to act exactly as government intelligence agencies have preprogrammed them to think and behave.

The technology exists right now to create a New World Order served by the zombie-like masses. Secret government agencies could easily utilize covert neurological communication systems in order to subvert independent thinking and to control social and political activity.

The National Security Agency's (NSA) electronic surveillance system can simultaneously follow the unique bioelectrical resonance brain frequency of millions of people. NSA's Signals Intelligence group can remotely monitor information from human brains by decoding the evoked potentials (3.50 hertz, 5 milliwatts) emitted by the brain. Electromagnetic frequency (EMF) brain stimulation signals can be sent to the brains of specific individuals, causing the desired effects to be experienced by the target.

A U.S. Naval research laboratory, funded by intelligence agencies, has achieved the incredible breakthrough of uniting living brain cells with microchips. When such a chip is injected into a man's or a woman's brain, he or she instantly becomes a living vegetable and a subservient slave. And once this device is perfected, the biochip implant could easily be converted by the Defense Department into an army of killer zombies.

Experts have said that a micromillimeter microchip may be placed into the optical nerve of the eye and draw neuroimpulses from the brain which embody the experiences, smells, sights, and voice of the implanted subject. These neuroimpulses may be stored in a computer and may be projected back to the person's brain via the microchip to be re-experienced. A computer operator can send electromagnetic messages to the target's nervous system, thereby inducing hallucinations.

Beyond all science-fiction scenarios, we could become a nation of zombies.

# GOLEMS AND TULPAS— PSYCHIC ZOMBIES

The Golem is the Frankenstein monster of Jewish tradition—it is, in fact, in the eyes of many literary scholars, one of the principal inspirations for Mary Shelley's *Frankenstein: The Modern Prometheus*. The Golem, however, is not patched together from the body parts of cadavers robbed from their graves, but it is created from virgin soil and pure spring water. It is also summoned, more than created, by those who purify themselves spiritually and physically, rather than by heretical scientists in foreboding castle laboratories who bring down electricity from the sky to animate their patchwork human.

The word "golem" appears only once in the Bible (Psalms 139:16). In Hebrew the word means "shapeless mass." The Talmudic teachings define the Golem as an entity "unformed" or "imperfect." The Talmud states that for the first 12 hours after his creation, Adam himself was a Golem, a body without a soul.

According to certain traditions, the creation of a Golem may only be accomplished when one has attained one of the advanced stages of development for serious practitioners of Kabbalah and alchemy. The *Sefer Yezirah* (Book of Creation or Formation), a guide book of magic attributed to Rabbi Eliezar Rokeach in the tenth century, instructs those who would fashion a Golem to shape the collected soil into a figure resembling a man. Once the sculpting has been completed, the magicians were to use God's name, He who is the ultimate creator, to bring the Golem to life.

Other instructions in the ancient text advise the magician to dance around the creature fashioned of soil, reciting a combination of letters from the Hebrew alphabet and singing the secret name of God. Once the Golem has completed its assigned tasks or mission, it may be destroyed by walking or dancing around it in the opposite direction and reciting the letters and the words backwards.

The Kabbalah gives instruction that once the Golem had been formed, it was given life by the Kabbalist placing under its tongue a piece of paper with the Tetragrammaton (the four-letter name of God) written on it. Other traditions state that one

The Golem is not patched together from the body parts of cadavers robbed from their graves, but rather, it is formed from virgin soil and pure spring water. It is also summoned, more than created, by those who purify themselves spiritually and physically (*art by Bill Oliver*).

must write the Hebrew letters *aleph, mem, tav* on the forehead of the Golem. The letters represent *emet* (truth), and once the characters have been inscribed on the Golem's forehead, it comes alive. When it has completed the work assigned to him, the magician erases the *aleph*, leaving *mem* and *tav*, which is *met* (death).

In his modern adaptation of the ancient text, Rabbi Aryeh Kaplan stresses that the initiate should never attempt to make a Golem alone, but should always be accompanied by one or two learned colleagues. Extreme care must be taken by its creators, for the Golem can become a monster and wreak havoc. When such a mistake occurs, the divine name must somehow be removed from the creature's tongue and it will then be allowed to revert to dust.

The most famous Golem is "Yossele," the creature created by Judah Loew Ben Bezalel (1525–1609) to help protect the Jews of Prague from the libel that the blood of a Christian child was used during the Passover Seder. There are many accounts of how Yossele saved innocent Jews from reprisals directed against them by those citizens who had been incited by the anti-Semitic libel.

Once the Golem had served its purpose, the rabbi locked it in the attic of Prague's "Old-New Synagogue," where it is widely believed that the creature rests to this day. The synagogue survived the widespread destruction directed against Jewish places of worship by the Nazis, and it is said that the Gestapo did not even enter the attic. A statue of Yossele, the Golem of Prague, still stands at the entrance to the city's Jewish sector.

## The Tulpa—a Mental Zombie that Can Rebel

Among the secret lore of the Tibetan adepts is the claim that phantoms or Tulpas may be created by those who have attained high mental and spiritual ability; they are sent to accomplish tasks or missions assigned to them by their creators. Once the adept has endowed the Tulpa with enough vitality to assume the form of an actual physical being, it frees itself from its creator's psychic "womb" and leaves to complete its assignment.

According to certain Eastern metaphysicians, thoughts, emotions, and mental emanations add to the strength of the Tulpa, enabling it to accumulate power and grow. The Tulpa may manifest apparent solidarity and vigor, and Yogis claim that they may even carry on intelligent conversations with these creatures born of their own minds. The duration of a Tulpa's life and its vitality are in direct proportion to the tension and energy expended in its creation.

Sometimes, however, even the most accomplished of adepts and magicians confess that the phantom, the Tulpa, becomes rebellious and may conduct itself independently of its creator. On occasions, the Tulpa may become something of a zombie-like monster. And in certain instances, the highly developed Tibetan magicians have been forced to admit that they have unconsciously set loose a phantom zombie to wreak havoc on unsuspecting victims.

## Tulpas May Roam the Earth Undetected

I have often theorized that the Yoga concept of the Tulp—the thought form that can appear to assume life independent of the human psyche that "feeds" it with emotions and mental emanations—might be responsible for many of the mysterious sightings reported of everything from zombies to werewolves.

Could it be plausible that many of the strange monsters that have been sighted around the world have been created by those who spotted them? Each individual's essential self may have the ability to influence and to shape a reality separate from that of the ordinary and the commonly accepted. It may require little effort at all for the transcendent self to skip blithely over, around, or through space and time and to manifest their own brand of Tulpa.

And, regarding space and time, it is clear that we really have absolutely no final definition of the true nature of time or of how many dimensions of time and space truly exist.

On some occasions, a Tulpa—whether consciously or unconsciously manifested—may appear so lifelike that its creator is amazed to learn that the phantom has traveled to other countries and interacted with people who were completely unaware that they were conversing with a spirit being and not the real person whom it mimicked.

Certain individuals have told me that while undergoing surgery they have "traveled" to other lands and have lived there several days, months, or years in the linear time of their operation's 40 minutes. One earnest storyteller said that he had even met, courted, and married a woman in those few minutes of time and that after he had recovered from the surgery, he traveled to that foreign country and claimed his bride, who had patiently awaited his return. These accounts are difficult to document—but then there is the case of Mr. Gorique.

In the summer of 1955, Mr. Erkson Gorique, a successful businessman in his fifties, decided to realize a long-nurtured wish to visit Norway and investigate the possibilities of importing china and glassware. Gorique had traveled widely but had never been to Norway. Each summer for several years he had declared his intention of making the trip to the land of fjords and icy streams, but something had always interfered with his plans and the journey had never been accomplished.

In July he landed in Oslo, asked a taxi driver to recommend a hotel. Gorique knew absolutely no one in Norway, and he was determined to conduct his business in a totally unplanned and random manner. One can imagine his astonishment when the desk clerk greeted him by name and expressed his pleasure at seeing him again.

Gorique left that bewildering encounter to walk into another scene even more baffling. The wholesale dealer whom he had planned to see about arranging for the importation of glassware smiled, shook his hand warmly, and said: "How wonderful that you did return, Mr. Gorique. You were in such a hurry the last time that you were here that we were unable to conclude the final details of our business."

The thoroughly puzzled American slumped into an easy chair and weakly inquired just when he was supposed to have been in Norway.

The perplexed Norwegian glassware dealer provided Gorique with full details of his previous visit. It was only when he could prove that he had never before traveled to Norway that the glassware dealer told Gorique that his desire to visit that country must have sent his *Vardogr*, his spiritual forerunner, on ahead.

As long ago as 1917, Wiers Jensen, editor of the *Norwegian Journal of Psychical Research*, wrote a series of articles on the Vardogr: "The Vardogr reports are all alike," he stated. "With little variation, the same type of happening occurs: The possessor of a Vardogr *announces* his arrival. His steps are heard on the staircase. He is heard to unlock the outside door, kick off his overshoes, put his walking stick in place, etc. The listening 'percipients'—if they are not so accustomed to the prelude of the Vardogr that they remain sitting quietly—open the door and find the entry empty. The Vardogr has, as usual, played a trick on them. Eight or ten minutes later, the whole performance is repeated—but now the reality and the man arrive."

## An Experiment in Raising Consciousness
## Brought a Visitor from Another Dimension of Reality

*Whether Jay and Janice summoned a visitor from another dimension of time and space or someone's Tulpa, they were left with a mystery that may puzzle them for years to come.*

*Jay and his girlfriend Janice were both off from work. Janice was out on the deck hot-tubbing in the Jacuzzi; Jay was inside playing video games.*

*In Jay's own words:*

I grew bored, and for some reason I placed a plastic water cup on top of a plasma globe lamp that sat on top of a speaker. I let the cup sit there for a minute, then drank from it.

I thought the water seemed like it had a "charge" to it and I drank it again. The next time I drank it I could definitely feel the electricity in my body.

Intrigued, I started putting my right hand on the top of the globe and my left on the base of the lamp. When you touch these lamps it will "arc" to your hand, and I could feel the electricity entering my palm when I breathed in. I had been reading a book by Master Mantak Chia about "sucking" chi (vital energy, also *qi, gi, ki*) up your spine by focused breathing exercises, so I decided to try it.

I must say that while I am familiar with chi and other metaphysical topics, I had never had any kind of experience worth noting before. So I'm breathing, and I noticed I could definitely feel some kind of power at the base of my spine. It felt like I was sucking it from the globe into my hand, down my front, and into the base of my spine. I also noticed a kind of electrical line looking down from the top on the electrode that wavered according to my breathing. I experimented with this and found that with focus the line started traveling clockwise around the surface of the electrode, faster or slower depending on my breathing. I also noticed when I breathed in, the electrode wasn't shooting off lightning bolts *per se*, rather I was drawing it in. As I breathed, I could feel the power creep up my spine—but I had to hold it where it was through focus, otherwise it would drop back down.

After doing this for a while, I got it so that the electrical line was spinning really fast and the lightning arms from the electrode inside the lamp started resembling

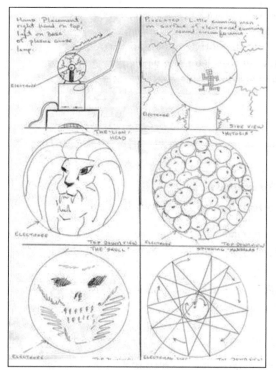

A drawing by the witness, who saw several images form within a lamp, including those of a man, lion, and an egg undergoing mitosis.

the spokes on a bicycle wheel spinning fast and the arms took on the shape of a mandala spinning. That's when the image of a little pixilated man appeared on the surface of the inner electrode, running around its circumference. Subsequent images were all monochrome green.

I was having a hard time believing this, so without telling Janice what I was looking at I called her in and asked her to take a look.

She got real quiet, and I could tell she saw it, too, but I had her tell me, "Yes, I see a little man running around."

I kept up the breathing and more images followed: a lion's head, what I think were eggs of some sort in mitosis; a Torus when I got the mandala to spin clockwise; and a skull when I got it to spin counterclockwise. As the energy got higher and higher up my spine, the mandala got more complex. Also as it got higher up my back, I felt lighter and lighter and my voice was getting higher.

I went for it, pulled it up to my skull, and it felt just like the accounts of Samadhi that I've read about. It felt like I knew everything and I was everywhere. I left my self behind and became one with the universe. Yeah, it sounds cheesy, but that's what it was like. It felt like some kind of electric fire inside of me.

Then I noticed the room losing its color and getting darker. At the same time, an interlaced reality was coming into view in an inverse proportion to the living room fading out. I didn't fully let the other reality come into play (it was still all shades of gray). There was something almost evil about it. It looked like some kind of stylized fairy-tale forest and there was some not so friendly type of creature watching me.

I slowed down the breathing, and my living room rematerialized. When I asked Janice later what she saw, she said it looked as if I were melting and she was genuinely scared that I might disappear. She also said she saw a black clawed hand reaching up to me from the floor. I didn't see the hand and I'm glad that I didn't.

It sounds like my vibration was raised to the point that by ingesting energy I had started to vibrate on a higher frequency and started to traverse these interlaced dimensions. Could that have been an astral plane? Who knows.

It was night now, and I am still goofing off when a woman with brown long hair and a green dress walks around the corner from the kitchen and walks up to me, talking about the lamp. I thought it was weird at the time, but in that dreamlike state I didn't question who she was or why she was there in our living room. There was nothing ethereal about this woman. She was absolutely tangible, and I thought she was a friend of Janice's. I was puzzled how she knew so much about what had just happened to me.

Later, I find out that Janice is wondering who this hot chick is who comes unannounced into our house? She, slightly annoyed, thinks the woman is a friend of mine.

I don't remember all the details of the conversation, but in a nutshell the pretty woman in the green dress told me her name was Ariel and she was an oracle. I got the image of priests around a crystal skull doing the "lamp thing" with the skull and calling upon her. She fed me info about geometry and a hand placement that would ramp up the output of the lamp. She moved behind me, and I could hear her voice in my ear behind me, guiding me. Janice later told me that it looked as if Ariel was on my back and making love to me. Janice got fed up and went to bed as she couldn't take any more.

This interaction with Ariel went on until morning. I started to feel like I'd been microwaved, like I was overcooked somehow. I went into the bathroom, and I looked at myself in the mirror, thinking there's no way that any of this happened. I actually thought for a minute that maybe I was the subject of a CIA experiment or something and they dosed me with some kind of gas that made me hallucinate.

So I go into the living room, thinking that there will be nothing there— and there she still is in full blown daylight as tangible and solid as ever.

Ariel wanted to continue our experiments, but it didn't feel right so I said you gotta go.

And she just walked back around the corner the same way she came.

I was worried about unplugging the lamp and going to bed as it felt like I had a huge amount of energy lodged in my body that I couldn't get rid of. I tried my best to wind down, reversing the process, but it didn't really help.

I went to bed and woke up later and my stomach was glowing phosphorescent green, and I felt terrible!

I got in the shower and Janice massaged my back. It felt like it all came out as I burped. Then we both forgot about everything that had happened that night!

It was about three days later when Janice asked who my friend was—and I immediately remembered everything.

"My friend? I thought she was your friend!'

Then we began to piece it together. Total weirdness. I also noticed what appeared to be distortions around the lamp for about a week afterward when the lamp was placed against a dark background. I swear it looked like little people around the periphery of the lamp —and they looked malevolent.

I've never tried this again, but I still have the lamp. I'm not sure if Ariel placed the thought of energizing the water in my head. It seems obvious to me that she was some kind of being that fed off of energy, just as we do— but she didn't have to digest solid food in order to break it down into metabolic components. She just withdrew energy straight from the human tap. In retrospect, it seemed as though she was trading information for energy to feed—a give-and-take situation. It never seemed evil. Pretty neutral, really.

I wonder if she was lying to me about being Ariel. Since the encounter, I have learned that Ariel is the name of a female archangel responsible for visions.

I still have yet to figure out what the images represented. Were they some kind of archetypal communication? And what's up with the running man? Maybe the egg cluster was some kind of life reference. I remember thinking the eggs looked like I was looking through an electron microscope at a cluster of divided human eggs. Lots of unanswered questions.

# ZOMBIES AND VOODOO MAGIC AROUND THE WORLD

In the 1870s, the territory of the Arikara, Mandan, and Hidatsa tribes lay west of the Missouri, from Heart River, North Dakota, to the Yellowstone and up to the mouth of Powder River, Montana. From there, according to the treaty made at Ft. Laramie in 1851, the tribes' land headed southeast to the headwaters of the Little Missouri in Wyoming, skirted around the Black Hills to the head of Heart River, went downstream to its junction with the Missouri. This territory saw few settlers until the 1880s when the U.S. government declared that the treaty signed at Ft. Laramie had not been ratified, and the tribes were moved to a reservation.

Although the concept of a zombie as understood by Voodoo priests and priestesses was not generally known to the Native American tribes, many of the early trappers, missionaries, and settlers to Arikara territory spoke of an incredible ritual of instant death and reanimation conducted by the tribe's medicine men.

### The Headless Warrior of the Arikara

Slowly, hypnotically, the crimson-daubed Arikara medicine man circled the lone brave, who stood as if transfixed on the raised log platform inside the sacred lodge.

Slicing softly through the air, reflecting highlights of a ceremonial fire into the faces of hushed onlookers, a razor sharp saber rolled lightly in the hand of the shaman as he peered into the face of the stoic brave before him—then he circled again.

Suddenly, with the fury of a rattler's strike, the medicine man's saber whirled once at shoulder length, then slashed off the head of the warrior on the platform.

The Arikara medicine man lopped off the head of a warrior standing on a platform in a sacred lodge, then completed the ritual by healing the man before the eyes of numerous blood-soaked witnesses (*iStock*).

In a macabre dance of death, the victim stepped forward, as if to leave, spouting great gouts of blood from the severed arteries that had moments before pumped life to his young face.

Screams filled the medicine lodge of the Arikaras as the brave's head struck the platform and rolled open-eyed to the packed earth floor of the log enclosure.

Many of the white women who had been invited to witness the Arikara medicine ceremony that night in 1872 fainted dead away at the ghastly sight. Some of their husbands fared no better, and welcomed the wifely swoons as a good opportunity for them to make an exit from the horrible scene they had just witnessed.

But for those whose curiosity was stronger than their revulsion, yet more astounding sights awaited them in the blood-spattered lodge.

Smiling with satisfaction, the medicine man picked up the head that had tumbled to the floor at his feet and walked among the remaining spectators, exhibiting the grisly proof that what had been witnessed was not some terrible dream or illusion.

Then, as swiftly as he had acted before, the shaman raised the headless corpse by its shoulders, sitting the gruesome head back upon the severed trunk, singing in ritual cadence a song to which he alone, among all men, knew the words.

As stunned witnesses watched, the brave, who moments before lay in grisly death, now stood, walked a few tentative steps, then ran about the platform, laughing hysterically, as though some great joke had just been told, and he had been its author.

White witnesses, including several soldiers who had just watched the entire tableau take place, were called upon to examine the brave. There were no marks to show where the saber had passed. The young Indian showed no effects of what the onlookers had seen with their own eyes moments before. It was as though none of it could have happened at all.

But then, there was the blood all over the lodge floor, and the blood that had spattered the audiences as they watched in horror. It was hard to explain that.

Western history recounts a number of recollections written down by white men who had been permitted to watch the saber ritual of the Arikara Indians, cousins to the Pawnees who practiced bizarre rites for which science today can offer no better explanation than some vague ability to induce mass hallucination among onlookers.

Yet pioneer trappers, soldiers, clergymen, and even frontier doctors saw for themselves the bloody rituals of the Arikaras and confessed their belief that what they had seen passed human understanding.

While the most dramatic part of the Arikara medicine ceremonies was the saber ritual, members of that deeply mystical tribe were also capable of performing other seemingly impossible feats.

A secret Arikara society to whom the rituals of fire had been entrusted often performed incredible rites which white men were permitted to observe.

Great fires were built upon a flat bed of stones several days prior to the ceremonies. Then, when the night of the ceremony arrived, members of the fire society brushed small paths through the still roaring logs and walked calmly amid the bed of white-hot coals that remained.

Above other portions of the great fires, large cauldrons of water had been placed to heat. When they had reached a thrashing boil, members of the Arikara fire society took turns immersing their arms into the boiling kettles to retrieve small items other members of the tribe tossed into the pots. For an incredible finale, as guests to the strange ritual looked on in speechless amazement, some of the more practiced braves coolly stepped into the cauldrons, sat down, and splashed the boiling water about themselves without apparent concern.

Some members of the Arikara fire society had also learned the secrets of oral fire manipulation, grasping hot brands from the fire and swallowing them without apparent harm.

Those early white men who had witnessed the unbelievable medicine of the Arikaras offered no explanation for what they had seen—and almost all made it a point to mention for posterity that they had not been drinking or had not taken leave of their senses the day on which they had been permitted to enter the sacred medicine lodge.

Today, science offers several possible explanations of the strange powers the Arikara seemed to possess. It is likely, anthropologists believe, that fasting and prayer ordeals which young Arikara braves put themselves through on the road to manhood made them latently susceptible to hypnotic manipulation by medicine men and also rendered them capable of self-induced hypnotic trance, as in the case of the fire society ceremonies. That, of course, may well account for what the Indians thought they saw, or felt, during medicine ceremonies. But what of the white men who witnessed a bloody head strike the dirt floor of the Arikara medicine lodge? That answer doesn't seem to come as readily.

### Ancient African Magic and the Missionary's Angels Lifted a Witch Doctor's Curse from Her Father

"**M**agic is our will to live," Beatrice Gompu said one afternoon as we had coffee in the college cafeteria after class. "We Africans look back now and stand amazed at the resources of our forefathers. They followed all kinds of occupations in search of power, security, and health. Magic was one of them."

A lovely and graceful young woman from Uganda, Beatrice and I became good friends when she enrolled in the writing class that I taught in a small midwestern college. Her father was a very wealthy man in her hometown in Uganda, and because she was the favorite child of her father's favorite wife, she had been allowed to travel to the United States to further her education. Her actual birth name was Mone, but she had acquired the name of Beatrice so she might be numbered among the Christian children and be allowed to go to a Christian school.

"Magic is completely integrated into all aspects of our life in my region of Uganda," she continued. "Magic is always there with us—alive, invigorating, but often very deadly."

"For instance, I found that the only thing that could stop a terrible curse that had been set against my father was my prayers to the angels of light," she told me. "On some level of knowing I felt that these angels had always been with me—long before the missionaries told me about them. Perhaps in Africa we equate them more often with nature spirits or devas, as I have heard some Hindu students call them. I believe that the word 'deva' is from the Sanskrit for 'radiant being.'"

When I agreed with her identification of the devic entities, I urged her to tell us the story of how angels had been able to rescue her father from a curse that had been set against him.

It seemed that Beatrice's father, Martin Gompu, had been ill for a long time, and no practitioner of Western medicine in the region was able to determine the exact nature of his illness. The village witch doctor had pronounced the sickness a very strange one and frankly admitted his inability to effect a cure.

Beatrice's father had always been a stubborn man, wild, strong, defiant, proud, and prosperous. It was natural that such a man should acquire enemies. The green-eyed monster of jealousy had prompted more than one business competitor to gaze with envy at the wealthy man with eight daughters, whose prospective sons-in-law would steadily assure him of even more wealth.

"Saja was the only jackal who had become jealous enough to try to kill my father," Beatrice said. "He was a weak, little man who was Father's principal rival in the village. And now it seemed that he had brooded upon Father's rise to prosperity until he could no longer sit passively by and let the fortunate man acquire more property and more possessions.

"Saja knew that he was far too puny and weak to fight my big, strong father physically, so he had sought out the most powerful witch doctor in the area and paid him to cast a dread curse upon him."

The curse had proved to be most effective. Beatrice told us that her father waged a ceaseless war against his unknown illness for nearly six years. If it had not been for his great physical strength, he surely would have died as he went from witch doctor to mission doctor to witch doctor in a vain attempt to find relief from his awful malady.

"At last Father was able to locate a witch doctor whose skill in magic was even more accomplished than the one that Saja had paid to curse him," Beatrice said, "and he was cured."

Many times after her father's recovery Beatrice heard Saja swearing and fulminating at him whenever the two of them met in the marketplace. Throughout all his afflictions she never once heard her father curse Saja or vow vengeance on the evil little merchant.

The young African woman found that the only thing that could stop a terrible curse and the demon that had been set against her father was her prayers to the angels of light (*art by Ricardo Pustanio*).

Beatrice also found it very ironic that Saja's nephew and only male heir, Amisi, was her brother John's best friend.

"I had also felt that Amisi, the little snake, was only trying to ingratiate himself to my family because he was aware that one day he and John would be the two central figures in the village, and his greedy mind envisioned a coalition between the two most powerful families," Beatrice said.

Beatrice was always appalled by the seemingly endless parameters of Amisi's greed. "Often he would bring baskets of fruits as gifts to our family—and then he would proceed to eat every piece of the fruit during the course of his evening visit."

The sinister Saja had not taken at all well to his being thwarted in his attempt to hex his chief competitor, Martin Gompu. After an extensive search of the outlying villages, he managed to find a witch doctor whose death-dealing curses were feared by the native people in villages far and near.

"Our father's terrible ordeal reached its climax one stormy night—a night of thunder, wind, and lightning, a night made for the working of Black Magic," Beatrice said.

"Father had been gone for several days on a long business trip. On this night of the violent storm we suddenly heard chanting outside our home. When we looked out the windows, we were astonished to see Saja and a fierce-looking witch doctor standing outside in the stormy darkness. A small crowd of men had gathered around them to watch the ensuing drama."

"This time I have you, Martin Gompu!" Saja's cackle sounded above the noise of the storm. "This time, my prosperous friend, you shall die!"

"If you fail this time, Saja," a voice mocked at him from the crowd, "you are not a man."

"I shall not fail!" Saja shouted at his unseen accuser. "No one can match the might of my witch doctor's magic!"

With shocked, incredulous eyes, Beatrice's family watched helplessly as Saja and his master witch doctor performed dark rites necessary to bring about the destruction of their husband, father, and head of the household.

A young goat was led into the magic circle by one of Saja's servants, and the witch doctor raised his angry features to the night rain, his lips mouthing curses, his red, devilish eyes burning beneath his protruding forehead and feathered headdress.

"There can be no escape for Martin Gompu," the witch doctor proclaimed to all within the sound of his harsh, croaking voice. "He will die in disgrace away from his home, and the curse will remain upon his family."

Beatrice said that she would never forget the way the witch doctor looked at them when he pronounced those hateful words. "The worm Amisi stood on the other side of the fence, and his pitiful expression seemed to plead with us to understand that he was helpless to come to our aid."

She confessed that she had screamed when the witch doctor slit the goat's throat.

"Everyone knew that as soon as the goat was killed in sacrifice, something horrible would happen to my father," Beatrice said. "The goat lay kicking, its blood spurting from its throat. The witch doctor beckoned, and Saja began jumping with his bare feet into the spilled blood of the goat. After he had performed his part in the ritual, each member of his family was made to observe the same blood curse against my family and all of our family."

That was when Beatrice began to pray the hardest. "I asked all those angels of light who were in the Bible and who the missionaries said were all around us, watching over us, protecting us, to stand guard over my father. As I said before, somehow I felt within my very soul that I had known the presence of those ancient guardian spirits before in my life, and I asked them please to manifest to protect my father on his homeward journey."

The witch doctor tossed the carcass of the goat on the sacrificial fire that had been built, and as he turned to leave, he made his final pronouncement of that terrible evening of storm and evil. "No one is to touch the goat meat," he said to the assembled crowd of onlookers and the members of Saja's family. "If any of you do so, the curse will be yours!"

Beatrice and her family, enveloped in grief and horror, huddled in their home. The ceremony had begun a few minutes before nine. The witch doctor had slit the

**The witch doctor tossed the carcass of the goat on the sacrificial fire and instructed them not to touch it, lest they be cursed (*iStock*).**

goat's throat and directed the curse at her father at exactly nine o'clock. It was now 10 o'clock. Their father—if he was unharmed—should arrive home at any minute.

Soon it was 11 o'clock. In terror the family of Martin Gompu watched the inexorable movement of the hands of the clock.

When midnight had passed, they retained their silent, prayerful vigil, but they had begun to fear the worst.

It was 2:45 AM when they heard the sputtering of "Odembo," the family automobile. Of all the men who had gone on the business trip, only Beatrice's father could drive a car. That meant that he was alive!

"Father and his companions were a physical mess," Beatrice remembered with a broad smile. "They were soaked, splattered with mud, and completely exhausted—but they were still alive."

As his family hugged and kissed him, Martin Gompu explained that a strange thing had occurred as they approached the main bridge over the river. A man with a lantern had jumped in front of the car with his arms outstretched, as if warning them.

When he applied the brakes of Odembo to miss hitting the man in the road, the car had slid into the ditch.

"When we got out of the car, the man with the lantern was nowhere to be seen," Beatrice's father said. "It was as if he had disappeared into the night."

Beatrice knew with a quickening of her heart that the stranger with the lantern had been a benevolent spirit being manifesting in answer to her prayer.

"While the rest of us were pushing the car out of the ditch, one of the fellows walked on ahead on toward the bridge." Martin Gompu continued his account. "He discovered that the rickety old wooden bridge had been struck by lightning from the storm and had collapsed into the river."

"If we had continued on, we would have slid into the rushing water instead of the ditch, and we probably have drowned. That fellow with the lantern had warned us and saved our lives. With the bridge out, we had to take the long way home. That's what took us so long."

"What time was that, Father?" Beatrice asked. "What time was it that you saw the man with the lantern and Odembo slid into the ditch?"

Her father shrugged, frowned, then smiled. "Yes, I remember looking at my wristwatch just before the man appeared on the road. It was exactly nine o'clock."

"That was the very moment that Saja's new witch doctor, a master of the dark forces, slit the goat's throat in front of our house and sent a death curse flying toward you, Father," Beatrice told him.

It seemed that she was the only member of the family who was able to find her tongue and explain the significance of the fortuitous accident to the bewildered man, who could only stare in amazement at his weeping family as they gathered around him.

"My prayer to the angels of light had been answered," Beatrice said, concluding her remarkable story. "A holy being bearing a lantern appeared on the road and prevented my father and his friends from drowning in the river."

"But the benevolent guardians performed a twist on the acts of the evildoers that I never would have thought of," she said.

"His family found Amisi the next morning quite dead. In his mouth was a piece of goat meat. He could not resist having at least one little bite of the sacrificial animal. By his so doing, his insatiable greed had transferred the effects of the witch doctor's curse from my father to him and his family."

### She Exorcised a Demon in a Madagascar Jungle

The Malagasy called her Ninebe, "The Great Mother."

It was an appellation which I knew that Solveig had earned in her more than three decades of missionary work in Madagascar. Whether she was looking after the

**Missionaries had tried to befriend the Malagasy people of Madagascar for years, but the natives became especially fond of the one they named "The Great Mother," Ninebe, who rescued them from a jungle demon (*iStock*).**

parentless in the mission orphanage, leading a hymn sing in a jungle clearing, or administering a bromide from her first-aid kit, Solveig had set an example for her adopted people.

When I first met Solveig, she was already 85 years old. She was still robust and filled with cheerful energy, and I marveled at the facility with which her mind could relate anecdotes about events which had taken place during the first days of her arrival in Madagascar when she was but a young woman in her early thirties.

"There is no word in the Malagasy language for 'love,'" she said, indicating but one of the many challenges that confronted her in communicating with the native people. "Love is central to the Christian faith. It would be impossible to tell of Jesus without telling of his great love for all humankind."

When missionaries arrive in a strange land, they sometimes discover that they may be on the firing line. Missionaries had been slaughtered and all Christians persecuted in an area where an overzealous cleric offended the indigenous culture by a rash and disrespectful act. Shortly before Solveig arrived in Madagascar, a Roman Catholic priest was killed when he made the mistake of ripping a charm from the neck of a tribal chieftain.

"You have to learn to know the people," Solveig told me. "You must learn their thinking: Most of all, you must show love."

Although she had won the hearts of many of the native tribespeople and had come to be known as the Lady Who Loves People, in addition to being called the Great Mother, she confided that she had not always been confident during her experiences in the field. There was the time, for instance, when she was confronted with her first case of demon possession.

It was quite late at night when she was aroused from her prayers by an urgent knocking on her door. There she found several of her carriers, one of whom was a Christian convert and a member of her congregation. He was the man whom she trusted to provide her with transportation through the jungle.

"Please come with us, Ninebe," begged the man.

Solveig followed the men outside and was soon confronted by the bizarre spectacle of one of the native bearers crawling toward her porch on his hands and knees.

"He has been possessed by a demon," the man nearest her whispered hoarsely.

"Cast the demon out of me, Ninebe," whined the afflicted one, who had by now reached her knees. "Cast him out—and I'll lick your feet!"

"That won't be necessary," the missionary told the man, involuntarily moving her feet several inches away from his slavering jaws.

Solveig, the Lutheran missionary lady, was confused.

She had heard all the learned dissertations about "demon possession" being but a primitive expression for mental illness. She had no doubt that this might often be the case.

Yet she sincerely believed that possession could be a very real thing apart from a mental aberration. And she sincerely believed that an essential element in the mission of Jesus on Earth was to cast out demons. After all, did he not give his followers his own promise that they could also cast out demons in his name?

And in the infinite duality of life on Earth, she knew there were angels of light and good. Did not that truth suggest that there were also angels of darkness and evil?

"My stomach!" wailed the man as he bent double with pain and collapsed on the ground at her feet. "The demon is in my stomach!"

Solveig hesitated. She was still undecided. "I'll get you a bromide."

"That will do me no good! Cast out the demon," the man pleaded.

Her converted carrier stepped close to her and explained to her in hushed whispers that the man had been sent to her as a challenge. The witch doctor in the demon-possessed victim's village had enlisted the aid of strong men to hold him down and pry open his mouth so that he might pour "devil medicine" down his throat.

"The witch doctor fears that you are becoming too powerful," the convert told her. "He fears your power of love, and he does not want to lose his control over the people. Everyone knows that he has sent a demon into this man. If you cannot cast out the evil spirit, all of the villages will see that the witch doctor is more powerful than you are."

Solveig looked closely at the man's face. There was *something* about his eyes—something very different from the glaze caused by either mental imbalance or a gastrointestinal disturbance.

She made her decision. She sent one of the men for the native evangelist and ordered the other men to carry the moaning carrier into the house.

Then, while a number of older village girls who stayed with her, and sang hymns, the missionary lady began to prepare for the ordeal, the duel with the witch doctor's demon.

It was a violent session of intense prayers with both Solveig and the native Evangelist beseeching the God of Love to cast out the demon that tormented the contorted man who lay before them.

During the course of the exorcism the demoniac's body levitated several inches into the air. The missionary lady kept her hand on the man's head and only increased the fervor of her prayers when his trembling body floated free of the bed.

At last the man was quiet, and after a time his eyes flickered open and he appeared to have regained consciousness.

"Do you know me?" she asked him.

The man grinned. "You're the Lady Who Loves People! And you have chased the demon out of my stomach."

Solveig uttered a brief prayer of thanksgiving. The ordeal was over. The witch doctor's challenge had been met. And she, with the help of the native Evangelist and God, had won.

"From that day on, the native witch doctors used to look at me with bullhead eyes," Solveig remembered with a chuckle. I grew bolder in dealing with those poor victims whom the witch doctors had possessed with their angels of darkness."

### A Terrible Marriage Proposal She Could Not Refuse

My Indonesian friend Jannes Lumbantobing was from a village on Samosir, an island in the middle of Lake Toba in Sumatra, Indonesia. We became good friends when we were college students, and we had some wonderful all-night bull sessions in his dorm room or mine. Some years back, he was visiting in the United States and stopped to spend a few nights with us. I could not resist bringing up the topic of how native Indonesians regarded hexes and witch doctors.

Although Jannes (who always preferred that I call him Jim) believed firmly in the existence of ministering angels of God, he had also seen the angels of darkness at

On the Indonesian island of Bali, the Witch Queen is known as Ranga. Many Indonesians still believe in witchcraft and hexes, though the culture has also been strongly influenced by foreign faiths (*iStock*).

work performing their painful enterprises against human beings.

"Christianity has brought many changes to my native Indonesia," Jim said as we relaxed with a soft drink in my study. "But in the outlying *angka huta* [villages], the old beliefs remain strong. Here the villagers may give lip service to the Christian God, but *mamele* [worship] of the old gods is observed with fervor.

"Although you are a student of such things and what some people call the 'supernatural,' Brad, you will agree that much of what I have shared with you in our many conversations over the years would be difficult for most Americans to believe. They live in the United States with their fast cars and their concrete highways. They believe themselves to be completely removed from the primitive and elemental. It is only in certain terrifying situations that Americans may be reminded that the dark powers are very potent. And if they should ever visit the environment of remote villages in Indonesia, Africa, South America, or Asia, they would observe a power of evil that can become formidable in the extreme."

When Jim was a teenager in his village, he witnessed a not uncommon phenomenon: The ugliest boy in his high school class fell in love with the prettiest girl.

What followed, however, would be judged very uncommon by most Western standards.

The boy began to court the young beauty and, quite understandably, was instantly rebuffed. The young man could hardly count on his good looks or his personal magnetism to help him out with the haughty object of his affections. But he had another advantage that transcended any and all physical properties: he was the nephew of the *datu*, the village witch doctor.

One day, during a study period at school, Jim noticed the rejected suitor stretch across his desk to pluck unnoticed a few loose hairs that lay on the shoulders of the desired girl's blouse.

At that time, young Jim had no idea why the frustrated lover boy would settle for some hairs from her head when he seemed to want the whole person. Jim did not yet have the faintest idea about such things as sympathetic or mimetic magic.

It wasn't until the conclusion of the series of strange events that had been set in motion by this simple act that Jim was made aware of such terrible projects of evil as shaping a figure in the likeness of one whom the *datu* wished to harm by hexing.

Jim was to learn that the effectiveness of the magic required strands of hair, nail clippings, blood—something that would form an unbreakable bond between the pretty young victim and the demons, the evil spirits, the angels of darkness, that had been set upon her.

But at that stage of his spiritual knowledge Jim was surprised when the girl was absent from school the next day.

Later, during the evening meal, Jim's father told him that the girl lay in a coma, unable to take either food or drink. She was asleep yet not asleep. Her eyes were open wide, unblinking. Over and over again she repeated only one word: the name of the *datu*'s nephew.

Within a week the girl was emaciated. She had eaten nothing, and she had drunk only the few drops of water that her distraught parents had managed to force down her parched throat.

The medical missionaries were helpless. Their Western medicines had no effect upon the hex. The girl became even worse after their visits. It was as if the creatures of darkness resented the ineffectual meddlings of another culture and took out their wrath upon the tormented body of the young girl.

In desperation the distressed father of the girl sought aid from three *datus* in a nearby village, but after taking his money and performing a number of worthless rituals and chants, the trio of witch doctors admitted that they were powerless to drive back the demons that had been set loose to torment the man's daughter.

The father could no longer avoid the inevitable confrontation with the *datu* of his own village, the very one who had set the horrid things of darkness upon his beloved daughter.

The *datu* remained impassive to the desperate man's pleas.

The fact that his daughter had been reduced to a hollow-eyed, babbling wretch was, he told the father, no concern of his.

The man fell to his knees and promised to give the *datu* what little wealth he had left.

At last the witch doctor, who had been feigning indifference, agreed to intercede for the man's daughter and to negotiate with the evil spirits that had taken up residence within her frail body.

Within a week the girl was smiling weakly in her mother's arms and calling feebly for rice and water.

However, it wasn't until the young girl had completely recovered from her mysterious delirium that the *datu* and his triumphantly grinning nephew arrived at her home.

"My nephew," the witch doctor said, indicating the ugly, hulking young man at his heels, "desires to marry your daughter."

The girl's parents were indignant and outraged by the *datu*'s words—even though they had not been unexpected.

"Never," replied the father, shaking his head emphatically. "My daughter is lovely and sweet-voiced. She can have the pick of any of the wealthy young men in the village."

The *datu's* eyes narrowed. "Ah, my friend, but she was not so lovely and sweet-voiced when you came begging to me on your knees for her very life. It would be a pity if the fever were to return."

The threat was obvious. The insinuation did not need to be stated any more clearly or elaborately. The *datu* had hexed the lovely girl once, and he was unhesitatingly prepared to work his evil on her again if need be.

The father stammered, his fists opening and closing in helpless rage. His wealth was depleted from the expense of the three unsuccessful *datus* in the neighboring village. And no one seemed able to combat the evil spirits that awaited the confident witch doctor's bidding. He knew that he had no choice. Although he was repelled by the very thought, he must give his daughter to the *datu's* nephew to be his bride.

"The *datu* had saved his daughter's life," Jim explained.

"According to Batak custom, one owes his life to someone who has helped him. There was nothing for the father to do but to accept the nephew's marriage proposal. The beautiful girl had to go through with the marriage or die.

"So you see, Brad," Jim concluded, "it truly is as you have so often said and written: whether in the United States or among the Batak, one must be wary of all manifestations of the dark angels and pray for protection from all evil spirits."

### The Monster of Glamis Castle

Princess Margaret of England's royal family was born in a haunted castle with its own grotesque monster-in-residence. While the British Isles can boast of many spectral visitants in its castle corridors, Glamis Castle is the only one that can claim an indestructible, flesh-and-blood monster that resides in a hidden mystery room.

Glamis is one of the most ancient of Scottish castles, and as it purports to be the actual scene of Macbeth's foul murder of Duncan, there is little wonder that the old fortress shelters a number of extremely active phantoms. For centuries, inhabitants of the castle claim to have seen ghostly reenactments of murders and agonizing deaths. Two ghostly dramas often seen played out are the death of the fifth Earl of Strathmore and the murder of another Earl of Strathmore over a game of cards in the castle.

One of the more foul deeds committed by a lord of Glamis Castle concerns the mass murder of a party of Ogilvies, who arrived at the castle and begged for refuge from a band of pursuing Lindsays. The Lord of Glamis pretended to be sympathetic to their cause and locked them up in a secret dungeon, promising to shelter them from the Lindsays and to bring them food and drink. What the treacherous Lord of Glamis actually did was to seal in the Ogilvies so they would starve to death.

Generations later, the current Lord Glamis, much less susceptible to tales of the supernatural than his predecessors had been, led a number of his servants in an investi-

**Glamis Castle is the only one in Great Britain that can claim that an indestructible, flesh-and-blood monster resides within its walls (*iStock*).**

gation of ghostly noises that had been disturbing the sleep of the household. They managed to trace the spectral sounds to a large room in an unused portion of the castle.

When Lord Glamis found a key to fit the ancient lock and pushed the door open, the aristocrat buckled to the floor in a faint. The wide-eyed servants, who caught their swooning lord, were horrified to behold a room filled with skeletons. From the position of the skeletal frames, it was easy to determine that they had died gnawing one another's flesh.

All chroniclers of Glamis agree that somewhere within its walls exists a secret room, and generations of servants, visitors, and inhabitants have sworn that they have heard the shuffling feet and hideous half-human cries of a ghastly monster as it emerges for its nocturnal prowling.

According to Augustus Hare, who visited the castle in 1877, there is a ghastly chamber, within a deep wall, that hides a secret transmitted from the fourteenth century, which is always known to three persons. When one of the triumvirate dies, the survivors are compelled by a terrible oath to elect a successor.

The monster, according to legend, was a future Earl of Strathmore, Lord of Glamis Castle, who, while innocent and in his mother's womb, received the brunt of a curse on the family—a curse which declared that he be born a half-human monster who should live in misshapen form for all eternity. When the child was delivered, it was indeed found to be a grotesque monstrosity, and the brutish baby was hidden away by his father in a secret room. Here, for nearly six centuries, three people have been selected to care and look out for the monster.

I was astonished when folklorist and occult expert Alyne A. Pustanio found a link between the Monster of Glamis and the infamous Devil Baby of New Orleans. Although we have dealt with one version of the Devil Baby in an earlier chapter, Alyne's remarkable research certainly requires examining the legend from another perspective.

### The Devil Baby of New Orleans

*Alyne A. Pustanio relates the following tale:*

What's that terrible howling, drowning out hurricane winds and honky-tonks? New Orleanians know it's none other than the Devil's own child, godchild of the Voodoo Queens!

This is at best a local legend, the origins of which are unknown. There are many who claim to know the real story and some who have tried to lay claim to inventing the story in order to capitalize on its ghoulish images. The story provided here is the product of the author's distillation of many versions of the tale and is entirely original in its telling.

In the early days of Marie Laveau's rise to fame, her clientele consisted mainly of country folk and free people of color whose long association with the practices of Hoodoo and root workers made her a natural attraction.

But at the height of her power, when her mystique was talked about constantly in fine salons throughout New Orleans, Marie Laveau was receiving visits from both Creole society and the upper-crust white-bread Americans. It was her service to this sector that embroiled her in one of the greatest legends of Old New Orleans: The Devil Baby.

Madame Laveau was often called to the fashionable home on Dauphine Street to delight and amuse the matron of the Creole family that lived there and her friends. This family had a beautiful daughter named Camille who, when she came of age, had many suitors. To her great disappointment, however, all of them were Creole. To most young women of her station, this would be a fabulous dilemma; but for Camille, it was truly disheartening. All her life she had been envious of the wealthy lifestyle of the Americans, of their fabulous homes built in the Northern style, and of their status and fine society, all of which they did not hesitate to flaunt.

Through her father's business connections, Camille befriended the daughter of an American family, Josephine Brody, who often invited Camille to her home for tea and other activities. It was on one of these outings that Camille, it is said, met the man who would change her life forever and gain her a place in haunted New Orleans' history.

Mackenzie Bowes was a Scotsman by birth, though the details of his life and how he had obtained his considerable fortune were obscure. He never commented on it and the shallow Americans in whose circles he moved with such ease were satisfied to know simply that he was "obscenely wealthy" and that the money was "very old," coming down from old Scottish lairds and some very lucrative family connections. He had arrived upon the steps of the Brody home in the company of August Brody, the eldest son, whom he had met in New York. He was looking for a place to settle down, the Brodys were told, and New Orleans, with its *joie de vivre* and continental flair, seemed just the place for a man like Mackenzie Bowes.

From the moment she laid eyes on the dark, handsome Scotsman, Camille was smitten, and she began to look for every opportunity to spend more time with the Brodys and their Scottish houseguest. It greatly pleased Josephine and her family when Bowes began to return Camille's interest with attentiveness and obvious devotion. Camille's parents, who also became regular houseguests of the American Brodys, encouraged the romance, hoping for a fine union for their daughter.

But not all were so delighted. In scorning her Creole suitors, Camille had certainly embarrassed them and for the most part wounded their pride; nearly all turned their attentions to other sultry Creole daughters. Nearly all, that is, except the intense Etienne Lafossat.

It did not please him at all that he had been set aside by Camille like a plaything that had outlasted her attention. As Camille's romance and her stature among the Americans grew, it was clear to all, including Etienne, that marriage was imminent. When Bowes threw off his Presbyterian faith and converted to Catholicism, the union was certain, and shortly afterward the bans were announced in St. Louis Cathedral.

All this Marie Laveau had watched with interest and she was not surprised in the least when Etienne came to her cottage on St. Ann imploring her aid. He wanted Camille back, he said at first, but when the Voodoo Queen shook her head and assured him it could not be so, Etienne ground his fist into the table and pronounced: "Then I want her dead!"

To his surprise, Madame Laveau laughed at his request. "You cannot know what you ask, boy," she said in her heavy Creole patois. "Go away! Do not trouble me."

Attempting to keep the Devil Baby of Bourbon Street at bay by placing a cross and a crucifix over a doll in his image (*art by Ricardo Pustanio*).

Etienne thought it through as quickly as his fevered mind could. "Then make her suffer, like she has made me suffer!" he blurted. "She goes to the Americans to make a spectacle of herself; make a spectacle of her for all to see."

Her patience spent, Madame Laveau looked darkly at Etienne and spat upon the ground, stamping the spot with her foot, "You will soon learn who is cursed, boy. Now, go I said!"

In the dark of her cupboard on St. Ann Street, Marie Laveau worked her charm. It would be months in coming, but Etienne Lafossat would have his revenge, and he would regret the day he asked for it!

On a bright October morning Camille became the bride of the dark, mysterious Scotsman in the halls of the great St. Louis Cathedral. All the high society of New Orleans, from both quarters, attended the fabulous wedding and the celebration at the family home afterward.

When Camille and Mackenzie returned from their wedding trip, the new bride was already pregnant. Beaming with delight, the handsome couple settled down in a home on the Rue Bourbon, not far from the French Market. While her husband went about his affairs in the day, Camille spent hours planning the nursery that would receive her child. Nothing could dim her enthusiasm or quell her excitement, except on one occasion when she happened upon Etienne Lafossat in the market. His scowl was so dark and intense that Camille became faint and her mother Marceline, who was with her, called for the carriage to take her home. The shadow passed. Or so it seemed.

Very soon after that unfortunate encounter, Marceline became restless in her sleep. Never one to be plagued by sleeplessness or dreams, she began to have vivid nightmares that would wake her in the middle of the night. Afterward, she would be so unnerved that she found it impossible to go back to sleep. She tried desperately to keep her troubles from Camille, not wanting to intrude upon the young woman's joy, but one day her daughter confronted her. When Marceline told Camille about her dreams and fitful sleep, the young mother-to-be was disturbed.

"My husband is having dreams as well," she told her mother. "He wakes suddenly in the night, calling for me, but he will not tell me what he has dreamed, or why he cannot sleep again."

This greatly troubled Marceline and when she had departed from Camille she spied a beautiful mullatress selling fish beside the road and this immediately put her in mind of Madame Laveau. As soon as she arrived home, Marceline sent out a servant with a message for the Voodoo Queen.

Within a half hour, the servant returned and announced that Madame Laveau was waiting to be admitted. Marceline went to the door herself and quickly brought Marie into the house. For what seemed like an eternity the two were closeted together in the parlor while Marceline poured out her concerns and told Marie every detail of her troubling dreams. When she added the details of Camille's distressing encounter with Etienne Lafossat in the French Market, a shadow passed over Marie's dark eyes.

"I believe the child to be in the greatest danger," Madame Laveau finally pronounced. "This is what the ancestors are telling me. When Camille is confined and the time of her delivery comes, I alone should be called to midwife her. Otherwise, I fear there will be a great evil laid upon this child. Even now I am not sure I can prevent it."

This troubled Marceline greatly and she could not understand the meaning of it, but assured by the Voodoo Queen that all would be well so long as she alone might bring the baby, Marceline put aside her fears. She watched as Marie's carriage clattered away down the flagstone streets, taking the great lady home to await the call.

Mackenzie Bowes was a dark and mysterious man and much about his past he kept to himself. Camille had accepted this when she married him. The most that she had been able to wrest from him was his connection to a family of Scottish lords called the Strathmores. She learned that he was in line to inherit a title and possibly a castle, "But several male heirs before me would have to meet untimely ends!" he had said with a playful wink.

So they would not be lord and lady of anything, thought Camille; but still, the idea of her child sharing in this noble bloodline was almost intoxicating. To the consternation of her husband, Camille launched into even greater effort and expense in making the nursery a fitting place to receive such a child.

One day, while looking through a Gazetteer, Camille came across a story about the Earls of Strathmore and the gloomy Scottish castle they called home. It was a cursed place, or so the article said, and had been associated for ages with the darkest form of malign arts. "Glamis," it read, "is purported to have locked within its walls the Devil himself!"

> She learned that he was in line to inherit a title and possibly a castle, "But several male heirs before me would have to meet untimely ends!" he had said with a playful wink.

This disturbed Camille, for combined with the dreams and fitfulness of her husband and mother, finding the article seemed to her an omen of some sort. She began to wonder, but soon all thoughts would turn to her delivery. Her first labor pains began, and she entered her confinement. Dutifully, Marceline sent for Marie Laveau.

Through a night of torrential rains, thunderclaps, and lighting breaking through the roiling skies, Camille spent a long and arduous labor. The ever-patient Madame Laveau did not once leave her side. She would soothe her through her pains and pat her head with a cool towel, always encouraging her. But it seemed that Camille's pangs were having a strange effect on Mackenzie as well, for as the labor increased and the delivery neared, Mackenzie became more and more agitated and nervous. He insisted upon being in the room, but Marie was not one to be bullied and no sooner did he step inside than he was put out again.

The Scotsman fidgeted as the time neared and would not be comforted. At last, unable to bear it, his mind seemed to completely collapse, and he ran from the home into the dark night. The Voodoo Queen mused darkly over this, sensing some other power at work against her own.

Camille suffered greatly from the labor and mercifully passed into unconsciousness before death came for her. Her grieving family was inconsolable when Madame Laveau told them that Camille could not be saved, but that the child had survived.

With her first glimpse of the infant Marie knew at once that a curse had been set on both mother and child, perhaps made more potent by the mysterious past of the

Strathmores. She immediately thought of only one person who might be responsible, but for the moment she knew she must focus on the grim task at hand.

She went in to the family and looked at them, telling them to prepare themselves for what they were about to hear and see.

"There is a curse upon this child and it has nothing to do with your poor daughter," she said. "This is the work of someone who hated this child enough to bring the devil out of hell to curse it, and though I have tried with all my power to prevent it, the evil has prevailed."

Then she revealed to the family the bundle lying in her arms. All present gasped in horror, including the family priest who had arrived in time to perform the last rites over Camille's stiffening body. In the arms of the Voodoo woman was not a plump and blushing human baby, but a grotesque and lurid imitation, a horror, an abomination.

Wails filled the room when the thing was exposed and all could see that where light tufts of hair should be were two lumps—the early roots of horns to come. Where little hands and feet should have been were the claws of some wild animal, like a possum or a raccoon. There were scales upon its body, though its genitals were perfectly formed and all could see it was a boy. But it was the eyes, the horrible, leering hell-like eyes that caused Marceline to faint in despair and Camille's poor father to turn his back.

Karen Beals, staff member of Haunted America Tours, holds a doll of the Devil Baby that was fashioned by Ricardo Pustanio (*art by Ricardo Pustanio*).

"Take it out of my sight!" he said to Marie.

"But Monsieur!" said the Madame. "What of his father!"

"ITS father has thankfully gone mad! The Ursulines took him in just an hour ago, ranting and foaming at the mouth. He is quite beyond our help!" was the heartless reply. "This is the curse of his family, NOT ours!"

"All curses come home to roost," Madame Laveau said obliquely.

"NOT this one!" the man barked. He pointed the way to the door.

"As you wish," said Madame Laveau, covering the little infant and holding it close to her. She left them there and passed out into the dripping, humid New Orleans night, making her way toward St. Ann Street, deep in thought.

Suddenly out of the shadows came the hunching form of Etienne Lafossat. Marie stopped suddenly but was not moved by the sight she saw: Etienne's own curse had, indeed, come home to roost. At least in this respect her magic had worked on the one who had been responsible for this evil.

He was hideously deformed, more like a devil now than a man. Where once a handsome Creole man had been, there was now only the bent and broken form of a demonic cripple. His face was so contorted that Marie thought he seemed more the father of the infant now dozing in her arms, and the justice enacted by the spirits became clear to her then. She smiled thinly.

"What have you done to me?" Etienne cried and lunged for her.

The Voodoo Queen held up a hand. "Stop!" she said in a commanding voice that stopped the fiend in its tracks. "You are marked for all to see, Etienne, for Camille has died because of your hatred. Now you may be testament to her life. Do you not recall? 'You do not know what you ask!' Go away, and do not show your face to me again. It sickens me!" With that, she passed into the night, and Etienne passed into obscurity.

A thought came to the Madame Laveau then and she turned quickly on her heel, making her way to Rampart Street and the familiar doorway of another infamous woman, Mammy Pleasant.

"Mammy" Pleasant was known to the Voodoo Queen simply as Mary Ellen, a relative by marriage of her patron, Christophe Glapion. Mary Ellen Pleasant would later go on to fame as one of the founders of the Civil Rights movement and to infamy as the Voodoo Queen of San Francisco.

When Marie had told her tale and shown the baby to Mammy, the little house rang with their laughter at what fools humans are to tamper with the will of the spirits.

"Ah! But he must be baptized!" Mammy said suddenly, jumping to her feet with excitement. "I know a priest who will do it right away! And I will stand for this child! It needs a godmother, after all!"

Marie Laveau stood up and rocked the dozing devil child in her arms. "I will stand, too. With us to protect him, none will harm him. It is, after all, the charitable thing to do!"

This is the legend of the Devil Baby, or so it is said; but the story does not end there.

It is rumored that throughout their lives Marie Laveau and Mammy Pleasant shared the care of the unwanted devil child between them. Sometimes the child would be kept with Marie at her home on St. Ann; other times, Mammy played host to it, and, it is said, even had a nursery made for it in her home. Town gossips whispered that the two crazed women used the baby to call to its true father, the Devil himself, who came to the house on Rampart Street to feast with his growing progeny on grisly banquets of animal sacrifices. But no one had any proof, and no one wanted to get close enough to find it.

Sometimes pitiful and chilling wails not of this earth would pierce the quiet of the Old Quarter, and whenever the rain would fall, reminiscent of the night of its birth, the baby would moan and howl incessantly, to the great disturbance of French Quarter residents.

Some who had heard dark hints of the origins of the baby's human father— Mackenzie Bowes—would often speculate that the curse of the Lairds of faraway Glamis had come alive again in New Orleans. The fact that first the Laveau and then the Pleasant families had cleverly concealed the existence of the child reminded these knowledgeable few of the legend of the Devil trapped in the walls of Glamis Castle far away, and they shivered when the suggestion was spoken aloud.

One stormy day many years later, however, the troubled residents of the Old Quarter began to notice that an uncharacteristic quiet had descended on the city. There were no howls, no moans or wailing, and shortly after this the old timers whose memories were long began to suspect that something had changed. Madame Laveau had died and Mammy Pleasant had moved with her husband, John James Pleasant, to San Francisco in pursuit of gold. Had she taken the cursed child with her?

Others told of seeing the Laveau family, led by Mam'selle Marie II, gathered together in St. Louis Cemetery No. 1, all dressed in black and standing in the rain, laying a small, nondescript box under the stones at the foot of Madame Marie Laveau's famous tomb. Could it have been the Devil Baby in the little makeshift coffin? Most people assumed this to be the case and the story passed on into the legends of New Orleans.

But there is a strange recent epilogue to the tale, or so some now say. If Mam'selle Laveau buried the Devil Baby with her mother back in the late 1800s then, some wonder, what's howling and terrorizing tourists and locals alike to this day?

Some long-time Quarter residents and historians have noticed that tales of the horrible wailing and moaning that once was blamed upon the Devil Baby have sprouted anew, and have even increased since the onslaught of Hurricane Katrina. There have also been reports of sightings of the ghoulish little thing scampering through the dark French Quarter streets.

Many might dismiss this as fantasy, but in an odd and troubling twist, residents and visitors to San Francisco also report seeing the shadowy form of a woman with a bundle in her arms wandering under the branches of the famous eucalyptus grove planted by Mammy Pleasant in the nineteenth century. Many claim to hear a baby's whimpering and a ghostly lullaby drifting from the scented darkness, just before the shadowy woman appears.

Can it be that these two great Voodoo Queens continue in death the duty they took on in life? Do these dark godmothers still take turns comforting the Devil Baby of New Orleans from beyond the grave?

# ZOMBIES AND MONSTERS OF THE APOCALYPSE

The term "apocalypse" means an "unveiling," a prophetic glimpse of the future. In popular usage, many people have confused the term with the "end times," the last days of life upon the Earth.

In apocalyptic thought, humankind's destiny is viewed as steadily unfolding according to a great design of God. The present is a time of trial and tribulation, and its meaning will only be made clear in the last days before the final judgment occurs.

Because of the current increase in interest in zombies—which are often portrayed as agents of some apocalyptic annihilation of humankind that leads to the end of the world as we know it—some zombie enthusiasts have discovered certain biblical passages that they suggest might indicate that zombies were mentioned in Holy Scripture. Herewith are some of the most commonly cited possibilities of the Undead in the Bible (Italics are mine):

> Here is what the Lord will do to those who attack Jerusalem: While they are standing there, *he will make their flesh rot and their eyes fall from their sockets and their tongues drop out. The Lord will make them go into a frenzy and start attacking each other,* until even the people in Judah turn against those in Jerusalem.
>
> Zechariah, 14:12–14. Holy Bible, Contemporary English Version (CEV).

These unfortunates certainly sound as if they are being threatened with zombification, but it really seems more like the Lord is turning their bodies to rot that will resist reanimation. According to Leviticus 26:27–29 (CEV): "If you don't stop rebelling, I'll really get furious and punish you terribly for your sins! In fact, *you will be so desperate for food that you will eat your own children.*"

Cannibalizing one's children has been known to occur throughout history, but the reasons are usually famine and poverty, rather than zombie hunger for human flesh.

Matthew 27:52–53 (CEV) reads: "The earth shook, and rocks split apart. *Graves were opened, and many of God's people were raised to life. They left their graves, and after Jesus had risen to life, they went into the holy city, where they were seen by many people.*"

This great event of reanimation that occurred at the death of Jesus has intrigued many individuals as they have pondered the Nazarene's crucifixion. Some Christian theologians explain that the awesome act of righteous individuals emerging from their graves to wander the streets of Jerusalem was only a temporary resurrection. The souls of the men and women of God will not truly ascend until Jesus returns after the great battle of Armageddon. It must be assumed that these reanimated corpses returned to their graves to once more lie in peace until the Great Day of Judgment.

## What is the Apocalypse?

In the Jewish tradition, apocalyptic thought presupposes a universal history in which the Divine Author of that history will manifest His secrets in a dramatic End-Time that, with finality, will establish the God of Israel as the one true God. The "end of days" (*acharit ha-yamin*) is bound up with the coming of the Messiah, but before he arrives, governments will become increasingly corrupt, religious schools will become heretical, the wisdom of the scribes and teachers will become blasphemous, young people will shame their elders, and members of families will turn upon one another. Then, just prior to the arrival of the Messiah, the righteous of Israel shall defeat the armies of evil and monsters that have gathered under the banner of Gog and Magog, and the exiles shall return to the Holy Land.

The advent of the Messiah promises a great Day of Judgment in which the dead shall rise from their graves to begin a new life. During the period known as the World to Come (*Olam Haba*), the righteous will join the Messiah in partaking of a great banquet in which all foods, even those previously judged impure, shall be declared kosher. All the many nations of the world will communicate in one language, the Angel of Death will be slain by God, trees and crops will produce fresh harvests each month, the warmth of the sun shall heal the sick, and the righteous will be nourished forever by the radiance of God.

To most orthodox Christians, the profound meaning of the New Testament is that Jesus Christ will one day return in the Last Days and his Second

**Zombies are often portrayed as agents of some apocalyptic annihilation of humankind (art by Ricardo Pustanio).**

Coming will prompt the resurrection of the dead and the Final Judgment. The heart of the gospels is eschatological, end-oriented. The essential theme of Jesus and the apostles is that the last stage of history, the end-time, was being entered into with his appearance.

But John the Revelator does present monsters in Revelation, the last book in the New Testament, and he provides a guidebook for the Christian on what to expect during the time of Tribulation. Specifically, the book was written for the members of the churches of Ephesus, Smyrna, Pergamum, Thyatira, Sardis, Philadelphia, and Laodicea in order to prepare them for what John the Revelator believed to be a fast-approaching time of persecution and the return of Jesus Christ.

The first terrible beings arrive when the Seven Seals are opened (Revelation 6:1–2) by the Lamb (Christ). This action discloses a conquering king astride a white horse, the first of the Four Horsemen of the Apocalypse. Some believe this to be Jesus, but since no good comes of his arrival, more contemporary scholars maintain that this is the Antichrist in disguise.

*Rising out of the abyss to block Christ's triumph at Armageddon is a monstrous army of demons, some resembling locusts and scorpions, others a repulsive mixture of human, horse, and lion.*

The Second Seal (6:3–4) reveals the red horse, representing civil war; the third, the black horse, symbolizing famine (6:5–6); the fourth, the pale horse, representing the suffering that follows war and famine. The Fifth Seal to be opened by the Lamb yields a vision of the persecution of the Church throughout history and during the Last Days.

When the Sixth Seal is revealed, it displays the coming signs of a great Day of Wrath when there will be earthly upheavals, a darkened sun, stars falling from the heavens, mountains and islands removed, and more strife and revolution throughout the nations.

The Seventh and final Seal releases seven trumpets that sound the triumphant blast signaling the approach of the final and everlasting victory of Christ over the Kingdoms of the World.

Rising out of the abyss to block Christ's triumph at Armageddon is a monstrous army of demons, some resembling locusts and scorpions, others a repulsive mixture of human, horse, and lion. This motley crew of hideous demons is soon joined by 200,000 serpentine-leonine horsemen capable of belching fire, smoke, and brimstone. Led by Satan, the once-trusted angel who led the rebellion against God in Heaven, the Prince of the World sets his legions upon the faithful to make their lives as miserable as possible in the End-Time.

To make matters even more complex for those who serve God, the greatest monster of all time, the Antichrist, appears on the scene pretending to be the Lamb, the Messiah. John the Revelator is told that this man, this Beast in lamb's clothing, can be recognized by a name, the letters of which, when regarded as numbers, total 666.

Although the term "Antichrist" is frequently used by those Christians who adhere to the New Testament book of Revelation as a literal guide to the time of the End of Days, which they feel is upon us, the word is nowhere to be found within its text. It is, however, very likely from the apostle John that we first learn of the Antichrist. In 1 John 2:18, he declares that the "enemy of Christ" has manifested and that many false teachers have infiltrated the Christian ranks, and in 2 John, verse 7 he declares that there are many deceivers already at work among the faithful.

In Hebrew legends, the Leviathan is a giant serpent, much like the Greek Ouroboros and the Midgard Serpent of the Norse. Symbolically, Leviathan could represent a great serpentine power that seeks to enslave the dwellers of Earth (*art by Ricardo Pustanio*).

At last Christ and his angelic armies of light destroy the forces of darkness at Armageddon in the final battle of good versus evil. Babylon, the False Prophet, and the Beast (the Antichrist) are dispatched to their doom, and Satan, the Dragon, is bound in a pit for a thousand years. With Satan imprisoned and chained, the Millennium, the Thousand Years of peace and harmony, begins.

Although Christ's Second Coming is said to be mentioned over 300 times in the New Testament, the only references to the Millennium are found in Revelation 20:2–7. Christian scholars disagree whether or not there will be an initial resurrection of the just at the advent of the Millennium and a second one a thousand years later, immediately prior to the Final Day of Judgment.

For some rather incomprehensible reason, Satan is released from the pit at the conclusion of the Millennium; and true to his nature, he makes a furious attempt to regain his earthly kingdom. His former allies, The Beast (the Antichrist), the False Prophet, and the hordes of Babylon, were destroyed at Armageddon, but there were some demons who escaped annihilation at the great battle who stand ready to serve their master. In addition to these evil creatures, Satan summons Gog and his armies of the Magog nations to join them in attacking the saints and the righteous followers of God. Although the vast multitude of vile and wicked servants of evil and grotesque monsters quickly surrounds the godly men and women, God's patience with the rebellious angel has come to an end. Fire blasts down from Heaven, engulfing and destroying the satanic legions and the armies of Gog and Magog. Satan himself is sent to spend the rest of eternity in a lake of fire.

## Monsters in the Old Testament

There is no shortage of monsters throughout the Old Testament. Prominent among them is Leviathan, who was a huge fishlike demonic entity who came into being during the fifth day of Creation. Although many scholars simply state that the leviathan was the Hebrew name for a whale, others point out several verses which indicate that the monster was so large that its diet subsisted on a whale a day. In other Hebrew legends, the Leviathan is a giant serpent that engulfs the entire planet, much like the Greek Ouroboros and the Midgard Serpent of the Norse. Symbolically, the Leviathan could represent a great serpentine power that seeks to enslave the dwellers of Earth.

So might it be with *Taninim*, a collective name for creatures such as sea monsters, crocodiles, or large snakes. These physical monsters could be symbolical of reptilian demons of great strength and might.

Rahab was said to be the guardian spirit of ancient Egypt. In some references, Rahab is the angel of insolence and pride, who commands such fallen angels as Belial, Mastema, Samael, and Uzza. Wherever he manifests, his mission is to create chaos. In Psalm 89, the God of Israel subdues the monster Rahab with his powerful arm and establishes His position as the Master of the heavens and the earth. It was common belief among the ancient Hebrews that the Earth was first controlled by the great sea serpent, Rahab.

Demons there were aplenty, slimy sea dwellers and hairy goat demons from the mountains:

"You offered sacrifices to demons (*Shedim*), those useless gods that never helped you, new gods that your ancestors never worshipped." Deuteronomy 32:17

"They sacrificed their sons and their daughters to demons (*Shadim*).... Then they poured out the blood of these innocent children and made the land filthy." Psalms 106:37–38.

"Don't ever … offer sacrifices to goat-demons (*Seirim*).... Life is in the blood.... That's also why I have forbidden you to eat blood." Leviticus 17:7, 11–12.

### *It Seems to Be Monster Time Again*

*Many students of the occult believe that the veil is growing thin between worlds and dimensions and that the inhabitants of other planes of reality or of hidden places on Earth are emerging to ready themselves for the Apocalypse.*

*I am grateful to Lance Oliver, founder of the Denton Paranormal Society and director/editor of the UFO Casebook, for providing the following account of a very strange creature that was sighted in the area of Copper Canyon in Texas.*

*As Oliver reported in UFO Casebook:*

Fellow DAPS investigators, Bob and Todd (names changed to protect their identity), came forward at our meeting on February 19 with a mind-blowing story. What follows is a recounting of what befell Bob on a fateful date this past January:

Having caught a late-night movie at a theater in the area, Bob dropped off his friend, Todd, before heading home. With the soaring price of gas, Bob decided to take a deserted country road which served as a shortcut back to his place.

Around 2:00 AM in the early morning of January 21, Bob drove east on Copper Canyon Road. Driving over a railroad crossing, at a sharp bend in the road, he saw something otherworldly suddenly appear from behind a tree to his left.

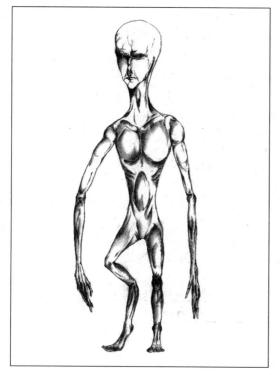

Lance Oliver, founder of the Denton Paranormal Society and director/editor of the UFO Casebook, provides a remarkable account of a very strange creature that was sighted in the area of Copper Canyon in Texas (*art provided by Lance Oliver*).

Slamming on his brakes, Bob was stunned as a thin, gaunt, hairless, long-armed, long-legged creature, was caught in the high beams of his headlights. Less than 20 feet away, this weird, five-foot tall, slumped forward, long-fingered entity darted smoothly across the road—alarmingly in two seconds flat! However, the real shocker came when it stopped under the yellow light of a streetlamp looming overhead, then turned, glancing in his direction!

As if the monster had the eyes of a cat, yellow light reflected back at Bob as he tried fighting off the fear of the unknown. A riot of conflicting emotions and questions flooded over him. What the hell was it? What was it going to do?

Even as all these fears began welling up within him, he stared wide-eyed and shaken, as the unexplained nocturnal visitor silently turned to his right and, thankfully, resumed his fast, gracefully sliding strides. Bob's mind whirled as he watched it quickly squeeze through the partially open gate of a driveway. Within moments, while Bob's lungs finally filled with short, agitated breaths, the thing vanished into a line of woods on the far side of a field to the southeast.

It was so difficult for Bob to come to terms, let alone grasp, what to do after seeing something so profoundly peculiar—especially at such point blank range. In an absolute state of shock, the rest of his drive home was a blur. Closing and locking the door firmly behind him, the true nature of reality of what he had seen wrestled with everything that he had personally ever known. Therefore, it was only natural that he refrained from openly sharing what had happened, fearful people would think him crazy.

Eventually though, days later, he told his friend, Todd. Being something of a hand as a graphic artist, Todd worked extensively with Bob to successfully reproduce the detailed illustration of the being that I've termed the Creature of Copper Canyon.

If Bob's sighting were not already amazing enough, earlier that very evening, around the stroke of midnight, Mary and I (Lance Oliver) witnessed a glowing, amber colored, chevron-shaped object zooming through the sky. The UFO appeared to only be about 1,000 feet up, and it moved like a stone skipping across the surface of the water. Looking up through our car's windshield, we watched the flying object travel southeast down McKinney Rd., for the approximate two seconds it was visible.

Remarkably, Tuesday, February 26, Bob phoned, saying he had found the ticket stub that I'd asked him to look for from the movie he had seen the night of his incident. A nagging suspicion became instant realization. The UFO sighting that we had seen had taken place a couple of hours removed from Bob's encounter with of the Creature of Copper Canyon!

For our part, I filed an official report of the UFO sighting with MUFON (the Mutual UFO Network) on January 21, which can be viewed and verified as a case file at the site http://www.mufon. com. By revealing this image of the creature and this story out into the arena of public opinion, we're hopeful that our observations and ongoing research into this bizarre chain of events may encourage others to come forward and share their accounts.

*After Lance Oliver published the account with the strange creature that his friend Bob had encountered, his newsletter was flooded with correspondance from individuals who claimed to have met similar entities on late-night travels. The following are two of those accounts:*

When I saw (the drawing of the creature), I tripped! I was returning to Houston from Reno (early '80s), driving through the desert, August 2:00 A.M., very bright Moon, about 60 miles per hour, watching out for range-roaming donkeys and horses. When I turned and looked to my right(husband and son sleeping in the back), there was this man-looking creature running right along-side of the car looking at me! I yelled "Wake up!" My husband jumped in the front. He saw it, too. And then without missing a beat, it jumped over the hood of the car and was gone!

The sketch was what we saw! It was very shocking to see something like that when you are with someone. But "Bob" seeing it by himself, how traumatic that would be!

It feels so liberating to be able to talk about this to others. I really don't care what other people say.

\* \* \*

The thing in Todd's drawing seems identical to an encounter I and others had at Bluff's Creek, in Van Cleave, Mississippi, in 1974. It was standing by a tree at the water's edge of a small beach area that could only be reached via a difficult footpath. There was only one parking area, and it was about four hundred yards from this area at the main beach.

There were no other cars there when we arrived. We had no flashlights, but it was a clear moonlit night and visibility was excellent. I was leading the others on the path through the growth to the smaller beach. I had just walked out of the brush onto the beach when those behind me gasped and whispered, "Ray! Stop!"

I did not see it standing there until that moment. I thought it was a tall, bald-headed man in the nude at first, as the moon had washed all color from the scene.

I was instantly frightened, and wondered what somebody would be doing out there, alone, in the dark, and at that time of night. I could hear those behind me starting to move quickly back to the parking area, and realized they were leaving me alone.

I said, "Hello!" in the loudest voice I could muster, and the thing turned its body to face me, keeping its head oriented towards me at all times. There were no frontal features. I was absolutely terrified and the sound of my friends crashing through the brush to get away reminded me that I was growing more alone with this thing by the second.

I spun and ran back to the car as fast as possible. There were four cars involved, and the other three were peeling away when I reached the lot. Those that rode with me were screaming for me to get the hell out of there. I tore the muffler off of my Vega GT flying over the ruts.

## The Roof-Hopping Monster of India

It seems these days that monsters are showing up everywhere. My friend and fellow researcher Paul Dale Roberts recently reported his conversation with Haaroon, an Indian, who currently resides in Los Angeles. Haaroon wanted to tell Paul about the mysterious animal that was attacking the people in Madhya Pradesh, India. Haaroon claimed to have seen the beast jumping from roof-to-roof with his own eyes while he was visiting his family in Madhya Pradesh.

**Haaroon:** The beast looked to be gray, hunched over. You know people with braided hair on sunny islands by Florida, this is the kind of hair it had.

**Roberts:** You mean dreadlocks?

**Haaroon:** Yes, I think dreadlocks. This monster has dreadlocks, bright red dreadlocks and shiny bright green eyes.

**Roberts:** What was this creature doing, when you saw it?

**Haaroon:** It leapt from one rooftop to another. At one point of time, it looked at me. It kind of snarled. It has big teeth, pointy teeth.

**Roberts:** What was the size?

**Haaroon:** Size like big dog, maybe German shepherd. It ran on two stubby legs. Sometimes it runs on all four legs, all stubby legs.

**Roberts:** Did it do anything else besides jumping from roof-to-roof?

**Haaroon:** Sure, it zap in air! You know zap in air. It goes away. It is gone. If you close eyes for one second, it is gone.

**Roberts:** Are you saying it vanished, it disappeared?

**Haaroon:** Yes, vanished.

Paul did some additional research and learned that there were many recent reports coming out of Madhya Pradesh of a mysterious beast that has been attacking people.

"I do not know if there are any other descriptions of this beast, but according to Haaroon, he saw the creature first hand and his description of the beast is very frightening," Paul said. "I wonder if this creature is some kind of multidimensional being?"

## Monster of Darkness

*The following contribution was written by Tuesday Miles, a highly regarded psychic sensitive, writer, and radio host who specializes in exploring the paranormal.*

The thought of night seeping around each corner always used to give me such an eerie chill throughout my body. After all, monsters never come out during the daylight—they hide or would melt if the sun were to hit the creepiness of their evil body.

I had finally accepted my psychic gifts. At first I had prayed, begged, and pleaded. I was willing to do a trade if only God—or whoever was listening—would take these pain-in-the-butt gifts. I did not ask for them, nor was I sent a manual on how to use them. Take them away from me! Return me to my old normal self.

My prayer requests fell on deaf ears. I tried to reason with myself that being psychic couldn't be all that bad. I could handle seeing a ghost or two— maybe three, tops.

For some reason I no longer would venture out in my backyard after dusk. I did not like the feeling I experienced during the daylight, but the nighttime was even worse. There was the eeriness of seeming to have 100 pairs of eyes following me around. There was a terrible odor which I thought was the smell of death. The sound of growls would come from somewhere. And then the deep serpentine sound of a hiss. I just knew something was lurking around out there—and I didn't quite understand if its intentions were to harm me or to send fear throughout my body.

When I was going through my spiritual awakening, I remember sitting at the window in my den area, watching the plants in the backyard move, as if someone or something was walking among them. The branches of the smaller trees that I had planted would bend as if something had grabbed them and pulled them down.

I would get up and run to the backyard, checking what exactly was out there, *who was doing this, and how they could disappear so fast.*

I even blamed the neighbor behind me that he had rats in his trees.

I would sit for hours, watching the monsters who were invisible fly around in these balls of light, then form into the kind of fog that only the deep woods of the South could create.

Was I insane? This would be the only way that I could accept what I was going to witness one night in my backyard.

I yelled for the dog, "Come on girl, come with me while I water the backyard lawn."

It was summer time. The house was too hot. Trying to conquer my fear of the darkness, I asked my husband to walk me out to the backyard and help me to grab the hose. I made sure all the bright flood lights were hitting every inch of the space that surrounded me. The sound of the crickets, mild at first, started to grow into this intense sound of a warning, as if they were saying to me: *Run, you must run now!* I could feel

The strange visitor had brilliant gold eyes, almost as if the eyes were lasers. It had strange spots all over its body. It had no hair, and its body looked as if it belonged to a lizard, a reptilian creature (*art by Ricardo Pustanio*).

this overwhelming sense of danger that comes with that moment just before you slowly move to turn around, adrenalin starting to pump through your heart, fear moving every nerve in your body.

The scream, the gasp, that fear as I turned to look behind me, squinting because of the flood lights bouncing off my pupils. "What the hell!" I said out loud as I took two steps back.

The creature's mouth was open to bare jagged teeth.

I glared at it the way you try to intimidate an enemy in front of you.

I froze. I was not sure if I should run. Would it run after me?

All of a sudden I felt like I was dinner. Neither one of us was going to move.

Then it happened. It moved, and I ran and screamed.

I did not know ghosts or spirits still had teeth, I had not seen them before. The gold eyes, almost as if the eyes were lasers, the strange spots all over this entity's body. It had no hair, and its body looked as if it belonged to a lizard.

I ran into the house, leaving the hose on the ground with the water running. I grabbed my husband, telling him to close the door and lock it.

He turned [and] asked me to fill him in on what the hell was going on?

I told him that I had just seen an alien. I swear to God it was an alien. I am not sure what type of alien, but I swear it was not human. It was big and ugly and it had awful teeth.

He went to go look out the window, returning with an "I don't see anything. Look."

I knew the only thing for me to do was to go back out into the backyard. I grabbed a small bat in my left hand, my pepper spray in the right hand. I opened the back door and tried to push my husband to go first. We both went hand-in-hand back to the very spot where I had seen the monster, the lizard- looking alien. We both froze before we moved around the corner.

It was then I realized that I was showing fear, so I told hubby to go back into the house. I would be okay—and if I wasn't he would listen for me to scream again.

I could see the water from the hose running towards me, flooding the backyard grass. I walked up the three steps and peeked around the corner where the ugly monster stood .

I asked, "Why you are here? What do you want?"

The thing said nothing.

"Do you understand me?" I asked.

This time the head moved, looking behind its self. The body turned so that I could see the side view of it. I could swear that this monster thing had a tail on it, although it seemed part of its legs.

I wanted to ask it a million questions—then my head started feeling strange, as if something was pulling information from my third eye. I no longer felt the urge to speak. I was communicating from inside my mind. I did not understand what was spoken to me—although I knew I was answering the questions I had been asked.

I turned to look behind me, and when I turned back it was gone. Not a trace of it anywhere.

I have been told it was a reptilian, a type of species in the alien spectrum. The reports of these types of aliens have mostly been negative. They are not the kindest types of aliens. My question was what did it want from me, and why was I able to see it and not my husband.

Was this a spirit, a reptilian spirit? I do not know—but I have learned that all things are possible.

# AZAZEL AND THE WATCHERS—
# SLAVEMASTERS OF EARTH

*Respected psychic and radio personality Julia Cole told me that over the course of her life she has experienced sporadic encounters with a being that she has dubbed "the Watcher," a very tall, very dark, spirit being with large saucer-like green eyes, that appears as if it is wearing a long, ragged, hooded cape.*

*According to Julia:*

The first encounter that I recall was in 1969 when I was nine-years-old and while I was taking a bath. Its message was: "We are watching you." My second encounter came a year later late one night while I was lying in bed. The being pronounced the same message.

The next two encounters came in 1972 while my kid sister and I were staying with our oldest sister while our mother was in the hospital. The one encounter during my stay there was late at night and occurred outside. The second encounter, both my kid sister and I were involved.

I didn't see the creature again until Thanksgiving night 1985. I was eight-and-a half months pregnant with my twins and spending the night at my dad's house.

My next encounter was in 1988. My only eyewitnesses were my oldest son who was four-and half years old, my three-year-old twins, and a friend who was spending the night.

Two years later, I came in contact with two men dressed all in black. Yes, I actually met the Men in Black! It was in the middle of the night. I had just moved into my new apartment. My telephone had not yet been turned on, and I was looking for a pay phone that actually worked when I came in contact with these beings. Their presence, I felt (and still feel), had connections to the Watcher.

In 1991, the Watcher reappeared to me. I had just come back from dropping my three boys off to spend the weekend with their grandmother. I didn't feel its presence until I went towards the bathroom.

In the "Watcher Angel Tarot" by Michelle Belanger and Jackie Williams, the Emperor represents Azazel, who taught humankind weapon-smithing and warfare (*art by Jackie Williams*).

My initial response was that someone had broken in and was hiding in the shower. Don't ask why I did it, but I rushed in, flipping on the lights, and ripped off the shower curtains.

There was no one there but me. But I could still feel it.

As I stood there, I saw it begin to take form.

I ran out of the apartment and across the street to where my fiancé lived, and waited for him to get home from work. A three-hour wait by the way!

A year later, as four of the neighbors and I sat playing cards, the apartment grew frigid cold. The A/C was not on. But the apartment was getting cold fast.

We all checked the vents, hot air was blowing out, but the entire apartment was getting colder. We could see our breath at this point.

This lasted only a few minutes. As we all began to sit back down, one of the ladies jumped back up and yelled that something had grabbed her arm. Right before our eyes, several long bruises began to appear across her forearm. It looked as though someone had her arm in a tight grip. We could see the skin being pressed down.

I was the first to see the Watcher appear. Soon, the others saw it as it slowly came into focus in the middle of my living room.

I didn't see this thing again until 1998. Its visit was brief, as was its oft-repeated message: We are watching you. Each time this thing has appeared, that has been its message, a brief notice that I am being watched.

In 2003, I encountered a lizard person. I think I frightened the poor creature with my screaming! But it had manifested much earlier in the day—in broad daylight—and I had encountered the Watcher in the evening hours. Again its message was "We are watching you."

Later that evening, I was on my way home from work when I came in contact with a very tall lizard person. When I first saw it, it looked like the Watcher. It was dressed in a long black-hooded cape, so I assumed it was the Watcher.

I had to walk through the Galleria to get to my bus stop. At that time of night, there were very few people around. I hurried through, and just as I reached the door, the lizard person caught up with me.

It reached out for me as the door to the Galleria began to close. The lizard person called out my name, telling me it needed to speak to me.

I fell face first onto the pavement, screaming for help. By the time the security guard showed up, it was gone.

The next time I would encounter the Watcher would be April 2006. In the fall of 2007, it had become bolder and tormented me for a week. It didn't come alone. This encounter lasted nearly two months, and nearly cost me my life.

It was during this time that I knew that I had to make a conscious decision to rid myself of this once and for all. The Watcher had returned full force and with company. This all began after I had volunteered to look into a paranormal investigation to help prove its validity. My friend John Zaffis, a well-known paranormal researcher, was instrumental in saving my life.

In the summer of 2008, I was called in to help an associate whose three-year-old son had been experiencing a dark entity for period of time. When I had confronted the entity, I was taken aback by its nonchalant attitude. It claimed that it knew me and asked if I remembered it.

Truthfully, I don't know if it was the same entity as The Watcher. Perhaps it was one of its brethren? All I know it shook me up.

## An Ancient Race of Serpent People

We can surely understand why Julia Cole would be shaken by the return visit of a being that had been watching her all of her life. In our files we have many accounts of men and women who testify that they have been visited by "Watchers" ever since they were very young children—and a high percentage of them state that their strange overseers were reptilian in appearance.

There are many accounts of wise "feathered serpents" and serpentine or amphibious culture-bearers teaching primitive humankind in the ancient texts of numerous religions and societies. Legends of these "Watchers" having sexual union with human women and men and producing children are also not uncommon.

In the Hindu and Buddhist traditions, the Nagas are a proud, handsome race of serpent people who dwell in Naga-Ioka, their splendid, underground bejeweled kingdom. Although an ancient race of serpent people figure in the myths and traditions of many cultures, in the Hindu and Buddhist traditions, the Nagas are semi-divine beings with many supernatural powers. Because both the male and female members of the Naga are physically attractive, legends of intermarriage with surface humans abound, and in the past, many noble families of India claimed a Nagi ancestor.

## The Grigori, the Watchers

The apocryphal book of Enoch tells of the order of fallen angels called "Watchers," "The Sleepless Ones," or the Grigori. The leader of the Watchers was called Azazel

**Temperance: Zaquiel (purity) stands in a balance between flesh and spirit, the earthy and the spiritual (*art by Jackie Williams*).**

(in other places, Semyaza or Semjaza) who led 200 Watchers down to Earth to take wives from among the daughters of men. It was from such a union that the Nephilim, the giants, the heroes of old, as well as the ancient practitioners of sorcery were born.

If we were to read the creation story in Genesis from the historical perspective of our current awareness of genetic engineering, the interaction between the Grigori and the fair daughters of men could assume a rather different interpretation.

If those alleged lustful fallen angels of Genesis were actually extraterrestrial visitors conducting experiments on the female members of the developing strain of *Homo sapiens*, then rather than decadent heavenly beings sinning with Earth's daughters, they were scientists carrying out the directive of their superiors to provide nascent humankind with a genetic boost.

It is difficult not to be fascinated by the passages about the *Nephilim*, the Hebrew word used to describe demigods—or men of great renown—those who were said to be the offspring of the Sons of God and the daughters of men.

Interestingly, the word used to denote true giants, as far as great stature was concerned, was *Rephaim*. The Israelites found such giants among the Canaanite inhabitants of Palestine. Among these *Rephaim* were the Anakims of Philisa and the Emims of Moab. Goliath was a Gittite, a man of great stature and bulk, but he was not a *Nephilim*.

Perhaps the Grigori interfered with the evolution of humankind to create a species of slaves to accomplish their manual labor on Earth. Indeed, they could have genetically altered humankind to produce a convenient food source. Science fiction authors have toyed with the concept of humans being tasty morsels from the Damon Knight short story "To Serve Man," which was one of the most popular episodes of *The Twilight Zone*, to the popular television series *V*, recently remade for a new viewing generation.

Other researchers have suggested that the fallen Sons of God came as Cosmic Puppet Masters, fashioning their own world of worshippers. Indeed, if they are paraphysical beings who were thrown out of "Heaven" after a failed rebellion against a superior force, they may have wanted to genetically alter an evolving species that would be hardwired to recognize them as their benevolent monarchs.

According to certain apocryphal literature, Azazel and the Grigori taught their human wives to cast various spells and to practice the arts of enchantment. They imparted to the women the lore of plants and the properties of certain roots.

Azazel did not neglect human men, teaching them how to manufacture knives, swords, shields and a vast array of weapons and tools of destruction.

Amaros selected a group of humans to whom he taught the power of magic and the elements of alchemy.

Baraqiel pointed to the stars and taught those humans following his gaze upward how to perfect the art of astrology.

Kakabel had been one of the Lord's most faithful followers, but he, too, joined the ranks of the Grigori and gathered an army of 365,000 Watchers to do his bidding.

Penemue instructed humankind in the skills of writing and learning.

Shamsiel had once been one of the most loyal of the angels of the Lord, entrusted, along with Hasdiel, to be a chief aide to Uriel as custodians of the Garden of Eden. He, too, became a Watcher and began to teach humans about extraterrestrial worlds. Allegorically, Shamsiel or Azazel was the serpent that tempted Adam and Eve (humankind) in the Garden of Eden.

## A Great Prehistoric War
## between Warriors of Light and Darkness

If the Grigori once ruled the Earth as physical beings, ancient scriptures indicate that those angels who had remained loyal to the Lord in Heaven descended to Earth in attempt to restore the natural evolution of the planet. Some scientists today believe that Sodom and Gomorrah may have been destroyed by an ancient nuclear blast. As early as the 1960s, Russian scientist Matest M. Agrest had suggested that the cities were fused together under the searing heat of a pre-Paleolithic atomic explosion.

In Genesis 19:1–28, we are informed that Lot is waiting by the community gate of Sodom when two angels approach him. Some scholars conclude that Lot must have made prior arrangements to meet these heavenly beings. After their meeting, he escorts the entities to his home where they are fed and lodged.

Such researchers as Professor Agrest maintain that if these angels were wholly spiritual beings, they would not have been interested in an evening meal, nor in a bed for the night.

Later, when the coarse men of Sodom pound on Lot's door and demand to "know" his visitors sexually, the angels appear to employ some kind of unusual weapon which instantly blinded them and blotted out their lust.

When Lot is informed by the heavenly representatives that Sodom will soon be destroyed, he chooses to remain in the city. Neither Lot nor other members of his family seem to take the warning seriously.

However, when the morning sun rose, the angels urged Lot and his family to flee at once.

And, in the aforementioned passages from Genesis, we read the following: "The men [angels] laid hold upon his hand, and upon the hand of his wife, and upon the hand of his two daughters. The Lord being merciful unto him; and they brought them forth and set him outside the city.

"And it came to pass when they had brought them forth aboard, that he said, Escape for thy life; look not behind them, neither stay thou in the plain; escape to the mountains, less thou be consumed hast thee, escape thither; for I cannot do anything till thou come hither."

Those who subscribe to Professor Agrest's theory believe that a nuclear device had been triggered and the "angels" had been assigned to lead Lot and his family away from the blast area.

### The World Shuddered, Scorched by Terrible Heat

Other ancient texts mention flying machines, advanced technology, and terrible weapons wielded by the Grigori and other gods.

The sacred Hindu hymns, the *Rig-Veda*, constitute some of the oldest known religious documents. The splendid poetry tells of the achievements of the Hindu pantheon of gods; and one passage tells of Indra, a god-being, who was honored when his name was turned into " India."

Indra, who became known as the "fort destroyer" because of his exploits in war, was said to travel through the skies in a flying machine, the *Vimana*. This craft was equipped with awesome weapons capable of destroying a city. The effect of these weapons seems to have been like that of laser beams or some kind of nuclear device.

Another ancient Indian text, the *Mahabharata*, tells of an attack on an enemy army: "It was as if the elements had been unfurled. The sun spun around in the heavens. The world shuddered in fever, scorched by the terrible heat of this weapon. Elephants burst into flames. The rivers boiled. Animals crumpled to the ground and died.

"The armies of the enemy were mowed down when the raging elements reached them. Forests collapsed in splintered rows. Horses and chariots were burned up. The corpses of the fallen were mutilated by the terrible heat so that they looked other than human. Never before had we heard of such a ghastly weapon."

There are many traditions that speak of a war between the forces of light and darkness which raged in humankind's prehistory. Perhaps there were rival extraterrestrial or multidimensional forces that fought for dominance over prehistoric Earth.

According to some traditions, the Sons of Light vanquished certain Dark Magicians who sought to enslave developing humankind. Whatever may have caused such a violent conflict, there exists awesome evidence around our planet that someone was exercising power of formidable energy.

Throughout our globe there are accounts of sand melted into glass in certain desert areas, of hill forts with vitrified portions of stone walls, of the remains of ancient cities that had been destroyed by what appears to have been extreme heat—far beyond that which could have been scorched by the torches of primitive human armies. Even conventionally trained archaeologists who have encountered such anomalous finds have admitted that none of these catastrophes have been caused by volcanoes, by lightning, by crashing comets, or by the conflagrations of humankind.

### Evoking the Grigori

In Enochian Magick, the practitioner, seeking to summon the Grigori, employed words of power which allegedly had been passed down in an oral tradition from the times of Enoch. The actual evocation began with the chanting of the appropriate words, which varied from spirit to spirit. These words of power were said, by their very sounds, to exert a strong emotional effect. A famous example is: *Eca zodocare iad goho Torzodu odo kilale qaa! Zodacare od sodameranul Zodorje lape zodiredo ol noco mada dae iadapiel!*

The Judgment card in the "Watcher Angel Tarot" represents the biblical Flood that destroyed the Watchers and all their works (*art by Jackie Williams*).

These words from the Enochian language, believed by magicians and other occultists to predate Sanskrit, is also believed to be the language of the Grigori. These words were addressed to the fallen angels that the Magi believed would assist them in their magic and they translate as follows: "Move, therefore, and show yourselves! Open the mysteries of your creation! Be friendly unto me, for I am servant of the same, your God, and I am a true worshipper of the Highest."

In all chanting, recitations, and litanies, the impact of a group is far more impressive than that of a single voice, and the Enochian practitioners always sought a group that consisted of seekers of like dedication. When properly performed, such rituals have a powerful impact on the emotions. This is heightened by measured walking around the inside of a magic circle, and dancing.

### The Legendary Hermes Trismegistus and His Emerald Tablet

In alchemical/magical tradition, powerful secrets of alchemy were found inscribed on an emerald tablet in the hands of the mummy of Hermes Trismegistus, the master magician and alchemist, who had been entombed in an obscure chamber of the Great Pyramid of Giza. The preamble to the key that would transmute base materials into precious metals and gems was the dictum that "It is true, without falsehood, and most real: that which is above is like that which is below, to perpetrate the miracles of one thing." The writings of Hermes Trismegistus were considered by the alchemists as a legacy from the master of alchemy and were, therefore, precious to them.

The discovery of the Emerald Tablet at Giza is quite likely an allegory. The alchemists, who were concerned with the spiritual perfection of humankind as well as the transmutation of base metals into gold, commonly recorded their formulas and esoteric truths in allegorical form. Today we know that there was no single personage named Hermes Trismegistus and that the Leyden Papryus discovered in the tomb of the anonymous magician contains the oldest known copy of the inscription from the legendary Emerald Tablet, which is itself a description of the seven stages of gold-making.

Hermes, who is called Trismegistus, "three times the greatest," was a deity of a group of Greeks who once founded a colony in Egypt. This transplanted god drew his name from Hermes (Mercury to the Romans), the messenger of the Greek hierarchy of deities and the god who conducted the souls of the dead to the underworld kingdom of Hades. The Egyptians identified Hermes Trismegistus with Thoth, who, in their pantheon of gods, was the divine inventor of writing and the spoken word. These same Greek colonists developed an interest in the old Egyptian religion, then went on to combine elements of their Hellenistic beliefs, add fragments of Judaism and other Eastern belief constructs, and set about creating a synthesis of the various theologies. A vast number of unknown authors worked at the great task of composing a series of esoteric writings, all of which were attributed to the mythical figure of Thoth-Hermes. Eventually, Thoth-Hermes became humanized into a legendary king, who supposedly wrote the amazing total of 36,525 volumes of metaphysical teachings. In the third century, Clement of Alexandria reduced the total to 42, which he said he saw in a vision which enabled him to condense the total of texts to 42.

### *Calling on Angels ... or Demons in Disguise?*

The science of alchemy was introduced to the Western world at the beginning of the second century of the contemporary era. Zosimus of Panapolis, self-appointed apologist of alchemy, cited a passage in Genesis as the origin of the arcane art: "The sons of God saw that the daughters of men were fair." To this scriptural reference, Zosimus added the tradition that in reward for their favors, the "sons of God," the "Watchers," the Grigori, endowed these women with the knowledge of how to make jewels, colorful garments, and perfumes with which to enhance their earthly charms.

The seven principal angels whose favor the alchemist sought to obtain for their transformation of base metals into gold were Michael, who was able to dissolve any enmity directed by negative entities toward the alchemist; Gabriel, who fashioned silver and foresaw the future; Samuel, who protected against physical harm; and Raphael, Sachiel, Ansel, and Cassiel, who could create various gems and guard the alchemist from attack by demons.

However, members of the clergy were skeptical that the alchemists were truly calling upon angels, rather than demons in disguise, and they recalled the words of the Church Father Tertullian (c. 160–240), who confirmed earlier beliefs that the "sons of God" referred to in Genesis were evil perverters of humans who bequeathed their wisdom to mortals with the sole intention of seducing them to mundane pleasures.

## The Universe Is Teeming with Angels and Demons

The essence of Abramelin Magick is to be found in *The Sacred Magic of Abramelin the Mage*, which was translated by MacGregor Mathers from a manuscript written in French in the eighteenth century. The work purports to be much older, how-

The Hermit, a wise teacher. In the "Watcher Angel Tarot," the Hermit is associated with Penemue, who is said to have taught humanity the wisdom of writing (*art by Jackie Williams*).

ever. It was dated 1458 and claims to be translated originally from Hebrew. The text reveals to the adept that the universe is teeming with hordes of angels and demons that interact with human beings on many levels. All the vast array of phenomena on Earth are produced by the demonic entities, who are under the control of the angels. Humans are somewhere midway between the angelic and the demonic intelligences on the spiritual scale, and each human entity has both a guardian angel and a malevolent demon that hover near him or her from birth until death.

Abramelin Magick provides instruction to the initiates of the "Magic of Light" which will enable them to achieve mastery over the demons and place them under their control. Abramelin the great Magus learned how to accomplish such a difficult task by undergoing a process of spiritual cleansing and the development of a powerful will.

In addition to spiritual and mental exercises, Abramelin discovered words of power that can be arranged in magic squares and written on parchment. With the proper application of these magical squares, the magus can command the demons and order them to assist him in the acquisition of earthly knowledge and power. By applying such magic words as "ABRACADABRA," Abramelin magicians believe that they can gain the love of anyone they desire, discover hidden treasures, become invisible, invoke spirits to appear, fly through the air and travel great distances in a matter of minutes, and animate corpses to create zombies to serve them. Abramelin magicians can heal illnesses or cause diseases, bring about peace or war, create prosperity or poverty. They believe that they can shapeshift into different animal or human forms.

## *Eliphas Levi and the Power of Tarot*

Eliphas Levi (Alphonse Louis Constant) was born in France about 1810, the son of a shoemaker. A pious boy, his parents soon decided that little Alphonse should be educated for the life of a parish priest. Constant became a deacon, took a vow of celibacy, and seemed destined for a quiet life in the clergy. But then his life suddenly assumed a very different course when Father Constant felt that somewhere along the ages the theologians of the Church had confused Lucifer, the bearer of Light, with Satan, the Prince of Darkness, and had judged him unfairly. Such a liberal attitude to the angel who led the revolt in Heaven did not sit at all well with his superiors, and Father Constant was expelled from the Church.

Alphonse Louis Constant assumed the identity of Eliphas Levi and began to devote his time to an intensive study of alchemy and the occult. Very often his focus was on the *Kabballah* and the Tarot, believing firmly that the ancient cards depicted a concise summary of all the revelations that had come down to humankind through the ages.

Levi saw in the symbolism of the Tarot cards the key to the Egyptian hieroglyphs, the mysteries of Solomon, and the truths hidden in the apocryphal text of The Book of Enoch and the scrolls of Hermes Trismegistus. To do a spread of the Tarot cards, in Levi's opinion, was to establish communication with the spirit world. To seek within the Tarot might bring the serious magician a clue to the manipulation of the natural and divine energy that permeated all of nature. The existence of such a force, Eliphas Levi believed, was to discover the Great Arcanum of Practical Magick.

His *Doctrine of Transcendental Magic,* published in 1855, was followed by *Rituals of Transcendental Magic* in 1856. Eliphas Levi died in 1875, esteemed by many and hailed as the last of the alchemists. Others have criticized certain of his writings by suggesting that his imagination may in some instances have surpassed his actual knowledge of the arcane.

Azazel and the Grigori may have lost a great battle in prehistoric times that forced them to withdraw to other dimensions, but they certainly did not lose the great eternal war. The deceitful, exploitative entities continue to visit our world in order to complete their master plan—to enslave humankind. Those humans who believe that they can command the demonic intelligences are falling into a trap that was set for the unwary and the arrogant in prehistoric times. Those who believe that they can master the Grigori with spells, chants, and rituals are only hastening an apocalyptic event that may decimate the entire human species.

# DOES THE RISE OF THE ZOMBIES HERALD ARMAGEDDON?

For decades, tourists from all over the world have visited Tel Megiddo in great numbers, attracted by the site's apocalyptic mystique and the old battleground's significance as the place where the fate of ancient empires was decided with the might of sword and spear. The Israel National Parks Authority work in close coordination with the Megiddo Expedition and the Ename Center for Public Archaeology of Belgium in offering visitors a dramatic perspective of the history of Armageddon.

As the Millennium approached in the last months of 1999, Israeli police were presented with an unusual and potentially deadly problem that could affect the entire world. Fundamentalist Christians began to arrive in large numbers so they could be in Jerusalem when Armageddon occurred. These extremist Christians had equated the advent of the new Millennium with the end of the world and the return of Jesus, and they wanted to be in the Valley of Megiddo to fight on the side of the angels against demonic hordes when the last great battle between good and evil took place. When it became apparent that some of the more fanatical Millennialists were prepared to precipitate a conflict and initiate Armageddon if "the Lord should tarry," Israeli police had no choice other than to escort a number of these Christian warriors to the airport and demand that they leave Israel.

Revelation 16:16 declares Armageddon, "the mound of Megiddo," as the battlefield where blasphemers, unclean spirits, and devils join forces for the final great battle of the ages between their evil hordes and the faithful angelic army of Christ. The inspiration for such a choice of battlegrounds was quite likely an obvious one for John the Revelator, for it has been said that more blood has been shed around the hill of Megiddo than any other single spot of Earth.

Located 10 miles southwest of Nazareth at the entrance of a pass across the Carmel mountain range, it stands on the main highway between Asia and Africa and in a key position between the Euphrates and Nile rivers, thus providing a traditional meeting place of armies from the East and from the West. For thousands of years, the Valley of

**Are signs of more and more zombies an indication that we are approaching Armageddon? (photo by Shannon McCabe).**

Mageddon, now known as the Jezreel Valley, had been the site where great battles had been waged and the fate of empires decided. Thothmes III, whose military strategies made Egypt a world-empire, proclaimed the taking of Megiddo to be worth the conquering of a thousand cities. During World War I in 1918, the British General Edmund Allenby broke the power of the Turkish army at Megiddo.

Most scholars agree that the word "Armageddon" is a Greek corruption of the Hebrew *Har-Megiddo*, "the mound of Megiddo," but they debate exactly when the designation of Armageddon was first used. The city of Megiddo was abandoned sometime during the Persian period (539–332 B.C.E.), and the small villages established to the south were known by other names. It could well have been that John the Revelator, writing in the Jewish apocalyptic tradition of a final conflict between the forces of light and darkness, was well aware of the bloody tradition of the hill of Megiddo and was inspired by the ruins of the city on its edge.

By the Middle Ages, theologians began to employ "Armageddon" as a spiritual concept without any conscious association with the Valley of Megiddo. Armageddon simply stood for the promised time when the returning Christ and his legions of angels would gather to defeat the assembled armies of darkness.

In the fourteenth century, the Jewish geographer Estori Ha-Farchi suggested that the roadside village of Lejjun might be the location of the biblical Megiddo. Ha-Farchi pointed out that Lejjun was the Arabic form of Legio, the old Roman name for the place. In the early nineteenth century, American biblical scholar Edwin Robinson traveled to the area of Palestine that was held at that time by the Ottoman Empire and he became convinced that Ha-Farchi was correct in his designation of the site as the biblical Megiddo. Later explorers and archaeologists determined that the ruins of the ancient city lay about a mile north of Lejjun at what had been renamed by the Ottoman government as the mound of Tell el-Mutasellim, "the hill of the governor."

### *Charles Manson—the Fifth Angel of the Apocalypse*

The Christian extremists who sought to prompt Armageddon into occurring at midnight on December 31, 1999, were certainly not the first group of individuals who tried to precipitate the last great warfare between good and evil. Charles Manson, who saw himself as the Fifth Angel who would be given the key to the pit of the abyss in Revelation, sent forth a number of his followers, after he had stolen their minds and turned into virtual zombies with plans to ignite an apocalyptic revolution that would lead to Armageddon.

Manson, who was called Satan, God, or Sweet Daddy-O by his young female disciples, seemed to be born under an unlucky star on November 11, 1934. His unwed mother was a teenage hustler who picked up tricks in cheap roadhouses and bars. Shortly after Charles' birth in Cincinnati, Ohio, his 16-year-old mother and her brother were convicted of mugging some of her clientele, and she was sent to prison.

While his mother was jailed, the baby was sent to his grandmother's home in McMechen, West Virginia. Later, the child lived with a quarrelsome uncle and aunt.

When he was eight years old, his mother was released from prison, and Charlie joined her as she drank in bars and hustled men. The two of them lived in rundown apartments on the ugly side of the city.

By 1945, his mother had found a traveling salesman who promised a steady relationship, but her lover did not consider young Charlie to be part of the arrangement, and she tried to place him in a foster home.

Later, the state authorities made him a ward of the county. He was sent to the Gibault School for Boys, a custodial institution for homeless or wayward boys. Charlie escaped after 10 months.

Thus began a cycle that would continue for decades. Charlie kept running away from reform schools, and the authorities kept catching him and bringing him back. Finally, he ended up in the reform school at Plainfield, Indiana—the toughest in the state. He escaped from there 28 times.

In the early 1960s, Charles Manson stole and cashed two U.S. Treasury checks. He was promptly apprehended and sent to the federal prison at McNeil Island, Washington.

It was here that Charlie began to explore offbeat philosophies and the occult. He developed an interest in Scientology and a mish-mash of pseudoscientific mysticism.

Manson also liked to play his guitar, and he learned that he could influence his cell mates with music. He worked hard, attempting to train his voice, and he began to write his own songs.

When Charlie walked out of prison in March 1967, a whole new world had been created while he was behind bars. The Flower Children had launched the hippie movement. The Haight-Ashbury section of San Francisco had become the golden glory land for the hippies.

**Charles Manson's rough childhood was excellent preparation for a life of crime, but he took it to the next level, seeing himself as the Fifth Angel of Revelations (*art by Ricardo Pustanio*).**

Charlie had spent 22 years of his life in state or federal prisons. Uneducated, untrained, and barely able to read, Charlie emerged with not the slightest evidence that he had been rehabilitated. He came out of prison a resentful, hostile man. The only thing that he had learned in his years of confinement was how to steal cars, how to pass bad checks, and how to pimp. Charlie got himself a hillside pad and started to collect his followers.

One of his first recruits was an attractive, long-haired, 19-year-old brunette named Patricia Krenwinkel. A 1966 graduate of Los Angeles High, she had gotten a job as a file clerk and bought a car. She was considered a reserved, conservative young woman by all who knew her, but when she met Charles Manson, she was transformed instantly into a cult camp follower with no will of her own. Krenwinkle had fallen under Manson's mystical spell so quickly that she abandoned her automobile in a parking lot and left without picking up her paycheck.

Manson collected a number of young enchanted women around him. They were primarily female dropouts, seemingly drawn to the mystical minstrel who appeared to control them with a power as great as the most commanding Voodoo priest. A few young men also joined his cult, and the group became known as the "Charles Manson Family."

Gullible, emotionally disturbed, and often very immature, the young men and women who gave obeisance to Manson's creed believed that he was the messiah of the New Age. So many of the empty, confused youth who roamed America in those days were devoid of values, and they longed for someone who could make them feel desirable and worthwhile.

Charlie was a magical man to those desperate, seeking young people who came to sit at his feet. Charlie knew the answers to everything.

Manson led his cult in weird chants. He adopted mystical rites from other traditions and shaped them to his own unique personality. He began to make prophecies, and anyone who doubted or questioned his godlike stature was threatened with expulsion from the group. To his young followers, Charlie seemed so wise, so ageless that they figured that he just had to be a being from another planet.

In May, 1968, with the hippie scene fading in San Francisco, Manson and his clan of subservient young disciples headed south toward Los Angeles. Led by their mystical guru, the flock of young people converted an old school bus into a rolling pad, and they drove to Los Angeles. The bearded, long-haired cultist planned to make a fortune as a songwriter and a musician.

In the film capital, Manson and his nomads met and moved in with 34-year-old Gary Hinman, a musician. The Hinman home was labeled the "pig farm," a refuge for weirdos.

A year later, Hinman was murdered by Manson's followers when he tried to toss the Family out of his home. The killing of Hinman is believed to be the first murder perpetrated by Manson and his cultists. The musician was discovered slashed to death in his home. The bloody words "political piggy" was scrawled on the walls of the death house.

*Author's note: Even today, more than four decades after the Tate-Bianca murders, many police officials believe that graves of other Manson Family victims might be at the cult leader's Death Valley base. In addition to disobedient Family members, some investigators suggest that a number of teenaged runaways, hitchhikers, and individuals who innocently stumbled upon Manson's hideaway may have been murdered by the Family.*

After leaving the "pig farm," the Family established several bases around Los Angeles, including the Spahn Ranch, a former Hollywood set for such television series as *Bonanza* and *The Lone Ranger*; a camp in Canoga Park, named the "Yellow Submarine" in honor of the Beatles; and the desolate Barker Ranch in Death Valley.

Manson pestered people he thought could give him his big break in music, such as Terry Melcher, son of actress-singer Doris Day. Strange as it may seem, some music world insiders remember that someone did arrange studio time and a kind of audition for Charlie.

Boyd Rice, San Francisco's "King of Noise Music" and a passionate Mansonophile, claims to be in possession of nearly nine hours of Manson music, which he recorded in his cell at Vacaville in the early 1980s. The songs are known collectively as *Charlie Manson's Good Time Gospel Hour*. Manson ruled his Family as the supreme tyrant. If he liked something, so must everyone in the group. If he directed his hostility toward an object or a person, the others were expected to develop their hatred. If he declared that sleeping in the nude was right, then everyone must do it. When he decided something was wrong, then that practice was forbidden.

Manson initiated the new female members of the commune, and he spent their first day in the Family making love to them. If the new girl refused to engage in oral-genital sex, she was expelled. Manson claimed that oral sex was an important indicator that the girl had been liberated from her middle-class sexual inhibitions.

In Manson's cosmology, he and all of humanity were God and Satan at the same time. He also professed that every human was a part of all others, which, in his philosophy, meant that individual human life was of no consequence. If you killed a person, you were just killing a part of yourself, so that made everything all right.

It is generally thought that Manson knew some techniques of hypnotism, but he appeared to believe more fervently in the power of motions and gestures. In the manner of a ritualistic magician, he felt that certain of his motions, movements, and gestures could create particular responses in other people.

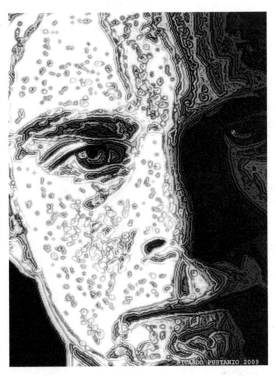

Manson was said to control his followers with a combination of hypnotism and his skill in influencing people with motions and gestures to elicit desired responses (*art by Ricardo Pustanio*).

Manson made his brainwashed followers feel most important when he told them that they had a mission that had been set forth 2,000 years ago in the Book of Revelation. He confided that he was the fifth angel who had been given the key to the pit of the abyss.

Reading from Chapter 9 of Revelation:

> And the fifth angel sounded, and I saw a star from heaven fallen unto the earth: and there was given to him the key of the pit of the abyss. And he opened the pit of the abyss: and there went up a smoke out of the pit, as the smoke of a great furnace; and the sun and the air were darkened.... And out of the smoke came forth locusts upon the earth; and power was given them, as the scorpions of the earth have power. And it was said unto them that they should (hurt) ... only such men as have not the seal of God on their foreheads.... And in those days men shall seek death ... and they shall desire to die, and death fleeth from them. And the shapes of the locusts were like unto horses prepared for war; and upon their heads as it were crowns like unto gold ... and they had hair as the hair of women, and their teeth were as teeth of lions. And they had breastplates, as it were breastplates of iron.... And they have tails like unto scorpions, and stings; and in their tails is their power to hurt men.... They have over them as king the angel of the abyss: his name in Hebrew is Abaddon, and in the Greek tongue ... Apollyon. The first woe is past: behold, there are to come yet two woes hereafter. And the sixth angel sounded.... Loose the four angels that are bound....) And the four angels were loosed that had been prepared for the hour and day and month and year, that they should kill the third part of men....) And thus I saw the horses in the vision, and them that sat on them, having breastplates as of fire and brimstone: and the leads of lions; and out of their mouths proceedth fire and smoke and brimstone. By these plagues was the third part of men killed.... For the power of the horses is in their tails; for their tails are like unto serpents.... And the rest of mankind who were not killed ... repented not of the works of their hands, that they should not worship demons, and the idols of gold, and of silver, and of brass, and of stone, and of wood.... (Revelation 9:1–21, condensed by the author from the American Standard Version of the Bible).

Manson believed that England's Fab Four, the Beatles, were the "locusts" that had manifested to herald Armageddon: They had faces like men, but hair like women; their breastplates were their guitars; the powerful lyrics of many of their popular songs were as "fire and brimstone" to more conventional society.

The "angels" loosed to kill a third of humankind were select members of his own Family that he would send out at night out to slaughter specially selected victims, which, would in turn, set off a revolution that would result in the killing of one-third of the population of the United States. His angels of death were told not to worry about reprisals from society against them. They were to remember that he held the key to the abyss, a secret cave in Death Valley. Within this cave they would find a wonderful land of milk and honey and flowing spring water.

Then came the fateful night of August 8, 1969, when Manson sent his angels of death—Susan Denise Atkins (d. September 24, 2009), Tex (Charles Watson), Linda Kasabian, and Pat Krenwinkel—to the mansion at 100050 Cielo Drive. They had two changes of clothes. One was their "creepy crawlies," black costumes that they wore when they crawled around inside peoples' homes.

Armed with knives and a gun, Watson drove the girls toward the Sharon Tate-Roman Polanski mansion. Susan Atkins remembered Watson explaining to them that the house had once belonged to Terry Melcher, Doris Day's son. Although Melcher no longer lived there, their mission was supposed to be part of a plan to frighten him. Terry had given his word to Charlie on some things and didn't come through, and Charlie wanted to scare him.

When they pulled up in front of the mansion, each of the girls was armed with a knife. Watson parked the vehicle, snipped the mansion's telephone wires, then led the Family members on a terrible orgy of murder.

The cultists were surprised when Steven Parent walked down the driveway from the caretaker's cottage. Watson rushed to the young man's automobile, fired twice, and killed him.

The assassins next moved toward the mansion. Watson forced open a window, crawled inside, and opened the door for his companions.

Voityck Frokowsky, a Polish film producer, was asleep on a couch in the living room. Awakened by the intruders, he stared in drugged disbelief at their creepy-crawly outfits and demanded to know who they were.

One of the girls told him that they wanted money. Frokowsky said that he would give them all the money he had. He fumbled for his wallet, couldn't find it, then remembered that it was on the desk.

Watson pulled out his pistol. "Don't move," he commanded. "Don't move or you're dead. I'm the devil, and we're here to do my business."

The disturbance alarmed Sharon Tate and the other guests, Abigail Folger, the Folger's coffee heiress, and Jay Sebring, the hairdresser to the stars, who were brought into the living room. The very-pregnant Tate was wearing a short, see-through nightgown with a halter beneath it. She wanted to know what the intruders were going to do with them.

Watson did not hesitate to pronounce their deadly mission: "You're all going to be killed!"

Sebring studied the five armed strangers. Perhaps his practiced eye could determine that they were on LSD or some other drug for he made the decision to fight for his life. He was shot, stabbed, and collapsed dead in the living room.

Although Frokowsky had been bound on the couch, he managed to break the nylon cords that tied him. One of the girls stabbed him again and again as he raced out of the house, screaming for help.

Watson pursued the wounded man, clubbed him with the pistol, then shot him in the back.

Abigail Folger was stabbed as she tried to run toward the caretaker's house on the southern edge of the grounds. She was slashed to death on the lawn.

Sharon Tate battled two of the girls, but was overpowered and forced back on a couch. "All I want to do is to have my baby," she pleaded.

"Kill her!" the girls chanted. They continued to stab and to slash at her body even after she lay dead on the floor.

Someone in the Family dipped a towel in the blood that flowed from Tate's breasts, and a red-stained "PIG" was scrawled on the mansion door.

The multiple murders were discovered by Winifred Chapman, a maid at the home, when she walked up to the Hollywood mansion early on the morning of August 9, 1969.

During a search of the grounds, the police awakened William Garretson, 19, a caretaker employed by the owner of the secluded villa. Bewildered and sleepy-eyed, Garretson informed the police that he tended to the house and grounds and looked after things when the tenants, Tate and her husband, film producer Roman Polanski, were away.

The police interrogated Garretson thoroughly. The young man had been present while five people had been viciously murdered and he claimed to know nothing about the terrible carnage around him.

Tate's husband was located and informed of the slayings. He was in London working on a script for a new movie, but in attendance at a party when he received the terrible phone call.

It is now a matter of historical record that the police arrested members of the Charles Manson "Family" and charged them with the grisly massacre of Sharon Tate and her friends. Still feverish from the massacre, the Family had also murdered Leno and Rosemary La Bianca.

After a long, bizarre jury trial, Manson and a number of his followers were sentenced to lengthy prison terms. Never once did the girls in the Family acknowledge any wrongdoing on the part of Charles Manson. His magic and enchantment maintained their hold on the young zombies who had killed innocent individuals to begin Manson's great push toward Armageddon.

## The Contemporary Zombie Plague

In the vast majority of zombie movies since George A. Romero's *Night of the Living Dead* in 1968, the undead rise from their graves craving the flesh of the living because of some kind of "zombie plague." In some cinematic presentations a virus is

In cinematic versions of the "zombie plague," one of three scenarios is usually played out: 1) the great pandemic comes from outer space and infects the population of Earth, 2) a radiation from some source affects those humans already dead in lying in their graves and awakes in them a desire to eat the living, or 3) some deadly manufactured virus escapes from a laboratory and begins to kill its victims and transform them into cannibals (*art by Bill Oliver*).

created in a laboratory and somehow escapes the test tubes to turn any human who comes into contact with the deadly strain into a grotesque killing machine. The zombie deserves our pity, but there is no way that we can help it in its agony. It only wants to eat our brains.

In other versions of the "zombie plague," the great pandemic comes from outer space and an extraterrestrial virus or some kind of radiation affects those humans already dead and lying in their graves. For some very unnatural reason, the corpses leave their resting places and seek human flesh. In each of these various presentations, the terrified living are forced to barricade themselves in some kind of secure environment and somehow fight off the ever-increasing waves of the undead who wish to feast on them.

As we have emphasized throughout this book, the zombies of fiction and cinematic horrors are not *real* zombies, and the very idea that our friends and relatives whom we have respected and loved should rise from their graves to eat us is very unsettling. Such a concept is also very upsetting to those devout believers of the Judeo-Christian-Islamic faiths who are taught to expect a resurrection of the dead after a Judgment Day.

To look at the current zombie fad from another perspective, what if those who visualize the kind of Undead that cinema-goers are so fond of are actually having premonitions of a societal future that may occur if some foul laboratory or government does release a biochemical weapon that will cause mass annihilation of human life?

### *Is the Zombie Plague a Prediction of Our Future?*

Germ warfare, also known as biological warfare, is not a new concept. In the Middle Ages, opposing armies would catapult diseased animal and human corpses into their foes' encampments or over their city walls. When the Black Death, the bubonic plague, nearly decimated Europe's population in the fourteenth century, attacking armies flung excrement and bits of diseased corpses over castle walls.

Use of biological weapons was outlawed by the Geneva Protocol of 1925, but reports of the uses the Japanese Imperial Army made of such weapons on Chinese soldiers and civilians began to filter out of Asia to Great Britain and the United States. During the war years of 1937 to 1945, the infamous Japanese Unit 731 conducted gruesome experiments that resulted in the deaths of an estimated 580,000 victims.

In 1941, in response to the bioweapons that were developed in Japan and Nazi Germany in the late 1930s, the United States, the United Kingdom, and Canada established their own biological warfare program and produced anthrax, brucellosis, and botulinum toxin that could be used in war. In 1942, British tests with anthrax spores contaminated Gruinard Island, Scotland, so that it could not be usable for 48 years.

In 1972, the Biological and Toxin Weapons Convention reinforced the prohibition of all chemical and biological weapons. The international ban pertains to nearly all production, storage, and transport of such biological agents; however, numerous researchers believe that the secret production of such weapons actually increased.

In 1986, a report to Congress stated that the new generation of biological agents includes modified viruses, naturally occurring toxins, and agents that are altered through genetic engineering to prevent treatment by all existing vaccines.

The Department of Defense admitted in 1987 that regardless of treaties banning research and development of biological agents, it operates 127 research facilities throughout the nation.

The U.S. military was frequently accused of using various biological and chemical weapons in the Gulf War in 1991. Often mentioned was the charge that "BZ," a hallucinogen, was sprayed over Iraq, causing its citizens to surrender as totally passive, drooling, troops with vacant stares.

In 1994, it was revealed that many returning Desert Storm veterans are infected with an altered strain of Mycoplasma incognitus, a microbe commonly used in the production of biological weapons.

In 1996, Department of Defense admitted knowledge that Desert Storm soldiers were exposed to chemical agents.

In 2004 dangerous "super bugs" were popping up out of nowhere. Suddenly there were cases of flesh-eating bacteria, fatal pneumonia, and life-threatening heart infections—seemingly all caused by mutating strains of Staphylococcus aureus that shrugged off penicillin as a duck shakes off rain.

With the advent of genetic manipulation, deadly designer viruses can be created. Through the sorcery of recombinant engineering, the highly contagious influenza virus could be spliced with botulism or the toxin from plague.

The smallpox virus is said to be particularly amenable to genetic engineering. The deadliest natural smallpox virus is known as Variola major, and it would especially deadly now because the disease was eradicated from the planet in 1977. The smallpox vaccine dissipates after 10 to 20 years, so unless someone has had a reason to be vaccinated against the disease, no one today is immune. The last known human case of smallpox appeared in Somalia, but no one can guess how many canisters of the lethal virus reside in laboratories awaiting deadly use in biological warfare.

Some researchers name the Ebola virus as the ideal biological weapon, because it has the potential of killing nine-out-of-ten infected humans within three weeks of contact. The virus first emerged in three European vaccine production laboratories virtually simultaneously in 1967. Leonard G. Horowitz says that the virus was named the "Marburg virus," after one of the vaccine maker's home in Marburg, Germany. Scientific consensus has it that this virus arrived in Europe in a shipment of nearly 500 African monkeys from Kitum Cave near the West Nile region of Central Africa.

In April 2005, the World Health Organization reported an "Ebola-like" virus spreading rapidly through seven of Angola's 18 provinces. The initial outbreak appeared to have spread from a pediatric ward about 180 miles north of Luanda. Most of the victims of the virus were children. Over a dozen health care workers had died from the disease, and those who remained were deserting hospitals and clinics. In one village, terrified people had attacked members of the World Health Organization out of fear of catching the disease.

The zombie may be our Other Self that we choose to treat with disdain and contempt—the mindless, subservient Self, that one day will rise up and takes its revenge on our carefully ordered vision of our world and our dream of immortality (**art by Ricardo Pustanio**).

In the fall of 2009, we faced the yet-unknown force of the H1N1 virus. If this should be discovered to be yet another designer drug, then we might wonder if a zombie-type virus, a pandemic that would steal the free-will and minds of the masses might not be far behind.

## The Zombie: Our Evil Twin

The contemporary cultural fixation on the zombie has made him become our evil twin. The zombie is the Other Self that we choose to treat with disdain and contempt—the mindless, subservient Self, that one day rises up and takes its revenge on our carefully ordered vision of our mores, our morality, and our dream of immortality. We have met the zombies in our fears, and we will soon join them in their graves.

The vampire is an evil being whose supernatural powers allows it to look like a human for the length of time it requires to drink our blood. But a zombie is one of us, rendered mindless by a clever sorcerer.

The werewolf is shape-shifter, seized by a horrible hunger for human flesh and possessed of a strength that permits it to savagely slash and devour its victims. But a zombie is one of us unwillingly enslaved and exploited by a cruel master or stricken by a deadly virus.

The Gaia Hypothesis, named after the ancient Greek Goddess of the Earth, became popular in the 1960s and thousands upon thousands of people warmed to the idea that the Earth is not simply a planet that supports life, it is itself alive. Gaia continually improves the conditions for life through a series of biological and biochemical feedback systems that maintain the best possibility habitability of the planet.

However, in his article in *New Scientist* (June 20, 2009), Peter Ward argues that our planet may not be a nurturing mother of life like Gaia, but perhaps a more murderous mother like Medea, the sorceress and princess who killed her own children. Ward, a professor of biology at the University of Washington in Seattle, sees that life on Earth is ultimately self-destructive. Gaia's "evil twin" is its Medean tendency to "pursue its own demise, moving Earth ever closer to the day it returns to being sterile."

In his new book from Princeton University Press, *The Medea Hypothesis: Is Life on Earth Ultimately Self-Destructive?*, Ward states that two lines of research are especially damning to the Gaia Hypothesis: "One comes from deep time—the study of ancient rocks—and the other from models of the future. Both … suggest that life on Earth has repeatedly endured 'Medean' events—drastic drops in biodiversity and abundance driven by life itself—and will do so again in the future."

If Ward is correct in suggesting that our planet pursues its own demise and that one day in the future Gaia's Evil Twin will usher in the mass extinction of Earth as we know it, we may wonder if the sudden great popularity of the zombie is a precursor in the human mass consciousness that will permit those who heed its warning to begin to craft a new science of survival for our species?

# Appendix:
# VOODOO QUEENS AND KINGS

*I am grateful to the following writers/researchers who helped compile the material in this Appendix: Dawn Theard, Aylne A. Pustanio, Donald Authement, Ricardo Pustanio, Lisa Lee Harp Waugh, Karen Beals, and the staff of Haunted America Tours.*

In 1996, seeking to prove that Voodoo may be used for good, High Priestess Sallie Ann Glassman called upon the gods of Voodoo to help rid their New Orleans neighborhood of drug dealers and crime. Sallie Ann and her business partner Shane Norris, both practitioners of Voodoo, had enough of the soaring crime rate when they were robbed and attacked.

About 100 people gathered outside their store one night and they led a procession to the nearest street corner. They set up an altar in the middle of the street using a sewer cap as its base. Against the background of beating drums and flaming torches, Sallie Ann performed a ritual to dispel any evil intent. Then she knelt before the altar and made an offering of rum, cigars, and bullets to Ogoun La Flambeau, the Voodoo god of war, fire, and metal.

Within a very short period of time, the Voodoo ritual had worked wonders. The crime rate dropped from 70 burglaries per month to about six. Before the ceremony, crack could be bought at seven houses. After the ritual, only one crack house remained.

Captain Lonnie Smith of the New Orleans police department, who witnessed the Voodoo rite, agreed that something seemed to have worked. And as long as they were getting positive results from Voodoo, he was all for it.

## Sanite DeDe, New Orleans' First Voodoo Queen

The first Voodoo Queen in New Orleans of whom there is any record was Sanite DeDe, a young woman from Santo Domingo who may have arrived as a slave sometime in the early 1800s. Once in New Orleans, she bought her freedom through the power of her secret hexes and Hoodoo Voodoo.

By around 1815, she was holding rituals in her brick-lined courtyard on Dumaine and Chartres Streets, just walking distance from the St. Louis Cathedral. The rhythmic beat of the drums could be heard inside the great church during mass, and it was because of this that the Church brought pressure upon city government to forbid any religion that was not Roman Catholic to be practiced within the city limits. It was at that time that Congo Square, now known as Armstrong Park, became the location where the early Voodoo worshippers would hold their rituals—which the *Times Picayune* described as "serpent worship" amidst "uncontrolled orgies" (February 1932).

## Dr. John, Man or Mystery?

The mysterious Dr. John has blended so completely with his legend that it is difficult at times to determine if he was a real flesh-and-blood person or some other dimensional entity that visited New Orleans only to create zombies and initiate Voodoo Queens. According to certain recorded accounts of the day, he was a true Voodoo King of enormous power who had been a Prince in Senegal before coming to New Orleans. Others state that Dr. John's full name was John Montenet and that he was a freeman of color who wielded great influence in the city. It is said that he owned extensive property, was married to several beautiful wives, kept a harem of lovely mistresses, and fathered as many as 60 children.

Whether or not he was a Prince from an African nation, he was unquestionably an accomplished African priest who became the most famous Voodoo Doctor in New Orleans in the period from about 1810 to 1840. Dr. John was said to be able to predict the future, cure illnesses, cast spells, and create zombies to serve him as laborers and sex slaves. Even more incredible, Dr. John was rumored to have the power to "zombify" instantly those unfortunate individuals who angered him or who appealed to his sexual desires.

## Dr. John and Marie Laveau

Dr. John ruled New Orleans with Sanite DeDe until he began to mentor a captivating young woman named Marie Laveau, who supported herself as a hairdresser while gaining a widespread reputation as a Voodoo practitioner.

Marie Laveau succeeded Sanite DeDe as the ruling Voodoo Queen of New Orleans around 1830. No one in the hierarchy of Voodoo priests and priestesses disputed Laveau's assuming the position of authority, for it had become known among her peers—as well as both the common folk and the aristocracy of New Orleans—that she was extraordinarily gifted with powers of sorcery.

Marie Laveau and Dr. John have been mentioned numerous times in this book. Many of the claims made about the two remarkable figures have lifted them to the realm of supernatural figures who still maintain a powerful hold on the city of New Orleans. Although the feats of Dr. John have elevated to the near-status of a Voodoo god, the fame of Marie Laveau has surpassed that of her mentor, and hers is the name most associated with Voodoo in the entire world.

In her ordinary human incarnation, Marie married Christopher Glapion, a freeman of color, who worked as a cabinet maker while she styled the hair of her clients, some of the wealthiest women in New Orleans. It is recorded that the couple had 15 children and that one of their daughters, also named Marie, would assume her mother's throne as Marie Laveau II, the Voodoo Queen of New Orleans, in 1869. Most authorities agree that Marie I died in 1891.

## Queen Bianca, the Ruling Voodoo Queen

Queen Bianca has been the reigning Voodoo Queen of New Orleans since 1983, when she received the title from Liga Foley, her aunt by marriage who claimed to be a granddaughter of Marie Laveau.

Queen Bianca has presided over the secret Sosyete (society) that the Laveaus originally founded, carrying on the legacy of true New Orleans Voodoo. Bianca has said that the Grande Sosyete did not die with Marie Laveau I or Marie II, it just went underground; therefore, only the inner circle of followers and devotees know of its secrets, rites, and ritual locations.

Each year—sometimes twice a year—Queen Bianca will host a ritual in which the Monkey and Cock Statues created in honor of Marie Laveau are blessed and charged. In this ritual, which always takes place outdoors in a highly secret location, Queen Bianca

will invoke the spirit of Marie Laveau, becoming possessed by the powerful Voodoo Queen. Through Bianca, her modern day counterpart, Marie Laveau is able to be present with her devotees and personally blesses the Monkey and Cock Statues, which protect the followers from evil and any curses directed against them during the course of a year.

The highly secret vodusi of Queen Bianca's Sosyete present the living, channeled Marie Laveau the first Monkey and Cock Statue of each year as an offering. This ritual is said to take place once each year, usually around April 30 or May 1. Other offerings preferred by Marie Laveau are also presented and accepted by her spirit through the powerful Queen Bianca.

The first Monkey and Cock Statue remains with the powerful Mambo throughout the year until the time of the next ritual when it is ceremoniously broken in favor of another. Often, however, Queen Bianca and her vodusi will repeat the ritual in the fall of the year, coinciding with harvest festivals and Samhain rituals. The location for each ritual is a closely guarded secret, shared only with members of the Sosyete at the very last minute when they are summoned to assemble. This is one of the most

**Queen Bianca (art by Ricardo Pustanio).**

powerful examples of continuing devotion to the great Marie Laveau surviving in New Orleans today.

Bianca began learning the ways of New Orleans Voodoo and Santeria at a very young age. Because she devoutly studied numerous ancient paths and traditions, she quickly became very well known as one who specialized in rare New Orleans original Voodoo occult items and personally made magical fetishes, small Voodoo statues, and good luck charms.

Go to the official Bianca the Voodoo Queen of New Orleans Website at http://www.thehouseofVoodoo.com/.

## Mambo Sallie Ann Glassman

Counted as one of the 20 most active Voodoo practitioners in the United States, Priestess Mambo Sallie Ann Glassman, a woman of Jewish-Ukrainian heritage, is known for promoting positive thoughts through her Voodoo faith. She is also a historian on Voodoo tradition and its roots in Haitian Vodun.

Mambo Sallie, who was well-versed in the teachings of the Kabala and ritual magic, began studying New Orleans Vodou in 1975. In her *New Orleans Voodoo Tarot/Book and Card Set,* she writes that she discovered "a vibrant, beautiful, and ecstatic religion that was free from dogma, guilt or coercion."

Mambo Sallie has been practicing Voodoo in New Orleans since 1977. In 1995, she traveled to Haiti and underwent the week-long "couche" initiation rites. She returned to New Orleans ordained as Ounsi, Kanzo, and Mambo Asogwe—a High Priestess of Voodoo.

Mambo Sallie is the founder of La Source Ancienne and the Island of Salvation Botanica, a resource for Voodoo religious supplies and a showcase for her Voodoo-inspired art.

You can find her website, Island of Salvation Botanica, at http://www.feyvodou .com/.

## Priestess Miriam Chamani

Priestess Miriam Chamani gives Consultations and African Bone Readings both in person and via the telephone. She specializes in Voodoo Weddings, Damballah for Healing, and Erzulie for Love. Priestess Miriam designs Voodoo Dolls and Kits tailored to each person's needs and desires.

Priestess Miriam was born and raised in Mississippi, where she experienced the power of mysterious spiritual forces, beginning in early childhood. Around 1975 the power of the spirit called strongly to Priestess Miriam, leading her to many spiritual orders and ultimately to a seat at the Angel All Nations Spiritual Church. There she increased her knowledge of spirit and explored metaphysical concepts and teachings.

In 1990, Priestess Miriam and her late husband, Oswan Chamani, settled in New Orleans, where they founded the Voodoo Spiritual Temple, the only temple of its kind in the city at that time. The Temple is located next to Congo Square, and its rituals are directly connected to the those performed on Congo Square by Marie Laveau and Doctor John. It is the only formally established Spiritual Temple with a focus on traditional West African spiritual and herbal healing practices currently existing in New Orleans.

Upon the death of her husband, Voodoo Priest Oswan Chamani, on March 6, 1995, Miriam Chamani continued her husband's Belizan Vodou and herbalism traditions in addition to her own spiritualist practices, and she pursues many of the inclusive trends of Black Christian Spiritualism, seeking to serve all peoples, regardless of race or belief.

Visit Priestess Miriam Chamani's website at http://www.Voodoospiritualtemple .org/.

### Voodoo Mambo Ava Kay Jones

Voodoo and Yoruba Priestess Ava Kay Jones was an attorney by trade before she chose the path of her true spiritual calling. One of only twenty practicing Voodoo Mambos in the United States, Ava Kay Jones has enthralled locals and visitors alike with her dynamic presentation of authentic Voodoo rituals as practiced in the days of Marie Laveau. Priestess Ava is also the founder and featured performer of the Voodoo Macumba Dance Ensemble, a performance group of drummers, dancers, fire-eaters, and sword and snake dancers. Priestess Ava and Voodoo Macumba have performed in movies, at festivals, and, most notably, in the Superdome conducting blessing ceremonies for the New Orleans Saints.

Jones, who was raised Catholic, says she is still very much a Christian. She was ordained as a Voodoo priestess in Haiti in 1985, and as a Yoruba priestess in 1989. She is frequently interviewed on the subject of Voodoo, which she says is misunderstood due to inaccurate portrayals, fear, and prejudice. She says she is committed to educating the public about the faith she has so deeply embraced.

The official Ava Kay Jones website can be found at http://yorubapriestess.tripod.com/.

### Rev. Mother Severina Karuna Mayi Singh

Rev. Mother Severina Karuna Mayi Singh practices Vodoun and Yoruba traditions, as well as Sufism and metaphysical practices. She is also the founder of the New Orleans Voodoo Crossroads Dance and Drum Ensemble, a popular troupe performing at festivals, Voodoo weddings, and other events.

RICARDO PUSTANIO 2009

Rev. Mother Severina Karuna Mayi Singh (art by Ricardo Pustanio).

The Voodoo Crossroads was founded in 1991 as a vehicle for the dissemination of true and accurate information about the beliefs and practices of the Voodoo religion in New Orleans. She offers products and services in the tradition of New Orleans Voodoo.

The official site is http://www.neworleansVoodoocrossroads.com/.

## Bloody Mary Millan

Mary Millan, known as "Bloody Mary," was born on the bayou and was reared in the Crescent City. Mary, who has earned the title the "Poet Priestess of the Spirit of New Orleans," inherited a rich tradition of spirit contact, clairvoyance, and healing.

A recipient of spirit visitation since she was a child, Mary learned to channel these spiritual powers into her work in Vodoun and Magick. Bloody Mary is devoted to educating the cautious public about the teachings of Vodoun and the "unique gumbo" that comprises the city of New Orleans.

Her official site is http://www.bloodymarystours.com/.

## Queen Margaret

Queen Margaret taught in public schools in her home state of Louisiana, and she employed the spiritual gifts with which she had been blessed early in her life. She has devoted her life to helping to bring peace, love, and light into the world of everyone whom she has met.

Well known as a historian, teacher, medium, and counselor, she is currently employed as a tour guide and reader at the New Orleans Historic Voodoo Museum.

Visit the Queen Margaret website at http://www.Voodoomuseum.com/staff.htm.

RICARDO PUSTANIO 2009

Queen Margaret (*art by Ricardo Pustanio*).

## Armando, King of New Orleans Voodoo

Armando begins his day with a Voodoo grave ritual at the tomb of Marie Laveau. Armando is a devotee of the special style of Voodoo practice employed by Prince Ke'eyma, known popularly as "Chicken Man." Prince Ke'eyma is said by some authorities on Voodoo to have founded one of the largest secret sosyetes since the one created by the legendary Voodoo Queen Marie Laveau. The Cult of the Chicken Man, according to many, survives today because of the devotion of Armando.

Armando's apartment on the edge of the French Quarter is dominated by a large portrait of Prince Ke'eyman, who took the Cuban orphan under his wing and taught him the ways of Voodoo. Armando is proud to have received the power of Chicken Man's legacy as his chosen priest, but also to have ceded him the right to become the guiding force of the secret sosyete. Although Chicken Man died just a few days before Christmas in 1998, a full Voodoo Burial and New Orleans Jazz funeral was held for him in January 1999. His ashes are kept in Priestess Miriam's Temple on Rampart Street.

Armando does not believe in permitting those not practicing Voodoo to observe performances of the rituals. His detractors argue that Armando is against public demonstrations of Voodoo because he does not wish anyone to share the special rites taught to him by the Chicken Man.

Many individuals have reported seeing the spirit of Chicken Man all over the city of New Orleans, and Armando is upset about those who create fabrications about the True King of Voodoo. However, he is secure in the knowledge that Prince Ke'eyama's followers know that his Voodoo was the real thing and that it will stand the test of time.

**Armando the King of New Orleans Voodoo (*art by Ricardo Pustanio*).**

# BIBLIOGRAPHY

Abanes, Richard. *End-Time Visions*. Nashville, TN: Broadman & Holman, 1998.

Bach, Marcus. *Inside Voodoo*. New York: Signet, 1968.

Barker, J.C. *Scared to Death*. New York: Dell Books, 1969.

Brandon, S.G.F. *Religion in Ancient History*. New York: Charles Scribner's Sons, 1969.

Buckland, Raymond. *Buckland's Complete Book of Witchcraft*. St. Paul, MN: Llewellyn Publications, 1986, 1997.

Budge, E.A. Wallis. *Egyptian Magic*. New York: Dover Books, 1971.

Canon, M., and S. Hutin. *The Alchemists*. Translated by Helen R. Lane. New York: Grove Press, 1961.

Crim, Keith. *The Perennial Dictionary of World Religions*. San Francisco: Harper Collins, 1989.

Davies, Jon. *Death, Burial and the Rebirth in the Religions of Antiquity*. London and New York: Routledge, 1999.

Ferm, Vergilius, ed. *Ancient Religions*. New York: Philosophical Library, 1950.

Goetz, William R. *Apocalypse Next*. Camp Hill, PA: Horizon Books, 1996.

Harvey, Graham. *Indigenous Religions*. New York: Cassell, 2000.

Huxley, Francis. *The Invisibles: Voodoo Gods in Haiti*. New York: McGraw-Hill, 1966.

LaVey, Anton Szandor. *The Satanic Rituals*. New York: Avon, 1972.

Lissner, Ivar. *Man, God and Magic*. New York: G.P. Putnam's Sons, 1961.

Marks, John. *The Search for the Manchurian Candidate: The CIA and Mind Control*. New York: Times Books, 1979.

Masters, R.E.L., and Eduard Lea. *Perverse Crimes in History*. New York: Julian Press, 1963.

Meyer, Marvin, and Richard Smith, eds. *Ancient Christian Magic*. San Francisco: HarperSanFrancisco, 1994.

Middleton, John, ed. *Magic, Witchcraft, and Curing*. Garden City, NY: Natural History Press, 1967.

Quigley, Christine, and Christ Wuigley. *The Corpse: A History*. Jefferson, NC: McFarland, 1996.

Seligmann, Kurt. *The History of Magic*. New York: Pantheon Books, 1948.

Shaw, Eva. *Eve of Destruction: Prophecies, Theories and Preparations for the End of the World*. Chicago: Contemporary Books, 1995.

Smith, Huston. *The World's Religions*. New York: Harper San Francisco, 1991.

Stanley, John. *Creature Features Strikes Again. Fourth Revised Version*. Pacifica, CA: Creatures at Large Press, 1994.

Steiger, Brad. *Medicine Power: The American Indian's Revival of His Spiritual Heritage and Its Relevance for Modern Man*. New York: Doubleday, 1972.

———. *The Werewolf Book: The Encyclopedia of Shape-Shifting Beings*. Farmington Hills, MI: Visible Ink Press, 1999.

———. *Real Vampires, Night Stalkers, and Creatures from the Darkside*. Canton, MI: Visible Ink Press, 2010.

———, and Sherry Steiger. *The Gale Encyclopedia of the Unusual and the Unexplained*. Three volumes. Farmington Hills, MI: The Gale Group, Inc., 2003.

———, and Sherry Steiger. *Conspiracies and Secret Societies: The Complete Dossier*. Canton, MI: Visible Ink Press, 2006.

Unterman, Alan. *Dictionary of Jewish Lore and Legend*. New York: Thames & Hudson, 1991.

Wilson, Andrew, ed. *World Scripture: A Comparative Anthology of Sacred Texts*. New York: Paragon House, 1995.

Zachner, R.C. *Encyclopedia of the World's Religions*. New York: Barnes & Noble, 1997.

Real Zombies, The Living Dead, and Creatures of the Apocalypse

# INDEX

Note: (ill.) indicates photos and illustrations.